New Riders

New Riders Publishing,
Indianapolis, Indiana

World Wide Web

TOP

1000

Presented by Point Communications

Edited by R.F. Holznagel

World Wide Web Top 1000

By Point Communications and R.F. Holznagel

Published by:
New Riders Publishing
201 West 103rd Street
Indianapolis, IN 46290 USA

Printed in the United States of America   2 3 4 5 6 7 8 9 0

CIP data available upon request

Warning and Disclaimer

This book is designed to provide information about the World Wide Web. Every effort has been made to make this book as complete and as accurate as possible, but no warranty or fitness is implied.

The information is provided on an "as is" basis. Point Communications and New Riders Publishing shall have neither liability nor responsibility to any person or entity with respect to any loss or damages arising from the information contained in this book or from the use of the disks or programs that may accompany it.

Publisher	*Don Fowley*
Publishing Manager	*Jim LeValley*
Marketing Manager	*Ray Robinson*
Managing Editor	*Tad Ringo*

Acquisitions Editor
Alan Harris

Development Editor
Suzanne Snyder

Production Editor
Sarah Kearns

Associate Marketing Manager
Tamara Apple

Acquisitions Coordinator
Tracy Turgeson

Publisher's Assistant
Karen Opal

Cover Designer
Karen Ruggles

Book Designer
Sandra Schroeder

Manufacturing Coordinator
Paul Gilchrist

Production Manager
Kelly Dobbs

Production Team Supervisor
Laurie Casey

Graphics Image Specialists
Jason Hand
Clint Lahnen
Laura Robbins
Craig Small
Todd Wente

Production Analyst
Bobbi Satterfield

Production Team
Heather Butler
Dan Caparo
Kim Cofer
Jennifer Eberhardt
Tricia Flodder
Aleata Howard
Joe Millay
Erika Millen
Beth Rago
Erich J. Richter
Regina Rexrode

Indexers
Chris Cleveland
Brad Herriman
Mary Jane Frisby

About the Editor

R.F. Holznagel is oddly well-suited to edit a volume on something as scattered as the World Wide Web. He did his first computing on a Commodore Pet in 1978, and progressed to programming in the Fortran language before abandoning computers to earn a history degree with honors from Willamette University.

In the early 1980s, Mr. Holznagel plunged into the film industry as a production coordinator and, later, as a writer. He emerged with a 1992 Emmy Award for scripting the CBS television special *A Claymation Easter Celebration*. He promptly left television to wander the emerging realm of computer multimedia, editing Mindscape's *20th Century Video Almanac* in 1993. He has since written for many companies, including Brøderbund and Compton's NewMedia. He is also a four-time champion on the game show *Jeopardy*.

Mr. Holznagel lives in Portland, Oregon with a wingback chair and several potted plants. His offline interests include newspapers, wood-chopping, and big breakfasts.

Trademark Acknowledgments

All terms mentioned in this book that are known to be trademarks or service marks have been appropriately capitalized. New Riders Publishing cannot attest to the accuracy of this information. Use of a term in this book should not be regarded as affecting the validity of any trademark or service mark.

Acknowledgments

A book of this size is a delightful undertaking. We're especially grateful to those Internet users who have visited our Web site, read our reviews there, and pointed us toward their own favorite sites.

Our 1995 staff included the following fine reviewers: Tom Braman, Ron Deutsch, Eric Elia, Allison Ellis, Mark Glaser, Lance Gould, Bob Hassett, Jeffrey Hoffman, Jay Kee, Heather McLatchie, Carlo Panno, and Ron Rasmus.

Several crack writers provided additional material and revisions to this book: Hawkins Dale, Katharine English, James Fitch, Greg Galcik, Gloria Mitchell Brophy, Susan Sorensen, and Derek Willis.

Mark Simmer provided special technical advice and lunchtime counsel to go along with his excellent writing. Paul Hehn produced lively reviews and some of the project's funniest e-mail.

Erik Arnold has been a stalwart of design and debugging in the database department; my hat is off to him. Jon Yi and Eric Choi also labored valiantly in the vineyards of programming and Web design. Todd Whitney spent many hours talking with Webmasters and arranging screen shots. Alicia Marziali spread the word about Point, and her tips led to several of these reviews. Christina Kitze did a fine job of wrangling spreadsheets while involved in a more personal production of her own. Lynne MacVean's excellent proofreading and coordination were invaluable; she also provided the Italian translations needed for everyday life.

Our guide at New Riders, Alan Harris, was especially helpful in polishing this book to its current shiny state.

Finally, special thanks are due to Chris Kitze, who started this ball rolling in the first place and who has kept it speeding along with many well-placed shoulder thrusts. It's been a kick to work with him, and with the entire crew.

R.F. Holznagel

Contents at a Glance

Table of Contents

Introduction

The World Wide Web is a gigantic all-night bowling alley with lanes crossing every which way and pins crashing and flame-colored balls whizzing by every few moments.

Or: the Web is a gigantic Palace of Versailles with elaborate halls and thousands of different doors, some of which open to reveal empty closets, but some of which lead to jugglers and royal astronomers and courtiers caught in various states of undress and visiting dignitaries in funny collars making speeches.

Or: the Web is a gigantic, complicated junior high school cafeteria with a million picnic tables, 10,000 different lunch lines, seniors lobbing soft-boiled eggs at freshmen, and everybody jabbering at the top of their voices all at once.

Take your pick. The metaphors for the Web will probably last as long as the Web itself. Whatever you call it, it's a big amazing world out there.

At Point Communications, we set out a year ago to make sense of it all by finding and reviewing the best of the World Wide Web. We've seen a lot in that time, from the college freshman showing off snapshots of his high school sweetheart, to the wreck of the *Titanic*, to the murky quagmires of the U.S. Legal Code. At each stop, we poked around, chatted with the natives, and then rated the site accordingly. What you'll see in this book are the best 1,000 of those Web pages.

Point is an independent company based in New York City. Keeping up with the Web is what we do for a living (and what most of us do in our spare time, too). Our staff is spread out across North America and includes some long-time Web fanatics, some professional writers and journalists, and even a few college students. The mixture roughly approximates the makeup of the Web itself, and we think this helps make our reviews useful to a general audience.

Here are some of the questions we ask ourselves when we visit a new home page:

- Is the content excellent? Just how broad, deep, and amazingly thorough is the information? Is it accurate? Complete? Up-to-date? Are there good hot links? Does it break new ground?

- Is the presentation impressive? Is the page beautiful? Colorful? Easy to use? Does it lead visitors through the information nicely? Does it use video, audio clips, and original graphics?

- How was the overall experience? Was it fun? Was it worth the time? Will we recommend it to friends? Will we visit again ourselves? Soon?

Many of the home pages you'll find in this book have it all: slick visuals, deep content, and the wonderful attitude that makes for a great experience. Others score especially high in one area—the "Internet Movie Database," for instance, isn't much for fancy visuals, but has a phenomenal amount of info about films and actors. And some sites, like the "Amazing Parrot Cam," are included because they're just silly fun.

Point makes no distinction between commercial, private, or student pages—excellence is our only standard. (And in case you were wondering, Point and its staff are entirely independent. Those who make our list don't pay for the privilege or otherwise have an influence on our reviews.) All these sites *do* share a single trait: a strong, distinctive flavor of their own. That's the mark of a good creative effort in any field.

We've put these reviews in categories that make the most sense to us, starting with Entertainment and ending with the Weird and Wonderful. Those who enjoy browsing can pick a category and see what's available. If you have a precise curiosity, you'll find a wonderfully exhaustive index to every little thing in the back of the book. If you're like most people, we suspect you can open this volume at any page and find at least one site (if not four) that will interest you. The URL of each site is provided, of course, so you can easily launch yourself on the Web.

Of all the wild metaphors for the Web, the launch pad is perhaps the best of all. The goal of Point reviews, after all, is to help you start an expedition to your own discoveries on the World Wide Web.

When you do find great new sites, we hope you'll tell us about them, too. Our Web page at **http://www.pointcom.com** features ratings and reviews of the top five percent of all Internet sites, including daily reports on brand-new Web pages. We generally have something new and interesting going on every day of the week. And, of course, so does the Web.

Enjoy the ride!

New Riders Publishing

The staff of New Riders Publishing is committed to bringing you the very best in computer reference material. Each New Riders book is the result of months of work by authors and staff who research and refine the information contained within its covers.

As part of this commitment to you, the NRP reader, New Riders invites your input. Please let us know if you enjoy this book, if you have trouble with the information and examples presented, or if you have a suggestion for the next edition.

If you have a question or comment about any New Riders book, there are several ways to contact New Riders Publishing. We will respond to as many readers as we can. Your name, address, or phone number will never become part of a mailing list or be used for any purpose other than to help us continue to bring you the best books possible. You can write us at the following address:

New Riders Publishing
Attn: Publisher
201 W. 103rd Street
Indianapolis, IN 46290

If you prefer, you can fax New Riders Publishing at (317) 581-4670.

You can also send electronic mail to New Riders at the following Internet address:

aharris@newriders.mcp.com

NRP is an imprint of Macmillan Computer Publishing. To obtain a catalog or information, or to purchase any Macmillan Computer Publishing book, call (800) 428-5331.

Thank you for selecting *World Wide Web Top 1000*!

Entertainment

Entertainment

Entertainment seems to bring out the obsessive side of Web fans. How else to account for the existence of the Game Show Page, with its Vegas-style odds sheet for each and every game of chance on *The Price Is Right*? And when it comes to obsession, music and musicians are especially hot Web topics. Groups like R.E.M. and Nine Inch Nails generate hundreds of electronic 'zines and high-octane arguments among fans; when the Grateful Dead's Jerry Garcia died in 1995, a dozen memorial pages appeared the same day. And commercial record labels like Geffen create some of the Web's slickest promo pages.

The humor segment of this chapter is also a great spot for adventurous surfers. As in real life, the "humor" can be a mixed bag, but some of the Web's craziest places call this category home.

books and comics

books and comics

The Art Comics Page

http://www.cais.com/artcomic/home.html

Books and Comics

Acollection of comics and a springboard for comics artists, this scores points for good use of the medium, even if the the material isn't wildly funny. Maybe that's what makes it *Art*. A wide selection of "mini-comics" are sampled and available for subscription, although without that homemade 'zine charm of cruddy photocopies, such comics as "Flashers" and "Relatives" have all the zing of an oatmeal taco. Jokes from newsgroups are also a regular feature, and hit-and-miss funny bits like "Bumper Stickers" (*Prune Juice Shall Set You Free*) may make you want to hit-and-run. On the upside, ambitious comics creators can find grant applications for the Xeric Foundation, whose purpose is to support artists by guiding them through the world of self-publishing, from binding to marketing. This is a great resource, to be sure, but we can't help but wonder if writing grant proposals sucks the yuks out of these artists.

Jane Austen Information Page

http://uts.cc.utexas.edu/~churchh/janeinfo.html

Books and Comics

We have seen the future of Cliff's Notes in this Jane Austen page. English majors will adore the complete hypertext versions of *Pride and Prejudice* and *Love and Friendship*, as well as annotated versions of several others like *The Watsons* (an uncompleted novel) and *Lady Susan* (here called her "wickedest tale"). The creators of this site at the University of Texas have stocked the pond with Austen information, a long biography, maps, and more, tossing in even minor works and letters. We highly recommend first viewing the "How to Use This Document" section, or risk getting lost in the sea of links; the "short" table of contents is longer than most author sites offer in their entirety. The links are lavish and the details fairly reek of early England. Every great author should have a page like this one.

Author, Author

http://www.li.net/~scharf/author.html

Books and Comics

If you're looking for sites that deal with literature or famous authors on the Web, this is an excellent place to start. Author, Author is simply a well-organized pointer to sites of substance, most of which prove to be worthy of a visit. Connect directly to individual author pages from Erasmus to A. Conan Doyle to Tom Robbins, or to concise directories of those on whom many resources are available (Mark Twain, Shakespeare). A brief history of the Internet is included as window dressing, and the section "Internet Tools and Vocabulary" isn't too helpful, with short but meaningless definitions such as, "the World Wide Web is the graphical environment of the Internet." (Yeah, that explains it!) Stick with the literary links here and you'll go places.

Welcome to Author Author!

AwardWeb: Collections of Literary Award Information

http://ivory.lm.com/~lmann/awards/awardweb.html

Books and Comics

Dominated by science fiction, AwardWeb offers current lists of major literary awards. (It's also where we learned that the crew of Apollo 11 was given a special 1969 Hugo Award for "The Best Moon Landing Ever.") Laurie Mann maintains this excellent source, catalogued by year and by decade with winners of laurels like the Arthur C. Clarke Award (best science fiction published in Britain), the Bram Stoker Award (from the Horror Writers' Association), or the James Tiptree, Jr. Award (for literary work that "explores or expands gender roles"). If this all seems a bit mainstream, more adventurous readers might explore the European Sci-Fi Awards *or* the French Sci-Fi Awards here (because, you know, the French aren't *regular* Europeans). A list of Newbery Medal winners for children's literature is also here, once you have waded through all that science fiction. Although a bit dry in presentation, this is one heck of a resource for recommended books and a font of trivia for tome gobblers.

Banned Books Online

http://www.cs.cmu.edu/Web/People/spok/banned-books.html

Books and Comics

Here's a marvelous group of texts that have at one time or another been banned in the United States or elsewhere. Joyce's *Ulysses*, Voltaire's *Candide*, and of course the Qu'ran and the Bible (banned in the Soviet Union from 1926 to 1956) have all fallen victim to censorship. This site responds by publishing the complete texts of more than 20 such works. The site authors point out that Aristophanes' ancient anti-war play *Lysistrata* was banned by a military junta in Greece as recently as 1967; today it's online here. To illustrate that books still get banned (especially in schools), the site includes a list of "Most Frequently Challenged Books of the 1990s," perhaps the only "literature" list where *Of Mice and Men* and *Huckleberry Finn* share space with *Cujo*.

The Book of Bitterness

http://www.webfeats.com/sealander/Bitter_Book.html

Books and Comics

This kooky anthology promises "unflinching accounts of a world that doesn't work" by writers "cursed with the ability to see the world as it is." Relationships, whether with lovers or nations, are the main ingredient, and such vitriol doesn't come without a little of, shall we say, "adult language." Actually, these stories are kind of funny. "Little did I know when the Significant Other was eating his sub... that little microorganisms were waiting to attack his digestive system that night," writes a miffed Arkansas woman of a vacation gone sour. We get the impression that the essence of bitterness is to keep your tongue in your cheek without biting it off, and to spew venom before yielding to despair (which isn't, after all, *that* entertaining). Struggling artists, four-kilometer walks in the rain, yuppies toting worn-out copies of *The Celestine Prophecy*—they're all here, along with a survey that could help you discover a bitter side of yourself.

Bullets and Beer: The Spenser Page

http://mirkwood.ucc.uconn.edu/spenser/spenser.html

Books and Comics

Spenser, mystery author Robert B. Parker's fist-fighting Boston detective, is the hero of over a dozen novels, all of them known for their swift action and tough-guy wit. Uncommonly comprehensive in scope, this site offers not only character descriptions and favorite lines, but also an annotated list of the novels, citing and explaining the literary references that pepper Parker's novels (he was a lit professor in Boston). This seems mighty highbrow for a character who's punching and wrassling bad guys with guns all the time, but it somehow isn't as pretentious as it sounds. In the mid-80s, Spenser had a TV show, and there have been a number of TV movies made with the same cast (Robert Urich as Spenser, and Avery "Captain Sisko" Brooks as Hawk); these are briefly covered here, though they rightfully take a back seat to the novels.

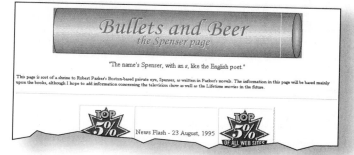

Children's Writing Resource Center

http://www.mindspring.com/~cbi/

Books and Comics

Brought to you by the "mom and pop" group that publishes *Children's Book Insider*, this site offers a gathering place for published authors, beginners, and those who just dream of writing for kids. Suppose you've written a story you think is every bit as good as "Grandma's Yummy-Tummy Ooey-Gooey Alphabet Cookies"—get a hot tip here on a new small press in search of submissions. A section on latest trends can protect you from embarrassing yourself (pack away that "Saddam the Snowbunny Goes to Congress" you've been working on: talking animals are *out* these days). You'll also find sound advice on agents, and a glossary that demystifies some pesky publishing terms like "SASE" ("self-addressed, stamped envelope") and "trim size" (the outer dimensions of the final product). Topical issues, like book-banning in public school libraries, are debated in weekly surveys. Good information that's easy to access.

The Collected Works of Shakespeare

`http://www.gh.cs.usyd.edu.au/~matty/Shakespeare/index.html`

Books and Comics

It's doubtful Shakespeare envisioned people scrolling through *The Tempest* by way of CRT screen, but this wordy site lets you

> ### The works of the Bard
>
> I picked these up some time ago from a server in England. Some of them required very minor work to be a in a consistent format--Act instead of ACT in some places, for instance--but such things have been fixed. You can browse through the list below or fill in the form to search for specific phrases.
>
> This site has been nominated among the top 5% of sites according to the Point Communications web survey. I've improved the interface as a result.
>
> Fill out the form (instructions) or, if your browser lacks support for forms, use the non-forms search to search the works of Shakespeare. Choose the plays/items you wish to search, the amount of context and enter the search text itself. This interface is new. If you have problems please contact me and use the old forms interface.
>
> Number of lines of context: 5   Search for
>
> | ☐ Histories | ☐ Tragedies | ☐ Comedies | ☐ Other |
> |---|---|---|---|
> | 2 Henry VI | Titus Andronicus | The Two Gentlemen of Verona | Venus and Adonis |
> | 3 Henry VI | and Juliet | The Taming of the Shrew | The Rape of Lucrece |
> | | | Errors | Son |

do so. The Bard's histories, comedies, tragedies, and poems are ready to read here. Most are presented in plain text, although several favorites like *Hamlet* have been converted to HTML, making it simple to access that famous speech (you know the one we mean). The plays are the attraction here, but the poetry section includes "A Lover's Complaint" and "Venus and Adonis," in addition to the sonnets. Perhaps this site's greatest function is its glossary of Shakespeare-speak. It's always good to know the correct definitions for bat-fowling and cony-catching, after all.

Comic Book and Comic-Strip Home Page

`http://dragon.acadiau.ca/~860099w/comics/comics.html`

Books and Comics

Pow! Wham! It's the nexus of all comic book home pages, Batman! This is a complete and super-exhaustive listing of comics on the Net, plus comic-cons, 'zines, and more! Beyond mainstream "heroes" like Sandman and the Transformers, the lists of links include pages on contemporary alternative comics artists like Dan Clowes ("Eightball") and Evan Dorkin (the comic/sardonic "Milk & Cheese"). Good coverage of European comics and Hong Kong anime. Kind of non-graphic for a comics page, but why quibble? It's ALL here. (We must confess, though: we STILL don't "get" Tintin.) Modern comics fans should take a look at the anachronistic rules from the Comics Code Authority, which includes such oft-trampled guidelines as, "If crime is depicted it shall be as a sordid and unpleasant activity," and "All characters shall be depicted in dress reasonably acceptable to society." Oh, but if they were only around today to see "Tank Girl" or "Cerebus!"

Commotion Strange

http://ecosys.drdr.virginia.edu/~jsm8f/commotion.html

Books and Comics

Commotion Strange is the newsletter by which Anne Rice communicates with her "Dearly Beloved Readers," because, in her words, "I hate and loathe with all my heart all the journalists who have written lies about me... I want to take control!" This site is the archive of the newsletters, full of not-so-controlled ramblings from Rice ("you have to love God greatly and deeply in order to be a true blasphemer, I think"), as well as unequivocal thumbnail reviews of movies she digs (*Interview with the Vampire*, for instance). Some bewitching photos of the author and her creepy-looking house in New Orleans are about the only visual stimulation here, but fans surely must love to hear Anne's rebel opinions. It's not often such a popular author gets down and friendly with the fans—just one big, happy, vampire-loving family.

Commotion Strange:

Anne Rice's Newsletter to Her Fans

Commotion Strange is a newsletter that Anne Rice has started to communicate directly with her fans. This page contains the archives of the text of the newsletters. So far there hasn't been much in the way of graphics, but if there are in the future I hope to scan them in. I have tried to preserve the way in which Anne wrote. For example, the frequent use of all caps is hers. I've also left in typos such as her unique spelling of laser disk (lazer disk). The newsletter is sent on an irregular basis. It can be obtained by sending a postcard to:

Anne Rice
1239 First Street
New

The Coupland File

http://www.interlog.com/~spiff/coupland/

Books and Comics

This gushing fan page for Douglas Coupland, the proud Canadian credited with coining the term "Generation X," presents him as one of that crowd's "best writers." Here we find that Coupland "refuses to own furniture" and is quite capable of spinning tales about "computers, life at Microsoft, and Legos all at once." Consider his strange comments ("Paper mail is like Mary Tyler Moore looking at a steak, and the price, and tossing it into a grocery cart"), and browse through some of the most endearing examples of his writing. That he can turn a phrase is no question, but the interviews with him and articles by him may have more prosaic types muttering "yeah, yeah, yeah—the silly punk." Nonetheless, here you can judge for yourself: is he a literary whiz kid, or simply this week's Brett Easton Ellis?

Dark Horse Comics Page

http://www.teleport.com/~dhc/
Books and Comics

The guts of this promotional site is the "Dark Horse Online" section, with its industry news and features (including a gallery of cover art), and press releases. Dark Horse, still in its first decade, has catapulted to the top of the multimedia entertainment heap with its string of successful comics, graphic novels, movies, and TV cartoons (the new *The Mask* on ABC). These guys have their fingers in more pies than Simple Simon at a bake sale. You won't see much of their critically acclaimed content here, but you're promised a media blitz on movies like *Barb Wire*. This site's mainly for industry insiders and the fiercest of fans. Purists who once championed the company's little-guy image may be disappointed by the new "let's sell *Mask* dolls" attitude.

The Dilbert Zone

http://www.unitedmedia.com/comics/dilbert
Books and Comics

"Dilbert" is fast filling the space left by "The Far Side" in the hearts of comics readers across America. This home page has the huge advantage of being written by Dilbert's creator, cartoonist Scott Adams. He details his meteoric rise to the height of cartoonist fame, from the rejection letter at age 14 from the Famous Artists School (you know, the "Draw Cubby" folks) to rejected pre-Dilbert cartoons, on up to the pinnacle: a licensed vendor list and advertisements on his Web site. Take a photo-tour of the creative process, which begins at night ("If I don't sleep with my mouth wide open like this, I won't get enough oxygen to the brain and I'll end up drawing 'Family Circus'). This is every bit as funny as the comic strip.

Disney Comics

http://www.update.uu.se/~starback/disney-comics/
Books and Comics

This Swedish site from Per Starbäck is an exhaustive history of the Disney character comics. Visitors can learn Donald's middle name (Fauntleroy), get a subscription to *The Duckburg Times*, or listen to scholarly debate about Scrooge McDuck's ethnicity ("Even though Scrooge is of Scottish heritage, there are... no indications that he speaks with a Scottish accent"). Profiles of the artists include Carl Barks, the undisputed King of the Duck comics, and funny and fascinating notes by Don Rosa, Barks' modest successor. Rosa on Barks: "...all he got from Disney was a slapstick hothead who threw walnuts at Chip 'n' Dale. What Dell/Barks did with the character is a miracle." Most Americans probably can't get too worked up over the "Duck Universe," but these comics are wildly popular in Europe. A group of German "Donaldists" even debate such hot issues as "how come that ducks show sometimes teeth and sometimes not?"

Fried Society

http://www.catalogue.com/comix/fried_society/

Books and Comics

A weekly comic strip by Los Angeles artist Chris Kelly, *Fried Society* has a skewed look at the struggle of being a Generation Xer. Dating, temping, even hemorrhoids all pose problems for twentysomethings (of course, the latter can be alleviated by "Preparation X"). Like most contemporary comics, this is a strip about modern woes and growing up, from the pitfalls of party prattle to the mysteries of puberty ("One minute you're blissfully playing in the backyard... the next minute you're suddenly stamped with a number from 1 to 10 representing your sex appeal.") Besides the new strip, you can catch up on previous weeks' strips from the catalog. We suggest the *Adventures in Temping* strip, a hilariously accurate portrayal of the bruising, low-pay world of the temporary work force.

Inkspot

http://www.interlog.com/~ohi/inkspot/

Books and Comics

Inkspot is a mammoth list of links to resources primarily for writers of children's books: workshops, style manuals, trade associations, and publishers, just to name a few. This has plenty to offer kids, too, from entertainment to sound advice for young authors. If the business end of it all gets a bit heavy, site creator Debbie Ridpath Ohi includes quotes from other writers (Noel Coward: "I'm bored by writers who can only write when it's raining"), lists of online literary magazines, and a hefty selection of diversions, such as lists of bestsellers and award winners. Many other areas of the book world are featured here, including Horror, Mystery, Romance, and Technical/Scientific, all with the purpose of helping you sell your book or other online writing.

The Inkwell

http://www.unitedmedia.com/inkwell/

Books and Comics

United Features Syndicate, who bring us "Dilbert" and scores of other comic strips, here trot out their stable of editorial cartoonists for a few quick yuks. Ten nationally syndicated political cartoonists are featured, though with only one panel per artist—why not *dozens*? The joy here is the consistently high quality of cartoonists such as Pulitzer winner Steve Benson, Jim Berry (creator of "Berry's World," now in its fourth decade), Ed Stein, and Dick Wright. The artists' statements, which we assume the marketing department put them up to, read like typical art show blather, about the "healing quality" of cartoons, and so forth, or "a meaningful image that will leave an impression on the public debate," and so on. Fellahs, just give us more panels! We promise we'll still buy the newspaper!

Into the Wardrobe: The C.S. Lewis Page

http://sleepy.usu.edu/~slq9v/cslewis/index.html

Books and Comics

Works by and about Clive Staples Lewis (see why he went by "C.S."?) are the foundation of a well-made site on this author (*The Chronicles of Narnia*) and sometime theologian (*Mere Christianity*). The inclusion of his nonfiction writings and speeches make this more than simply a bookish tribute. (Utah State's John Visser maintains this page with the help of other Lewis scholars.) The annotated bibliography, several quotes, and even sound clips with Lewis himself increase the appeal and provide a forum for ideas, as well as an appreciation for the man who put Christianity into a modern context for millions of readers.

Literary Kicks

http://www.charm.net/~brooklyn/LitKicks.html

Books and Comics

"If Generation X is like Woodstock, the Beat Generation was like a small dark tavern at two in the morning, with a bunch of old jazz musicians jamming on stage and Jack Kerouac buying rounds at the bar," explains Levi Asher, who has developed this impressive tribute to some of his favorite writers. Asher wisely keeps his distance, with biographies of Beat authors Kerouac and Ginsberg that don't portray them as heroes, but as guys who wrote some good stuff in spite of their sometimes glaring lack of *cool*. He's not blind to their literary faults either, noting that while what they wrote is sometimes brilliant, "a lot of it sucked." Selected writings are provided for the uninitiated, and Ginsberg fans *and* critics should love the parody "Yowl," an updated version of his classic poem. Asher works in some fantastic links—his own—on topics like Bob Dylan, San Francisco, and Buddhism.

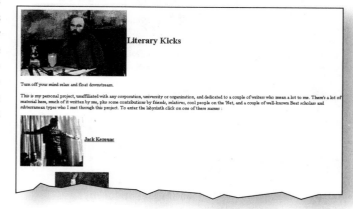

Nadia

http://utd500.utdallas.edu/~hairston/nadiahp.html

Books and Comics

This is an amazingly complete compendium of plots, graphics, and music for the Japanese anime TV series, *Nadia: The Secret of Blue Water*, an adventure series based "very loosely" on Jules Verne's *20,000 Leagues Under the Sea*. Nadia, a 14 year-old circus acrobat, seeks the stolen gem Blue Water, the only link to her mysterious past. Along for the ride is her sort-of boyfriend, Jean, also 14, an "inventive genius." The series ran for just one year, from 1990 to 1991, but was hugely popular in Japan, popularity that carried over to the U.S. crowd of anime fans. If you thought "Japanimation" started and ended with "Speed Racer," the richness of Nadia and the anime genre as a whole may astound you. Fans beware: the page tries not to give away too much of the story, but lets some pretty big spoilers slip through.

The Non-Stick Looney Tunes Page

http://www.tncnet.com:80/~jmccarthy/

Books and Comics

This monument to Warner Bros. cartoons goes beyond the characters to feature details of the men who created cultural icons such as Bugs Bunny, Daffy Duck, and Foghorn Leghorn. The essentials are here: filmographies, video and laser disc resources, and even current TV listings for the U.S. A list of cartoons from "Bosko and Honey" (1930) to "Miss Priss-I Say-Miss-Prissy" (1950), and on up to the easily forgettable "Rapid Rabbit" (1969, when things were getting bleak in the cartoon universe) includes selected voice samples of the "stars" from the Golden Era under directors Chuck Jones and Friz Freleng. Other members of the Warner crew, like Robert McKimson, Bob Clampett, Tex Avery (directors), Mel Blanc (the man of 1,000 voices), and Carl Stalling (the wild and wonderful music director), are also noted for their contributions.

The Non-Stick LOONEY TUNES Page

[TEXT ONLY]

NOTE: This page is *ALWAYS* under construction

Warner Animation Info

- Available Titles on Video
- Laser Disc Information

Project Bartleby

http://www.cc.columbia.edu/acis/bartleby/

Books and Comics

This site bills itself, not incorrectly, as the "public library of the Internet." Named after a Herman Melville book (*Bartleby, the Scrivener*), this resource provides online access to out-of-print classics and poetry to visitors. Bartlett's *Familiar Quotations* has several Internet homes, most of them unofficial (for that matter, illegal), but can the same be said of Walt Whitman's "Leaves of Grass" or the complete poems of William Wordsworth? Probably not. A growing collection includes John Keats' *Poetical Works* and all 12 books of George Chapman's 1857 translation of Homer's *Odyssey*. Poetry is the main subject, but a collection of presidential inaugural addresses is a welcome addition, including this portion of Zachary Taylor's message: "So far as it is possible to be informed, I shall make honesty, capacity and fidelity indispensable prerequisites to the bestowal of office." Project Bartleby is where your mom would hope you'll spend your time online.

COLUMBIA UNIVERSITY

PROJECT BARTLEBY

Project Bartleby: The Public Library of the Internet

Bartlett, John. 1901. *Familiar Quotations, 9th ed.*
Chapman, George, trans. 1857. *The Odysseys of Homer.*
Dickinson, Emily. 1896. *Poems.*
Inaugural Addresses of the Presidents of the United States. 1989.
Keats, John. 1884. *Poetical Works.*
Melville, Herman. 1853. *Bartleby, the Scrivener. A Story of Wall-street.*

Queensboro Ballads

http://levity.willow.com/brooklyn/

Books and Comics

This "Web album" by Levi Asher spins tales of life in the "humble and mostly unloved part of New York City" called Queens. Designed to look like something you'd find in the "free" bin at the used record store, this is a collection of personal writings, autobiographical "songs" about things like crummy jobs and lonely people. They reveal an unabashed city boy who revels in wearing black sneakers to his day job in the heart of Wall Street, tweaking beeper-bearing stuffed shirts who need to take a meeting before deciding it's a nice day. The first "single" is a photo essay of people on the subway, set to the words of two Beatles songs. Another track breezes in disgust through Long Island's Walt Whitman Mall. ("Whitman wore khakis.") It's a high-fidelity read with the charm of a scratchy old record album.

Superguy

http://www.halcyon.com/superguy/index.html

Books and Comics

Here's a dizzyingly complex (and mostly text) online comic book. "Superguy" is a collaborative writing project in which dozens of superheroes with names like Cholesterol Man and Spandex Babe interact in a fantasy world (or "altiverse") and fight villains like Blenderhead and Dr. Robert Unethical. Since the late 1980s, over a dozen authors have continued to add new characters and new stories; the creative process here seems so convoluted that apparently some of the writers don't even know what their characters look like! No matter, neither will you—with a few exceptions, visuals are conspicuously absent! You can read installments by joining an e-mail mailing list, and *try* to follow the adventures of Captain Non Sequitor, Wonder Grunion, or Dangerousman ("Roaming the country in his car, the Dangerousmobile, he sought out crime and blew it up but good").

Tank Girl

http://www.dcs.qmw.ac.uk/~bob/stuff/tg/

Books and Comics

In the year 2033, water is a scarce commodity. But have no fear: H20 is protected by Tank Girl, a little Red Robin Hood with heavy armor and a mutant kangaroo for a boyfriend. This shrine to the raggedy British comic book heroine, the creation of Jamie Hewlett and Alan Martin, offers detailed info on her original appearances in *Deadline* magazine, the subsequent Vertigo mini-series and Dark Horse graphic novels, and the 1995 movie starring Lori Petty. The comics section covers all the strips, with some hints on how to find them or order them from *Deadline*. Since the movie's release, the amount of Tank Girl merchandise has, of course, increased exponentially, but not enough for hardcore fans, who here present their "wish list" of items from the benign to the appropriately nasty.

Thomas Pynchon

http://www.pomona.edu/pynchon/index.html

Books and Comics

Pynchon admirers from Pomona College have done their homework on this elusive and reclusive author, and the result is a real treat. Thoughtful examinations of Pynchon's work include essays on peripheral themes like V2 rockets and entropy, and the entire site is peppered with amusing, Pynchon-esque diversions. Like prizes from a Crackerjacks box, some of these are gems and some are duds. Besides covering his major novels *The Crying of Lot 49* and *Vineland*, we are treated to several previously uncollected works, from short stories and magazine articles to liner notes for a 1994 Spike Jones album. Personal information about the author (a rare commodity) is presented with fitting unobtrusiveness, including trivia treasures like Pynchon's love of *The Brady Bunch*. On the serious side, Tim Ware's remarkable concordance to *Gravity's Rainbow* is just one impressive feature of this fine site.

The J.R.R. Tolkien Information Page

http://www.lights.com/tolkien/rootpage.html

Books and Comics

If this site is any indication, there's a correlation between interest in the Net and fascination with the works of J.R.R. Tolkien. And this site should satisfy all your Tolkien needs, linking you to sites delving much further than tributes to *The Hobbit* and

The Lord of the Rings. The frequently asked questions (FAQ) guides are so lengthy, they had to create a "less frequently asked questions" list just to keep up. Archives include all of Tolkien's works, plus language resources and even games related to the *Rings* trilogy. Graphics include paintings, illustrations, and photos, and this is the ONLY place we know of to find those elvish fonts that are so much in demand (wink, wink). The only downside is trying to connect to these far-flung sites—they seem to be constantly busy.

Tool User Comics on the Web

http://www.tooluser.com/
Books and Comics

High quality is the strength of this home for Tool User Comics, a "shareware comics" outfit that mixes commerce and comics. It's pretty righteous, really, as most of the proceeds (and they're not a lot) go directly to the artist. For just a couple of bucks, you can subscribe for up to a year of online comics. The samples aren't skimpy, and the stable is healthy, with high-quality art and content. Some of these scanned pen and ink drawings are too darned hard to read (Stan Mack's "Real Life Funnies" is gray and washed out, just like real life), but if you like what you see, offers to subscribe are everywhere. Nina Paley's popular (and rightfully so) "Nina's Adventures" is top drawer stuff, and Ruben Bolling's "Tom the Dancing Bug" is reliably funny, and guarantees "no dancing bugs!" Check out his "Malibu Firefighters," sample. Battling the 1993 wildfires, entertainment-savvy firemen must decide whether to save Bob Newhart's house or Sean Penn's. ("I say we let it go west. I've seen reruns of *The Bob Newhart Show*, and frankly it hasn't held up.") The peculiar interactive "Little Failure" is 16 drawings that can be arranged randomly; this means it can be read a bazillion different ways, at your whim, and there always seems to be some magical logic to it. A couple of bucks isn't much to experience what could be a strong future for online comics.

Mark Twain Resources

http://web.syr.edu/~fjzwick/twainwww.html
Books and Comics

With this resource for Twain sites, Jim Zwick is emerging as the Web's "Mark Twain Guy." Zwick has collected online exhibits (his own "Mark Twain on the Philippines" is one), texts, scattered writings, and cartoons, and even spots where you wouldn't expect to find the cigar-chomping, quote-mongering literary

continued

Mark Twain Resources continued

giant (for instance, *Star Trek: The Next Generation* and *Babylon 5* episodes). Twain said, "My books are water; those of the great geniuses is wine. Everybody drinks water." Now millions more have access to the well. Although there's little flash to this site, it is generously sprinkled with Twain quotes, from the celebrated ones to this less-famous comment on Hawaiian volcanoes: "The smell of sulfur is strong, but not unpleasant to a sinner."

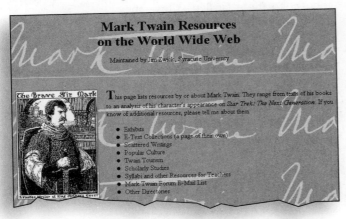

Speculative Fiction Clearing House

`http://thule.mt.cs.cmu.edu:8001/sf-clearing-house/`

Books and Comics

This catalog, specializing in science fiction and horror, had us shouting "Extensive!" and "Comprehensive!" at each other across the office. This is a great starting point for the genre, loaded with links both mainstream and offbeat, whether you seek gay/lesbian/bi sci-fi, something in the Mexican/Latin American genre, or myth and fantasy. This is also a writers' resource, with publisher and trade association information. Lists of awards, electronic texts, and episode guides to sci-fi TV shows round out the archives, which are as thick as Daleks at a "Dr. Who" convention. If you're looking to buy, we recommend the Bookstore section for its helpful descriptions of those in your area. Hundreds of bibliographies on authors from Arthur Conan Doyle to Bruce Sterling and links galore to author pages make browsing pleasantly overwhelming.

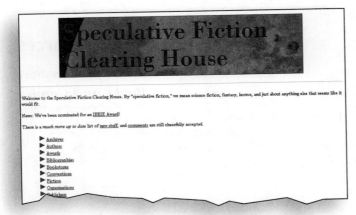

The Unofficial Jack Chick Archive!

`http://dig.netcentral.net/vx/chick/jackhome.html`

Books and Comics

Anyone who's ever ridden a bus or spent too much time at a laundromat has probably read at least one of Jack Chick's little religious comic books. This "fan" (or "anti-fan") page gleefully examines the work of Chick, publisher of dozens of religious tracts and newsletters over the past few decades. Chick's comics are "obsessed with hell and the more gruesome aspects of the gospel." Archived mini-tracts and comic books are the centerpiece here, but fans ("Chicklets") can also hear the voice of Jack Chick in sampled sound files. The Webmasters (who are themselves Christians) poke fun at elements in the tracts like Chick's fear and loathing of the Catholic church, elements they believe represent the worst side of fundamentalism. Other common Chick motifs, they note, include a "bad person or devil laughing HAW! HAW!" and "God as a giant light-bulb-headed judge."

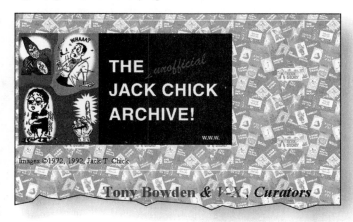

WebComics Index

`http://www.cyberzine.com/webcomics/`

Books and Comics

Bucknell student David de Vitry created this site "so that normal netizens like you and me could easily find most all the comics on the Net." He's collected and presented scores of dailies, weeklies, and editorial cartoons. They include the latest episodes of popular dailies like "Dilbert," and samples from and links to Web sites "Dr. Fun," "Buzz the Fly," and "Lily Wong," among others. Both online entries and familiar newspaper strips are available, like the weird oldie "Marmaduke," the new weirdie "Rose is Rose," and "Soft Targets" (a kind of contemporary Canadian "Pogo"). This site is well-organized and well-executed, with lots of pretty colored background to spice up what is really simply a comics directory. For some reason, Web comics tend to be PG-13 material or stronger, and the selection here is no exception.

Web of Lost Souls

http://www.jr2.ox.ac.uk/~nowen/index.html
Books and Comics

This is the official page of Clive Barker, prolific writer, filmmaker, playwright, artist, and the man who added "Pinhead" to our modern pantheon of bogeymen. Best known for the *Hellraiser* series of movies and comic books, Barker is a grand champion in the nightmare division, and better at the grisly and gruesome than at crafting puns: "Every body is a book of blood; whenever we're opened, we're red."

Well, hardy-har-har, Clive, you handsome scamp! The scary, gory images are the best thing on this comprehensive site, which includes *plenty* of merchandise. The lists of books, comics, plays, and stories are informative, but a bit of a tease. Other than some comments about his own artwork, you don't get to *read* much Barker, and the text is more charming than chilling. The movie section, however, is great.

Welcome to Wayne Manor

http://www.books.com/batman/batman1.htm
Books and Comics

Though not the "official" Batman page, these folks have gone all out with a site that would make the Penguin squawk with jealousy. Enter the Bruce Wayne Gallery for images from early Batman appearances in *Detective Comics* through TV to, of course, the films. Dark Knight purists might balk at the absences of Frank Miller's work and the dominance of movie stills, especially those from the bloated and

over-hyped *Batman Forever*. This is the world of entertainment, however. And after all, which of Batman's many incarnations has made more (and *cost* more) money? The Library features a fistful of books and audiobooks, with leads on where to purchase them online, and the Conservatory has sound files of the TV themes of the '60s *Batman* and the '90s *Batman: The Animated Series*.

games

Contests on the Web

http://polvo.catalogue.com/contest/contests.html
Games

More than 100 contests on the Web are linked on this page, with prizes ranging from T-shirts to $20,000 giveaways.

The site's updated frequently, and is broken out into several categories, such as Scavenger Hunts, Games, and Trivia. Some contests require no skill ("fill out a survey and you'll be entered in a drawing for the Grand Prize!" stuff), while some require creativity, like the "Worst Experience with a Salesperson" essay contest. Most links only have the name of the contest listed (so, unfortunately, you have to hit each one to find out what it's about), but some have general descriptions provided. But hey, aren't you willing to do a little clicking for a brand-newwww carrrr? The Webmasters also add amusing commentary in random places.

Chinook

http://web.cs.ualberta.ca:80/~chinook/

Games

Chess gets all the glory and the high-strung champions, but checkers still reigns as the game that is easiest to learn and hardest to master. Don't take our word for it: jack into Chinook, this world championship checkers program. Chinook's endgame database totals over 443 *billion* resolved positions, including the one where you dump the board onto the floor. Don't doubt that this monster is formidable. Chinook isn't just a Web toy provided for our amusement; it's the fruit of many years' labor by a team of researchers at the University of Alberta.

You may have to wait for a game, because only one person can play at a time; while you do, you can check out the comprehensive library of information and links to checkers fanatics worldwide.

Welcome to *Chinook*, a world championship checkers program developed by a team of researchers led by Dr. Jonathan Schaeffer of the Department of Computing Science at the University of Alberta, Edmonton, Alberta, Canada. *Chinook* is the by-product of a research effort started in 1989 into game-playing strategies. This project has had two goals:

Cindy Crawford Concentration

http://cad.ucla.edu:8001/concentration

Games

Modeled (so to speak) on the TV game show, this amusing diversion uses supermodel Cindy Crawford for all the game pieces. (It's from a UCLA student, natch.) You choose two game squares from a board of 16, and they flip around to reveal pictures of the Indiana Bombshell (or whatever Ms. Crawford's nickname is). To win, match up the identical photos. Don't expect any instructions on site, but you'll pick it up. We wouldn't be so sexist as to comment on the photos, but the programming is just achingly gorgeous. The site can be difficult to get into, but it's worth swinging by some night when you're up late: it's a clever use of the Web. It's also a classic waste of time.

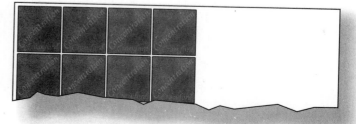

The Dockingbay

`http://www.csd.uu.se/~johnn`
Games

Somewhere between *Star Trek* and a high-quality CD-ROM game, John Nilsson awaits. The Swedish computer-science student stars in his own space-age

fantasy, asking surfers to begin at a ship's docking bay and aim to find Nilsson's private quarters. It's a fun trip, and worth the wait for the pictures to load: we've seen graphics of this quality in off-the-shelf home games. Clicking on buttons and feeling one's way through a slick, brutish environment, lucky surfers will arrive in about 15 minutes. At least that's our experience (and we didn't even read the tips on Nilsson's home page!). But after milling about in Room 6, we wondered what was going on in the other locked rooms. Does John have other keys he's not telling us about?

DoomGate

`http://doomgate.cs.buffalo.edu/`
Games

DoomGate is on the Net, and it's just WAD the doctor ordered. (That's a Doom-junkie pun.) Here you get all the latest shareware releases of DOOM, DOOM II, and Heretic; spoilers, cheat codes, and screen shots; utilities, editors, and add-ons; more WADs than you can count; themes that cover everything from *The Simpsons* to *Star Trek*; plus a kazillion

docs and FAQs, including "The Wadster's Guide" and "DEU For Dummies." Stop us when you've had enough. There's even a section on iFrag (for playing DOOM over the Net). If none of this makes any sense to you, you can safely skip this site, which is really aimed at dedicated DOOMsters. In that sense, this page is to DOOM what Stonehenge is to Druids.

Doug's Myst Page

Are you, or someone you love, caught in the throes of Myst-eria? Then check this hint guide to the popular CD-ROM puzzle game. Unlike some hint pages that merely walk you through the game, this one has a zillion links that show you just a little bit of needed info at a time. If you can avoid the temptation to read ahead and spoil everything for yourself (didn't even know there was a Dunny Age, did you?),

this site's just what you need when you're really stuck. Doug himself has no connection to creators of Myst; he just wanted a better helping hand. As he puts it, "This set of pages is the kind of resource I wish I had had when I was solving the game." Amen. If only we'd known about this earlier, we could have saved 100 hours of our lives.

The Electronic Arts Web

Electronic Arts has long been a popular game creator for home game systems and computers. Their stunning pages make extensive use of graphics (maybe *too* extensive—even fast-linked Webbers may get tired of the huge load time each page requires), and provide access to new product releases, game demos, and affiliated companies. You can search for demos of games like "Hi-Octane" or "Magic Carpet II" by company or by

platform (Sony, Nintendo, Sega, 3DO). And if you already own an EA product, a customer support form is provided for help with any technical difficulties you might be having. The site includes a nice little history of the video game industry, reminding aficionados how far things have come since Pong was produced by Atari in 1977. Highly creative.

Game Page of the Universe

http://www.pht.com/games.html

Games

According to the *Hitch-Hiker's Guide to the Galaxy*, the universe is "bigger than the biggest thing ever, and then some." The Game Page of the Universe is similarly sized, having games, links, demos, and new releases on the Net, updated daily; plus a really big, fully automated FTP site where you can see file sizes, statistics, and ZIP contents before downloading. This way, you can tell if "Superhero League of Hoboken" would really be your cup of tea before you take the time to download it. The text colors they've chosen can be an eyestrain (if you're using a browser that can understand color-change messages), but if you're a serious game player, you're probably used to that particular pain anyway. Though dense and having a definite PC-compatible slant, this page will thrill just about any type of computer gamer.

The Games Domain

http://wcl-rs.bham.ac.uk/GamesDomain

Games

Could there be a more complete source than this for the home computer gamer? The Games Domain has built its popularity on its huge array of direct links to games and tip sheets around the Internet. You'll find pointers to games, mailing lists to discuss games, and resources to help you play games; or, if you can't solve your own file transfer software, you can download files directly through your Web browser. In recent times, the Domain has added The GD Review, an online magazine "by gamers, for gamers" with the hottest reviews and sneak peeks available. (We don't know if they're really "the hottest"; that's just according to these guys). Programmers will like The Nexus, with its links to resources for creating games. Face it: you're not a true gamer if you haven't memorized the location of this site.

Gid's Web Games

http://inferno.cs.bris.ac.uk/~gid/games.html

Games

Gid's Web Games is a cool game site dedicated to the aimless pursuit of multiplayer games and solitaire. Try your mouse at Webtris, a multiuser variation of Tetris (which doesn't become a game of strategy as much as a race to access the game computer first), or play a few rounds of "marble solitaire," a jump-the-pegs sort of game where you aim to leave only one marble on the board. Or take a shot at the Cube or Blobs, a couple of pan-dimensional brain-teasers. As interesting as the games are, they can be awkward with a Web interface: for most games, you click on a piece and load a page, then click where you want the piece to go, which loads another page. A fast connection and Netscape are almost essential here.

GNU Web Chess

http://www.delorie.com/game-room/chess/

Games

This page is a quick 'n' dirty way to play chess against a computer. You can find other automated chess games on the Net, but they generally involve telnet sessions, logins, and other Internet arcana. Here, you only need Web browsing software to start playing a robotic opponent immediately. You simply fill out a quick form with who goes first, the computer's "thinking time" (how smart your opponent will be), and the graphics size you prefer. In seconds, you're locked in combat. To test it, we fool-ishly lost a pawn and a bishop in the first five moves, and got a rook rammed down our throat for our trouble. Don't forget to delete your game when you're finished (it's only polite).

Chess Game 12146.1 - Delete Game

Your Move: [   ] GO Hint Help
Sample moves: a2a4 e7e8q o-o o-o-o
Board: Text Small Medium Large

LucasArts Entertainment Company

http://www.lucasarts.com/
Games

Just as the LucasFilm company is known for the wildly popular *Star Wars* and *Indiana Jones* movies, The LucasArts company is known for its wildly popular computer games based on those movies. This site showcases the software created by LucasArts, and provides lots of dirt for the avid game player. For example, in *The Adventurer*, their semi-regular promotional magazine, we learned that Rebel Assault II was made with studio-shot action sequences with real actors. (Sure, this is old news now—but hey, we were the first on our block to know about it.) Demos and "sneak peek" screen shots of upcoming games are provided, and where better to get the latest scoop than the company's own press releases? Seeing this site may set you to sharpening your résumé for the Human Resources division provided here.

Name That Tune!

http://www.omg.unb.ca/~glenn/nameThatTune.html
Games

In the spirit of the famous game show, Name That Tune! gives you ten short sound clips from various songs, and asks you to identify the song and artist. Sounds simple—but if you could have correctly identified "When You Walk In The Room" by The Searchers, you would have scored much better than we did. There's a new collection of songs every week, and each set has a theme, like "Hard Rock in the 80's" (sic) and "The British Invasion Continues." The winners are posted every week as well. If you don't feel like competing, but want to test yourself anyway, you can check the archive for previous weeks' sound clips. You can't win fabulous cash prizes, but it's fun regardless. You'll need a browser with sound support to play.

Can you... *Name That Tune???*

TOP 5% OF ALL WEB SITES POINT

TOP 5% OF ALL WEB SITES POINT

Play this week's contest
Check last week's answers
This week's players
Last week's players
The All-Time Players List
Information on how to play
News (last updated *Monday, September 11th, 1995*) and statistics
I need YOUR feedback!
Check out the new contest archives!

Zarf's List of Interactive Games on the Web

http://www.cs.cmu.edu:80/afs/andrew/org/kgb/www/
zarf/games.html

Games

Zarf has collected a bunch of links to interactive areas on the Web and organized them here for your fiddling enjoyment. The list is split into two main areas: Interactive Games, which usually have some goal or way to win, and Interactive Toys, which don't necessarily have a purpose, but are fun to play with. Each link has icons describing what the games will demand from your browser (forms, color, image maps, and so on) and some have extra notes as needed (like "requires a fast connection"). We wished there were more subdivisions; everything loads up on one page, which makes it a little cumbersome. If nothing else, it proves that the Web holds more Tic-Tac-Toe, Maze, and Mastermind variants than you will ever need.

humor

Annals of Improbable Research

http://www.improb.com/

Humor

This may be science at its funniest, as students at MIT collect and distribute some of the best science stories ever. AIR hands out the IgNoble awards (which "should not be confused with those other prizes") to such dignitaries as the co-authors of "The Constipated Serviceman: Prevalence Among Deployed U.S. Troops," which kept numerical statistics of bowel movement frequency. They even have some fun of their own: burying a "time caplet" containing, among other things, McDonald's fries, Internet Barbie (a half-naked doll with fiber-optic cables for hair), and a running shoe. Of course, they placed all these items in a trash compactor before putting them into the caplet. AIR is a great reason to go into science (or perhaps to avoid it at all costs).

Automatic Complaint Generator

http://www-csag.cs.uiuc.edu/individual/pakin/complaint

Humor

This amusing little utility saves hours of fretting: simply type the name of whoever bugs you, and out pops a random complaint letter riddled with verbose insults. Example: "a day without [target here] would be like a day without temperamental contemptible absolutism." Taking the historical perspective, we selected "King George III" as our target. The resulting letter was oddly accurate, calling his friends "sexist misogynists" and declaring, "He will draw unsuspecting boneheads into the orbit of ungrateful undesirables long before he can convert me into one of his subordinates." Another try, this time aimed at our landlord, was even more on the mark. The sentences are created via odd "context-free grammar" machinery, described in a "nerds-only" page. It ain't "Give me liberty or give me death," but it's a start.

Centre for the Easily Amused

http://www.islandnet.com/~cwalker/homepage.html

Humor

Picture, if you will, a crack team of scientists in white lab coats exploring the Internet for the most astounding sites on the Web. Now forget it, because you're way off. It's just Canadian authors Cathie Walker and Brian Leslie, browsing around the Web and finding those sites that are silly, strange, or just plain stupid. All their selected sites follow a common thread, however—they're a delightful waste of your time. The pair offer links to dumb spots such as the Pez Home Page, the Random Monty Python Skit Server, and, of course, the Belch Page. You don't have to do any hard work if you don't want to— they select a "Short Attention-Span Site of the Week" every seven days (or so) for your benefit.

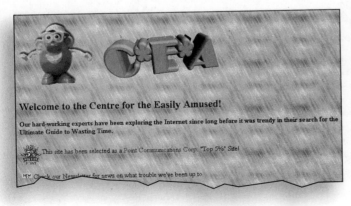

Confession Booth

`http://anther.learning.cs.cmu.edu/priest.html`

Humor

Guilt-ridden surfers worship this wacky site that lets you confess your sins to an unseen cyberpriest. The interface is a simple multiple-choice form, so don't expect visual miracles. You get to select what sort of sin you've committed, from murder and adultery to "fish in microwave" and "didn't put printouts in bin." After you spill all the juicy details, you're given a penance such as "Teach your parents again how to program the VCR." Or the priest may just tell you, "Never mind, I've done that myself." (Why doesn't this happen in real life?) Want to see how the other sinners fare? Take a peek at the (huge!) Scroll of Sin for previous confessions. The site's slogan says it all: "Bringing the Net to its knees since 1994."

Dr. Fellowbug's Laboratory of Fun & Horror

`http://www.dtd.com/bug/`

Humor

Dr. Fellowbug's Lab is a collection of weird and funny sites, all produced by the Web design firm Downtown Digital. Sites include the Keepers of Lists, who can show you the "Top 81 Things Kirk Would Say While Changing A Tire" ("Must... get... lug... bolt... off!"), and the ghoulish Letter R.I.P. (a hangman-style puzzle with a twist). You'll also find a surprise or two: clicking on a balloon tied to a rat's tail leads you into a little comic strip involving the rat and an executive. This isn't exactly chock-full of useful information, but what's here is great fun. And the artwork is terrific! You have to like a company that pours this much energy into just horsing around.

The Dysfunctional Family Circus

http://www.thoughtport.com/spinnwebe-cgi-bin/dfc.cgi

Humor

" "Family Circus" comic strip fans have fair warning. This page portrays the "heartwarming cartoons drawn by Bil Keane, gone horribly awry." Webmaster Greg Galcik takes existing "Family Circus"

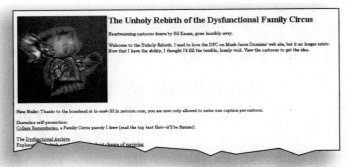

cartoons and then prints suggestions for alternate captions from site visitors. (Dolly, saying her prayers in bed, now chants: "la, Shub-Niggurath! The black goat of the woods with a thousand young!") Galcik makes it pretty clear that he is the boss here, giving guidelines for which captions have the best chance of surviving. Of course, if any comic strip is ripe for this kind of satire, it's the preternaturally cheerful "Family Circus," a strip that practically begs for an irreverent response. Many are *quite* funny and (no surprise) many are also naughty, and some are just plain weird.

Evil Little Brother Excuse Generator

http://www.dtd.com/excuse/

Humor

Your evil little brother always seemed to get out of trouble, didn't he? Leaving you holding the bag, right? This site lets you put his Unholy Power in *your*

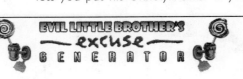

hands for a change. From "I never return your calls" to "Sorry I burnt down your house," this Evil Little Brother zips to the rescue with an apology, a rationalization, and a spiteful grin. You choose a general description of your problem, then type in the recipient's name and other excuse-specific details. Forgot your mother's birthday? Key in the appropriate information and receive a custom phrase of rapprochement: "I have made a kelp cake stuffed with gnocci, your favorite, if I remember correctly." It's strange, but it's fun.

Fidel for President

http://www.slugs.com/imagesmith/fidel/

Humor

We're *glad* the folks at Image-smith have nothing to do all day but create winning Web pages like this one. Who knows what they'd be capable of if they were really unleashed in the American political arena? Even if you choose not to join "Team Fidel," you'll be swept up in the excitement of this presidential campaign for Castro, "The Ultimate Washington Outsider." You can hardly escape the logic: Castro knows the Contract for America because "America's had a contract out on him for more than thirty years." Politics is also merchandising, and Team Fidel is prepared with shirts, bumper stickers, and bubble-gum cigars for sarcastically spendy sums. Even the links are jokes, and pretty good ones at that. Semper Fidel!

Guess the Evil Dictator and/or Television Sitcom Character

http://sp1.berkeley.edu/dict.html

Humor

"Pretend to be your favorite evil dictator or television sitcom character and I'll try to guess who you're supposed to be," invites this page (the creation of a cleverly twisted Berkeley student). It's like Twenty Questions: you just answer yes or no to queries like "Do you work in a news room?" and "Are you a landlord who favors leisure suits?" Believe it or not, the server swiftly and correctly identified our chosen characters, first Jack Tripper from *Three's Company*, and then Benito Mussolini. (And aren't they related?) Conclude what you like about the predictability of dictatorship or TV stardom, but there's no arguing this is just the kind of delightful waste of time the Web accomplishes best.

Imagine's Joke Board

http://www.best.com/~imagine/jokes/
Humor

Readers rate jokes (from "not funny" to "herniatingly funny") at this knee-slapping site. Search for new jokes, popular jokes, high-rated or low-rated jokes, or by topic. As with so many Web humor sites, many of the jokes are in poor taste—but they're offensive in four languages! Headlining itself as "not just jokes," the site has branched out a bit from its jokes-only origins: the WhiteBoard News sections provides strange news items from around the world, like the story of Dan Anderson, whose dog was the best man at his wedding. You can submit your own jokes, or if you want a challenge, you can hit the Interactive Jokes area, where a lead-in is provided and you get to enter your own punchline.

Inert Net Grave Near Mars

http://www.wordsmith.org/awad-cgibin/anagram
Humor

The Inert Net Grave Near Mars is not a space-station cemetery; rather, it is an anagram for "Internet Anagram Server." (An anagram is a "word or phrase made by transposing the letters of another word or phrase.") The interface is simple: you enter your word or phrase, hit Enter, and the program does its magic. No bells and whistles, but none are really needed. An excellent bet is the "Anagram Hall of Fame," which offers up such delicacies as "Clint Eastwood = Old West Action." Politically stinging anagrams are always enjoyable: "William Jefferson Clinton = Jail Mrs. Clinton: Felon wife." The page also offers an automatic device that will anagramize any words you feed it. Kudos to site author Anu Garg... or should we say, A Rag Gnu?

Keepers of Lists

http://www.dtd.com/keepers

Humor

The Keepers describe themselves as "a secret society dedicated to the creation and maintenance of lists." Each day a new list appears, and visitors vote on their favorites. You're also able to enter your own addition (if your ego can withstand the possibility of everyone voting it down). Because anyone can enter anything, you have to expect some stupidity, but there's plenty of good pickings, too: the "85 Ways to Describe the Internet to Grandma" included "It's like being able to check on the chickens without leaving the house," and "It's like reading a paper, only you go blind faster." Past lists have included "Top 139 Favorite Childhood Toys" and "Top 66 Talk Show Topics that use the word Gorgonzola." Some good, some lame, lots of laughs.

The Capt. James T. Kirk Sing-a-Long Page

http://www.ama.caltech.edu/~mrm/kirk.html

Humor

In psychedelic 1968, William Shatner (Captain Kirk from the original *Star Trek*) recorded an album called "The Transformed Man." The choicest cuts are reproduced here, and some of them sound like Shatner was being transformed on the spot, or maybe being pulled inside-out. Shatner's renditions of songs like "Lucy in the Sky with Diamonds" must be heard to be believed. Hundreds of reviews (you can enter your own) will tell you what others think of Shatner's "singing" (i.e. he "makes Michael Bolton look like Howling Wolf.") You'll also find smaller snippets of three other *Star Trek* alumni who have also taken the musical plunge, but none of their efforts are nearly as embarrassing as the Captain's incredible "Mr. Tambourine Man." We love you, Bill, but we laughed out loud and had our own "jingle-jangle mornin'."

Magic 8-Ball

`http://www.resort.com/~banshee/Misc/8ball/index.html`

Humor

You remember the Magic 8-Ball: the leaky plastic billiard ball with crystal blue water in the middle that prophesied the future? It's a pop-culture icon for most kids born between 1960 and 1975. Well, this Web version is just as cheesy—and almost as irresistible, at least for a time or two. You can query the "Ultimate Oracle" here courtesy of some friendly computer geeks from Santa Cruz, California. Our choices: "Will we finally meet that blonde with the great calves at the gym?" ("Better not tell you now.") "Will mohair come back into vogue?" ("Without a doubt.") And "Will this site score highly?" ("My sources say no.") Ah, guess again!

Mediocre Site of the Day

`http://minerva.cis.yale.edu/~jharris/mediocre.html`

Humor

You can't swing a virtual cat by the tail without hitting a Best or Worst of the Web site these days—but what about the semi-interesting land in-between? This terrific page was "created to pay homage to the middle 98%—the mediocre, the so-so, average sites." Author Jensen Harris personally chooses a mediocre site of the day for visitors to peruse; we can't imagine a more anti-exotic site than the "Dentistry in Florida" page. The folder of previous sites is a treat for the giggle-inducing site names alone: try Poultry Science, The Cleveland State University Police Department, and *Asian Bride Magazine*. Harris maintains "mediocrity is not boring," and here he twists your arm half-way to agreement.

Mirsky's Worst of the Web

http://turnpike.net/metro/mirsky/Worst.html

Humor

The "Gong Show" of the Internet, this site shamelessly parades the absolute worst Web pages naked down the Infobahn. As you enter this Hall of Lame, Mirsky offers this Dante-esque warning: "You are in for the opposite of a treat." How wrong he is! This pantheon of camp, buffoonery, and ineptitude is a browser's delight. He serves up two to five spectacles per day, so there's always a lot to browse. And Mirsky himself adds amusing asides that tease, cajole, and are generally mean to the creators of these sorry sites. His comments don't give away the surprise, though: "I don't see how anyone can answer this without full-body nudes" leads to a page where a user is conducting a poll on whether his sister looks like him wearing a wig. As he puts it: "If it isn't Mirsky's, then it isn't the worst!"

News of the Weird

http://www.nine.org/notw/notw.html

Humor

Chuck Shepard, a syndicated columnist, makes a weekly collection of, shall we say, unusual news items from around the globe. Take, for instance, the Kansas City man found guilty of murder and sentenced to death, plus life in prison, plus another 315 years. Or consider the court case where the defendant's attorney argued for low bail because his client would not flee. At that moment, the client ran from the courtroom and led deputies on a one-hour chase. (He's back in jail.) This site presents his column in full every week (but it's delayed by two weeks, because the papers get it first). If you prefer not to hit the Web site to check for updates, instructions on having the column mailed to you are provided. The layout is simple, even ugly, but the reading is irresistible.

The Palindrome Page

http://www2.ecst.csuchico.edu/~beej/palindromes.html

Humor

Aha! Oho! (Well, they're a start.) This is, quite simply, a gigantic list of phrases that read the same forward as backwards, listed in length order from "Kayak" to a 543-word variation on the well-known "A man, a plan, a canal—Panama" palindrome. Author Brian Hall has added some contemporary examples—like "Age, irony, Noriega" and "Lisa Bonet ate no basil"—to punch up the well-worn classics like

continued

The Palindrome Page
continued

"Madam in Eden, I'm Adam." There's also a few bonuses, like palindromes in languages other than English, and "acoustic palindromes" (phrases that sound like themselves, if you were to record them and play them backwards). This is a treat for fanatics, an amusing diversion for the rest of us. But then again, "We panic in a pew."

The Random Haiku Generator

http://www.ip.net/2d/Haiku/haiku.html
Humor

Haiku is a very distinguished type of Japanese three-line, non-rhyming poetry. This site has terrific fun with the idea (while no doubt trampling on the sacred spirit of haiku masters everywhere) by enabling surfers to enter one random first, second, or third haiku line. The lines must be five, seven, and five syllables, respectively, so if you can count to seven, you qualify as a modern poet on this page. (Just like in real life!) The computer throws together submissions into an endless series of addictively fractured haiku (or is it "haikus"?). Sure, there are the Net's usual dopey obscenities, but the best combinations can be oddly effective: "Phil Donahue sucks / I'm taking over the world / Pop will eat itself." If that's not insightful, we don't know what is.

The Spam Haiku Archive

http://www.naic.edu/~jcho/spam/sha.html
Humor

Here you can get a taste of inner peace through poetry devoted to that all-American pink meat in the blue can, Spam (which, as anyone can tell you, is a registered trademark of the Hormel Foods Corporation). These Haiku have from-the-gut emotions and language as slippery as the jelly lubricant/adjunct that Spam fans know so well. One biting (so to speak) example: "Millions starve in Chad/U.S. sends massive SPAM aid/ Millions starve in Chad." The site includes hundreds of selections (loosely organized into topics such as "Cannibalism" and "Childhood trauma"), surely the world's most extensive collection of lunchmeat poetry. The site includes links to other Spam sites, where Spam is *also* a registered trademark of the Hormel Foods Corporation.

Welcome to the SPAM Haiku Archive!

SPAM, that mysterious and irresistably repulsive food product, has spawned a post-modern, cross-cultural literary form: the **SPAM haiku**. This WWW site was created so that anyone who comes under the influence of this enigmatic porcine muse can share his/her poetic epiphany with the rest of the world. Even if you are not inspired to contribute to the archive, you can browse through and marvel at the works of genius that SPAM has motivated in others.

- Go to the archive.
- Submit a SPAM haiku to the archive.

Spatula City

http://www.wam.umd.edu/~twoflowr/index.html

Humor

Based on a comedy concept by "Weird Al" Yankovic, this silly site has fun and fiction down every aisle, creating the same overwhelmed feeling you get from a real superstore. To fill all your spatula needs, head over to Aisle 1, where "Spatula City stocks only the latest advances in spatula technology." The shelves are stocked with dozens of fantasy spatulas, from "Swiss Army Spatula" to the "Five Spatulas of Fury." Spatniks will flip at the chance to submit their own models. In Aisle 3, the "Silly Zone" lives up to its name, with cute jokes that are witty, if a bit over-wrought. The bells and whistles in the "Black Light Special" are guaranteed to waste your time, and that's the point. This is a great-looking place stocked with non-sense, and chuckles come with almost every selection.

The T.W.I.N.K.I.E.S. Project

http://www.rice.edu:80/~gouge/twinkies.html

Humor

The Twinkie page is the brainwave of a pair of engineering students at prestigious Rice University, who applied standard engineering tests to, well, Hostess Twinkies. Their deadpan experi-mental technique gets funnier and funnier as they try various experiments, from Rapid Oxidation (attempts to set fire to a Twinkie) to our favorite, the utterly moronic Gravitational Response test (Twinkies dropped off high buildings). Each experiment is replete with technical details and pictures of the ongoing procedure. Be sure to catch the Turning Test, where they use a control subject (a sophomore) to determine whether Twinkies are intelligent. (The conclusion: Twinkies are "not sentient in any way we can understand.") And, if you're entirely baffled by all the technical Twinkie jargon, you can read the haiku interpretation of the test results. Intelligent stupid fun.

Wall O' Shame

http://www.milk.com/wall-o-shame/

Humor

Webmaster Dan Bornstein presents wild and wacky tales at this site—all true, he says, and indeed the stories are often credited to a news service or some such source. The material is the kind urban legends are made of: "A hunter in Uganda is being sought by local authorities for ille-gally hunting gorillas. He shoots them with

continued

Wall O' Shame continued

a tranquilizer gun and dresses them in clown suits." Some samples aren't so cutesy, however. Sellers of the Polytron, an industrial-strength mixer used in laboratories, thought this phrase was just what they needed to sell their product: "Only the Polytron reduces an entire mouse to a soup-like homogenate within 30 seconds." (Yeesh!) Bornstein calls the Wall o' Shame "an attempt to characterize the erosion of our world," so apparently we're having a laugh at the expense of a crumbling society, here. But hey, the stories are still a lot of fun.

WALL O' SHAME

"Before I read the Wall O' Shame, my vocabulary was small. Now, it's big."
-Satisfied customer Alan Asper aasper@andersen.com

Guest Book / Sign & Feedback / Linkers / Submissions

This is my attempt to characterize the erosion of our world by displaying *true* stories and tidbits that are just too nonlinear.

Normal Shamefulness

- 90% Body Odor
- Albert de Salvo
- Anarchy In Action
- Appropriate use of Gorecki's Third

movies

Alien, Aliens, Alien3

`http://dutial.twi.tudelft.nl/~alien/alien.html`
Movies

Subtitled, "The Art of Survival," this site covers more than the three *Alien* movies—it has the skinny on POTENTIAL stuff. Unused scripts (including the now-legendary William Gibson script) are right alongside the scripts of the first three movies, and of course the FAQ is rife with rumors. For true fans, the vehicles and weaponry are presented here like a Pentagon brochure. The gallery for H.R. Giger (the artist who designed the Alien) has more than just monster pictures, and the movie stills include those french-kissing "Facehuggers," ribcage rebels the "Chestbursters," and the rather selfish "Queen Alien" and her eggs by the dozen. Woo!

ALIEN WAR

The ultimate attraction for every Alien fan in **London, England** on Piccadilly Circus... There is an 'official' Alien War Page under construction which is located HERE.

Pictures, Info and Sound

Description of the alien's lifecycle.

Pictures from the movie Aliens.

Various pictures about the Alien trilogy and games.

A directory with pictures of and by Giger.

Another site, with Alien Traced Art...

Let's visit a collector: *Roman*

SOUNDS from Aliens in .au format
SOUNDS from Aliens in WAV format...

A sample of 450Kb... Alien: The Beginning

Buena Vista Movieplex

http://www.disney.com/
Movies

Forget about Siskel and Ebert. This page from Buena Vista pictures (a division of Walt Disney) brings you previews of coming attractions right on your computer. Click on MoviePlex and you're treated to either "Sneak Peeks" (Quicktime movies, with sound) or full-fledged trailers for several of Buena Vista's current releases. Film clips, however, are just the beginning. You can also listen to interviews with various stars or take a look at production notes, film credits, and promotional stills. When you've had your fill of movies, Buena Vista also offers the paltry-by-comparison TV Plex and Walt Disney Records (why were we not surprised to learn that Disney's in the record biz too?). You need a high-speed connection or an amazing amount of patience to really enjoy this site.

The Cannes International Film Festival

http://www.interactive8.com:80/cannes/welcome/
welcome.html
Movies

With everything from restaurant reviews ("some of the best bouillabaisse to be had anywhere is at Tetou in Golfe Juan") to the French translation of industry phrases (*Mon assistante appellera ton assistante* means "I'll have my people call your people"), this site is an informative and quirky look at life on the French Riviera. For a real hoot, take a look at the list of the film festival jury members. Where else but Cannes '95 would you have found cult director John Waters and Pulitzer Prize-winning author Nadine Gordimer at the same event, let alone swapping opinions about the merits of various films? Sponsored by Tanqueray, this page not only demystifies the international film market, but it also includes gossip about films and stars, plus how-tos for getting appropriate Cannes credentials.

Fast Times at Ridgemont High

`http://wizvax.net/truegger/fast-times.html`

Movies

This site captures the fun and wit of the 1982 movie that showcased comically obnoxious California teenagers in their natural habitat—high school and the mall. The film made Sean Penn a star and made his character, Jeff Spicoli, a cinema icon for airhead surfer dudes. (The film also launched the careers of Phoebe Cates, Jennifer Jason Leigh, and Judge Reinhold.) Sound samples of Spicoli and the script (and book) excerpts are still funny. Rather than long movie clips to download, a clever "filmstrip" method revisits some of the best film moments. Trivia abounds, including the fact that writer/director Cameron Crowe (*Singles*) posed for a year as a southern California high school student to research the book on which the movie's based. It's rather odd, in fact, how interesting the movie still is.

Hitchcock—Master of Suspense

`http://nextdch.mty.itesm.mx/~plopezg/Kaplan/`
`Hitchcock.html`

Movies

While this site contains a great collection of facts and trivia from Alfred Hitchcock's 50-year film career (we had absolutely no idea that he directed nine

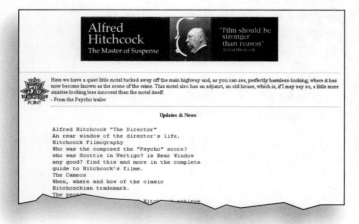

silent films between 1925 and 1929), fans will find only fair-to-middling details on the films themselves. Not to worry, though. The page has terrific coverage of favorite Hitchcock actors like Cary Grant and Grace Kelly, as well as a good bio on The Plump One himself. Best of all, the site offers a complete list of the oddball cameo appearances Hitchcock made in nearly all of his movies. ("*Spellbound* (1945): Coming out of an elevator at the Empire Hotel, carrying a violin case and smoking a cigarette, 40 minutes in.") Good quotes, too. ("I didn't say actors are cattle. What I said was, actors should be treated like cattle.")

Hollywood Online

http://www.hollywood.com/
Movies

Hollywood Online is one of several sites gunning to become *the* online guide to Tinseltown. And with a plethora of multimedia clips, promos, and notes on several of the newest and hottest films, it has a good start. The page is hype-heavy and studio-friendly, no question; it's a form-over-substance situation. Still, the on-demand trailers for the latest blockbusters are almost irresistible if you've got the high-speed equipment to handle them. Somewhat out of context, but still fun, is the guide to Hollywood Luxury Homes, where you can take a gander at some high-ticket real estate. Interested in that Malibu colony mansion? It's yours for a song—as long as the song happens to be "If I Were A Rich Man."

Internet Movie Database

http://www.msstate.edu/Movies/welcome.html
Movies

This tremendous movie guide is compiled by Internet users for Internet users. Visitors will find crew lists, running times, actor bios, gaffes and goofs, and much more, all shot through with hyperlinks for easy reference. The site claims to cover more than 50,000 films, plus thousands of TV series. Since the information comes from Web users, the quality is sometimes fabulous and occasionally lame. Still, what do you want for free: Shakespeare? Look up a great thespian like Martin Balsam, for instance, and you'll learn that he recently starred in an Italian parody called *Silence of the Hams* along with Mel Brooks, Phyllis Diller, Rip Taylor, and Larry Storch. (No kidding!) Then you can learn that Rip Taylor has since appeared in *Private Obsession* with Peetie the Dog. Then you can see Peetie's filmography. (Just the one film, sadly.) Then you can... well, this is just scratching the surface. A delightful, unique-to-the-Web resource.

The Internet Movie Database

formerly (and incorrectly) known as the Cardiff Movie Database

All information provided here originates from the users of the database. ..an example of how the internet community can provide for itself.

Recommended reading for new users...

James Bond Movie Page

http://www.dur.ac.uk/~dcs3pjb/jb/jbhome.html
Movies

Producer Albert "Cubby" Broccoli once said, "It was estimated recently that half the world's population has seen a James Bond movie." If you're on the right half of that equation, you'll find this page as tasty as a vodka martini shaken and... well, you know. Fabulous density here; metric tons of info and links. The film summaries include categories like "Bad Guy sidekick" and "Best Gadget/Gimmick." There's also a section devoted exclusively to those sleek Bond autos. (WannaBonds can contact Neiman Marcus for a limited-edition BMW 23 Roadster, the agent's new German (!) auto-of-choice.) Plenty of chat about the newest Bond, Pierce Brosnan. Is he tough enough? Good photos and no-nonsense presentation make this a great movie page.

Mel's Godzilla Page

http://www.ama.caltech.edu/~mrm/godzilla.html
Movies

This Godzilla fan site is as towering and hulking as the flame-spewing matinee idol himself. Flip through the Great One's filmography (*Godzilla Raids Again*, also known as *Gigantis, The Fire Monster*, a.k.a. *Godzilla's Counterattack*), or see him fighting off Mothra and taking a death-ray hit from shiny nemesis SuperMechaGodzilla. A stat sheet shows results from some of history's major monster matches. In their first meeting, Godzilla managed only a Kaiju Retreat against the Sea Monster; but in the rematch, it was lights out for the Sea Monster when Godzilla scored a Kaiju Kill. In fact, all the best Godzilla opponents are here, from first-string contender Rodan to Manda, a monster your "grandma could whup." We can't shriek enough about this colorful, funny, and content-rich page.

The Movie Clichés List

http://www.well.com/user/vertigo/cliches.html
Movies

The Movie Clichés List is a triumph of content over presentation. Giancarlo Cairella doesn't go in for fancy graphics, but he's put plenty of energy into this laundry list of filmdom's greatest repeating phenomena. The list covers dozens of topics, ranging from war (you'll never survive if you show someone a picture of your sweetheart back home), to chess (supposedly brilliant players always miss one-move checkmates in critical games), to schools (teachers are always interrupted mid-sentence by the end-of-class bell). Anyone who's been to more than 10 movies will recognize something here. Great stuff, even if it does leave out how every window in Washington, D.C., has a view of the Capitol.

Movie Link

http://www.777FILM.com/

Movies

This is an online version of MovieFone, the nationwide service that offers show times and ticket sales for movies now playing. Movie fans from all over can enjoy the trailers, posters, and plot synopses of current movies, or check the Parent's Guide to find out which "R" movies the nippers may try to sneak into. The big selling point, though, is that users in major U.S. cities can order tickets from participating theaters right online. Could this be the future in moviegoing? You watch a few previews (if you have the time to download them), decide on a show time at the local theater, and buy tickets without having to leave your monitor. Of course, you still have to haul your body, and your date's, to the theater to actually see the movie.

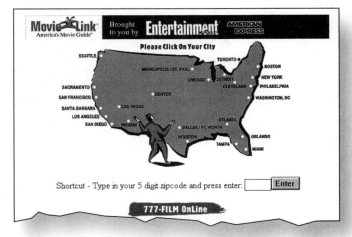

The Official Interactive Guide to the Academy Awards

http://guide.oscars.org:80/

Movies

This page is loaded with known and little-known facts about Oscar winners (*Forrest Gump* was up for almost twice as many awards as any other 1994 film), plus clips and images galore. We learned a lot from the Academy of Motion Picture Arts and Sciences link (the calendar of upcoming events is only beneficial if you live in L.A.), but our favorite stop is the trivia game. Name the only actor nominated for an Academy Award twice after his death! Better still, which *three* actresses used sign language in their Oscar acceptance speeches? Here's a gimme: Walt Disney is the all-time Oscar champ, personally collecting 26 statuettes before his death in 1966. Actually, you might try reading this page during the dull moments in the next Academy Award telecast.

Off-World (A Blade Runner Page)

http://kzsu.stanford.edu/uwi/br/off-world.html

Movies

This is one of many fan pages for *Blade Runner*, one of the most influential sci-fi movies of the 1980s. Some loved it as a visionary work of great importance, some hated it as a schlocky, updated Raymond Chandler rip-off. This page is for the admirers, who'll love the images and the wrangling over whether or not Deckard (Harrison Ford) was really a replicant (android). Serious studies include an essay on the architecture in the film and a Washington State University Study Guide of the book *Do Androids Dream of Electric Sheep?* by Philip K. Dick, on which the film is based. Great links to various *Blade Runner* resources, with leads to image and sound files from the movie, as well as the original script in its entirety. Good stuff!

Picture Palace

http://www.ids.net/picpal/index.html

Movies

This New Jersey cinema shop may just be the cult film lover's court of last resort. Proprietor Steve Kramer sells rare, questionable, and frequently downright lurid videos and laser discs, and his love of the stuff makes even window-shopping terrifically informative. (And Kramer promises to verify all orders via e-mail within 24 hours of receiving them.) You won't find skin flicks here, unless you count 1950s pinup girl Bettie Page's film loops, but Chaplin and Keaton classics abound, plus posthumous tribute packages to Ginger Rogers and other recently departed icons. Good sidelights, too, like the interview with Patrick Nagel on the craft and business sense of American art today. Odds seem good that if Leonard Maltin says a film is out there, but the teenager behind your local video counter gives you a blank look, you'll find it here.

No Paper Waste In Virtual Space! With at least 13 shipping centers and over $15 million in inventory at our disposal, we can track down what you need if it's currently in release. Just let us know your interests or use Netscape for our 30,000-title MonsterBase.

Videos/Lasers/CD-Roms

The Picture Palace Newsreel: Sept. 19th - 26th

The big news in home video this week is six new releases in the *Dr. Who* series. "More Than Thirty Years in the Tardis", "Time and the Rani," "Curse of Peladon," "Seeds of Doom" and "Arc of Infinity" are priced at $19.98 apiece ($24.98 in Canada), but the double cassette "Inferno" is $29.98 ($34.98 in Canada). These will be followed in December by another handful. On our site we present some pre-teen Spielbergs (or would that be Camerons?)! Quentin Crisp has personally autographed copies of *The Kissing Booth* just for us. We've also updated our dead letter collection. We've also supplemented our bargain videos section with some of Tarkovsky's bigge... ...ns ...ts: *The Story of Boys & Girls*, the first film of China's new cinema, and other international

The Rocky Horror Picture Show

http://www.cs.wvu.edu/~paulr/rhps/rhps.html

Movies

Thanks to this site, you won't make the faux pas of arriving for the midnight showing of that granddaddy of cult movies, *The Rocky Horror Picture Show*, without rice, toilet paper, or toast. Most people know that the *Rocky Horror* experience involves more audience participation than viewing; in fact, if you've ever seen the spectacle, you know better than to try to understand the movie or listen to the soundtrack. Here novices (are there any left?) are guided through dialogue and songs like "The Time Warp," and offered parenthetical audience cues (most use adult language) along with "traditional" responses. It's no substitute for the real thing, but conscientious students who carefully study the script won't be embarrassed by tossing their cold weiners prematurely screenward.

Star Wars

```
http://force.stwing.upenn.edu:8001/~jruspini/
starwars.html
```
Movies

"A long time ago in a galaxy far, far away..." If those words stir nothing in your heart, stay away. This is THE site by and for fans of the *Star Wars* films. The

> **News and frequently asked questions about the Star Wars galaxy.**
>
> 🌐NEW! The Star Wars Collecting FAQ
> 🌐NEW! Plans for Indy IV may be Dead
> 🌐NEW! How to Subscribe to Star Wars Insider Magazine
>
> - New Trilogy News (New FAQ v 2.0)
> - The New Updated Star Wars FAQ
> - Frequently Asked Questions ver 4.10
> - Kenner Star Wars Toy Line Update
> - Spielberg's Company Dreamworks to Produce New Trilogy?
> - An Article on Skywalker Ranch
> - Future Dark Horse Comics Star Wars Projects
> - Star Wars Card Game in Works
> - John Williams Retires From Boston Pops
> - ANH Theater Re-Release Confirmed by L.A. Times
> - A Report From the Star Wars Summit
> - Lucas: New Trilogy Should be Released In '98 or '99

collection is admirably, amazingly thorough; these rabid fans even discuss composer John Williams' retirement from the Boston Pops. The online scripts include an early George Lucas draft titled *The Adventures of the StarKiller*, and the FAQs are full of delicious rumors about a new *Star Wars* trilogy (with Kenneth Brannagh as Obi Wan Kenobi?). And where else but in the trivia section could you learn where to look for a brief glimpse of Carrie Fisher's birthmark during *The Return of the Jedi*? Good-looking, stuffed with detail, a delight from start to finish.

Universal Cyberwalk

```
http://www.mca.com
```
Movies

The Universal Studios Cyberwalk is a flashy neon sign of a site, and isn't it nice to know you can still depend on Hollywood for a great sense of glitter? The Cyberwalk is a fine showcase for MCA/Universal coming attractions, with categories like V/IP (films), the Universal Channel (TV productions), and AMP magazine (MCA records). As an added bonus, if you're looking for that perfect gift, you can browse Spencer Gifts ("the people who made Lava Lamps cool again") online. Yup, it's a PR site, but a handsome one with video clips, stills, audio, and lots of star power. Come prepared to wait, though: all that multimedia means lots of slow loading. Only YOU can decide how many minutes of life you're willing to spend waiting for a "personal message" from Arnold Schwarzenegger.

music

American Recordings

http://american.recordings.com/

Music

This site for the genre-splicing American Recordings label rises way above the promotional purgatory ambiance that hexes many of its peers. (It's fun! What a concept!) A monster "Web Wide World of Music" machine generously links you to artists as oddly familiar as ABBA and as unfamiliar as Zen Cats. And an on-site 'zine called Virus has great headlines ("God Sues Michael Jackson") among other notes. American's PR efforts are genuinely creative, too. (A promo for the band Swell includes a word-search game with names of 53 bands it has been compared to in reviews.) Listen to the latest from Johnny Cash and MC 900 Foot Jesus, and watch videos for "the generation that wants to see what MTV can't show." With an invitation like "Run your fingers through these digital furballs," who can resist?

Aussie Music Online

http://www.aussiemusic.com.au/

Music

Aussie Music Online is a comprehensive guide to tunes down under, and it's got a charming personality. (But does everybody really say "G'day" down there, or is it all a gag?) Divided between a magazine and a shop, the site sings with weekly charts and news blurbs ("INXS singer Michael Hutchence sold his Sydney house for $270,000..."), but it will also help you locate an obscure Australian record label, or pick up Radio Australia via shortwave or satellite. Authoritative views from some of Australia's leading rock journalists pad the site, while a down-underground 'zine adds the balance of some indie-musicologists on an amusing mission to "destroy accepted journalistic standards." When you're ready to shop, the record store displays the latest Aboriginal releases.

Aussie Music Online

The Best in Australian Music

● **An introduction to AMO**
   A brief outline of what AMO is about and how to get around

 **Good news for Aussie music**

   AMO has been rated in the top 5% of all Web sites
● **AMO's Music Magazine**
   Information, contacts, news, views and where to hear Aussie music
   An intro   AMO's Music Magazine

Alan Braverman's Beatles Page

http://turtle.ncsa.uiuc.edu/alan/beatles.html
Music

With the breadth of information available on the Fab Four, it's refreshing to find a compact fan site like this one, which pulls together the most fascinating trivia and offers links to the rest. See the beloved "Butcher Cover," which gives new meaning to the phrase "rare image." (It features—no kidding!—smiling Beatles seated amongst doll parts and cuts of meat.) Join the ongoing "Norwegian Wood" debate by listening and deciding for yourself: "Does John burn down her apartment or relax by the fire?" The random coincidences surrounding the "Paul is Dead" hoax are examined here in enough detailed exposition to send Oliver Stone reeling. (These folks know the words to Beatles songs *backwards*.) And a graphical chart reveals identities of all the curious figures on the *Sgt. Peppers* album cover—even those whose faces were blotted out.

The Blue Highway

http://www.magicnet.net/~curtis/
Music

This encyclopedic road-trip of the blues "winds past the plantation barrelhouses of the Mississippi Delta to the south-side clubs and tenements of

The Blue Highway

. . . winds past the plantation barrelhouses of the Mississippi Delta to the south-side clubs and tenements of postwar Chicago. While it's a somber trip, humbling, even distressing, it's also enchanting and joyful—and reassuring in its success.

The history of the blues is more than a musical chronology. The blues was born the day the West African shoreline fell from the horizon. It was raised amid the institutionalized savagery of the Deep South and flourished in the dark heart of America's largest cities. We owe the blues to those who bore the pain of enslavement behind the frightful shadows of our collective soul. *The Blue Highway*, then, is dedicated to the men and women who traveled beyond our ignorant place, and to those who could not.

postwar Chicago." The roadside attractions: 20 of the masters who shaped the blues. Meet Robert Johnson "at the crossroad where they say he struck a deal with the Devil," and John Lee Hooker, who, pushing 80, continues to innovate. Sorrow-soaked audio samples include "St. Louis Blues" from Bessie Smith and "Hoochie Coochie Man" from Muddy Waters. In fact, "Muddy's Cabin" (well, a picture of it anyway) features guest-chat appearances by greener blues celebs like Poppa Chubby, Keb' Mo', and G. Love. One spirited entry in the site's guest book exclaims "BLUES IS MY THANG!" Even if it's not yours, this is an enchanting journey to take.

CDNOW

CDWOW is more like it. This online superstore offers a mind-blowing collection of music and related products (over 65,000 items and two-day delivery), but it also includes some invaluable information resources—like a guide for building a classical-music library, and a dictionary with definitions for musical terms from acappella to zither. The scope of the CD database is almost unbelievable. A search under Donald Fagen (one of our own favorites) turned up his personal biography, a discography with descriptions and star ratings, and a list of import titles (even telling us that his Japanese EPs were not in stock, but could be backordered). It also revealed a Fagen video we didn't know existed. Multiply this entry by every jazz, pop, country, and classical artist you can think of, and you get a sense of this site.

Classic Rock Photo Gallery

This fascinating photo gallery is part of the private Web site of Robert Altman (not *that* Robert Altman—this one used to shoot covers for *Rolling Stone*). The emphasis is on the performers of late '60s and early '70s: a youthful Jerry Garcia clutches his guitar in Golden Gate Park, and a downright boyish Neil Young looks the spitting image of the grunge rockers who are singing his praises (and his songs) these days. The adjoining Celebrity Wing is also worth a tour for its striking portraits and funny stories about people like Joe Montana, Kirstie Alley, and Groucho Marx. (It was during Marx's interview with Altman that made the famous remark, "the only hope for Nixon was his assassination.") This is a real treasure for anyone who likes portraits, rock history, or modern culture in general.

Classical Music Home Page

http://www.webcom.com/~music
Music

Here's the "How to Buy Classical Music CDs 101" class that you never had. The bad news: "The diversity, complexity, and even the mystique of classical music can be rather intimidating." The good news: "You can enjoy what you're hearing without knowing exactly why." Author Dave Lampson (an Oklahoma trumpet player who gave up performance for nuclear engineering and mathematics) will help you understand why you like what you're hearing, and much more. If you don't know Schubert from shinola, you will learn here that most classical pieces fall into four basic categories: orchestral, chamber, keyboard, and vocal. (And we thought they were pretty, ugly, creepy, and the William Tell Overture.) Lampson recommends boatloads of recordings based on first-hand experience and availability. He won't send you on a hunt through flea-market bins, however: "If it isn't out on CD, it isn't available."

Countdown: An Opera for the Nuclear Age

http://www.xs4all.nl/~yavelow/docs/CnDnIntro.html
Music

Commissioned and performed by the Boston Lyric, this "first computer-assisted opera" weaves a musical yarn of love, pregnancy, and nuclear war. For this showcase site, the 28-minute production has been divided into 16 logical chunks, enabling you to listen to all of the music as you follow along with the libretto. It's a riot. A cheesy sci-fi overture is perfect for the setting in an underground missile command silo where, amidst general chaos and operatic cries of "red alert," the command comes to push the button. As usually happens in these situations, personal revelations surge. (Oh, the drama!) And it's near impossible to resist a baritone belting out lines like "They will transfer you out of hazardous duty!" to his pregnant infatuation, the mezzo soprano, who wails back, "I wouldn't mind getting out of this hole in the ground."

The Death of Rock 'n' Roll

http://weber.u.washington.edu/~jlks/pike/DeathRR.html

Music

Bizarre, messy, and early deaths are a long-standing rock and roll tradition, as pointed out at this site. (It's subtitled "Untimely Demises, Morbid Preoccupations, and Premature Forecasts of Doom in Pop Music.") Untimely death, it suggests, is what ties Elvis Presley to the Rolling Stones to the Sex Pistols to Slayer. Offering excerpts from a book of the same name (for sale here, natch), it chronicles more than 50 dead rockers and still doesn't seem all-inclusive. But it *is* fascinating material. Your morbid bone will be tickled with such blood-curdling tales as Billy Murcia (of the New York Dolls) drowning to death in coffee. And to cap off the surrealism, the site includes a photo of Elvis shaking hands with Richard Nixon. This is one of the few Web pages where heroin gets its very own link.

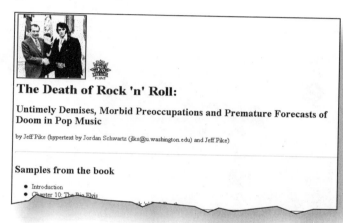

DiscoWeb

http://www.msci.memphis.edu/~ryburnp/discoweb.html

Music

Paul Ryburn ("the only University of Memphis faculty member with a fully operational disco ball in his office") pays campy tribute to the era of the Bee Gees, Gerald Ford, and powder-blue leisure suits at this delightful site. Ryburn pines for the glory days, spinning off his personal top 101 disco nuggets, lest we forget "Funky Town" and "Boogie Wonderland." But he also keeps tabs on the current tour activity of platform-soled troopers like the Village People and K.C. and the Sunshine Band ("hear 'Shake Your Booty' and 'Y.M.C.A.' performed live!"), and provides info on an International Leisure Suit Convention. A "Disco Around the World" folder is an essential for disco jet-setters, who can find out where to experience "Funky Friday" when in Greenville, S.C. Giddy fun.

elektra.com

http://www.elektra.com

Music

This big, colorful promotional site attempts to make you feel as though you're "wandering the halls" of Elektra Entertainment. Thus, the chat area becomes the "water cooler," the bulletin boards become the "soda machine," and so on; you can visit the receptionist ("Hi!"), or meander over to publicity ("My name is Shelby. I am the media mouthpiece for Ween..."). But the most fun to be had in this place comes from rummaging through the archives, where you can listen to Adina Howard sing "Freak Like Me," or watch a smashing video by the Breeders. Every once in a while, the site also lets you chat with Elektra artists. A recent celebrity session with earthy Natalie Merchant found her making statements such as, "Don't like eggs. But am not morally opposed to them."

jump to lo-bandwidth version

Elektra Entertainment Group

click to enter

ELEKTRA.COM

Expecting Rain

http://bob.nbr.no/

Music

Emanating from just below the Arctic Circle, this Norwegian (!) site is awash in esoteric facts and features on Bob Dylan. Hear "Bob sounds" (like an answering-machine message) and learn about his "Highway 61 Interactive" CD-ROM. Along with answers to the obligatory Frequently Asked Questions, the Webmaster incorporates a massive Bob Dylan Who's Who of 400 people connected, however remotely, with Dylan and characters from his songs. (We must say that one fan's suggestion that Bob was thinking about Jeffery Dahmer when he wrote "Baby Blue" seems a bit of a stretch.) Less arbitrary is the site's Dylan Atlas, which maps out scenes and locales mentioned in Dylan songs, from Armageddon to Williamsport. Shockingly, Dylan has never mentioned in song the Webmaster's hometown of Mo i Rana, Norway.

FenderWorld

http://www.fender.com/

Music

This home page for the famous Fender Guitar company doubles as something of a shrine for rock history: without Leo Fender and his revolutionary Stratocaster, rock just wouldn't be the same. Here, you'll find not only Frequently Asked Questions, but peeks at Fender fashion, dealer addresses, and a way to determine the age of most Fenders. In a chat area, we discovered which Strat Jimi Hendrix used, and why Kurt Cobain finished sets with a black Strat. (That's the hip nickname for the Stratocaster, by the way.) And in a com-pany history, we read that musicians "discovered that by carefully positioning the Stratocaster's switch between settings, the signals from two pickups mixed and produced snarling nasal tones that rede-fined electric guitar sound."

Geffen/DGC Records

http://www.geffen.com/

Music

Refreshingly devoid of PRattle about the David Geffen Company and its paper-pushing minions, this promo site puts the spotlight where it belongs: on the artists. Weezer, Nirvana, and Sonic Youth are among the so-hip-it-hurts acts featured here. Folders for more than 20 bands contain whimsical biographies ("Like a demonic Energizer bunny possessed by a superhuman work ethic, White Zombie keeps going and going"), sound clips, and videos (see Courtney Love's "Doll Parts" in action at the Hole page). The Geffen folks have a good sense of humor, too. The "Vintage 80s" folder greets visitors with text in a ghastly, archaic font. "No, you didn't launch telnet by accident," reads the narrative. "In the true spirit of nostalgia, we wanted to... remind you how lame com-puters looked in the 80s."

The Grateful Dead

http://www.cs.cmu.edu/afs/cs.cmu.edu/user/mleone/web/dead.html

Music

This fine Dead-ication invites you to "Go on, my friend, do anything you choose," and offers a daunting array of options. Read song lyrics to "I'm a Hog for You" and "Wharf Rat." Listen to the crowd bubble up as the Dead plunk into a performance of "Cosmic Charlie." Download some groovy dancing bear screen savers or Mac icons (peace signs, Zig-Zag packages, and so on). The excellent directory of bootleg tapes (a way of life for Deadheads) appears to be the ultimate list of what's out there and what's not, and a database of set lists covers what songs were performed at concerts between 1972 and 1995. With sections like "The Live Taper's Survival Guide" and "Tape Trading Information and Etiquette," the site begins to feel less like a fan page and more like a community. Touching tributes to Jerry Garcia, too.

Hip Hop Reviews

http://www.ai.mit.edu/~isbell/HFh/reviews/000-toc.html

Music

Charles Isbell, the self-proclaimed "homeboy from hell," hosts this amusing house-party of Hip Hop criticism. Isbell doesn't just *review* the lastest releases, he *dissects* them, phrase by phrase. And when the current crop grows thin, he isn't averse to going back in time to revive a classic like N.W.A.'s *Straight Outta Compton*. ("I think to myself: 'Damn. Ice Cube? What kinda stupid name is that?' That doesn't stop me from restarting the track, though, before I even got to the next verse.") Isbell's rating system is amusingly cryptic (he rates A Tribe Called Quest "Phat-plus," but gives MC Hammer an ice-cold "WhickerChairWack"), and his blow-by-blow reviews make perfect sense. We also dig his notes on profanity levels: "You could let your mother listen to it, but I wouldn't."

Hyperreal

http://www.hyperreal.com/

Music

Hyperreal is "a home to alternative culture, music, and expression," with a heavy emphasis on rave culture. (In case you're still in the dark about rave, a humor section explains, "You know you're a raver when... you have trouble naming five friends who are not pierced somewhere.") This site provides information for daze, and it serves as a flop-house for a dozen noisy 'zines like *Urb* and *Slurp*. A Spirit of Raving Archive includes enlightening rave testimonials ("When I reached the dance floor, it was as if all thoughts were wiped from my mind"). A database lets you track down a rave party in Africa, or list one of your own. A Raves in the News index includes breathless reporting on the phenomenon by such unlikely sources as the *Dayton Daily News* and the *Financial Times*.

Internet Rockhouse

http://www.rockhouse.com/

Music

The Rockhouse provides a cheap online crash pad for bands and musicians throughout 12 countries, "no matter how crappy or amateur you think you are." For a small fee, new acts are provided with a home page and a variety of services to help them get launched. The "rooms" are dedicated to genres (blues, classic, folk, punk) and services (equipment wanted, record labels)—each with its own news, gig reviews, calendar, and search function. On a recent visit to the Blues Room, a contest asked voters to choose between member sound samples for "best blues diddler." The site looks grungy (in keeping with the low-budget theme), but it also has some big ideas and valuable services.

Internet Underground Music Archive

http://www.iuma.com/IUMA-2.0/pages/home_page/homepage.html

Music

This interactive Underground Music Archive is flashy, gadget-heavy, and loaded with fan info and consumer details on more than 500 unsigned, independent musicians. A guided tour stops off at the burgeoning "Santa Cruz geek community" from which the archive sprung, and the impressive bands and artists section lets you experience an amazing range of new music; from Club Baby (they're "all the rage with toddlers and tykes") to Ganser, a punk trio inspired by the Carpenters. A publications section leads to fine 'zines like *Addicted to Noise* and *Strobe*, and neat user features let you do things like display a personal top-ten list. The graphics—it's that Betty Crocker motif again—are a tad oafish, but the site's sprightly features more than make up for that.

I.R.S. Records

http://www.underground.net:80/Rocktropolis/IRS/
irsclubfront.html

Music

Housed in the rock and roll fantasy theme park of Rocktropolis, this well-lit promo site steps "back into the future" with the independent record label that launched bands like Concrete Blonde and R.E.M. (I.R.S. was "anti-established in 1979.") The site is arranged like a multilevel nightclub, so you can hit the Main Stage for a history of the Go-Go's ("little punkettes with green and purple hair who slashed and painted their clothes and wore trash bags for dresses"), or cool off in the Hemisphere Lounge with fresh voices from a new generation of traditional Irish folk music. Downstairs, the Tribal Basement flashes neon party lights and pulsates with samples of white-hot club hits like "Let Me Be Your Underwear." The Hall of Fame has some nice cover-art from classic I.R.S. albums.

Jim Santo's Demo Universe

http://www.popes.com/demou/

Music

Since 1989, Jim Santo has chronicled the "peculiar" world of unknown-band demo tapes in his "Demorandum" column for the cutting-edge music mag *Alternative*

Press. With this, his own site, Santo invites the Internet community to join his quest for music's strange and undiscovered. Specifically, geniuses and hacks alike are welcome to send demos for consideration here. More casual surfers can check out daily reviews or read Santo's columns from *Alternative Press.* His style is best described as pungent: "Rural Swine roadhouse punk-rock comes on like 20 million gallons of spilled hog waste." (Didn't Ed Sullivan say that once?) He's also capable of more traditional critic-speak; Minion Project's songs "would be considered ambient were they not so subliminally distressing." All in all, this is a nice demonstration of the Web's do-it-yourself spirit.

Live Aid—A Celebration

http://www.herald.co.uk/local_info/live_aid.html

Music

British site creator Melanie Dymond Harper does not pretend to be affiliated with the official sponsors of Live Aid, the July 1985 international mega-concert for Ethiopian famine relief. Her site "is merely an attempt to remind people of the great day that was Live Aid." The program—dubbed "the greatest show on Earth"—featured dozens of top pop stars performing at Philadelphia's JFK Stadium and London's Wembley Stadium, with various performances from around the world zapped via satellite. The performers (including Phil Collins, bat-gobbler Ozzy Osbourne, and anyone who was anyone in 1985) are remembered here in exact order and time of appearance, with a link to a fan page if one exists. (Yes, Ozzy has one.) In the spirit of the event, the site also links to various world hunger resources.

Megadeth, Arizona

http://bazaar.com/Megadeth/megadeth.html

Music

This promotional site has a lot more personality (and a lot less headbanging hype) than you might expect. Heavy-metal band Megadeth recorded its *Youthanasia* album in a warehouse outside Phoenix; hence the site's title. Apparently this was a monumental event, as publicity photos were snapped by the esteemed Richard Avedon, and the publicity bio was penned by best-selling author Dean Koontz. ("These guys pass the imaginary Godzilla test... If he stepped on Megadeth, believe me, he'd know he stepped on something.") The site is loaded with "Meganews" ("*Youthanasia* Banned!"), provocative images, tunes, and videos. Visitors can amuse themselves by downloading some cool Mac wallpaper, or playing a game with cowpies. Be sure to commemorate your visit by sending one of the site's funky digital postcards.

Metaverse

http://metaverse.com/
Music

Among its many dazzling features, the Metaverse presents live "cybercasts" of major events (from cross-country bike races to rock-your-brains-out beach parties), replete with videos, sound, and commentary. It's all a production of On Ramp, Inc., the pet project of former MTV VJ Adam Curry, who gives a daily dose of "Cybersleaze" here (like news of an off-Broadway production based on Courtney Love's Internet postings). It's a mix of fascinating news and commercial promotions, with enough meaty factoids to hold your attention. And Metaverse happens to be the official online home of 4616 Melrose Place, where you can flip through "Billy & Brooke's Wedding Album." A note from Heather Locklear, nay Amanda, declares it "the hippest address in all of LA!" And we understand it's just best not to argue with her.

Montreux Jazz Festival

http://www.grolier.com/festival/montreux/
Music

This appropriately cool site from Grolier features history, jazzy gossip, and sound bites of live performances from the world-famous Montreux Jazz Festival in France. The History folder is an amazing collection, with dates, performers, highlights, and original poster artwork from each year of the festival. Click on 1971 and learn that more than 300 musicians were featured, including Aretha Franklin, Roberta Flack, and King Curtis (who was killed two months later). The striking posters from each year since 1967 could stand alone. (David Bowie designed the 1995 poster, which depicts the bombing of Hiroshima.) A photo essay takes you on "a day in the life" of the festival, and you can test your jazz knowledge with a neat multiple-choice quiz. How many times *did* Miles Davis play Montreux?

MTV

http://mtvoddities.viacom.com

Music

The majestic purveyor of *Beavis & Butt-Head* and *The Real World* (and sometimes even music videos) now has a place on the Net. Not surprisingly, the MTV site is graphics-heavy (though super-slow), more promotional than substantial (a virtual plug-fest for shows like *Most Wanted Jams*), and often disappointing. Just like MTV itself! Still, also like the channel, there's somehow enough eye candy here to keep you dropping by. Cool animated QuickTime movies are provided—strange and colorful all, though up to 10 megabytes in size. (You can always turn on the TV while you wait for the download.) On our last visit, a "Beach Cam" projected images every few minutes from Malibu. Big

bonus: full transcriptions of *The Week in Rock* make viewing MTV News anchors Kurt Loder and Tabitha Soren unnecessary.

The Unofficial Nine Inch Nails Home Page

http://ibms15.scri.fsu.edu/~patters/nin.html

Music

The quality of this tribute to rockers Nine Inch Nails is so slick that it feels like it's coming straight from a PR hack. Not the case: it's a fan site—part of the "ninternet," where "ninnies" go to play. Along with answers to urgent Frequently Asked Questions (bandleader Trent Reznor's favorite candy: Reese's Peanut Butter Cups, creamy style) and scattered concert memorabilia (an autographed

wristband, after-show-reception passes), the site tosses up a mind-numbing spread of morbid videos and audio samples for songs like "Happiness in Slavery" and "March of the Pigs." With albums like *Pretty Hate Machine*, this band can be pretty gloomy; the music is not for all tastes. But Nine Inch Nails should hire this Webmaster and make the page "official."

Nirvana Web Archive

http://www.ludd.luth.se/misc/nirvana/

Music

The Webmaster spent more than a year gathering Nirvana data and imagery from various Internet sources for this impressive index. Borrowing a quote from the late Kurt Cobain, he says, "I've seen it all, I was here first," and we believe him. Gossip items (Cobain's suicide note notwithstanding) are largely shucked for guitar tablature and top-form trivia here. The archives reveal the existence of a Muzak version of "Smells Like Teen Spirit," and that Cobain bought his burglar alarm *and* his speakers from Radio Shack. A special section commemorates "MTV Unplugged in New York," Nirvana's last official recording, with an assortment of sounds and images. A picture gallery traces the band's meteoric (and despised) rise to superstardom. The transcriptions of muddled song lyrics ("When I was an alien / Cultures weren't opinions") are a welcome bonus.

Rhino Records

http://cybertimes.com/Rhino/Welcome.html

Music

Rhino Records' online catalog is just what one would expect from a label that has cornered the market on quirk and kitsch. The site offers shopping, browsing, and amusing trivia forays—and it favors out-of-favor genres like spoken-word, folk, and Cajun. A novelty section features the hot temptation *Benzedrine Monks of Santo Domonica: Chantmania* (they chant "Theme from the mMonkees"). And the video catalog incudes classics from all-time worst director Ed Wood (*Orgy of the Dead*, anyone?). As for, um, serious music, each decade is represented by a photograph (the '70s employ Tony Orlando's mug) and album covers. Rhino is absolutely out of its mind to squeeze Otis Redding into the "One Hit Wonders of the '60s" category, but this spirited catalog still makes for an absolutely fabulous shopping spree.

The Rock and Roll Hall of Fame

http://www.rockhall.com/

Music

The Rock and Roll Hall of Fame and Museum may be "loud, fast-paced and thrilling," but its namesake home page isn't quite that exciting. Inductees like Ricky Nelson and Frank Zappa are presented here encyclopedia-style, with sketch drawings, brief bios, and audio files reminiscent of what you hear in the headphones at a natural history museum. Perhaps the best deal here is the "Bloodhound," which searches the hall's text archives. We asked for "Peter Frampton" and found a news story about his 1992 "classic rock reunion" concert with Bachman-Turner Overdrive and (unbelievably) Foghat. That function alone makes this worth the visit for rock fans. If you want to experience George Clinton's "Atomic Dog" shoes and white fur "Dr. Funkenstein" coat, however, you'd best hop on a plane to Cleveland.

Southern Folklife Collection

http://ils.unc.edu/barba/sfc.html

Music

Here's a site the Hatfields and McCoys might actually agree on. (Is there such a thing as gangsta bluegrass?) Southern Folklife is stocked with tidbits culled from the grand ol' collection at the University of North Carolina, whose library houses one of the world's largest holdings of traditional music. The sections on old-time string bands, gospel/spiritual music, and early country are bristling with archival photos and sound samples. Hear an academic demonstration of early Hillbilly music, trace the roots of modern country/western back to high-pitched nasally immigrants, or soak up the history of the Fisk Jubilee Singers, one of the first African-American gospel groups. The designated blues segment is surprisingly anemic, but the Southern Folklife is a nice shady spot for anyone interested in music history.

The Ultimate Band List

http://american.recordings.com/WWWoM/ubl/ubl.shtml

Music

There are lots and *lots* of bands listed here, with links to their resources around the Web. Whether this really is the "ultimate" list or not, it's pretty impressive—the 700 kilobyte complete list includes bands as popular as The Cure and as obsure as Abe Lincoln and the Swingin' Stincolns. (Right next to Paula Abdul!) You can also list, for instance, country-western bands only, or bands that have their own newsgroups. Each band's info is organized on a "card," and the site maintainers promise the card URLs will never change (a great way to link to the info of your favorite band, as Net sources always mutate). It's all part of the Web Wide World of Music page.

people

The David Bowie File

http://liber.stanford.edu/~torrie/Bowie/
People

In addition to being an excellent resource for David Bowie trivia, Evan Torrie's fan page is also a gas. A "Quote of the Day" quizzes surfers daily on Bowie lyrics, while "Click Your Heels" will take you to a randomly selected Bowie song like "Port of Amsterdam," from the album *Pin Ups*. Fans can stop by for the latest tour information and (rumored) release dates for new singles and CDs. Hundreds of the prolific singer/writer's songs are on file here, hooked to a terrific Bowie-lyric search engine; the impressive array of pictures includes Bowie performing mime in the '60s (weird!) and an expressionistic self-portrait. Before you depart from the site, you can hear David (over the roar of a crowd) say, "Thank you very much, bye bye, we love you."

Boy George Homepage

http://www.umich.edu/~geena/boygeorge.html
People

Wow. Not only are we impressed with the utter completeness of this tribute site to '80s flash-in-the-pan Boy George, but we're impressed that anybody is still interested in the man—er, boy—at all. If you like George, you'll be glued to this page's full color photos, current Boy news ("Boy George faces possible lawsuit from ex-lover"), audio song-of-the-month feature, and tons of articles on George (including one where he reveals to whom he lost his virginity—what a frightening thought). George himself was impressed enough with the site to send a letter to Webmaster Sherri Slotman, promising that "I'm back and ready to rock." Don't miss the nasty things BG has said about his fellow rock icons; Slotman cleverly assigns each dish a "Bitchiness Rating" of one to ten.

The William S. Burroughs File

http://www.hyperreal.com/wsb/index.html
People

Everyone's favorite heroin-addict-turned-Beat-novelist-turned-sneaker-spokesmodel arrives on the Net at this site. Burroughs wrote the hallucinatory 1959 novel *The Naked Lunch*, inspiring several generations to explore their own minds (and veins). Thanks to Malcolm Humes, proprietor of this page, you can explore the man and his musings, and even listen to a few audio clips of Burroughs mumbling and rumbling. Online texts include, appropriately enough, Burroughs on "The Electronic Revolution," as well as a rather creepy 1992 *Esquire* article in which he and filmmaker David Cronenberg discuss some mutual obsessions like poisonous insects, painkillers, and the nature of evil. As the man who deemed that "language is a virus," Burroughs surely deserves a place in cyberspace.

The William S. Burroughs Inter*NetWebZone*

"Language is a virus..."

"We must find out what words are and how they function. They become images when written down, but images of words repeated in the mind and not of the image of the thing itself."
– *W.S. Burroughs*

THE BURROUGHS FILE: An electronic reference guide to works of *William Seward Burroughs*, his literary works, record... ...samples, and other publications.

Elvis Costello

http://east.isx.com/~schnitzi/elvis.html

People

One of the United Kingdom's best punk-era angry young men was born Declan Patrick MacManus, but you know him better as Elvis Costello. To know him even better, stop by this wonderful Costello kiosk built by fan Mark Schnitzius. Offerings include an amazing, album-by-album compilation of song lyrics, some with guitar tablature; the usual "what's he up to?" news; links to home pages of "artists often mentioned in the same breath as Elvis Costello" (Bob Dylan, the Beatles); links to "other EC-related stuff," including a page done by Warner Brothers; instructions on how to get some decent fanzines; and the news that Costello recorded his first album, *My Aim Is True*, with Clover, an American country and western band whose singer was Huey Lewis!

Dead People Server

http://web.syr.edu/~rsholmes/dead/index.html

People

You're having a big party, and naturally you want to invite Abe Vigoda. But is he still alive? Well, thank heavens for the Dead People Server, which is just an alphabetical listing of "interesting celebrities who are, or might plausibly be, dead." When we checked in last, Bea Arthur was still alive, as was the actor who played "Mikey" in Life cereal ads. Fred MacMurray, on the other hand, was not. The exact date and cause of death are sometimes listed, depending on the whim of Webmaster Rich Holmes; Kurt Cobain, for instance, gets the entry "Dead. Angst. 4/8/94." And the jury's still out on Elvis, of course. This fascinating list is not for all tastes, but bookmark it and you'll be surprised how often you find yourself tuning in.

Elvis Home Page

http://sunsite.unc.edu/elvis/elvishom.html
People

Those living "down at the end of Lonely Street" can always tug on their blue suede shoes and cruise the info highway to this Elvis fan page. It's undergone some legal plastic surgery at the "request" of the Elvis estate's lawyers. (Author Andrea Berman thoughtfully includes a copy of that threatening letter here.) Pick through the legal rubble and you'll still find some fun stuff here, including the King's last will and testament, a message for Austrian Elvis fans, and a global pen-pal connection. Take a gander at the Elvis Tales to find out what fans around the world have to say about their favorite singer, from sightings at small-town 7-11s to testimonials of adoration, "We admire you, Elvis. Please, return to our planet." Amen.

Virtual Voyager—In Search of Elvis

http://www1.chron.com/voyager/elvis/
People

Is Elvis a religious icon? Does his soul live on in the body of a 21-year-old Vietnamese impersonator? To find out, we took a virtual voyage with David Galloway, a writer and content developer for the *Houston Chronicle Interactive*. The site details his visit to the First Annual International Conference on Elvis Presley, "six days of intensive Elvisia" at the University of Mississippi (with side excursions to Memphis and Tupelo). Galloway turns the trip into a personal quest to find Elvis, and he tracks the magic of the "poor old boy from Mississippi" with unusual vigor, even by the standards of Elvis fanatics. Galloway's witty travelogue ("Day 3: Elvis goes to College") is never dull, and breathes new life into an entirely worn-out subject. Bonus: a collection of fantastically tacky portraits of the King displayed at the "Velvet Gallery."

The Unofficial Harrison Ford Stuff Page

http://www.mit.edu:8001/people/lpchao/
harrison.ford.html

People

The graphics (from *Blade Runner* to the *Star Wars* and *Indiana Jones* trilogies) and audio clips ("Laugh it up, fuzzball!") are a lot of fun, but it's the unexpected nuggets about Ford's personal and professional life that make this site truly enlightening. George Lucas, for instance, is reportedly working on a—can it be?—fourth *Indiana Jones* script for Ford. Links here include an article describing the young Ford ("Harry"?) as a shy C student who "toiled in obscurity" as a lowly audio-visual assistant and had trouble getting dates. (Starring in seven of history's top 25 grossing films is one way to cure the latter problem.) Ford is married to *E.T.* writer Melissa Matheson, and this site also contains an interesting look at how spouses of famous men deal with their situations.

The Completely Unauthorized Hugh Grant Page

http://ucsub.colorado.edu/~kritzber/new/hugh/
hugh.html

People

This page satirically "devoted" to the suave-yet-stumbling actor is thin on material, but a real kick in the pants (something Mr. Grant once could have used on Sunset Boulevard). Site creator Blake Kritzberg really doesn't worry too much about the facts; Grant's eye color is listed as "blue, green, or brown. Most likely blue or green," and his nationality is "evidently British." But then, the facts just wouldn't be as fun as a filmography that includes titles like *The Unbearably Sexy Babe Who Went Up a Hill But Came Down a Mountain.* Kritzberg also replaces Grant photos with her own crude sketches, and insists that no pictures of Grant's *Four Weddings and a Funeral* co-star Andie MacDowell will be accepted, "unless she's being squashed under Gerard Depardieu or something similarly unpleasant."

KeanuNet

http://www.interport.net/~eperkins/
People

Absolutely koo-koo for Keanu (Reeves, who else?), this most righteous site delves into every exposed aspect of the actor's life. Discover that Keanu means "a

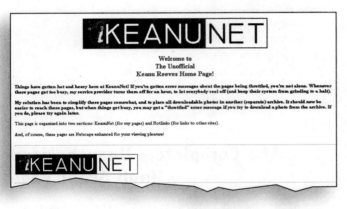

cool breeze over the mountain" in Hawaiian, and that even *he* pronounces it wrong. Get the dirt on the "folk/punk" band for which he plays guitar, and, naturally, choose from a variety of dashing photos. "What's New With Keanu" provides news about Reeves's upcoming movies as fast as he can churn 'em out, including some handsome official-looking press releases. Visitors also get recommendations about where to find even more Keanu trivia (a London publisher has put out a book on the lad, if you can believe it). Don't expect grist for the gossip mill, however. The Webmaster says there's no need to e-mail your rumors, "unless you've got pictures!"

The First Greg Kinnear Page

http://pages.prodigy.com/NY/kinnear/kinnear.html
People

"You loved him on *Talk Soup*," insists this page, "Though it wasn't for long, you couldn't believe your good fortune when he did both *Talk Soup* and *Later*. And now, you hear he's going to be in the movies!" (Perhaps somebody needs to turn off the TV and get some fresh air?) Still, there's plenty of good info here on wry TV host Greg Kinnear, including a list of every guest on *Talk Soup* from the first visitor, Julia

Louis-Dreyfus, on February 28, 1994. The page also dishes the dirt on topics like Kinnear's Beverly Hills villa (a steal at $1.4 million, sources say) and his silver screen debut in a remake of *Sabrina*. Nice transcript of his chat session on America Online. (Kinnear on his ties: "NBC has forced me to make bad fashion choices. I'm a victim.")

Alt.Fan.Courtney-Love FAQ

http://www.mordor.com/rcmaric/clfaq.html
People

Addictive heroine Courtney Love is famous for a lot of things, not the least of which are her notorious postings on the Internet. The Love letters are presented here in a rolling monolith of text—she forwarded many of them to the Webmaster herself—and they make for a fun read. Love trades thoughts with fans, swears like a longshoreman, and shoots barbs at rock stars like Eddie Vedder and Trent Reznor. ("Quote Reznor in the same sentence as my husband and I'll find you at your (expletive) community college and hack your grades to F OK?") She also defends her messy spelling and punctuation: "As if I were preparing myself for a future CLERICAL position!" Loads of information on her music here, too. "Frank language" would be an understatement here.

Steve's Madonna Page

http://www.buffnet.net/~steve772/maddy.html
People

This Web shrine to Madonna offers news, video, and audio clips (including her cameo "No way!" on a *Wayne's World* episode), all compiled by her main fan Steve. The amazing Madonna-lyric link features a Top-100-words-from-Madonna's-lyrics counter ("you" was the runaway champ, with 913 uses when we last checked in). Steve also provides a page for fans to trade or sell Madonna memorabilia. On our last visit, the News and Rumors page speculated about the title and contents of an upcoming album ("Old Age Madonna"?) and reported that Madonna and Courtney Love "had some words" after the 1995 MTV Video Music Awards. And among the 25-odd shots of the Material Girl is at least one nude shot, which might help to explain the author's "buffnet" Web address.

The Meg Ryan Page

http://web.cs.ualberta.ca:80/~davidw/MegRyan/meg.cgi
People

Even the hardest-core Meg Ryan aficionados may not know that she turned down the lead in *The Silence of the Lambs*, ranked number 11 in her high school graduating class, and was dubbed the "ragbag doll of the year" by Mr. Blackwell in 1988. In addition to an audio archive (yes, it includes *that* moment in the deli with Billy Crystal), this page offers dozens of magazine spreads, notable

continued

The Meg Ryan Page continued

quotes ("I came away from *When Harry Met Sally*... realizing I was a whole lot more like Harry than Sally"), and a filmography. (Who knew she played Lisa in *Amityville* 3D?) An ongoing poll lets fans vote on favorite Ryan films; they can also discuss just why they find her irresistible, including that "little nose crunch thing she does."

Winona Ryder

http://www.duc.auburn.edu/~harshec/WWW/Winona.html
People

Creator Eric Harshbarger says he's obviously a big fan of Winona Ryder and the gorgeous opening photo collage helps explain why. (We hear she can act a little, too.) This page is absolutely loaded with photos and sound clips ("I just killed my best friend!"), but Winona's filmography is also quite complete, with links to everyone even remotely associated with her movies and whatever info on her upcoming projects is available from the Hollywood trade mags. In fact, the impressive catalog of magazine and newspaper articles on Our Favorite Actress would make any periodicals librarian proud; reading through every interview at this site would be an all-day project. And what do you know: her real name is Winona Horowitz! Reality bites, indeed.

Ring-a-Ding Ding! The Frank Sinatra Page

http://www.io.org/~buff/sinatra.html
People

For those who croon along with Old Blue Eyes (he makes us feel so young!), it's *certain* to be a very good year. This page is the last word for Frankophiles, created by William Denton, a Sinatra buff who's doing it his way. Fans can read the crooner's views on rock music ("sung, played, and written... by cretinous goons"), get his recipe for spaghetti sauce, or just sigh over a few photos. (Frank looks a bit tired in the '93 entry.) Not only does this site contain lyrics for all the old Sinatra favorites, it also lists songs that merely allude to him (Paul Anka, T-Bone Walker, and The Pogues are a few who pay homage). Loads of links to Sinatra "societies" and newsgroups, and regular updates on new CD releases of old classics.

Orson Welles

http://www.voyagerco.com:80/CC/gh/welles/intro.html

People

At the tender age of three, when most of his peers were struggling with potty training, Orson Welles was reading Shakespeare. You'll find some good Welles trivia in the brief bio at this handsome site, but the real prize is an in-depth look at the masterpiece *Citizen Kane*. This "making of" page includes movie stills, a brief synopsis, a description of the filmmaking process (the makeup artist designed a plastic foam nose "addition" for Welles, which he liked so much that he wore it in subsequent films for years). Images aplenty throughout, including one of a glaring, black-clad Welles standing over a microphone as "The Shadow." The Voyager Company's ultimate goal here is to get you to buy movie laser discs, but this page stands nicely all by itself.

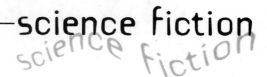

science fiction

DreamWatch Online

http://www.pavilion.co.uk/UniversalFlavour/DreamWatch/

Science Fiction

This online monthly version of the British paper magazine is devoted to "telefantasy"—that is, television shows that are science fiction or fantasy. It celebrates popular shows from the U.K. and the U.S., such as *Dr. Who*, *Babylon 5*, *Blake's Seven*, *Highlander*, and of course *Star Trek*. Each month a new issue offers reviews and news, and DreamWatch Online has expanded to include feature films. The reviews are sensible, not simply fan gushings. A review of *Waterworld*, the Kevin Costner adventure film, gives the lowdown without the high-brow: "when all is said and done, he's just an athletic guy with funny toes and a yen to be alone." A sci-fi database weighs in alongside the magazine archives as a great resource guide, with articles and interviews about the shows, the stars, and the creators.

Espana's Science Fiction Page

http://WWW.Catch22.COM/~espana/SFAuthors/index.html
Science Fiction

This is a great place to begin your sci-fi hunt on the Web. An alphabetical listing of authors makes searching this small field a snap. Although the bibliographies provided are easy to use, information about the authors isn't dazzling. If an author has a big presence on the Web, the file will be thick. Names like Arthur C. Clarke and William Gibson tend to get plenty of attention, but the lesser-known R.A. Lafferty got three choppy sentences. Likewise, the entire electronic text of Edwin Abbot's *Flatland* can be found from here, but Philip K. Dick gets short shrift, with only a dozen novels listed. Regardless of the skimpy biographical information and sometimes incomplete bibliographies, this remains a good site for beginners, much easier to use than a larger reference sources, and much prettier, too.

The Klingon Language Institute

http://www.kli.org/
Science Fiction

OK, we admit it! We can't resist recommending this crazy page! The Klingon Language Institute is a non-profit organization (for real!) dedicated to promoting and developing the Klingon language—that's right, the lingo grunted by the original bad guys in the world of *Star Trek*. At one point, the producers hired an actual linguist, Dr. Marc Okrand, to create a real-sounding language for the rib-headed behemoths. Okrand went on to write a book called the *Klingon Dictionary*, thus kicking off the whole craze. Here you can hook up with like-minded speakers and find out how to order the audio tape "Conversational Klingon." (Really!) The KLI is also translating the Bible into Klingon, and restoring the complete works of Shakespeare to the "original Klingon." These folks have no doubt heard all the jokes by now; you've got to like their unabashed enthusiasm.

Links of Interest to Fandom

http://www.greyware.com/sfrt3/sflinks.htm
Science Fiction

Every now and again on our virtual travels, we stumble onto a site with links to just about every-doggone-thing in a particular field of interest. This is that site for "Science Fiction, Fantasy, Horror, Anime, and Gaming," maintained by the GEnie Online Service and the Argon SF Society. "Mundanes" (non-fans) looking around should skip right to the Sci-Fi Fanspeak Dictionary, or they may be lost amid the fannish jargon. This incredibly comprehensive (or ridiculously bloated, depending on your perspective) resource includes lists for "fannish" publications and groups, from the Irish Science Fiction Association and the Klingon Assault Group, to Timebinders, the Society for the Preservation of the History of Science Fiction Fandom (or TSPHSFF, pronounced "tisfisfuhfuh"). This is for fans who want to analyze *fandom*, not just simply read sci-fi.

Lysator Science Fiction & Fantasy Archive

http://sf.www.lysator.liu.se/sf_archive/
Science Fiction

This site consists largely of reviews from Usenet groups, those average Joes and Janes discussing books, short stories, movies, and 'zines. On the one hand, it's a tremendous source of information on hundreds of authors. On the other hand, the reviews presented are a real mixed bag, ranging from the well-written to the frightful. Although the reviews are from "fans," many are negative, revealing more about the reviewer than the topic. Such comments as "I'd be totally embarrassed if I'd written it," don't exactly illuminate the novel (in this case, Michael Crichton's *Sphere*, which *is* a stinker), and some remarks are just plain strange: "It annoys me the same way that a key-change in a song does." As a source for fanzines and sci-fi publications, however, the site *is* worthwhile.

Phantasmagoria

http://www.lehigh.edu/~tpl2/phantom.html
Science Fiction

Mausoleums, eyeballs, cackling pumpkins, and Michael Jackson are all incorporated into this fantastic online horror gallery—brought to you by, of all

things, the Jaycees of Bethlehem, Pennsylvania! Phantasmagoria is their annual Halloween kid-friendly event du horror (largest in the Keystone State!), taking up two full city blocks! Primarily a fundraiser for over 20 non-profit organizations, it also provides a "safe haven" for kids (yow!). But who needs to go out (and pay nine bucks!) when you can play a game of "Alien Carnage," fool around with some "Bloody Fonts," or download "Scream Savers" right here on the computer? Visit the Phantasmagoria Graveyard for these and more, including dozens of creepy sound files like "Head Being Smashed" or "The Thing that Couldn't Die." It's a beautiful online creepshow.

Sci-Fi Channel: The Dominion

http://www.scifi.com/
Science Fiction

The Dominion is the Sci-Fi channel's unearthly presence on the Web, a slick promotional page offering program guides, series information, chat boards, and more. Visit "The Creature" for the current month's viewing tips, with understated reviews like this one for the mime-filled William Castle movie, *Shanks*: "Marcel Marceau (in a dual role) stars as a mute puppeteer and an old scientist who brings dead animals back to life with electricity.

Very interesting film." The Sci-Fi Channel features mostly old TV shows (from *Kolchak: The Night Stalker* to *Max Headroom*), but the "magazine" here, *Sci-Fi Entertainment* features news and reviews on more current happenings, such as feature films and Japanese anime and manga. The Free Zone includes sound and movie clips for those unlucky folks without cable, and The Trade Zone offers merchandise hounds mugs, T-shirts, and posters.

Science Fiction Resource Guide

http://sundry.hsc.usc.edu/hazel/www/sfrg/
Science Fiction

This site offers links to virtually every galaxy in the sci-fi universe. We're talking *Cheap Truth* (an electronic cyber-punk fanzine), Silly Little Troll Publications, and whimsical oddities like "WWWF Grudge Match (Enterprise vs. Death Star, Khan vs. Lex Luthor)," plus scads of archives and newsgroups. This collection of sci-fi-related pages is far more inclusive than most of its competitors, with rarely recognized sites that feature African-American, French, Japanese, Jewish, and Gay and Lesbian fan pages. Wonderfully presented, and because each item contains a brief description of the site, there is less "linking to the void;" you'll actually have an idea of what to expect. A small but worthwhile section is "Art and Artists," including Frank Kelly Freas, winner of 10 Hugo Awards and granddaddy of post-WWII science fiction cover art.

Tor SF and Fantasy

http://www.tor.com/index.html
Science Fiction

Tor books has been one of the top publishers of sci-fi and fantasy for the last decade. They have plenty to crow about here, with two finalists for the 1995 Hugo Award, John Barnes (*Mother of Storms*) and Nancy Kress (*Beggars and Choosers*), among their authors. For eight years running, the site reports, Tor has been selected Best Publisher by sci-fi consumer polls. The publishing schedules and sales offers are pretty standard, but the clear explanation of imprints (a group or "line" of books) is a miniature lesson in publishing. Tor, by the way, is "a venerable English word for an outcropping, a butte, a promontory or high hill," and not an acronym for "Take Over Rackspace" or "Terrific Online Resource."

University of Michigan Fantasy and Science Fiction Page

http://www.umich.edu/~umfandsf/
Science Fiction

Created by U. of Michigan Professor Eric Rabkin and his inspired students, this site is "dedicated to assisting scholars" in their pursuit of fantastic knowledge. Budding scholars can find a collection of essays on futuristic and sci-fi classics taught in English 313, such as: "Frankenstein," "The Left Hand of Darkness," and Philip K. Dick's delightful "Ubik." Common themes in speculative and science fiction are outlined, as in Rabkin's bibliographical "History of Utopian Literature," covering texts from Plato's *Republic* (380 B.C.) to James Gurney's *Dinotopia* (1992). The more useful attraction here, however, is the library of multimedia materials and an electronic books index, an impressive collection of accessible online texts including sci-fi ancestors such as H.G. Wells' *The War of the Worlds*, Oscar Wilde's *The Picture of Dorian Gray*, and *Edgar Allen Poe's Collected Short Stories*.

tv and radio

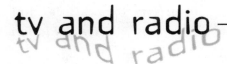

BBC Home Page

http://www.bbcnc.org.uk/index.html
TV and Radio

No doubt the British Broadcasting Corporation (BBC) has its share of dopey programs, but everything here looks quite cracking to an outsider. (And isn't it cute how they spell it programme?) The BBC has made a firm commitment to online technology, and that shows in this slick site. We recommend a trip through the catalogue of BBC TV shows: some merely offer episode lists, but others, like the children's program—er, programme—"Blue Peter," have delightful Web presentations. Even Americans can enjoy discovering what's on the telly tonight overseas. And in the great British tradition, the BBC gives equal time to its radio shows and provides special searches for educational productions. One disappointment: where's the BBC's signature Big Ben chime?

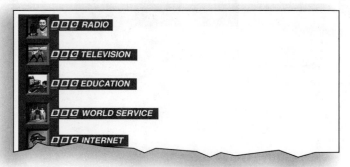

The Unofficial Brady Bunch Home Page

http://www.teleport.com/~btucker/bradys.htm

TV and Radio

As if the stage play and movie weren't enough, you can now revisit the sunshine days of *The Brady Bunch* on the Web. The site features pictures (including, of course, the famous 9-cell Brady grid), song clips, and semi-cynical episode guides. (Episode 56:"Marcia lands the part of Juliet in a school play and becomes possessed by Shannen Doherty.") The list of *Brady Bunch* articles and interviews doesn't always differentiate clearly between the '70s sitcom and the 1995 movie, but includes some fun stuff: a quick psycho-analysis of the show's characters portrays Alice, the housekeeper, as "trapped within the expressionless blue uniform she was always forced to wear." (At last, a dark side to Brady life!) The Bradys' staying power in the public consciousness is amazing—and a little frightening.

Bravo U.K.

http://www.uaep.co.uk/bravo.html

TV and Radio

This is a wonderful Web site for fans of cult movies and weird TV shows. Bravo is a satellite cable television channel in the United Kingdom and Ireland specializing in just such topics. Obsessed viewers of *Twin Peaks*, *UFO*, and *The Adventures of Robin Hood* can dig up excellent trivia, download photos and video clips, and get crisp, satisfying episode synopses. First-time viewers should take care: the site suggests you "assume that all episode guides contain 'spoilers' (crucial plot information that may spoil your enjoyment of the programme)." But isn't it worth being spoiled to learn exactly what unflattering nickname the *Twin Peaks* cast had for Joan Chen? (We'd blush to mention it here.) With good background info on *The Critic*, *Madman of the People*, and *The Saint*, among many others, this is exactly what a cult channel site should provide.

CBS

http://www.cbs.com

TV and Radio

CBS, once as plain as a tweed sport jacket, now has one of the hippest TV sites on the Net. The CBS home page stacks a bank of colorful TV screens and turns your mouse into a remote control. You get a program guide, pictures of CBS stars, a CBS sports schedule, and a link to "CBS News Up to the Minute," which has its own server ("Senior Citizens on the Net" was one segment recently featured here). CBS spares no expense to hype its shows old and new, from *Sixty Minutes* to *Central Park West*. The star feature is the Dave Letterman page, which offers last night's "Top 10 List" and actual pictures from Dave's historic interview with Madonna.

Comedy Central

http://www.comcentral.com/

TV and Radio

Cable TV's renegade comedy channel asks visitors to "Keep your arms and legs inside the browser and PLEASE don't feed the llamas." (Monty Python-style nonsequiturs are all the rage here.) Gimmicky-but-cute show promos include "E-Therapy with Dr. Katz," where visitors can describe their emotional state to the doctor (choose from selections like "Deliriously happy" and "Like I want to vomit"). The often-funny text is the best reason to visit here; descriptions of the channel's shows like *Exit 57* and *Politically Incorrect* can be shallow at times. Other pluses include video clips from *Saturday Night Live* and *Mystery Science Theater 3000*, online shopping for funny products (a pen is billed here as a "handheld inkjet printer"), and a wonderful mail room.

Warning! You are about to enter the Comedy Central Totally Free World Wide Web Site. The opinions expressed here do not necessarily reflect those of the known universe. All participants are required to be up to date on all their vaccinations. Keep your arms and legs inside the browser and PLEASE don't feed the llamas.

Discovery Channel Online

http://www.discovery.com/

TV and Radio

This cable channel's excellent nature and lifestyle programming (and that of its sister, the Learning Channel) translates beautifully here. Start your education by checking the on-air schedule—we like to know when *National Geographic* is on so we can hum along with the theme song. A searchable database weaves through topics like nature, science, and exploration, and contains some wonderful stories like "Breaking the Ice," a critical look at polar icebreakers. You may even be able to find stories here before they're turned into finished Discovery productions: on our last visit, a team of arctic explorers was checking into the site with daily reports (and pictures!) on its trek across the tundra. This is easy and *totally* fun to navigate. And still growing!

Matt Messina's Frasier Page

http://www.umich.edu/~messina/frasier/

TV and Radio

Among other things, this excellent episode guide lists all the movie stars and celebrities whose voices have appeared as talk-radio callers on the show, including Kevin Bacon and Lily Tomlin. Wonderful photos of the cast include an adorable photo of Moose, the dog who plays Eddie, in a "Must-See TV" tote bag. (Moose, we learned, is a wire-haired Jack Russell terrier, although "it is possible that Eddie is a different breed than the dog who plays him.") Emmy nominations and wins are listed here, and short bios of the series' producers describe the "usual three-and-a-half years' starvation" two of them suffered while breaking into the scriptwriting business. Fans will appreciate the "Niles and Maris Trivia," which includes a short list of "Excuses as to Why We Don't See Maris."

Fox World

http://www.foxsports.com/
TV and Radio

In the TV network business, Fox has become one of the "big four." Fox shows its pride at this glitzy site. Fox Sports is the heart of the site, offering minute-by-minute coverage of NFL games while they're in progress, plus updated news and stats. The Kids Network offers program schedules and fan clubs, and the Fox Entertainment section offers a chat area.

There's certainly enough to do here, and it's all aimed at increasing your interest in Fox TV programs. But the sometimes slow-loading graphics are far from the fast-moving visuals of a typical Fox program, and the contrast may be a bit of a jolt. The best parts here are the jazzy opening page and top-notch NFL coverage; the rest can wear thin quickly.

fX

http://www.delphi.com/fx/
TV and Radio

This is the Web site of fX, Fox's foothold in the basic cable industry. Their various live segments are broadcast from a seven-room apartment in New York; in keeping with their "just walk in" offer to viewers, they provide a visual tour of the apartment here, as well as the story of its renovation from a second-floor china showroom. Also included are bios of the on-air talent (including audio and video

clips) and a program schedule. The extensive episode guides for all the old syndicated series on the channel somewhat belie the "fresh, new approach to television" fX claims to take, but they're fun for nostalgic types. With shows like *Fantasy Island* and *Hart to Hart*, this is like a catalog of what twentysomethings used to watch when their parents were out for the evening.

The Game $how Page

http://silver.ucs.indiana.edu/~wlambert/GameShows.html

TV and Radio

It's a neeewwww car! Game show fever is hard to avoid when you stop at this infectiously fun fan page. The main events are the links to worldwide pages for game show classics like *The Price Is Right* and *Jeopardy*, and overseas offerings like popular exchanges from the show, featuring such network-approved euphemisms as "making whoopee." A trivia quiz asks, among other things, what game show G. Gordon Liddy appeared on as a celebrity Britain's *Going for the Gold*. You'll also find obsessively detailed information on game shows no longer on the air, including *Hollywood Squares*, *Card Sharks*, and *Password* (all five versions). The section on *The Newlywed Game* includes a few contestant. And, for our third place contestants, check out the "Birthdays" folder, with the natal days of Wink, Monty, Alex, and Bob.

The Jihad to Destroy Barney on the Worldwide Web

http://www.armory.com/~deadslug/Jihad/index.html

TV and Radio

Billed as "The Internet's Leading Anti-Barney the Dinosaur Web Page," this large and mostly hilarious site leads the mentally unbalanced in their holy war against the excessively cute public-TV dinosaur. There's a load of single-minded rant from "The Jihaddi, Who Have Functioning Cerebrums (tm)"—based on the premise that Barney "isn't just bad, or even merely evil, but is downright UNHOLY," and that he and his "sponge-minions" can be warded off with such talismans as McDonald's shakes and Pez candy. There are lame but fun interactive Barney-destroying games, drawings of the "purple felt demon" in world-destruction mode, and links to the alt. barney. dinosaur.die.die.die newsgroup. Don't miss the lengthy FAQ, with questions like "Are Rush Limbaugh and Barney the same persona?"

Joyce Loves Conan

http://www.rbdc.com/~hgambill/conan.htm
TV and Radio

" **M**y love for 'Late Night with Conan O'Brien' did not begin on first sight," admits Joyce Wankable. But now she's solidly in Conan's camp: "I much prefer his humble style to Letterman's arch demeanor and morning DJ ethos." Wankable's excellent site has abstract reviews of every show (and even has a stable of volunteers who each cover one day of the week). The Conan Moment of the Week features a favorite photo from recent shows (we once found actress Famke Janssen using Conan to demonstrate her "deadly rib crush"). Joyce also praises the bits she digs, like the recurring appearances of Wo Lee Pi, the fictional "Lenny Bruce of China, who delivers his monologue in Chinese and then (through a translator) makes a savage mockery of Conan's naive American values." Pleasingly obsessive.

Late Show with David Letterman

http://www.cbs.com:80/lateshow/lateshow.html
TV and Radio

The star feature of Dave's quick-hitting page is the Top Ten List taken from last night's show. (True fanatics can search the archive of every list since the show began; the show's writers have also picked their early favorites in a list of "The Top Ten Top Ten Lists From Dave's First Year on CBS.") Brief staff bios include some weird items: for instance, stage manager Biff Henderson got his nickname when his mother's friend "had a dream involving a boy named Biff." You'll also find guest lists and the week's top monologue quips ("Larry King announced the date of his next marriage—June 25th. Also the one after that—Nov. 17th"). No heavy substance here, just slick graphics and laughs.

Mayberry, My Home Town

http://www.w3-design.com/frank/mayberry/
TV and Radio

In Mayberry, the only request is that you pull up a chair and "jaw awhile" on the front porch. Besides exhuming Aunt Bee and Floyd the barber, the Webmasters (one of whom has a thing for getting his picture taken with Don Knotts) have fun pointing out politically incorrect Barney Fife behavior: "Andy, if you flew a quail through this room, every woman in here would point." An episode guide lists titles for 249 Andy Griffith shows; if you think you've seen 'em all (or most, or some), try out the trivia quiz, which asks questions like "What is engraved on the back of Barney's anniversary watch?" and "How long can you park on Main Street?" The most obsessive can join a chapter of the Andy Griffith Show Rerun Watchers Club.

Mentos—The Freshmaker!

http://www.best.com/~dijon/tv/mentos/

TV and Radio

This brilliant page offers, believe it or not, witty and detailed analysis of all known Mentos TV commercials—you know, the ones where life's little difficulties are solved by enterprising young people with the aid of "the Freshmaker." The site offers synopses and made-up titles for each ad, and so much more! You'll find "concrete proof" that the ads are German in origin (look for the Munich street sign in the "3 Second Car Jacking" ad), complete jingle lyrics, and minutiae delivered with the cool detachment of academia: "The shape of a Mentos candy is disklike, with an elliptical bulge in the middle. They measure 3/4" in diameter and at their largest point, 6/16" tall." Site visitors have written in to announce such undertakings as "hammering out a 'freshness defense' for criminal acts committed under the influence of Mentos." Cheerfully obsessive! Fresh!

Monkees Home Page

http://www.primenet.com/~flex/monkees.html

TV and Radio

Did you know that Ensign Chekov was added to *Star Trek* because Gene Roddenberry wanted a young heartthrob like Davy Jones to reel in the teenage audience? That fact and many others turn up on this incredibly detailed home page celebrating the "Prefab Four." This fond look back at "the '60s pop culture phenomenon that started out as a TV show about a band and became a band without a TV show" recaps the television adventures of the Monkees and includes plenty of info and trivia. (Do you know which unreleased Monkees song appeared in the film "Easy Rider"?) Visitors can also find the chord progressions of "Daydream Believer," read the script to *Tales* (the sequel to Monkee movie *Head*), or just find out what the boys are up to nowadays.

Monty Python Home Page

http://www.iia.org/~rosenr1/python/
TV and Radio

This Monty Python "pointer index" extends its finger to the various Web archives that touch on the legendary comedy troupe. Yes, they have original airdates of the *Monty Python's Flying Circus* series. Yes, they have complete scripts of *Monty Python and the Holy Grail* and *Life of Brian*. Yes, a "concordance of all 45 episodes" lets you read sketches ("Crunchy Frog," "A Man With Three Buttocks") compiled from the published Python oeuvre. You'll also find song lyrics ("When you're chewing on life's gristle, don't grumble, give a whistle!") and links to sound bytes from the show—nudge, nudge, know what we mean? The Webmaster even gets in a few surprise kicks of his own. It's nothing like the real thing, of course, but there's plenty here for trivia buffs and "Pythonologists."

Muppets Home Page

http://www.ncsa.uiuc.edu/VR/BS/Muppets/
TV and Radio

A smiling picture of late great Muppeteer Jim Henson welcomes you to this unofficial homage to the funny, fuzzy creatures. This repository of Muppet trivia answers questions like "What are the names of the two old geezers/critics in the balcony on the TV show?" (Statler and Waldorf, natch.) Occasionally the authors are reduced to guessing: just what *is* Gonzo, anyway? ("Sort of like a turkey, but not much.") Strong points here are the exhaustive reviews of Muppet TV and movie appearances, and list upon list of individual Muppet performers. However, the scant illustrations (no doubt prevented by copyright entanglements, or perhaps eaten by the Cookie Monster) and sophisticated tone make this much more for adult fans than for tykes.

NBChttv

http://www.nbc.com
TV and Radio

The TV network that glamorized a peacock's backside displays this colorful site to lure users away from the Web and back to programs like *Friends* and the *Tonight Show with Jay Leno*. The name "httv" plays off the customary "http" you must type to get here, although it seems more a stretch than cleverness. But once past the identity crisis, you get complete program schedule hit shows like *ER*, plus details like the real name of the dog that plays "Eddie" on *Frasier*. (It's Moose, if you must know). The news and sports sections will disappoint you if you're looking for headlines or scores; all you get is a promo of on-air personalities. Still, this site's worth visiting as a curiosity, and for the great searchable database of NBC program information.

NPR Online

http://www.npr.org/

TV and Radio

Newshounds who feel guilty because they prefer Garth Brooks to Bosnia during their morning commute have nothing to worry about: thanks to this National Public Radio Web site, they can get NPR's distinguished news anytime. In addition to the day's highlights (via text or audio), this page also includes a guide to member stations throughout the U.S. and overseas.

True fans will be happy to discover a number of links to home pages for popular NPR programs like *All Things Considered*, *Morning Edition*, and *CarTalk*. And despite the typically low-tech approach to many of NPRs programs, the network does a masterful job of creating an interactive forum for its listeners here.

NYPD Blue

http://src.doc.ic.ac.uk/public/media/tv/
collections/tardis/us/drama/NYPDBlue/index.html

TV and Radio

Perhaps in Dave Chapman's native England, this show should be called *Bobby Blue*. But it isn't. That hasn't kept Chapman from writing this tribute page, which has photos of the *NYPD Blue* cast, descriptions of the characters, a list of the series' awards and accolades, and more. The VERY detailed episode guide has shows broken down by subplot, plus liner notes from newsgroup member Alan Sepinwall, who isn't afraid to call 'em like he sees 'em: "I was shocked by the fact that Steven Bochco and David Milch, the series' creators for cryin' out loud, would churn out such a generic plotline," he complains of one episode. Sepinwall is also responsible for the drinking game included at this site (whoever "has" Detective Andy Sipowicz has to take one drink whenever he makes a racial comment). Even without drinking, this is a superior site for fans.

Simpsons Archive

http://www.digimark.net/TheSimpsons/index.html

TV and Radio

The real fun here is in the Groups and Lists headings, where the minor *Simpsons* characters get their day in the sun. (Check the Stellar Acting Career of Troy McClure, or the ongoing discussion of Smithers' sexuality.) You'll also find the usual overboard discussions of mysteries like the true location of the Simpsons' hometown (Springfield has a garage/shop called "Smog Check"... so it must be in a state that actually enforces emissions laws.) And the episode archives point out background gags from each show ("Did you notice... Michener is on sale for $1.99 a pound?") It's all fun, created by devoted fans of the show around the Web. Note: if you've never seen the show, you won't follow much of the action here. Text only, due to the usual pesky copyright problems.

Sound Bytes: WWW TV Themes Home Page

http://www.tvtrecords.com/tvbytes/

TV and Radio

The thought of chortling along with TV-show theme songs at the computer may be a bit embarrassing, but it's likely to happen if you visit this silly site. Most have been recorded directly from the TV set, but that doesn't really harm the fun. From *Absolutely Fabulous* to *WKRP* and *Barnaby Jones* to *The X-Files*, they're all here (the outrageous exclusion of *Benson* and *Joanie Loves Chachi* notwithstanding). You can browse the offerings by genre: Westerns includes favorites like *Bonanza* and Rawhide, as well as some oddballs like *The New Kung Fu*. And who could live without their own recording of the slinky jazz-cheese Siskel and Ebert theme music? Still not satisfied? Try the recordings of commercials. And the Webmaster takes requests!

Space Ghost

http://iquest.com/~cshuffle/sghost/

TV and Radio

Space Ghost is the animated, yellow-caped, black-hooded, interplanetary crusader who has been doing the TV thing since 1966. (The original episode guide here features phrases like, "When the twins and Space Ghost arrive, they are attacked by Locar's metal-eating locusts, who make short work of the Phantom Cruiser.") Having conquered his longtime enemies Zorak and Moltar, SG now hosts the late-night tongue-in-cheek talk show *Space Ghost: Coast to Coast* on the Cartoon Network, where he has interviewed David Byrne, Bobcat Goldthwait, and Carol Channing. (Thankfully, not all at once.) Not many images here, but plenty of show trivia and quotes: "I don't want to sound arrogant, but who among the current crop of late-night talk show hosts can truthfully say they've evaded the entire Council of Doom?"

Space Ghost

Space Ghost, the yellow-caped, black-hooded interplanetary crusader, has been on television since 1966. He currently hosts the late-night talk show *Space Ghost: Coast To Coast* airing Fridays at 11:00 PM (ET) on the Cartoon Network.

Major renovations underway. Watch your step...

Check this stuff out:

- Learn about the original *Space Ghost* televison show.

Star Trek: The Next Generation

http://www.ugcs.caltech.edu/~werdna/sttng/

TV and Radio

As with most *Star Trek* fan pages, this one works much better as a hot spot for insiders than as an intro for beginners. As such, though, the detail is magnificent. Review every Emmy award! Check the precise episodes in which Captain Picard quotes Shakespeare! The trivia notes are great fun, with directions on how to create the "transporter effect" on video, a discussion of money in the future (what *are* the officers betting for in those poker games?), and the information that everyone's least favorite TNG character shares a name with the show's creator (whose full name is Eugene Wesley Roddenberry). A catalog of in-jokes records various cute stunts the art department pulled over the years, like recreating Oliver North's uniform on an evil-nemesis type character in the show's first episode (filmed just after the Iran-Contra hearings). A very entertaining site.

Star Trek: Voyager

http://voyager.paramount.com/VoyagerIntro.html

TV and Radio

Are you fit for duty? The holographic doctor frowns at you through cyberspace as you enter this home page for Paramount's latest *Star Trek* enterprise. Your training begins with complex color photos of the spaceship, background on the crew, and enough *Star Trek* facts to choke a Roddenberry. (Did you know that Trekkies are listed by name in the *Oxford English Dictionary*?) Use a "control panel" to navigate through the mission log (episode guide) or to visit Personnel for a rundown on the characters from *Voyager*. The interface is lovingly designed to Trek standards, the TV schedules are kept discreetly in the background, and you even get an evaluation from the holographic doctor who tests your knowledge. And did you know that 13 *Star Trek* books are sold every minute in the United States?

TV Net

http://tvnet.com/TVnet.html

TV and Radio

Wondering how many rolls of gauze they use each week on *ER*? Curious about German soap operas? TV Net is the place to start your search. It's a deep-and-dandy library of TV home pages, shop talk, jobs, and data on national networks. International, too: on our last visit, an overseas report offered the horrifying news that Susan Powter is available on European TV. There's plenty here for professionals, and home viewers will find news and chat opportunities galore. TV Net is an excellent resource that covers everything, gossips with the best, and stays crunchy even in milk. OK, we made that last one up, but what's TV without a commercial? We give the TV Net experience a 42: as they say on *American Bandstand*, it's easy to dance to.

Last updated October 3, 1995

Congratulations anyone link to **TV Net**.
TV Net is your starting point for Television Hot Spots.

KCBS 2neT

Join the ongoing discussion on The OJ trial in:
OJ Chat
Review the Simpson Case Webstyle

TVNET TRIVIA   **TV CHAT**

The TVplex

http://www.gigaplex.com/wow/tv/index.htm

TV and Radio

Who could possibly want more than interviews and crystal-clear color photos of today's top TV stars? (Don't answer that.) The TVplex—part of *The Gigaplex*, a "whopping 600-plus page Webmagazine devoted to arts & entertainment"—offers exactly that. On our last visit, a hilarious interview with Paul Reiser of *Mad About You* revealed how he met his wife: "She walked over and introduced herself. I couldn't talk. Not that I was that much in love, but I had an olive stuck in my throat." Other subjects have included Julia Louis-Dreyfus, Henry Winkler, Bob Saget, and the predictably uninhibited Roseanne: "I have lots of roses and flowers on my back. I'm slowly losing my total mind at the tattoo parlor." The weekly Studio Briefing also recaps happenings in the world of entertainment. Can be a tad hype-y, but it's fun overall.

The Unofficial Reboot Page

http://www.inwap.com/reboot/

TV and Radio

Here's all you need to know about "Reboot," a weird Canadian computer-animated cartoon series. This unofficial fan page features piles of information, as well as sound files, teaser clips and toys. A map of Mainframe, a kind of cyber-opolis where "Reboot" takes place, bounces you around with ease, and character descriptions separate the good guys (Bob, the hero, Dot Matrix, and her brother, Enzo) from bad guys (Megabyte and his Viral Binomes). Episode guides are incredibly complete, and the teaser clips are accompanied by text of the dialogue. Even the opening theme audio is paired with a shot-by-shot description of the visual sequence. The cartoon is a light romp with plenty of computer-driven puns (like that one), some of which you may have missed while watching—catch up to them here.

Vanderbilt Television News Archive

http://tvnews.vanderbilt.edu/
TV and Radio

It's not easy keeping up with Tom, Dan, and Peter, but a dedicated group of folks at Vanderbilt University have "systematically recorded, abstracted, and indexed national television newscasts" since August 5, 1968. This amazing "ever-expanding collection" now holds over 23,000 newscasts. Visitors can, for instance, search the 1993 database for the word "Buttafuoco" (though why they'd *want* to is another question). Vanderbilt also accepts videotape loan requests from scholars and teachers, although it's possible that your chosen historical moment isn't available: the Television News Archive Newsletter points out that no tape exists of Nikita Kruschev pounding his shoe on the table at the United Nations ("there were no cameras present at the U.N. on that day in 1960"). There's still plenty here to browse. And that's the way it is.

The Wild Wild West Episode Guide

http://www.uvm.edu/~glambert/twww1.html
TV and Radio

Obsessive, opinionated, and amusing, this site is a shrine to the TV show that made Robert Conrad a star by "blending elements from 'The Man from U.N.C.L.E.,' James Bond, and the ever popular western." (Webmaster Gary Lambert claims *The Wild Wild West* was taken off the air by CBS not because of ratings, but because it was too violent.) The site has just a few photos and sound clips, but provides seemingly endless trivia and background: air dates (both for the show's first run and for its syndicated reruns), technical credits, plot summaries of each and every episode, links to biographies and filmographies for all the lead actors (plus some minor ones), even a list of the programs that other networks put up against *The Wild, Wild West*. Good stuff.

Wonder Woman Home Page

http://www.knowsys-sw.com/Mike/WonderWoman/
TV and Radio

Lynda Carter may not have been the first (nor even the only) Wonder Woman, but even we have to admit she's one of the best. This page is as much an homage to Ms. Carter as to the comic book heroine, and it's full of super stuff. (Yes, there's a nice photo of her in that little suit. In fact, there are many photos of her in that little suit.) We were simply dazzled by not one but THREE separate versions of the television theme song ("In your satin tights, fighting for your rights...

Wonder Woman!"). Fans have written in with such obsessive questions as why you never see alter ego Diana Prince turn into Wonder Woman when her hair is done up, rather than in a ponytail. The thrills and spills keep on coming in a few QuickTime adventures, including rare footage of Wonder *Girl*.

X-Files: The Truth is Out There

http://www.neosoft.com/sbanks/xfiles/xfiles.html
TV and Radio

Stuffed with audio and visual treats about the hit sci-fi TV series, this page avoids being snide toward the uninitiated. But only hardcore viewers (known as "X-philes") will enjoy the dozens of sound-bites or the chatty FAQs, which not only note Special Agent Mulder's habit of shelling sunflower seeds, but also mention that he shares that habit with his father. It takes a while just to download the lists of available pictures, which range from images of the show's photogenic stars to stills of spooky special effects to related "art" (like the comic strip "Foxtrot," which sometimes makes *X-Files* references). The many pieces of "fanfiction" (in which fans write stories featuring the show's characters) have us convinced that there is *something* out there, stripping eager writers of punctuation skills.

Buzznet

http://www.hooked.net/buzznet/
'Zines

An absolutely superior cyber-zine, *Buzznet* is a pop-culture maelstrom spewing chunks of cool music, travel, art, science fiction, and the bizarre. Each story is masterfully designed with pulsating (and sometimes unnerving) graphics. The music section concentrates primarily on alternative, hip-hop, and world beat, and the record reviews tend to take on a language all their own ("Reverbed dub beats are... supplanted by drifting ARP 2600 sequences that swirl into whirlpools of surprisingly aggressive rhythms or eddies of found sound"). But there's more fun to be found elsewhere: past topics have included knife throwing, and surfing in South Africa. Some of the 'zine's diversions—like a cryptic "Radiation Warning: Hot Dog Stand Virus" sci-fi feature—can be intimidating. But don't be shy: you'll probably enjoy the buzz.

In Orbit Around The Web

http://www.tcp.com/~prime8/Orbit/
'Zines

Patrick Farley, creator of IOATW, has discovered the true spirit of Web publishing: if you can't find what you want, make it yourself. Tired of what he sees as the same old harangues from liberals and conservatives, he envisions a world where "left" and "right" are outdated—his e-zine is a retreat for those who "quit being anarchists because there were too many rules." The result is, well, *out there*, but it makes for an exciting read. The premiere issue featured articles like "Who is Buckminster Fuller?" and "Fair is Fair," a proposal on unwed fathers. For a kicker, he proffered the "Senator Jim Exon Memorial Web pages," adorned with a pretty flower and dirty words. This is a highly personal, and thought-provoking, political manifesto.

Mr. Showbiz

http://web3.starwave.com:80/showbiz/
'Zines

Mr. Showbiz is a sort of happy conglomeration of facts and gossip about the ever-fascinating, ever-present world of entertainment. The creators, those busy folks at Paul Allen's Starwave Corporation, call this an entertainment magazine with moving parts. Mr. Showbiz is breezy, he's updated daily, and he's creative—on past visits, we've found amusing items like a comparison of recipes from the cookbooks of Oprah Winfrey and Vincent Price, and ruminations on the great cinematic art of defenestration (throwing people or things out the window). Hardened showbiz types will also find box office reports and other industry numbers. And heck, the page even has its own theme song! Professionally written, fast, funny... this is what we wish the "People" section of our daily paper was like.

The Muse

http://www.hyperlink.com/muse/

'Zines

This British 'zine—"a mirror of creative contemporary culture"—seems to cover Oprah just as easily as opera. (And please, no "fat lady" jokes.) The site reflects on various aspects of the arts with authoritative coverage that doesn't appear to discriminate against the low-brow fare. A feature entitled "A Look Back to Man Ray and the Surrealists" mingles comfortably with notes on Sylvester Stallone movies. And the site is adorned with quotes in equal parts Oscar Wilde and *Celestine Prophecy*. (It's also one of the few places we've visited to compare P.J. O'Rourke to Ghengis Khan.) This Muse is wordy and forthright—and it accepts original poetry submissions for publication! For those who like to gnaw on contemporary culture, this is a tasty bone.

Seconds Magazine

http://www.iuma.com/Seconds/

'Zines

A hot feature of the Internet Underground Music Archive, this online version of *Seconds* magazine is ambitious and irreverent in its approach to covering modern music. A "warning" label on our last visit screamed "Rock Stars Flaunting Their Alleged Immortality." But don't let that scare you off. Excellent—and polished—coverage of rock, rap, punk, and funk follows. Our last visit found features on alternative rock troopers Jesus and Mary Chain, "booty bandit" Bootsy Collins, and Van Halen vocalist Sammy Hagar (described as "still hard, sweet, and sticky"). Articles are presented in a user-friendly Q&A format with photos. And on occasion, *Seconds* strays from typical rock-'zine coverage: a tour through the archives turns up "groovin' guru" Allen Ginsberg attempting to describe the Beat Generation to the Lollapalooza Generation.

Soccer Riot Magazine

http://www.xmission.com/~gam/Riot/

'Zines

"Pretty much, I hate celebrities," writes *Soccer Riot* editor Jon Gillette, who sends sardonic e-mail messages to stars and publishes their responses. Pretty much, that's the gist of this irreverent 'zine. As for the name: "Soccer riots take place pretty much everywhere except for at Wal-Mart, where quality assurance is provided by kind, caring employees who are trained to help you find exactly what you need." The *Soccer Riot* employees (who get a big kick out of doing things like working erstwhile Karate Kid Ralph Macchio into an irritated funk) are kind and caring in their own way. They'll help you, for instance, find disturbing passages in computer manuals ("FTP stands for File Transfer Protocol. I am your master. I control your mouth and your arms"). It's thought provoking at times, but mostly goofball fun. Pretty much.

The Sonic Core

http://www.sonicnet.com/sonicore/

'Zines

Here you can grab "the best" of the alternative Net from a group of former New York City BBSrs. They've moved their board to the Web, and brought with them a jackpot of idiosyncrasies suited to all manner of unconventional palates. The chat zone features provocative sessions with artists like Meat Puppets, Laurie Anderson, and Talking Head David Byrne, who discusses the "Muzaking" of "Burning Down the House" ("I thought it was a pretty ridiculous idea... but they did it and I've yet to hear it in an elevator"). An animated cyber-musical, Ralph Steadman's "Project No. 1: The Fouling of America" puts a gruesome (but artful) spin on the mugs of Laurel and Hardy. For an encore, see why spooning, bikini waxing, and dumping your boyfriend have never been easier in the "Indie Rock Guide to Dating."

Urban Desires

This interactive magazine of "metropolitan passions" is a publication for people who might enjoy "Internet-based robotic gardening" or "interactive metafiction." (Read: people who live in cities, have computers, and are bored.) It all makes for a lively read, though. Past issues have included a prostitute's interview with forthright feminist Camille Paglia ("I would only put her book down to sleep, eat, or turn a trick") and a cheeky review of

Martin Amis' *The Information* ("Free dental work was part of the advance"). A style column relayed the "Confessions of a Flea Market Junkie," and an "Urban BBQ" food feature offered recipes and grill tips for those who have to sneak barbecues on fire escapes and high-rise rooftops. (None of this is really for kids, either.) Smart, sexy, and slightly twisted, *Urban Desires* is a fresh blast amongst the 'zines.

The Vibe

The Vibe is also known as "Adam Curry's The Vibe," in recognition of the hirsute ex-MTV veejay and grand poobah of the site. This compendium of music news, reviews, and sound bites is part of the mighty multimedia Metaverse site. It has a young target audience, but if you can handle salutations like "Welcome aboard dudes!!!!!!," you'll be rewarded with a worthwhile (and zany!) musical trip.

Discover what's hiding in celebrity closets, from Weird Al Yankovic's "Wonder Hamster" to Tori Spelling's "hot pants." Read rock audio reviews, or salivate over Curry's juicy gossip column, "Cybersleaze," which dishes up daily helpings of gossip. Or check out the Curry-Cam, which zaps a shot of Adam's casa (in New Jersey—"exit 153"), updated every minute. Fun stuff.

The (virtual) Baguette

The (virtual) Baguette is an interactive 'zine (in French and English) with a baker's rack full of some of the "wildest, strangest, Frenchiest content" you're likely

to find on the Web. A creation of Multimania productions, it's very funny, and very tongue-in-cheek. Find an exhaustive history of the Charentaises, a kind of

continued

The (virtual) Baguette continued

French footwear ("According to the Darwin theory of evolution, the ancestor of the Charentaise would be the wood clog"). Listen to magical music from a man who can play the guitar with his long toenails. (Yeesh.) Create French poetry with pull-down menus, and get instant English translations. ("The dog inflates step by step.") As they say, "You will need a (huge) bag to store all your catches, some salad, a snail horn and a gun."

Web Review

http://gnn.com/wr/
'Zines

This slick, insightful bi-weekly gives readers a look at "the world behind the Web" while chronicling the Web's influence on the world. Articles cover hot-button topics like politics ("Republicans dominate a new medium while Democrats fiddle"), while a Dialogue section finds readers sounding off on hot-button topics like child pornography online. Naturally, the publication also gives excellent reviews of Web sites ("Time Warner says Click Here, Did the Earth move?"). Good business coverage, too. And you can expect plenty of profiles on Webmasters and other "dreamers, innovators, and dominators" on the Internet. When it comes to the Web life, this is about as topical as it gets.

word

http://www.word.com/
'Zines

"Issues. Culture. Oh My!" is the sometime-subtitle (it changes) for this slippery smooth pop-culture 'zine aimed at the younger, electronically inclined generation. On our last visit, the interactive feature story "The Stevie Nicks Experience" put a new spin on the swirling '70s singer. (The delightful opener: "Most Fleetwood Mac music reminds me of waiting in a hot car while my mom shopped in the mall.") Elsewhere, visual entries like "Skateboard Jungle," a rotating grid of manipulated digital images, accompany soundbites from techno-funk rappers. A "Habit" department delves into things we love to hate (and love again). And in the "Desire" department, you can find "a real letter to an ex-lover," and a "Guy Talk" guru divulging sacred topics of "guy conversation." Wild words, great graphics, and frivolous fun for hours.

Global Village

Global Village

One of the first things people think of when the Internet is mentioned is "bringing the world together." The idea seems to be that we'll all spend our days chatting with someone in Minsk or Tasmania, and that when the time comes for the next world war, we won't go because half the people on the other side will already be our pen pals. Well, this actually might work. Certainly, anyone with a modem can now stretch their arms and touch the far side of the globe in seconds. And as this section shows, one of the best things about the Web is the way it enables anyone to spread the word about their own nation, their own culture, or their own beautiful home town.

The A–Z of Jewish- and Israel-Related Resources

`http://www.ort.org/anjy/resource/a-z.htm`
Global Village

This marvelous global collection is maintained by Webmaster Matthew Album, project coordinator for the British organization ANJY (A Network for Jewish Youth). This jump-station features sites ranging from the Abayudaya Jews of Uganda to the Zamir Chorale of Boston (so named after the Hebrew word for "nightingale"). A real variety of issues are tackled, from the horrors of the Holocaust (at least seven sites, including "Holocaust Denial & the Internet"), to the fundamentals of the "Jewish Belief Home Page," which offers selections from the Babylonian Talmud and Maimonides. Our personal favorite: a page "devoted to studying and collecting trivia relating to the Jewish religious/cultural odysseys of Shabtai Zisel ben Avraham, a.k.a. Bob Dylan." A masterful compilation.

The African-American Mosaic

`http://lcweb.loc.gov/exhibits/African.American/intro.html`
Global Village

This text-heavy, but still super page from the Library of Congress covers early black American history, from colonization to the Depression era of the 1930s. Visitors can read about the American Colonization Society, which by 1867 had sent some 13,000 free African-Americans to Liberia as part of an alternative emancipation plan. Visitors can follow Joseph Cinquez as he leads a slave revolt on the ship *Amistad*, or discover the significant contributions of African-Americans to President Franklin Roosevelt's Federal Art Project. Reproductions of rare original abolitionist artwork, plus artwork from the Works Progress Administration of the 1930s, is a nice touch throughout. This is a first-rate resource for black history and culture.

Alcatraz Island

`http://woodstock.rmro.nps.gov/alcatraz/index.html`

Global Village

The National Park Service maintains this great page on the infamous prison island. Here you can skip the real-world lines (there are 750,000 visitors annually) and take a virtual tour of the historic island that was once home to Al Capone and "Machine Gun" Kelly. Before Alcatraz hosted the likes of the Birdman, it was an Army fort, then a military prison whose inmates built the world's largest (at the time) concrete structure, only to live there when it was finished. The self-guided tour reveals more than a prison, with great views of the San Francisco Bay and features on local gardens and wildlife. No more inmates, no more Native American occupations, just banana slugs, deer mice, salamanders, and a dedicated National Park team.

Alchemy of Africa

`http://www.aztec.co.za/biz/africa/`

Global Village

Created by freelance writers Steven and Shannon Lipschitz, this site purports to be "the most valuable African Internet resource" around. In addition to a great graphic interface, the duo has assembled a broad South African events calendar (check out the Guinness Jazz Festival in Johannesburg), an online gallery featuring the work of contemporary African painters, and a marketplace where you can purchase everything from South African wines to a luxury waterfront apartment. A super facts book reveals population statistics, language, and currency info on more than 40 African countries, including Madagascar (brush up on Malagasy and French before your next visit). IRC fans can telnet to a real-time chat room, or just leave a message on the Web wall. But we particularly like the idea of spreading a little interactive love around the globe using "The Love Pages." Regular updates to "the best ten Web sites on the African continent."

Alexandria, Egypt

http://ce.ecn.purdue.edu/~ashmawy/ALEX/
Global Village

This is an enthusiastic introduction to the history and culture of Alexandria, "the shining pearl of the Mediterranean." Built on orders from Alexander the Great in the third century B.C., it remains the second largest city in Egypt and one of the cultural centers of the world. The page

الإسكندرية

Alexandria

expertly traces the history of the Ptolemies (a bunch of pretty powerful kings who liked to throw their weight around), and describes how Cleopatra miscalculated the strength of her ties with Rome. Maps and pictures of local architecture, like the fort of Qaitbay, amply illustrate the historical narrative. Never dull, the page even offers a listing of other Alexandrias around the world—the Ukraine alone has five similarly named cities. Webmaster Alaa Ashmawy keeps the entertainment levels at top volume.

American Indian Computer Art Project

http://www.mit.edu:8001/activities/aises/aicap/archive/aicap.html
Global Village

Turtle Heart, an Objibway artist in the Mojave Desert (and host of this site), tells us he has become a "scout" for the Internet. Traditionally, a tribe's scout was sent out to watch for important natural "signs"—some good, some not so good—

and report back to the Chief. The scout is an important member of the tribe, for he or she must be unusually perceptive, and able to decipher and interpret the unknown. He must also be a messenger, and here Turtle Heart shares Native poetry, prose, and song, while scouting for signs of Native life in the cyber world. Further explorations in the digital gallery reveal a stunning partnership between historical imagery and new art forms, bridging the gap between past and present. "We are the people of the ancient ones," writes the artist, "of the stars and the seasons of time, root and feather, and beyond." A most gratifying and enlightening stop.

The Bangladesh Home Pages

http://www.asel.udel.edu/~kazi/bangladesh/
Global Village

While some may think of this remote country only as the subject of George Harrison's fundraising concert in the late 1970s, this packed site from graduate student Zunaid Kazi enlightens on the Land of Bengal's diverse industry and recent economic recovery. (Export crops include guava and sugarcane, and the country now supports nine airports.) Among many sights and sounds, hear the roar of the royal Bengal tiger, or sing along with the Bangladesh National Anthem ("My Bengal of gold, I love you"). You can also take a lesson in "Survival Bengali" (er, "Ami bAnglAjAni nA"?), complete with sound illustrations. The grand tour includes a pictorial history and sections on national sports (kabbadi, anyone?) and food. Along the way, visitors can learn English translations for a variety of odd proverbs, like "Fish + Rice = Bengali."

Blucher's Boot Hill

http://www.fn.net/business/boothill/
Global Village

The Blucher Boots Company has rustled up a fine kettle of links to Western history, music, Indians, and rodeo. And horses. Did you know, for instance, that there's a National Cowboy Hall of Fame? It's been in Oklahoma City for nearly 40 years, founded by a Kansas City businessman as a tribute to cowboy performer and pundit Will Rogers. And what western page would be complete without an homage to arguably the greatest ever Hollywood cowboy, Tom Mix? (Hope we don't rile none o' you John Wayne fans... there's a spot for him, too.) The cow-embossed background decorated with rope and barbed wire is quaint, but we wouldn't say "no" to more pictures of, well, cowboys (and maybe one or two links to some Sergio Leone films). But git along to this fun site, anyway.

Bosnia Homepage

http://www.cco.caltech.edu/~bosnia/bosnia.html
Global Village

As a resource on "troubled Bosnia" (as they say on the TV news), this page is excellent. It links to just about every Bosnian Net source imaginable, including *Ljiljan*, a weekly Bosnian newspaper online, relief agencies, and devastating photos with titles like "Dare to Feel Thirsty" and "Mass Burial." The page has a decided anti-Serb bias (but then, much of the rest of the world seems to as well). Serb President Slobodan Milosevic, for example, can be found in the "Major War Criminals/Suspects" folder. Even with the bias, this remains an excellent page. A concise conflict timeline is provided, as are maps that illustrate subjects such as ethnic occupation and military front lines. And the "Culture, Academia, and Daily Life" folder offers a respite from hard news, with pieces on academic exiles, and artists working in war-torn Sarajevo.

The Brasil Page

http://charlotte.acns.nwu.edu/rio/brasil.html
Global Village

Bright graphics and comprehensive links combine to make this a pleasant and thorough Brazilian resource. (Much of the site is in Portuguese.) Direct links to government offices include the Ministry for External Relations (kind of like the State Department) and the Ministry for the Army. A "Portuguese for Travelers" guide teaches vital phrases like "Where is the bathroom?" and "I don't understand"; photo essays, including a "Greenpeace Visits Brazil Photobook," show off the country's life and beauty; and audio files resound the cries of exotic birds and samba music. (There's even a link to a *Swedish* samba page.) Odd humor turns up in the curious recipe for "Mother-in-Law's Eyes," built around a pound of pitted prunes. Museums, universities, publications, businesses... what a site!

Welcome to the Brasil Page!!!
We were recently recognized by Point Survey as being in the
"Top 5% of All Sites on the Internet." Thanks to all who sent in links,
and please help us grow by sending in any new sites you find while
exploring the Web. We hope to provide Internet citizens with a place to
go when World Wide Web resources containing information on Brasil
category in the index below

The Caustic Seattle Compendium

http://www.oz.net/~evad/
Global Village

Subtitled "an unflinching urban guide to Seattle living," this definitive virtual tour of the Pacific Northwest city has as much for the tourist as it does for the long-term resident who just "never leaves the house." (After all, "your inner child might be sensitive to light.") The Webmeister includes plenty of pointers to that favorite Seattle beverage, coffee—we'll have a double mocha, please—and recommends the famous Crocodile Cafe for sneak peeks into the urban grunge scene. (He also warns 20-and-unders against trying to pass off "bogus" IDs.) The site also sings the praises of "the treasures that await you when you spend some time searching for that super cheap something special" at the Chicken Soup Brigade, a Seattle thrift store whose profits go to help the city's needy and hungry. A complete, hip, and wonderfully irreverent handbook.

The Channels

http://www.channels.nl/
Global Village

Visitors to Amsterdam can hop on a virtual tram car, walk along the Damrak, or visit the Nieuwmarkt at this site from Netherlander Bas van Reek. In the city's famous OZ.Achterburgwal (or Red Light District), the curious can take a peek into Casa Rosso, the old erotic theater (and "a decent place in a 'dirty' district") or stop at the Erotic Museum (though there's nothing X-rated on this page). Van Reek's expert clickable map permits easy navigation from the Hobbemakade to the Muntplein, once home to the Holland Mint. For "an exciting evening in the trendiest neighbourhood in town," step into Blitz on the Rembrandtplein, "where everybody... feels welcome." Amsterdam seems to attract Web authors—compare this site with Moon City.

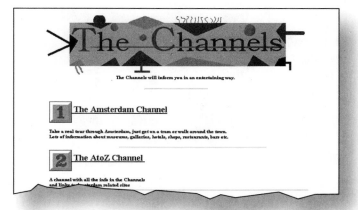

City.Net

`http://www.city.net/`
Global Village

Welcome to "the most comprehensive international guide to communities around the world," with links to more than 1,000 cities in over 200 countries and territories. Visit Ydre, Sweden ("closer than you think and easy to find"), and discover the legend of Urkon, the Monster ("more fascinating than fiction"); Skopje, in the Republic of Macedonia, reveals a history of determination and resiliency, despite its position on the Balkan route between Athens and Belgrade. And New York City? City.Net has over 20 links to Big Apple history pages, maps, nightlife, and relocation resources. If a country has no Web sites— Togo, for instance—the Webmasters provide links to relevant information sources, like the CIA World Factbook and ethnologue database. A super idea that just keeps getting better, all started by a couple of guys from Portland, Oregon over a margarita.

> City Net ━━━━━━━━━━━━━━━━━━━━━━━━━
>
> **September 23, 1995: 1048 cities and 543 other destinations online!**
>
> Welcome to City.Net, the most comprehensive international guide to communities around the world. City.Net is updated every day to provide easy and timely access to information on travel, entertainment, and local business, plus government and community services for all regions of the world.
> *- Kevin Altis and Nancy Tindle, Editors*
>
> **Please help improve City.Net by taking a few minutes to fill out our survey.**
>
> **Home || Contents || Regions || Countries || Index || Search**
>
> Top 10 destinations for last week (September 11 - September 17):
>
> 1. United States   6. France
> 2. California, United States 7. New York, United States
> 3. Germany   8. Italy
>   9. Paris, France

Culture and Entertainment

`http://udgftp.cencar.udg.mx/ingles/CUAAD-INGLES.html`
Global Village

The University of Guadalajara in Mexico sponsors this bright collection of paintings, poetry, music, photography, and cultural history from south of the border (the U.S./Mexico border, that is). Plenty of sound here, including the mystic sounds of a Nahua Aztec flute; you may want to whip up a cup of Mexican hot chocolate while waiting for lengthy downloads. Good cultural info, including a history of the Olmecas, mother folk of Mesoamerica. Especially lively is the story of the *Charreria*, a sort of rodeo celebrating the skills of the classic Mexican cowboy. Being from Mexico, this is written with certain assumptions you may not share ("When we think of Mexico, we automatically visualize that unique character, the Charro, with his black suit, guns, and wide hat."). No matter how you visualize yourself, this is a handsome page.

Faces of Sorrow: Agony in the Former Yugoslavia

http://www.i3tele.com/photo_perspectives_museum/
faces/exhibition.html

Global Village

A stunning virtual museum exhibit, "Faces of Sorrow" is harsh photographic testimony to years of war in the Balkans. The dozens of photos reproduced here, taken by 35 photojournalists from 14 countries, offer "indisputable pictorial witness to the searing effects of man's in-humanity to mankind." The exhibit, presented by Photo Perspectives—and sponsored by *Time* magazine in cooperation with the United Nations—is divided into six sections, including "Ethnic Cleansing," "Siege of Sarajevo," and "Faces of Rape." Even as the very idea of ethnic cleansing is horrifying, it becomes even more so as the viewer looks into the faces of innocent children targeted for slaughter. Hard-hitting, dismaying, and an amazing use of the Web.

Friends and Partners

http://solar.rtd.utk.edu/friends/

Global Village

Like a post-Cold war "Brady Bunch"-style mix-up-the-family story, this joint project—developed by American Greg Cole and Russian Natasha Bulashova—hopes to "at least in some small way promote better understanding between our nations." Transatlantic surfers can learn about Russian and American culture through language, music, art, economics, and more than a dozen other topics. A link to "Those Darn Accordians" (better known at home as "Vongole Fisarmonica") plays back a real Russian treat: a fanciful audio clip entitled "Lithuania." Check into a cool "hypertexted babblebox" for intra-continental conversations between Yanks and Russkies. (Guess we can't call them "reds" any more.) Remember, as the Russians say, "All are not cooks that walk with long knives." And vice versa.

Friends and Partners

Friends and Partners	History	Geography	Art Music	Literature	Language	More Information Resources
Telecommunications	"who's Who"	Services	Health & Medicine	Help! (user documentation)	Cyrillic Text	Weather
Education	Science	Funding & Exchange	Economics & Business	Tourism & Travel	"Life"	News

Click on any region of the image of interest to you.

In the top 5% on the net by Point Communications.

The Gathering of the Clans

http://www.discribe.ca/world/scotland/clans.html

Global Village

This site is one of the most complete packages of Scottish material on the Net. The Gathering covers things clannish and Scottish, from Celtic Christianity to gaelic lessons ("Tha sinn luath," yes?), to

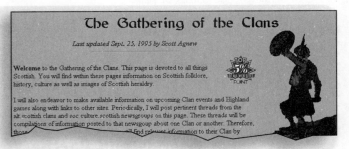

history, travel info, genealogy, gatherings, and Usenet groups like soc.culture. scottish. You'll also find images of various Clan crests and tartans, complete with thumbnail histories. The Clan Butters from Perthshire, we learned, were a bunch of pretty tough hombres in kilts; Queen Elizabeth II is now godmother to the eldest Butter daughter. And a Scottish site just wouldn't be complete without a dandy haggis recipe ("Clean stomach bag thoroughly and leave overnight in cold water...") and the poem "To a Haggis," by Robert Burns.

Guide to Museums and Cultural Resources on the Web

http://www.usc.edu/lacmnh/webmuseums/

Global Village

The L.A. County Natural History Museum has put together this catalog of worldwide cultural pointers. Travel to the ends of the earth and find "Live from Antarctica," a Web project for students

that explores life on the planet's coldest continent. Further north (and definitely warmer) is South America, where the *Museu de Arte e Etnologia* serves up plenty for ethnographers and speakers of Portuguese. And in Japan, link to the Hosokawa Museum of Classic Computers. Australia clocks in with Sydney's Fantasmagoric Museum, a collection of "mechanical fiction and fantasmic inventions" (and we wouldn't expect any less from the land of Tasmanian Devils). In North America, museums are broken down into six categories, including planetary science, archaeology, art, and history. All seven continents are amply represented, and entries seem to keep pouring in.

A Guide to the Great Sioux Nation

http://www.state.sd.us/state/executive/tourism/sioux/sioux.htm
Global Village

Here is the land of great leaders like Red Cloud and Crazy Horse—a place brimming with history, tradition, and spirit. It's South Dakota, home to the Great Sioux Nation, originally an alliance of seven tribes known as the "Seven Council Fires." This page details the Nation's rich history, and recounts ancient legends and mysteries from the sacred Black Hills and Dakota Badlands. We learned the distinct difference between Dakota, Lakota, and Nakota tribes, and discovered a valuable guide to "wacipi" (powwow) etiquette, which warns observers not to enter the sacred circle until invited, and to remain standing while the Sioux anthem is sung. Individual pages from the Cheyenne River, Oglala, and Rosebud tribes offer local travel highlights and cultural notes.

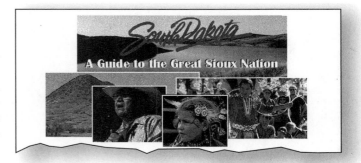

Historic Philadelphia

http://www.libertynet.org/iha/
Global Village

Tour the historic district of Philadelphia for a virtual look at the birthplace of the Declaration of Independence, spawned in the city with the "greatest density of history in all America." (Hey, what about LA, man?) The tour is pretty loose, the sequence dictated "by caprice," but it covers the usual and the unusual, from the Liberty Bell to the City Tavern, where John Adams and Thomas Jefferson would come "for a feast of reason and a flow of soul." (Translation: for a snort.) Landmarks such as Independence Hall sit proudly beside links to the Pretzel Museum and the Man Full of Trouble Tavern, as sure a sign as any that there's something here for nearly every taste and tenor.

Home Page for Hellas (Greece)

http://www.forthnet.gr/hellas/hellas.html
Global Village

If the phrase "It's all Greek to me" produces excitement rather than intimidation, this is definitely a trip you'll want to take. This gift from the Greeks lays out a variety of resources, from the Hellas Chess Club and the Orthodox Page to Greek Restaurants All Over the World. (Remember, when dining at the Acropolis in Brisbane, Australia, the attire is casual.) Even better, a clickable map will take you from the Macedonian stomping grounds of Aristotle and Alexander the Great (history lessons are included on both) to the warm Mediterranean waters of Crete, "with its sea, rocks, and gleaming plateaus" (or with its "full-bodied wine and pungent raki" for you dionysian types). You can also link to the Athens News Agency for the day's top news stories in English and Greek.

Home Page of the Netherlands

http://www.eeb.ele.tue.nl/dhp/
Global Village

All those names! Holland, the Netherlands, the Dutch... what gives? But these authors have a charming sense of humor about it, as they serve up Web links with amusing commentary. (A link to the CIA's World Factbook '94 is dubbed "what the CIA thinks it knows about us.") The site doesn't aim to be an exhaustive collection of pages, but rather an exhaustive collection of *interesting* pages. A clickable map takes you to an incredible *muziek* site in Rotterdam or shopping or browsing elsewhere. And the obligatory Frequently Asked Questions folder details the social and cultural peculiarities of the Netherlands. Hey, they call ATM machines "flappentaps"! And the definition of Dutch bravery? "Courage stimulated by drinking alcoholic liquor." Whatever they call the country, they seem to be having fun.

Human-Languages Page

http://www.willamette.edu/~tjones/Language-Page.html
Global Village

Sprechen Sie Deutsch? No? How about Gaelic? Tagalog? Urdu? Yo, didn't they teach you *anything* in school? Make up for it at the Human-Languages page, a colossal archive of Web sites about (and in) foreign languages. Depending on dialect, you may find Arabic learning tutorials, a Latin dictionary, or Bulgarian poetry. The Aboriginal Studies Electronic Data Archive holds dozens of dictionaries and word lists, and even provides pointers to Aboriginal software applications. Students of Cantonese will find instructions and software for displaying Chinese characters on Unix, Mac, or Windows platforms. An astonishing number of languages represented, right down to Rastafarian *patois* and Klingon. (Yes, Klingon.) C'est le grand home-page!

Hungarian Home Page

http://www.fsz.bme.hu/hungary/homepage.html
Global Village

When asked if there were extra-terrestrial beings, Italian physicist Enrico Fermi said "they are already among us—they are called Hungarians." The Hungarian Home Page is out of this world, as well. A clickable map provides speedy links to the country's Web and gopher servers, and virtual tours are provided of Budapest (where you'll see the Holy Royal Crown of Hungary) and smaller towns like Debrecen and Nyiregyhaza. A search engine will look up Hungarian translations of English words (and vice versa), and a timeline traces Hungarian history from the tribes leaving the Urals in the fifth century to the end of communist rule in 1990. The site also includes an exquisite cookbook—may we suggest the Curd Dumplings and Roasted Gooseliver Slices? And yes, there is a *great* goulash recipe.

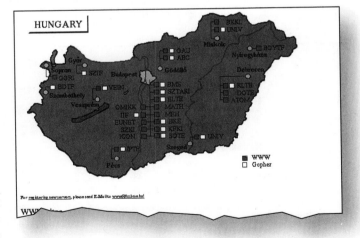

Interactive Tour of Tasmania

http://info.utas.edu.au/docs/tastour/tourhome.html
Global Village

Tasmania may be Australia's smallest state in both size and population, but this interactive tour of "Tassie" shows off the island's larger-than-life wilderness scenery. Visit the Great Western Tiers mountain range in the Central Highlands region, or visit the fertile Northeast, where poppies and hops grow. Excellent thumbnail descriptions and colorful photos of Tasmania's major tourist attractions are provided, like Marakoopa Cave (it claims to be the only glow worm cave in Tasmania open to the public—a claim we can't dispute) and the bustling Salamanca Market, where local traders sell everything from "honey to straw dolls" each Saturday morning. And yes, among a host of other bizarre marsupials, the Tasmanian Devil actually exits. And where to catch them in action? Trowunna Wildlife Park, natch.

Japan Infoweb

http://electra.cortland.com/electrazine/japantour/
Global Village

This superior multimedia e-zine covers Japanese culture with entertaining style. Among the site's informational features and history, you can get an art history lesson in Japanese painting, which

Welcome to the debut issue of the Japan Infoweb.

tells of the profound role Buddhism played in the shaping of the unique Japanese aesthetic sense. You can also learn to prepare Spinach with Sesame Seed Paste. A food glossary gives important cuisine terminology, and provides audio files to make sure you use correct pronunciation. A travel feature explores vacationing in Zen temples, and a philosophy feature suggests, "See into your nature and become Buddha!" Or you can see into the site's Marketplace and become a shopper! A Japanese Green Tea & Healthy Snack Set awaits, and it can be delivered right to your doorstep. Links are included to sites like the Japan Soccer League and a "roll your own sushi" page.

La France

http://web.urec.fr/france/france.html
Global Village

Vive le Web! This lovely clickable map of French Internet >servers scores high for its detailed renderings and sensible interface. Click on a region and up pops a magnified view, right down to cities and lists of dozens of sites. Even global access providers are listed. Our favorite link, "Nouveau," led to great tidbits about French companies and organizations like RegardsNet, which promotes communist and general discourses. The poem "UnderNet," asked what we find beneath the Net (or perhaps beneath our souls): *un _tat dans I'_tat?* ("A nation in a state of nature?") Beware: these maps take an especially long time to load, and you won't enjoy this site much if you don't read French (pronunciation not required).

LatinoLink

http://www.latinolink.com/
Global Village

Breezy graphics and upbeat, informed writing make this one of the liveliest ports on the Web for Latino art, culture, and political news. Up-to-the-minute immigration scoops explore legislative efforts to limit asylum for refugees, and in economic news, Latino business writers examine (for instance) the tenuous relationship between Mexico and Wall Street. Search LatinoLink archives to find out how Hollywood is embracing Latino filmmakers, and why record companies are hot to sign *merengueras*. All of the columns, stories, and images are by Latino journalists and artists from the U.S. and Puerto Rico, many of whom are regular contributors to *The New York Times* and *The Boston Globe*. All first-rate, front-page stuff.

Links to Scandinavia

http://www.infoserve.net/netquest/nordic/welcome.html
Global Village

Come along with your friendly guide Tor Rognmo for a smorgasbord of information on the chilly northlands. He offers links to sites in Sweden, Norway, Denmark, Finland, and Iceland, from "Jesper Lauridsen's Soccer Page" to the University of Helsinki. Browse the *Nordic Times*, an online publication covering mostly news from Norway, like lobbying efforts for the 2008 Olympic Games and a film production of the life of Nazi sympathizer Knut Hamsun. "Between Friends" offers e-pals the chance to get together: on our last visit, it was "Dallas, Texas calling Denmark," a claims analyst seeking online Danish companionship. We get the feeling that there are plenty of links to each country that *aren't* here, but the graphics are superior and this makes a fine "jump station" (as Tor says) for Scandinavians.

London Calling Internet

http://www.demon.co.uk/london-calling/content.html
Global Village

The distant echoes of the BBC (or the Clash) give this site its name. This well-done page presents London as the living city it is, not just a place full of old statues and royal family doodads. With counter-culture flavor, LCI dishes the U.K. skinny on everything from media news to film reviews, in a tone ranging from rudely irreverent to discreetly English. On British television: "If the BSC get wound up by the amount of sex and violence on the BBC, then surely Sky [a new satellite network] must seem like a vision of hell to them." A virtual tour of the Portobello Road Market captures some of the hustle and color of this unusual shopping district, while gems like "The Pixel and Paper Art Gallery" keep you up-to-date on local artistry. Some naughty language, but still a swell place to visit.

Losers' Guide to New York

http://www.sonicnet.com./sonicore/loser/loser.html

Global Village

Are you ready for New York, spacepunk style? This site makes an animated blast-off, complete with cyber-aliens on the attack and crash landings, from Planet Loser (where everyone is named Herman) in search of cheap eats, beer, and a cordless toaster (yup) in the Big Apple. Use a clickable map to navigate your way through losing NYC adventures, like a run-in with giant hissing roaches, a harrowing taxi ride, and a Polish vodka binge at Ludwika's Tavern. Activate your RealAudio Player for the best musical and narrative accompaniment a loser could hope for. Utterly groovy slide shows, animation, and superb audio clips make this unconventional tour simply one of the more truly interactive experiences on the Web. A word of advice from the Webmasters: "This site is BIG."

Madagascar

http://www.cable.com/madagas/madagas.htm

Global Village

"Tonga soa aty Madagasikara!" This popular phrase translates to "Where the hell is Madagascar???" (Just kidding.) Teknika Consulting in Toronto brings you this guide to the African "rainbow island," complete with a very hip connection to sites of Malagasy folk music. Discover "the fabulous roots-pop" of Tarika, and get an introduction to Justin Vali, "the ambassador of today's Malagasy music." And when you've had your fill of island rhythms, you can jump to the Madagascar factbook to learn that the island is about twice the size of Arizona (though it lacks Charles Barkley), or to the Usenet postings for the myth of a "man-eating plant" reported by missionaries. For a few monkeyshines in academia, swing by the site's Lemurs Pages, among them "Stanford University's Lemur Gallery" and "Duke University's Lemur Home Page."

Maui Interactive

http://www.maui.net/~kelii/MIA/MI.html

Global Village

Virtual surfers will shoot the curl over this great-looking page from Maui-ites Stuart Helmintoller and Rick Leong, who

are out to promote the island's many charms. Info on everything the Maui-bound could want (and then some), including a sunrise bike ride into a volcano (watch for erupting rock!), and a kayaking expedition in search of Moby Dick (watchers only, please). The Webmasters serve up a colorful interactive map of hot spots like "La Haina" (where you can enjoy a little skydiving) and "Molokini," where the best of Maui is evidently underwater. Links to *Maui Digital Magazine* and a wealth of photo and art exhibits make this as much fun for the armchair traveler as it is for the real-timer.

Michael's New & Improved Pacific Islands WWW Things

http://www2.hawaii.edu/usr-cgi/ssis/~ogden/ogden-newpacific.html

Global Village

Consider yourself *very* well-informed if you can find on your globe the Federal States of Micronesia. If you can't, fear not: the answer to that and a whole lot of other questions is right here. Each

Pacific island has a listing of online resources for languages, politics, geography, and even a few personal home pages. Just north of Australia is Papua New Guinea, a hotbed of political controversy and now the site of a World Bank-sponsored sustainable-farming project. Or travel to the furthest reaches of Melanesia to Fiji, where Kiribati is spoken fluently. Places you may never have known existed are all here: Palau, Tuvalu, Niue... when do we set sail? Links to island resorts take your virtual visit one step closer to reality.

Moon City

http://www.euro.net/5thworld/mooncity/moon.html
Global Village

"From raves to art, from club-hopping to coffee shopping," your trek through Amsterdam pop culture starts at this mellow spot. The page is a lively match between form and function. We used the clever Moon City Mission Control Bar to navigate our way around the site's universe: click on an exploding planet to connect with "Fifth World," a group of Amsterdam rave hosts who believe in the inalienable right to party. Point to the Great Pyramids and enter "MystiCity," an impressive collection of Amsterdam resources, and a direct link to the "Big Trippy Buddha," a painting by Herre

Hoogheimster that you can download right here. Nightlife, movies, museums, and yes, Amsterdam's famous red light district are all well-represented. Great spot for travelers.

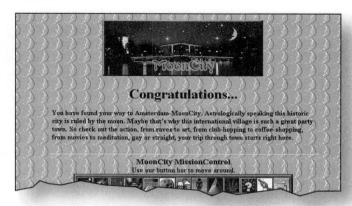

Nation of Hawai'i

http://hawaii-nation.org/nation/
Global Village

A hearty "E komo mai!" opens this informative page from native Hawai'ians (Kanaka Maoli) committed to restoration of their island's independence. This is a group of indigenous people who say they want to refute their "imposed" 1959 admission to the United States. They argue a pretty good case here, and offer full text and analysis of their own new Hawai'ian Constitution, ratified in January 1995. The Constitution, they say, decrees the fundamental right of each citizen to choose nationality and residence, and in a bold progressive move, declares "the right of

everyone to a healthy and sustainable environment." None of this has been acknowledged by the U.S. government, however. Will the U.S. flag drop to 49 stars? Stay tuned.

New Orleans Virtual Library

http://www.geopages.com/SunsetStrip/1202/
Global Village

This is really the easy way to travel the "Big Easy"—home to Mardi Gras, Anne Rice, streetcars named Desire, and cool cemeteries. Start with the limber backbone of this page (and the city), "Blues Chat," an amazing discography and music history lesson chronicling jazz legends from Louis Armstrong to the gutsy modern blues of Marcia Ball. Hundreds of cityscapes document New Orleans' evolution, including a view from space that shows how this delta town got its "Crescent City" nickname. Not just for tourists, the site also provides business and education information, movie schedules, and a five-day weather forecast (usually hot; *always* humid!), all with a groovy interface. Special bonus: art galleries chock-full of local work.

New Zealand on the Web

http://nz.com/
Global Village

A New Zealand Web marketing firm hosts this extra-cheerful page. "We have friendly people," assert the Webmasters, "almost perfect weather,

VIRTUAL TOUR OF NEW ZEALAND

NEW ZEALAND GUIDE BOOK

TRADE AND COMMERCE

great food, and even better wine." Take a virtual tour of the "land of the long white cloud" here. Visit the Art Deco City of Napier on the North Island, or truck down to the South Island for a view of beautiful Christchurch, where you'll learn of the irresistible Wizard who appears in the town square at 1 p.m. every weekday, resplendent in robes, to harangue the assembled crowd about his various causes. You can also bone up on New Zealand's 15 languages, including *Pukapuka* (which, at first glance, we mistook for a Trader Vic's appetizer). Nice collection of pages of "Kiwis at Home and Abroad."

North Cyprus Home Page

http://www.brad.ac.uk/~yysentur/.ncyprus/doc2.html

Global Village

Anchored in the cerulean waters of the Mediterranean, Cyprus is about 40 miles off the coast of Turkey—one of its mainland parents. The island has long been in the middle of a historical tug-of-war between Greece and Turkey, a problem that continues today and is covered here in some detail. This server comes from the Turkish realm, or "North" Cyprus, and covers the island's unique culture with a somewhat fixed perspective. The site still gives a top-notch glimpse of this "corner of Earth touched by Heaven," though. The island's people, language, and history are fleshed out in brilliant detail, from aerial shots of the island to pidgin Turkish lessons. A variety of links to Turkish and Turkish Cypriot home pages from across the world are also included here.

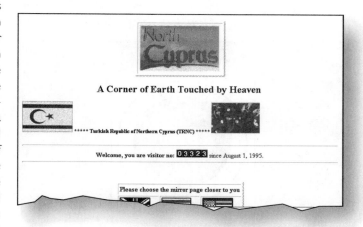

Nyiregyhaza

http://www.bgytf.hu/~komodi/nyiregy/

Global Village

Istvan Komodi, a student at Teacher's Training College in Ny_regyhßza, Hungary, hosts this virtual tour of his home town. Nyiregyhaza (*you* try to pronounce it) is the seventh largest city in Hungary, and the "cultural and economic centre" of Szabolcs-Szatmar-Bereg county, near the Slovakian border. Recorded history of the area dates back to 1326, and perhaps just as important, its first brewery was built in 1421 (marking its entry into "civilized" Europe, we presume). Komodi provides many more colorful details, like the fact that the city is home to 60 medical doctors and one county hospital, and eight colleges and vocational training centers. Plenty of snapshots keep up the visual narrative.

Oneida Indian Nation of New York

http://nysernet.org/oneida/
Global Village

This site is sponsored by the Oneida Nation, "one of the original members of the Iroquois Confederacy that dominated New York State and Canada 200+

Onyota'a:ka:

People of the Standing Stone

years ago." These "People of the Standing Stone" have proudly been part of a "sovereign political unit which predates the Constitution," and they back up that claim here. Long before American colonists won independence from Great Britain, Iroquois members of the Oneida Nation sported muskets and fought alongside revolutionaries. Visitors will find plenty of cultural and political information here, too, including audio samples of the Oneida language, the full text of Oneida/U.S. treaties, and an online museum exhibit of tribal artifacts. The "Chief's Kostoweh," a traditional deer-horn-and-turkey-feather headdress of the Iroquois leaders, is an impressive sight.

Paris

http://www.paris.org/

Global Village

We love Paris in the springtime; we love Paris in the fall... but boy, oh boy, do we love this *virtual* Paris from a team of Francophiles in (of all places) La Jolla, California! This page fairly glows with inside info on the Paris Ballet, the Paris Book Salon, the infamous Champs-Elysées and men with exotic names like Jean Francois de La Beaujardiere. Rich

photographs, maps of the city, histories, cafe reviews... you'll do everything but smell the fromage. Writer Richard Erickson's *Paris Journal* provides first-hand accounts of the Paris Music Expo ("more sound than music"), local politics, and tourist news. And gourmet shopping tips advise that the best truffles are still found at Pebeyre in Cahors (66, rue Frederic Suisse).

A Pictorial Round Trip through the Swiss Alps

http://www.math.ethz.ch/~zari/flight/
zariair/rundflug.html
Global Village

Take a "pictorial round-trip through the Swiss Alps" with math professor Alain Zarinelli. (It's safer than an actual drive down the Autobahn, and no lederhosen are required.) The site has fantastic photos of the Finsteraarhorn, the Schreckhorn, and the eastern edge of the famous Eiger. And aerial shots show off dandy views of the upper Rhine Valley. Zarinelli makes an amiable host, too: "At the end of the lake of Zurich," he instructs, "we make an orbit so that everybody can enjoy the beautiful sight and continue direction alps." (Hey, we said amiable, not "fluent.") When the trip is over, link to "Zari's European Aviation Server" to see how the good prof got all those terrific photos (and if you're inclined, take another trip in a "little hummin Grumman... just back from its summer hols").

The Polar Regions

http://www.stud.unit.no/~sveinw/arctic/
Global Village

Svein Yngvar Willassen, "a lover of the cold and remote," put together this information station on Earth's polar regions. A self-described "computer communication nerd," Willassen includes cool links to "Blocks of Ice," where you may frolic with a furry seal and learn how thinning of the ozone layer has affected the Arctic's natural ecology. "The Great Explorers" chronicles explorations dating back to the early 20th century (when Robert Falcon Scott trekked the Antarctic), and shows off the likes of Roald Amundsen and Fridtjof Nansen. Though "Bears, Seals, and Penguins" sounds a lot like a hockey league lineup, it's actually a study of polar wildlife, with super shots—and a few eerie soundbites—of arctic beasts.

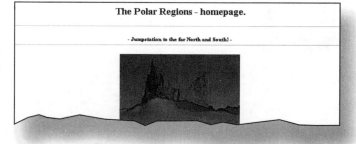

The Polar Regions - homepage.

- Jumpstation to the far North and South! -

Portuguese Home Page

http://s700.uminho.pt/homepage-pt.html
Global Village

Atruly beautiful, Old World-style map of Portugal helps visitors ferret out the nation's Web sites, most of which are

«Home Page» de Portugal / Portuguese Home Page

university scientific spots. But wait, there's much more, including news on human rights, international exchange rates for the Portuguese escudo, area codes, and facts about East Timor (a former Portuguese colony). See the flag, read the anthem, and get loads of information on national pastimes like futebol (soccer) and mountain biking. And choose from dozens of artistic photographs depicting the strangely beautiful countryside of Portugal. English-speakers will be dismayed to find that many of the links are introduced in English, but lead to text in Portuguese; this is far more effective if you speak the language. Still, the lovely presentation is the real winner here.

Serbia

http://www.umiacs.umd.edu/research/lpv/YU/HTML/srbija.html
Global Village

"The history of the people on Serbian soil has always been turbulent," and this site concentrates on everyday aspects of Serbian life. Recipes for many Serbian specialties are included, from the spicy

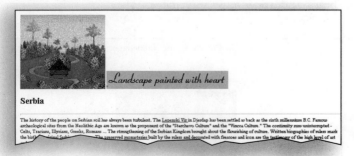

Landscape painted with heart

Serbia

The history of the people on Serbian soil has always been turbulent. The Lepenski Vir in Djerdap has been settled as back as the sixth millennium B.C. Famous archeological sites from the Neolithic Age are known as the proponent of the "Starchevo Culture" and the "Vincca Culture." The continuity runs uninterrupted - Celts, Tracians, Illyrians, Greeks, Romans ... The strengthening of the Serbian Kingdom brought about the flourishing of culture. Written biographies of rulers mark the birth ... The preserved monasteries built by the rulers and decorated with frescoes and icon are the testimony of the high level of art

appetizer "ajvar" ("always made during summer and early autumn, just after the paprika harvest") to "Pecceno prase" (roast suckling pig). And a poem on why women belong in the kitchen begins, "When a wife doesn't cook, children run to Grandma!" The site also offers excellent information on various Serb cities, including the capital city of Belgrade—the spot includes a movie on the house of Yugoslav parliament. Or you can visit a dozen Yugoslavian monasteries. With plenty of graphics and music and pronunciation files interspersed throughout, this makes for an educational experience.

Sweden Information

http://www.westnet.se/sweden/
Global Village

Here's a smorgasbord (we had to say it) of facts and maps from Sweden. For instance, let's talk inventors: "Sweden is the home country of unusually many inventions considering its small population," says the page, which goes on to cite the milking machine, the zipper, and dynamite as Swedish creations. (But can they put the three together?) The site features plenty of good dope on food (a recipe for meatballs!), language, and the arts as well. Hot exports like the chart-topping pop group Ace of Base and world-famous soprano Birgitt Nilsson get their due, and an "Absolutely Swedish" folder outlines the national character. "Foreigners sometimes think Swedish people are undercooled and formal," it explains, adding that Swedish people can be very emotional. "Especially after 2 a.m. in a bar." Well, we think this page is overcooled.

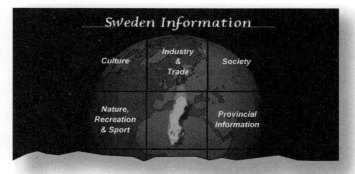

Switzerland

http://heiwww.unige.ch/switzerland/
Global Village

This dandy clickable map from the Graduate Institute of International Studies shows off sites throughout the three-tongued banking and wristwatch capital of the world. We can say that because Switzerland is one nation that doesn't seem to mind stereotypes. In fact, this site seems dead set on perpetuating them. "The most accurate public clocks... are those on the (train) stations, and the trains themselves are nearly as dependable," it explains. The links come in amazing variety: from individual cities (Bern and Lausanne) to engineering institutes and info-sources on hang-gliding and rave parites. Furthermore, you'll get a directory of Swiss banks, the current ski conditions, and an amazing "Pictorial Round Trip through the Swiss Alps." No holes in this site.

Tour Guide of Slovakia

http://www.sanet.sk/Slovakia/TourGuide/
Global Village

Slovakian art photographer Vladimir Barta "has traversed Slovak country many times and has an intimate knowledge of this beauty." (He probably has a cute accent, too.) Who better than Barta, then, to create this travel page. It's a stupendous effort, which took 10 years of "thorough search for the most beautiful and valued places in Slovakia to visit." The virtual tour is driven by both a simple outline (for adventurous surfers) and a clickable map, each with 29 numbers representing a special locale. Click on number one and visit the majestic Devin Castle (at the confluence of the Danube and Morava rivers, it serves as a symbol of friendly relations among the Slavic nations). Click on two and go to Hviezdoslav's Square in Bratislava. Or call up number 16 and discover that "Woodcarved crosses at Detva are the pride of the local cemetery." Travel by numbers is fun!

Tribal Voice

http://www.tribal.com/
Global Village

Tribal Voice is a Native American resource committed to the way of the warrior. The way is "narrow and arduous," quote the Webmasters. "Its foundation is the Word. For the warrior, his word becomes what he is... If he perseveres, great power and magic [are] given to him." Thorough lessons on the right use of "magic" and sweat lodges (an important part of purification rituals) accompany slightly tongue-in-cheek links to "The Heyoka" and "The Prophet" (which is also a super slideshow). For a moving glimpse of the contemporary warrior's journey, link to "The REAL Tribal Voice," a breathtaking visual and poetic landscape that successfully connects traditional Native wisdom with the modern world.

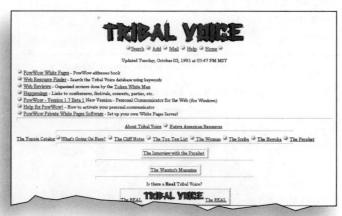

The Unofficial Haitian Home Page

http://www.primenet.com/~rafreid/

Global Village

Ralph Reid, a film student from Northridge, California, does an excellent job of conveying the essence of his native country with this site. His "virtual tour" of Haiti takes you to the crowded Iron Market, to a Port-au-Prince boulevard during rush hour, and on a beautiful beach stroll, where you can practically *smell* the millions of discarded conch shells. You can also check out Carol Guzy's Pulitzer Prize-winning photographs of Haiti, and groove to musical selections like Reginald Decastro's "Pou ou Ayiti." History buffs will want to take this site up on its Haitian history course, while others may be more inclined to gravitate to the Voodoo section. (Discover special days on the Voodoo calendar, like Legba Zaou, when "eating consists mainly of a black goat.") A fascinating page with a very strong flavor.

Virtual Jerusalem Tour

http://www1.cc.huji.ac.il/md/vjt/

Global Village

The Hebrew University hosts this tour through one of the world's oldest and most culturally rich cities. Step into "The Jerusalem Mosaic" for a concise record of the City of David, home to some of the greatest archaeological finds of this century, and the locus of Jesus' final ministry. Enter the Haddassah Hospital Synagogue for a bird's-eye view of 12 stained-glass windows designed by painter Marc Chagall, representing the Twelve Tribes of Israel. Remarkable photographs of the "new" and the "old" cities' landscapes show just how much of the original architecture still remains, while the city itself forges into the 21st century, its residents now facing some of the hardest political and social realities of its long and colorful life. A find for archaeologists, theologians, historians, and travelers.

Welcome to Central Park

http://mosaic.echonyc.com/~park/
Global Village

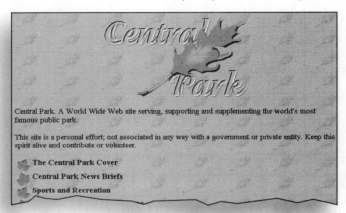

ow will proud New Yorkers react to the news that their beloved Central Park actually "required tons of topsoil to be moved in from New Jersey"? This is just one of many delicious tidbits from Jay Fayloga, the New York University student who created this site. Central Park news briefs keep residents up to speed on issues like banning all car traffic, and info on park-affiliated organizations, like the New York Road Runners Club and the Wildlife Conservation Society. Readers can post their personal park stories here, like Jay's account of bumping into (and knocking down) the same runner twice. Future plans include a bulletin board system, a community calendar, and sound and video bites. Can virtual pretzel bites be far behind?

Windows on Italy

http://www.mi.cnr.it/WOI/
Global Village

he title here is a little deceptive; even the site admits it offers "few pictures." The text-heavy package of Italian cultural and historical information makes this more of a research spot than a travelogue. But what a research spot it is! A clickable map whisks you directly to the region of your choice for a dense array of facts. Visit the Emilia Romagna region and discover its yummy claims to fame, like Parmigiano-Reggiano cheese, hams, and Lambrusco wine. And don't forget the *zampone*: a delicious pig's trotter stuffed with meat. From there you can go to the region's capital, Bologna, where you'll get a brief history, a rundown of monuments, and a list of famous people who once called the city home. And then... well, you get the idea. Sorry: no espresso listings. Yet.

Government and Politics

Government and Politics

Much has been written about the "electronic town hall" the Internet is supposed to bring to government: the new ability of citizens to gather information and talk directly to their leaders. So far, the governments have held up their end of the bargain, offering endless mountains of transcripts, trade pacts, and tax codes, right down to detailed specifications for "jumbo" olives. Citizens, doing their part, have generated equally large mountains of opinions, arguments, and just plain rants, especially about politics. 1996 will be remembered (or forgotten) as the first year that American presidential candidates hit the World Wide Web in search of votes. And attorneys (who are accustomed to dealing with mountains of information) have embraced the new medium as well. The Web may not be an electronic town hall yet, but it's at least an electronic water cooler.

american government

Browse the Federal Tax Code

http://www.tns.lcs.mit.edu/uscode/

American Government

Here it is, kids: Title 26—the Internal Revenue Code. These are the rules the IRS plays by, and if you're a U.S. citizen, you might as well know the rules, too. Sure, the title says "browse", but this is *complete* in a big way: the complete Table of Contents alone takes minutes to download. (A nifty search interface will help you get around that.) Once there, you can pick your favorite section, like Subtitle A, Chapter 5—Tax on Transfers to Avoid Income Tax. Many of the tax code documents are still in plain text rather than hot-linked HTML, but with the volumes (and volumes) of info available, that's no surprise. Your tax dollars at work!

Constitution for the United States of America

http://www.nauticom.net/users/whig/Constitution.html

American Government

"We the people..." yeah, yeah, yeah, the boring old U.S. Constitution, right? Guess again: this site puts a new spin on the old girl. For one thing, author Mike Goldman has provided an index. You want to get right to the passages about fugitive slaves or declaration of war? The handy index will point you right to Article IV, Section 2, Paragraph 3, and Article I, Section 8, Paragraph 11, respectively. Netscape users will enjoy the parchment-like background (nice touch). Another nice touch: this uses the original language—and spelling—of the document's authors. Thus, when you read that "The Senate shall chuse their other Officers," don't panic—our founding fathers just spoke a different language. A simple, useful site.

The FBI's Current "Ten Most Wanted Fugitives"

http://www.fbi.gov/toplist.htm

American Government

Eat your heart out, David Letterman—the FBI's been doing the Top Ten gig for years. And now you don't have to go to the post office to see photos and bios of these dangerous crooks. When we visited, Arthur Lee Washington topped the list (though the FBI insists that members of the list "are not ranked"), with scars on his neck, arms, wrists, and left thigh, and the classic label of "armed and dangerous." These creepy bios are backed by an excellent FAQ about the list, which was launched in 1950 and has had more than 400 members. "DO NOT ATTEMPT TO APPREHEND THESE FUGITIVES YOUR-SELF" says the page, advice that probably doesn't need to be repeated. On our last visit, however, the list had only nine members. What, there was nobody nasty enough to bump up from number 11?

The FBI's "Ten Most Wanted Fugitives"

WARNING: If you have any information concerning these fugitives, please contact the nearest FBI Field Office. Do not attempt to apprehend these fugitives yourself.

- Arthur Lee Washington, Jr.
- Donald Eugene Webb
- Leslie Isben Rogge
- Victor Manuel Gerena
- Mir Aimal Kansi
- Juan Garcia-Abrego

The Federal Web Locator

http://www.law.vill.edu/Fed-Agency/fedwebloc.html

American Government

The Federal Web Locator from the Villanova Center for Information Law and Policy wants to be your one-stop shopping center for federal government information on the World Wide Web. (It's a similar function to that offered by the Department of Commerce's FedWorld site.) Even though the VCILP is not a federal agency, it gets the job done very nicely. Hunting for the Naval Undersea Warfare Center? You can turn it up here. Or check under "Federal Government Consortium and Quasi-Official Agencies," and you'll find Web sites like the National Consortium for High Performance Computing, and the Smithsonian Institution. Plus the World Bank, *Congressional Quarterly*, and much more.

THE FEDERAL WEB LOCATOR

The Villanova Center for Information Law and Policy

"Federal Government information at your fingertips" (tm)

The Federal Web Locator is a service provided by the Villanova Center for Information Law and Policy and is intended to be the one stop shopping point for federal government information on the World Wide Web. This list is maintained to bring the cyber citizen to the federal government's doorstep. If you learn of a federal government site not listed, please mail us so we can add it. If you learn of a federal government on the Web. Also, please check out our

NASA Information Services via World Wide Web

http://www.nasa.gov

American Government

NASA's Web home page is dynamite. If you can't slake your space thirst here, you're just plain abnormal. Hot Topics is a great starting point, especially when a shuttle is up and flying. The "Pick of the Pix" gives popular pictures and even movies, including shots from the Hubble telescope (now in focus!). For a more advanced search, link to the Guide to NASA Online Resources. Teachers and students should also visit Spacelink, which is just for them. Be warned: it takes some effort to wade through the data and get to the juicy parts. (If NASA really wants to thrill the Web community, how about a link called The Most Cool Pictures and Stuff?) Still, this is just a terrific set of pages.

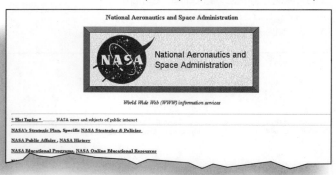

The National Archives Information Server (CLIO)

http://www.nara.gov

American Government

A peek at the first page here is discouraging: only a handful of links, no graphics, dull headings. But since the National Archives has kept federal records since 1774, this is a bit like opening Pandora's box. Census schedules, genealogy, the Federal Register... the list goes on and on. President Clinton has ordered the release of 44 million pages of previously classified documents from WWII and beyond, and a bunch of them are here. You'll also find few graphics and layers of lists to scroll through before you get to anything. (After all, they said declassify, not declumsify.) This is, in short, both our open society AND our modern bureaucracy in all their hypertext glory. Incidentally, the feedback page is called "Letters to CLIO"—somewhere behind this conglomeration is an alternative music fan with a sense of humor.

National Performance Review

http://www.npr.gov
American Government

Hobnobbing with Al Gore has never been easier than at this innovative democratic experiment devoted to reinventing government. You can send messages to the vice president himself in the online open meeting area (or to his aides, anyway), or search the more than 500 documents pumped out for the National Performance Review program. A recent addition is *Common Sense Government*, a status report on the workings of the NPR to date. For the most part, this reads like a public relations piece, but it's pretty lengthy and covers the Clinton camp's entire view on the program. Don't expect to reinvent your own federal agency and appoint yourself head honcho, though. This online brainstorming session is all about saving money, so you'd probably get laid off.

Thomas: Legislative Information on the Internet

http://thomas.loc.gov
American Government

If you believe in freewheeling democracy, the Thomas archive of the Library of Congress will fascinate you. Named after Thomas Jefferson, this text-only site delivers on a simple, elegant concept: take the Congressional Record of the U.S. and every pending bill before Congress and put it in a bazillion-gigabyte Web server. Good Netizens can research bills, follow the actions of bills sponsored by their own representatives, or just filibuster around. The home page includes a short section of Hot Bills, a weekly-updated listing of "major bills receiving floor action... as selected by legislative analysts in the Congressional Research Service." An excellent public-participation tool.

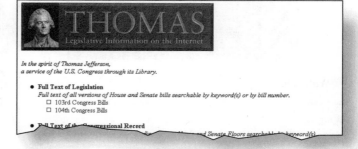

U.S. Bureau of the Census

http://www.census.gov

American Government

The U.S. population will grow by an estimated 183 people while you read this. (Sure, that's an old-fashioned opening, but it still works. Oops—here come another 19 kids!) Lovers of cold, hard facts will find a fascinating vault of knowledge here at one of Uncle Sam's best Web offerings. Huge databases are available for highly specialized searches, although it takes a bit of practice to do it right. If you're single, why not compile a rough estimate of your local dating possibilities by running a search for the number of unmarrieds in your age group and city as of 1990? (You'll still have to go out of the house to find them, though.) This is dense and often technical data—not for the faint of heart.

U.S. Department of Education

http://www.ed.gov/

American Government

You might even call this "the teacher's Net." The USDE *ought* to put up an excellent Web site, and they do. Government watchdogs will find the department's goals and programs spelled out, while K–12 front-liners stand to benefit from a comprehensive teachers' guide to "National Standards Projects," the "Eisenhower Regional Consortia for Mathematics and Science," special education and rehabilitative services, and more. The news section offers a quick-look view of press releases, transcripts, and funding opportunities. (And if you like the sound of "funding opportunities," a link to a gopher-based directory will show you plenty of other opportunities available.) Plus, there are a zillion (yes, Miss Hendershot, we know "zillion" isn't a real word) links to NASA, the National Agricultural Library, and on and on.

The U.S. Federal Budget

http://www.doc.gov/inquery/BudgetFY96/BudgetFY96.html

American Government

Could there be any other document so fully hashed and re-hashed in the history of Man? When you're talking big bucks like the United States Federal Budget, there's no way you can get away with simplicity. This site lets you download the whole 1.7 megabyte Federal Budget to your computer and browse to your heart's content. (With a fast modem, that could still take around an hour to receive.) Using the search form, you can also enter a few choice search words and play watchdog online. Despite the staggering national debt, we could find nothing when searching for words like "fat" and "pork." Keeping in mind how budgets work, terms like "miscellaneous" netted us dozens of listings for nearly every federal agency. This is a nice public service if you're long on patience.

> **THE BUDGET OF THE UNITED STATES GOVERNMENT**
> Fiscal Year 1996
>
> The Budget of the United States Government, Fiscal Year 1996 contains the Budget Message of the President and presents the President's budget proposals.
>
> Electronic access to the Budget of the United States Government, Fiscal Year 1996 is provided by STAT-USA, of the U.S. Department of Commerce.
>
> - Search the complete text of the Budget of the United States Government, Fiscal Year 1996.
> - Mid-Session Review of the 1996 Budget (HTML format)
> - View the Budget in Portable Document Format (PDF).
>
> containing the Budget of the United States Government, Fiscal Year 1996.

U.S. House of Representatives

http://www.house.gov

American Government

Those eager pups at the U.S. House of Representatives have beaten the Senate to the punch again, this time by setting up their own Web home page. (The Senate still has just a gopher.) There's enough data here to pack the Capitol rotunda: housekeeping notes like phone numbers and committee schedules, and high-minded stuff like ethics rules for members. Plus, a trip through this highly complicated info is a major reminder of how a government actually has to function. The House rules changes, for instance, are full of dramatic, ringing phrases: "In clause 6(i) of rule XI, strike 'paragraphs (a)(2) and (b)(2)' and insert 'paragraph (a)(2)'." That sort of reality check may be the best reason of all to visit this site.

> **U.S. House of Representatives Home Page**
>
> **Welcome to the U.S. House of Representatives' World Wide Web Service**
>
> The U.S. House of Representatives' World Wide Web service provides public access to legislative information as well as and to other U.S. government information

United States Information Service

http://www.usia.gov/usis.html

American Government

The job of the U.S. Information Service is to spread the word about the United States to those in other countries. So here, visitors can access full-text versions of the U.S. Constitution, Bill of Rights, and Declaration of Independence in English, French, or Spanish. Brief histories, an outline of the U.S. economic system, and a breakdown of branches of government are just the beginning; cultural exchange info is provided for foreign students, too. Along with expected lists (such as current events), there's some intriguing esoterica, like information on U.S. International Broadcasting, which includes the *Voice Of America*, and Radio and TV Marti, which broadcasts specifically into Cuba. An A-1 resource on all counts.

Welcome to The U.S. Information Service Home Page!

United States Postal Service

http://www.usps.gov/

American Government

The official USPS Web site has what you'd expect: consumer information (like the "correct" way to address mail, and the attendant guilt trip on all the time and money lost because people don't do it), some pictures of 1995 stamps, and the like. If you dig a little, though, you can find a gem or two: did you know that the agency holds auctions for unclaimed lost mail items? (The USPS gets junk sent incorrectly for free—and passes the savings on to you!) You'll even find helpful documents on how to sell supplies to the USPS if, for example, you happen to be a paper clip wholesaler. But hands down, the most useful part of this site is the zip code database, which will even give you those extra four digits you're always forgetting.

UNITED STATES POSTAL SERVICE.

ZIP+4 Lookup

This lookup will attempt to match the address entered. It will then standardize the address, add the proper ZIP+4 Code, and provide the county for that address. Your Web browser must support online forms in order to use the ZIP+4 Lookup. Click here for questions and comments.

Company Name (optional)
Urbanization Name (only used for Puerto Rico)
Delivery Address
City State and/or ZIP Code

Submit *(select when ready to submit)* Clear *(select to clear the form)*

List of State Abbreviations

The White House

http://www.whitehouse.gov/
American Government

Policy wonks will go ape over this virtual White House, where you can visit the Oval Office, meet Chelsea, review the entire GATT treaty, or just hear Al Gore say hello. Thrill to the stylish interface and the gigabytes of government documents, enough to satisfy any talk-show host or conspiracy theorist. Even Tipper Gore gets her own space (though sadly, the Gore daughters do not). Some of the most impressive detail comes in the "Publications" department, where you get same-day transcripts of White House press briefings, reprints of the president's remarks at prayer breakfasts, and much, much more. Of course, this tour is all official stuff, so don't expect to browse the president's mail or tour the First Bathroom. Still, this fine site is as close to the White House as you can come without a Secret Service frisk.

international government

African National Congress

http://www.anc.org.za/
International Government

This site straddles the line—successfully—between partisan political support of the ANC, South Africa's ruling party, and patriotic tribute to a unified nation. Plenty of important political details are here, including bills, press statements, and white papers, most of which are on gopher links. One page, "in the interests of openness, transparency, and democracy," invites you to send mail to the leaders of the ANC, using the direct e-mail addresses provided. That includes President Nelson Mandela, of course, with lengthy bio information— bet you didn't know his middle name is "Rolihlahla"! But there is also a clear black perspective of South African history: "Had it not, in fact, been for the arrival of the British forces, the Boers would eventually have been defeated in their quest to occupy, dominate, and enslave our country." Fascinating country; good Web site.

Brazilian Embassy in London

http://www.demon.co.uk/Itamaraty/
International Government

As odd as it may seem for a country's info source to be based in one of its embassies, it seems to be consistent with this Brazilian embassy's *modus operandi*: rather than stay behind its walls, this outpost embraces its surrounding and invites the world for a stay. The goal of INFOLONDRES, as this Web site is also known, is "spreading greater knowledge and deeper understanding about Brazil." This embassy site offers fabulous information on South America's largest nation: "Brazil in Brief," "Brazilian Foreign Policy," and a "Message from the President" himself. The detail of the embassy building itself is an embarrassment of riches: each room is described meticulously, accompanied by wonderful photos.

Bulgaria—Clickable Map

http://asudesign.eas.asu.edu/places/Bulgaria/map.html
International Government

Arizona State University student (and occasional judo-trophy winner) Plamen Bliznakov has created a Bulgarian resource site so complete, you won't believe your okos. (Look it up.) Links to "a very small Bulgarian dictionary," "Bulgarian Folk Dance," and even a "Bulgarian Joke Page" (in Bulgarian, but still a knee-slapper just for the concept) should satiate Bulgarians. Some links give you the feeling Plamen must've scoured the Net looking for all references to Bulgaria, because some are exceedingly obscure: the Bulgarian cuisine page in Asia, for example ("Dobar apetit!") and a place where you can pick up audio files of amateur Bulgarian folk singing. Also has an almost infinite supply of Bulgarian news and Usenet links, and, as the title promises, a clickable map of Bulgaria featuring WWW resources in Varna, Blagoevgrad, and the capital, Sofia.

Related Information Resources in Bulgaria

Click in a box to get corresponding WWW info or select server to connect to. Clicking outside the figures will connect you to the *"official" Bulgarian WWW page*.

EUnet
Varna

(ist)
(ist)
MGUA
Sofia

Blagoevgrad
AUBG

■ WWW page
● WWW server(s)
▽ ftp server(s)
△ gopher

Embassy of Canada

http://www.nstn.ca/wshdc

International Government

This official embassy site is a wonderful point of departure for exploring the Canadian superhighway: look for links to the House of Commons, the Supreme Court of Canada, Canadian political party sites, and extensive provincial sites. "Newscan," produced by the embassy's press office, sums up Canadian news for the week (fish and fishing treaties always seem to be big news). And, in keeping true to Canadian custom, the site is available in English and French (so surfing Canadians abroad should feel right at home). Internet tech-heads might be amused to note that, although the embassy is located in Washington, D.C., the server boasts a ".ca" address. Even on the Internet, an embassy is a little piece of its country.

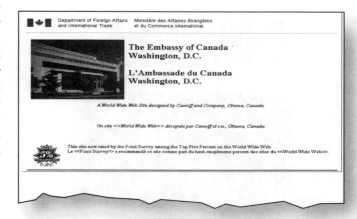

Embassy of Iceland

http://www.globescope.com/web/iceland/index.html

International Government

After a little digging, you find that this page is full of useful, interesting, and sometimes strange stuff. For instance: are questions about the proper disinfectant techniques for fishing equipment *really* that frequently asked? Political junkies can read up on the "Althingi," Iceland's parliament. Surfers will appreciate the map of Icelandic WWW servers and get a kick out of the links to almost 30 personal home pages of Icelanders worldwide. You can pick up a recipe for fried crullers, or hear the Icelandic national anthem on audio, with accompanying trivia about the author, Matthias Jochumsson. (But how did he manage to get the anthem to rhyme in both Islandic and English?) A wonderful experience.

Europa

`http://www.cec.lu/Welcome.html`

International Government

This Belgium-based server from the European Commission offers comprehensive links and info on the EU's goals,

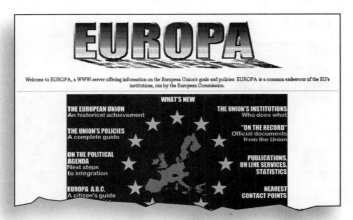

institutions, and policies. Some surprising notes hint at the EU's growing economic clout, like the fact that its gross national product is some ten percent higher than the U.S., and more than 60 percent higher than Japan. A nifty clickable map traces EU history and evolution. Best bet: the "Euromyths" section, where "Euro horror stories fall basically in three categories": completely untrue (the EU is forcing fishermen to wear hairnets aboard their boats); muddles or misunderstandings (Brussels did *not* try to halt production of prawn cocktail crisps); and those that are, essentially, true (the EC *has* proposed laws on lawnmower noise levels).

European Union

`http://www.chemie.fu-berlin.de/adressen/eu.html`

International Government

Just as music has the Artist Formerly Known As Prince, the globe has this group formerly known as the European Community. This comprehensive information station offers links to all 15 members of the EU. Each link leads to a central home page of the particular country, and each page is a clickable map of the various Internet resources available in that country. You can consider it a self-directed tour of the European side of the Internet—some of these links will take you to places you probably didn't even know had Web sites. Some of the pages have more than just the usual—Luxembourg's full-color map, for example, provides a visual listing of sites that provide tourist information, as well as the official Luxembourgian (Luxembourgish?) Web sites. Deep.

Free Burma

http://sunsite.unc.edu/freeburma/freeburma.html

International Government

"The country of Burma has been under martial law since 1962," announces this site, and since the late 1980s, the country has been known as Myanmar. This politically-charged page has a wealth of information on the country (whatever you want to call it): news stories, general national info, and a wonderful photo album of popular hero Aung San Suu Kyi, the 1991 Nobel Peace Prize Laureate who was under house arrest from 1989 to 1995 for resisting the military junta. An absolutely charming "Sights & Sounds" folder captures fleeting Burmese scenes, like the eggplant salesman who's seen it all, but escaped to the border. "He doesn't talk anymore. He just sells eggplants."

Welcome to Free Burma

The country of Burma
is lush, rich in natural resources
and home to dozens of peoples and cultures.
But due to a military government of isolationist economic mismanagement,
the people there live without their human rights and in extreme poverty.
The country of Burma has been under military dictatorship since 1962.

Free Burma *is a slogan, a hope, a certain number of web pages, and, until the people there are free and self-governing,... the only one there is .*

The Hill Times

http://resudox.net/paper/hill.html

International Government

This snappy, hard-hitting independent newsletter covers Canada's national parliament, much like *Roll Call* reports on the U.S. Congress. *Hill Times* is filled with investigative pieces that examine the business connections of Canadian senators and the latest government information online. "Hill Climbers" offers a who's who rundown on the movers and shakers in the Canadian government. It looks like a trade mag gossip column (all the names are in boldface), but this nicely explains the happenings in parliament in a conversational tone (which will hold your attention, unlike the average governmental text). A useful list of government-related sites is squirreled away at the bottom of this site, so don't assume you've seen everything. Great independent Web journalism!

THE HILL TIMES
CANADA'S PARLIAMENTARY NEWSPAPER

Welcome to the Web site of Canada's first and only independent government newspaper. This ever-evolving site is already the most convenient avenue for access to electronic information about Canada's Parliament, its politicians and their staff, and the federal bureaucracy. The editorial, advertising and circulation departments of The Hill Times can be reached by e-mail. The address is hilltimes@resudox.net.

Hill Climbers
Michaela Rodrigue runs down who's who on the Hill, who's on their way up and who's on the way out. All the latest ministerial, senatorial and departmental appointments.

Israel Information Service

http://www.israel.org/
International Government

Maintained by Israel's Chicago consulate, this site "serves as a clearinghouse of official and government information regarding the State of Israel and the Middle East." The superb searchable database offers details on everything in the country, from modern dance to the fact that 2.5 percent of Israelis live in a kibbutz (the plural is "kibbutzim," in case you were wondering). Also offers links to Middle East newsgroups, Israeli Web sites, including Yad Vashem (the Holocaust Remembrance Authority), and a Stamps of Israel page. The graphics are slick, perhaps because they're the product of an independent Web publishing firm. In fact, you'd think more governments would scrape together the money to produce quality sites like this.

Republic of Croatia

http://tjev.tel.etf.hr/hrvatska/HR.html
International Government

This site has a wonderful compilation of Croatian links (not as tasty as Polish links, but...). On our last tour through the clickable map of this boomerang-shaped country, we stopped in the coastal port of Split, where we found a small but interesting bunch of Croatian sites, including the Diocletian palace (built by the Roman emperor "exactly 1,700 years ago"). Other links outside Split include a Croatian tour guide with sound and video files, and a fabulous Croatian-English dictionary. Remember this phrase: "Gdje je najblizha tvrdjava?" ("Where is the nearest fortress?"). If you're not in Croatia yourself, expect slow connect times—but hang around for the stuff to load, because it's an interesting corner of the Web you probably won't hit otherwise.

"Sí, Spain"

http://www.civeng.carleton.ca/SiSpain/

International Government

Spain's Canadian embassy manages to maintain a sunny disposition while telling Canadians—and surfers—about Spain's history, population, culture, economy, and the other usual suspects. You might expect history to be dry, but much of this is just fascinating (did you know Spain went through a major political overhaul and restructured itself into 17 Autonomous Communities in 1978?). Heck, you can even download (and install to DOS) a Spanish course for beginners! The best section, though, deals with fisheries and the often bitter dispute between the two countries over fishing rights off the coast of Newfoundland. (The Spanish tone here is decidedly *un*sunny.) Political junkies will enjoy the dispute, and everyone else will enjoy the decidedly un-governmental feel to this government site.

Somalia—NomadNet

http://www.interport.net/~mmaren/index.html

International Government

Wow. Michael Maren is the author of this astonishing page, collecting information on the embattled nation of Somalia. And he's plenty angry, reproducing articles like the *Washington Post*'s "The Italian Connection: How Rome Helped Ruin Somalia." Maren also holds Western journalists somewhat responsible for Somalia's troubles because of their demand for action. "Somalia," he says," is the story of how the media fed a famine—with tragic results." However, he's not just media-bashing: a striking article by Ali Musa Abdi, a Somali journalist who wrote this piece several months before his arrest in September 1995, tells the bleak story of how third-world journalists often risk their lives to report the news. Excellent photos, behind-the-scenes info, and powerful letters from Somalis.

United Nations

http://WWW.UN.ORG/

International Government

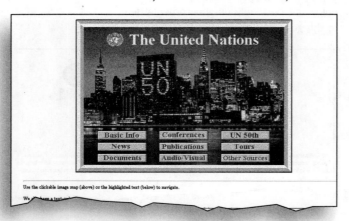

Use the clickable image map (above) or the highlighted text (below) to navigate.

The official UN home page counts its member nations (185 total, once Palau joined in December 1994) and tells you who named the whole darn organization in the first place (Franklin Roosevelt). It also serves up a pictorial history, seminal documents like the UN Charter, and the Universal Declaration of Human Rights, and not-so-seminal reports like the "United Nations Conference on Straddling Fish Stocks and Highly Migratory Fish Stocks." You'll also find plenty about UN50, the 50th Anniversary "programme" of the UN, including pictures of the anniversary ceremony, UN-sponsored concerts, expanded media coverage... Well, stop us when you've had enough. There's enough UN info here to satisfy surfers from all 185 nations.

law ───────────────────────────────────

American Bar Association

http://www.abanet.org/

Law

This is a can't-miss bookmark for any legal pro. The American Bar Association is the primary association of attorneys in the United States, so it's fitting that this site includes just about any information one could want about the legal profession, from notices about ABA meetings to a catalog of ABA publications. Detail is deep, but can be deadly dull: the ABA is made of over 2,200 entities, which "includes 22 sections, five divisions, and more than 80 commissions, standing and special committees, forums and task forces." Those who are so inclined can check the products and services of the Standing Committee on Legal Aid and Indigent Defendants. And for the layman, it includes a Legal Help Center to answer questions or help locate an attorney.

The Consumer Law Page

http://tsw.ingress.com/tsw/talf/txt/intro.html

Law

Caveat venditor! That is, *let the seller beware*, because this site is loaded with ready information to help consumers avoid fraud, defective products, and deadly chemicals. They'll find articles on Toxic Torts, excellent links to other consumer-oriented Web sites, and Federal Trade Commission brochures on everything from auto service contracts to generic drugs. There's also a collection of over 100 brochures, those little fact-filled pamphlets from various organizations you can never find when you're really like them—like the Home Buyer's Guide to Environmental Hazards from the U.S. Environmental Protection Agency. The list of over 500 law resources, sorted by subject, is worth the price of admission alone. A tip of the ol' non-toxic hat to the Alexander Law Firm, sponsors of this exemplary home page!

First Amendment Cyber-Tribune (FACT)

http://w3.trib.com/FACT/

Law

The First Amendment is perhaps the most-discussed part of the United States Constitution, and Charles Levendosky has created this fantastic guide to it. Most useful here is First Amendment Alert!, which includes weekly updates on the topic as it appears in state legislatures, courts, and Congress. If your timing is right, you can catch the page on Banned Books Week (generally the last week of September), which lists all books challenged in or banned from libraries around the U.S. (Some will leave you guessing—like the removal of the *American Heritage Dictionary* from classrooms in Washoe County, Nevada.) You'll also find Supreme Court decisions and a Q&A section where Mr. Levendosky or another scholar answers visitor questions. An amazing site.

International Constitutional Law

http://www.econ.uni-hamburg.de/law/home.html
Law

This Hamburg, Germany, University project contains the full constitutions of more than 30 nations, including Rwanda, Sweden, and Iraq. (Yep, Iraq has one.) A handy search function lets you compare similar provisions in the various constitutions. You can, for instance, learn how to impeach presidents around the globe! (For the record, the constitutions of France, the U.S., and Germany address the issue).

Although the title of this site seems to limit its scope to legalities, the page has plenty of current and background info on the countries it lists. The quick-look summary provides interesting tidbits about each country, including the correct noun and adjective forms for describing its residents (so you won't be socially awkward when discussing your Belarusian friends). Interesting idea, funky maps, too.

Internet Resources for Women's Legal and Public Policy Information

http://asa.ugl.lib.umich.edu/chdocs/womenpolicy/womenlawpolicy.html
Law

This meta-index of resources is a gold mine for anyone interested in hot public policy issues like women's reproductive rights, sexual harassment, and women in the military. It offers a link to the "Glass Ceiling Newsletter," a publication edited by a former placement professional, which reports on sex discrimination in the workplace. The Women of Color Resource Center explores minority issues, while the

Women's Environment and Development Organization (linked in five languages) examines women's roles in achieving world ecologic and economic sustainability. Domestic violence, parenting, children's issues, poverty, and disabilities are among other topics for which vast resources have been carefully assembled and summarized. A solid bookmark for legal professionals and women in general.

The 'Lectric Law Library

http://www.inter-law.com/
Law

Perhaps the most complete law library on the Web, The 'Lectric Law Library includes statutes, case law, legal forms, and the Library's own *'lectric Lawcopedia*. This is no musty, dust-filled citadel: at the home page, you're greeted by Ralf, the head librarian, who can lead you to either a "tour" of the library, or directly into the heart of the site, The Rotunda ("Its dome, as you can see, is covered with frescos by Michelangelo and my brother Randy"). And it's not just for the pros: the "Law for Business Lounge" and "Laypeople's Law Lounge" cover everyday legal matters like taxes, traffic tickets, and leases. Don't let the topic of the site fool you into thinking

it's boring; don't let its sense of humor fool you into thinking it doesn't mean business. A fine resource.

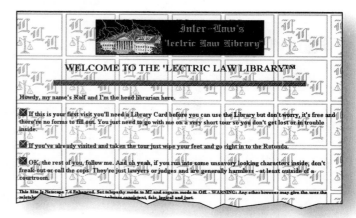

The Legal Information Institute

http://www.law.cornell.edu/
Law

The Legal Information Institute is well on its way to making itself one of the Web's best legal resources. The site contains a huge amount of legal material organized by topic, type, and source, from state statutes to recent Supreme Court decisions. (And who can resist titles like "Florida Bar vs. Went For It, Inc."?) A recent addition is the Federal Judicial Statistics interface, which lets you get statistics on over 3.5 million (!) federal civil cases over the last 15 years. The page also provides a list of occasional "special interest" pieces on topics like the "Proposed Examination Guidelines for Computer-Implemented Inventions from the U.S. Patent and Trademark Office." Another winning bookmark for scholars and legal pros.

NetWatchers Cyberzine

http://www.ionet.net/~mdyer/netwatch.shtml

Law

For the latest legal developments in cyberspace, the NetWatchers Cyberzine is the place to go. Editor Marshall Dyer offers his latest headlines, and then you settle in on the NetWatchers main page—a slick newspaper-style setup with all the news that's fit to serve. (A warning, though: the cover page will look sloppy if your browser doesn't support tables.) Among the zingers is a copy of a letter sent to the U.S. Department of Justice, which warns that Senator Exon could be arrested under the provisions of his own bill (because he carries a book of illegal photographs supposedly gathered from the Internet, and he's been passing it along to fellow senators). Things move fast in cyberspace, and this is not a bad way to keep up to speed.

Richmond Journal of Law and Technology

http://www.urich.edu/~jolt

Law

This University of Richmond publication aims to be a leader in examining the intersection of law, technology, and the Internet. (And the foreward's ringing endorsement by David Johnson, chairman of the Electronic Frontier Foundation, should be impressive enough to grab your attention.) The articles and essays in the first issue are lengthy, detailed, and of a quality you'd expect in any print journal, on topics including Apple vs. Microsoft and the fate of trademarks, contracts, and copyrights in cyberspace. This journal is also part of a coalition attempting to standardize citation formats for legal publications on the Web—a goal we would support if we ever actually read footnotes.

The Tax Prophet

http://www.taxprophet.com/

Law

Robert L. Sommers, a sole practitioner in San Francisco, has created this site to assist with the tax law blues. Here you can find the latest Hot Tax Topics, such as the (remote) possibility of a new flat tax on income. Also of interest (particularly to foreign citizens investing in the U.S.) is the foreign tax section. And if you've the urge to ask, "Who the heck is this guy to be giving me advice?" you can check for yourself: peruse the Tax Prophet's professional record and download any of his tax-related newspaper columns published semi-regularly in the *San Francisco Examiner*. In addition to cool graphics, this site also has a taste of interactivity: you can complete a test to see whether you owe Social Security taxes on your babysitter.

Web Journal of Current Legal Issues

http://www.ncl.ac.uk/~nlawwww/

Law

Here's an example of the legal profession using the Web to its full potential. This journal from Britain's University of Newcastle has everything one would expect from a respectable paper journal, from articles to case notes to book reviews with hypertext footnotes. Typical topic for study: the United Nations Commission on International Trade Law and its attempt to establish rules for corporate electronic data interchange. Most articles are similarly on the cutting edge of information law, though not all fit that mold: *The Marginalisation of Gypsies* was a lengthy dissertation on the prejudice against gypsies in the United Kingdom. This is filled with interesting essays that will easily consume more time than you have.

military

A-Bomb WWW Museum

http://www.csi.ad.jp/ABOMB/index.html
Military

"Fat Man" and "Little Boy" are the strangely whimsical names of the two bombs which fell on Hiroshima and Nagasaki in World War II. They're featured here at the A-Bomb WWW Museum by virtue of being the only two nuclear weapons ever used in wartime. This site was assembled by volunteers who "strongly believe that the world must learn about weapons of total destruction," and who hope nuclear weapons will never be used again. The site (necessarily) gives emphasis to the atomic bombing of Japan, but the authors make it clear that the site's purpose is not just to make the reader feel sorry for the people of the bombed cities, but to help build a better future by understanding the past. It's a complete (and sobering) site.

AirForceLINK

http://www.dtic.dla.mil/airforcelink/
Military

Although it holds plenty of spec sheets for aircraft, this official page of the U.S. Air Force is not just for fighter buffs.

Welcome to AirForceLINK, the United States **Department of the Air Force Home Page**, your first source for Air Force news and information.

● **AF delivers help to Caribbean**

Probably the best of the defense force Web pages, AirForceLINK has very cool graphics (much cooler than you'd probably expect from the military), and lots of general interest information. For example, most people know a sonic boom is caused by air compression in front of a plane going faster than the speed of sound, but here, you can get all the technical info you'd ever need (or possibly want). Links are "faster than an F-16," too. You may even have fun (we read about how goats have interfered with radio transmissions in Utah). Aircraft facts, air show pictures, and good links around the world.

E-HAWK

http://kuhttp.cc.ukans.edu/history/ehawk/

Military

Okay, so the name "Electronic Headquarters for the Acquisition of War Knowledge" is a long way to stretch for a snappy acronym (E-HAWK). But the page, compiled by two grad students at the University of Kansas, is a military buff's delight. E-HAWK catalogs U.S. and NATO home pages, along with hard-to-find military science files (like the "CIA Guide to Guerrilla Warfare" in Nicaragua). Meanwhile, the "Officer's Club" has a great listing of veterans associations and reunion registries. If you're looking for a historical perspective, check out E-HAWK's sister site, Mil-Hist, for a wealth of battles, blitzes, and bombardments. The site uses more than its share of odd color schemes, but it's an impressive independent effort.

Enola Gay

http://www.nasm.edu/GALLERIES/GAL103/gal103.html

Military

This Smithsonian National Air and Space Museum exhibit "commemorates the end of World War II, as well as the role of the Enola Gay in securing Japanese surrender." The Enola Gay is the famous plane that dropped the first atomic bomb on Hiroshima. This fabulous exhibit comes replete with text and photos. You'd have to go to the Smithsonian to see all the info and pictures, but in some ways this is better than an actual museum (plenty of info—and no screaming kids). Includes technical specs on the B-29 bomber, and answers a burning question we've all had for years: the Enola Gay was named after the pilot's mother. And if you do visit the actual exhibit, don't worry—this site promises that the "Little Boy" replica "contains no nuclear material and presents no radiation hazard."

The Enola Gay, the B-29 bomber used in the atomic mission that destroyed Hiroshima, went on display June 28, at the Smithsonian's National Air and Space Museum in Washington, D.C. The display commemorates the end of World War II, as well as the role of the Enola Gay in securing Japanese surrender.

The Enola Gay will remain on display at the National Air and Space Museum indefinitely. Admission is free but passes will be required for this exhibit. Same-day tickets for specific times of entry will be distributed at the museum every day. Museum hours are 10 a.m. to 6:30 p.m.

"It is particularly important in this commemorative year that veterans and other Americans have the opportunity to see the Enola Gay," Smithsonian Secretary I. Michael Heyman said. "The aircraft speaks for itself in this exhibit and, 50 years after its mission, it continues to evoke strong emotions, in those who look at it."

On Jan. 30 of this year, Secretary Heyman ended months of controversy when he announced his decision to replace a larger, interpretive exhibition with a less complicated display. "The exhibition you are entering does what I intended," Heyman says in his written introduction at the exhibit's entrance. "We have added some material on the Smithsonian's restoration of the Enola Gay and some explanatory material on the B-29 aircraft and the 509th Composite Group."

Images of My War

http://www.ionet.net/~uheller/vnbktoc.shtml
Military

This plain, text-only document contains first-hand accounts of a young soldier's experiences serving in Vietnam. Vet Ron Heller describes his war experiences with cool detachment and a soldier's black humor (at one point noting that his troops "had achieved the highest total body count in the battalion... I like to think that my leadership had something to do with it"). There are, of course, the inevitable nasty bits that come with any firsthand war account, but there's plenty of "how could that happen" military humor, like the sergeant who received a Purple Heart for stubbing his toe, and the lieutenant colonel who had his shower water replaced with Kool-Aid. (True stories!) This sharp-edged read will disturb the squeamish, but intrigue anyone interested in a personal account of military history.

Korean War Project

http://www.onramp.net/~hbarker/index.html
Military

This page dedicated to the Korean War also showcases the talents of creator Hal Barker, a photojournalist, writer, inventor, and founder of the Korean War Veterans Memorial Trust Fund. When you're not looking at Barker's photos or reading the first chapter of his book, "Return to Heartbreak Ridge," you can browse extensive links to Korean maps and history, casualty files, or U.S. military, government and veterans' groups. This site is also the host to *Please Bow To The Great Leader*, a travelogue by Australians Paul and Rick Bakker, who are aficionados of Communism (really!). "Stalinism," they say, "acts like a preserving agent, leaving countries like North Korea in pretty much the same state as they were 50 years ago. It's like a trip back in time, but whether it was to 1945 or 1984 we couldn't decide."

On The Road In Korea - Photography

Korean War Veterans Memorial Dedication Week

Military Secrecy

http://www.portal.com/~trader/secrecy.html

Military

"Despite the end of the Cold War, billions of dollars are spent in secret each year, without any accountability to the taxpayers." So says site author Paul McGinnis, who offers amazing links like "How Code Names Are Assigned." (A name "must be chosen with sufficient care to ensure that it does not express a degree of bellicosity inconsistent with traditional American ideals...") Visitors can download a virtual model of the Voyager (the so-called "mystery supersonic aircraft"), and amateur spies will appreciate the listing of radio frequencies for various military contractors. There's a few guides on how to assert your rights under the Freedom of Information Act to get documents from the U.S. government (and tips on traversing that incredibly twisty maze). This page is fun, fascinating, and a testament to free speech in America.

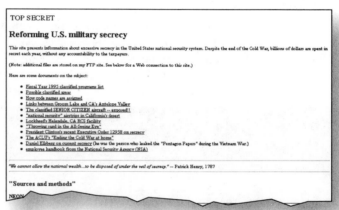

Vietnam Veterans Home Page

http://grunt.space.swri.edu/

Military

Created "to honor Vietnam veterans, living or dead, who served their country on either side of the conflict," this emotional site contains stories, poems, songs, maps, and narratives from many people touched by the war. Though we couldn't find any material from Vietnamese vets, the page does acknowledge, if not embrace, those soldiers on "the other side." Put together with "help from the platoon," the page has a casual, homey feel as it makes visits to the country of Vietnam and then to the Vietnam Memorial in Washington, D.C. Vets will appreciate resources like the "Lost & Found" page, an aid in searching for old war buddies, and "Reunions," a list of vet gatherings and other get-together sources. A provocative and engrossing page for all.

politics

Amnesty International Online

http://www.io.org/amnesty/overview.html
Politics

Amnesty International is one of the world's largest human rights watchdog groups. Here you can read about its current campaign to establish a UN-sponsored International Criminal Court, and its appeals on behalf of the victims of human rights violations in East Timor, where thousands of civilians have died following a military takeover. And what better way to dispense time-sensitive information than on the Net? AI's Urgent Action notices, which are requests for immediate action from plain folks, are frequently updated here (although summaries on the list page would have been helpful). Details are available here in English, French, or Spanish, and AI also offers an extensive library of documents and publications. Excellent list of links to other human rights info on the Net.

CCER National Budget Simulation

http://garnet.berkeley.edu:3333/budget/budget.html
Politics

Okay, Mr. or Mrs. John Q. Smartypants: you want the budget balanced? Go ahead. This fascinating interactive game actually lets you balance the 1995 fiscal budget—or try to. Brought to you by U.C. Berkeley, the site shows you the current federal budget, and lets you monkey around with different programs—cut defense, cut welfare, cut what you want. (We scrapped social security, Medicare, military spending, transportation, and international affairs, and came out just a few hundred billion dollars over-budget. What's so hard about this "politics" stuff, anyway?) You can take the Short Form, with 20 spending and six tax expenditures categories, or the huge, rolling Long Form, with those categories broken into 144 subcategories. A great site and a great public service.

The National Budget Simulation

Welcome to the National Budget Simulation!

This simple simulation should give you a better feel of the trade-offs which citizens and policy makers will need to make to balance the budget.

Crash Site

http://www.crashsite.com/Crash

Politics

Just like a real crash site, this site isn't always pleasant, but it *is* a spectacle for gawkers. Its cover page is set up like a splashy tabloid, and you're given low- and high-resolution paths (to save and burn bandwidth, respectively). Underground poster art, movies, and morphs are scattered across these pages like shattered glass on the avenue, highlighting alternative music, fiction, and politics. The bands highlighted are given extraordinary personal treatment (the Royal Trux pages are set up like an FBI surveillance report, complete with blocked-out agent names). The look of this page is great, yet some of the political humor is beyond Swiftian and it is hard to tell when the kidding stops, if ever;

"War as Entertainment" features a Top Ten list that's bitingly funny, but the movies here are certainly not. Because, you know, war is hell. Isn't it?

The Democratic Leadership Council and Progressive Policy Institute

http://www.dlcppi.org/

Politics

In an attempt to deflect an onslaught of Republican legislative initiatives, the Democratic Leadership Council (DLC) and its creation, the Progressive Policy Institute (PPI) have joined efforts to spread the "New Democratic message" throughout America. Their agenda includes "progressive ideas, mainstream values, and nonbureaucratic approaches to governing." (As opposed to the many parties who want regressive ideas and pro-bureaucratic approaches, we presume.) All kidding aside, one of the group's defining documents, the New Orleans declaration, outlines their philosophy, which seems to go against some stereotypical Democratic thinking. A library of texts significant to the DLC/PPI are available here—or you can order a printed copy of the exact same thing if *you* feel like being regressive yourself. Great page for policy wonks!

The Flag-Burning Page

http://www.indirect.com/user/warren/flag.html
Politics

Strike up the Diamond matches, granny! Click on the Stars and Stripes, and watch 'em sizzle! Before you get mad, virtual flag burner Warren Apel wants you to know he created this page *not* to encourage real-time torching, but to make a point about civil liberties. He's vehemently opposed to the so-called "flag amendment," making it a crime to desecrate Old Glory. "With all the problems facing America right now, it's hard to imagine how 252 Representatives and 50 Senators have found the time to sign this legislation..." As support, Apel offers a transcript of a bizarre, hour-long debate on the House floor that goes on wild tangents, including the name of the actor who played the Tin Man in *The Wizard of Oz*. Does Apel shed light on the topic, or just more heat? You decide.

Get out your Zippos, it's...
The Flag-Burning Page

Burn a Virtual Flag

The History of Flag-burning

The Purpose of this Page

Track Current Legislation

- Senate
- House

NewtWatch

http://www.cais.com/newtwatch/
Politics

The NewtWatch page marries political factoids, mean-spirited humor, and plenty of yuks to try to get under the skin of our House speaker. Miscaptioned photos, insults worn as a badge of honor (Gingrich spokesman Tony Blankley called NewtWatcher Matt Dorsey a "Third Wave slime"), and ethics complaints all make this an amusing stop for politicos. Especially effective is the rundown of Newt's office salaries and expenditures, up 30 percent over the previous administration (which Gingrich himself said was run by a free-spending Democrat). The page lists the salaries of everyone at Newt's office (Blankley himself makes nearly $2,300 a week!) and says, "An ancillary function [of the salaries list] is to foster resentment among Newt's staff." Gingrich fans should avoid this site: it's just not worth the high blood pressure.

Political Babble Generator

http://www.webcorp.com/polibabble.htm

Politics

"Haven't you always suspected that a randomly selected bunch of hackneyed phrases might have as much insight as the daily political babble?" asks this site. The Political Babble Generator tries to prove it through the "same distribution of three-word phrases as real speeches by Clinton and Gingrich." Sometimes it doesn't make sense, but then, the same is true of most speechmakers. If the computed speech *is* understandable in any way, you can submit that text to the Book Of Knowledge, a collection of sensical quotes spotted by other viewers. One favorite Clinton bit: "Tip O'Neill never forgot who he was, where he came from, or who they voted for change in our regulations? You bet we do. But we all agree that the real credit belongs to the fire." New random speeches are cranked out every 10 minutes.

W Clintov and Gingov

Haven't you always suspected that a randomly selected bunch of hackneyed phrases might have as much insight as the daily political babble? Clintov and Gingov prove the truth of that suspicion by generating randomized "speeches" that have the same distribution of three-word phrases as real speeches by Clinton and Gingrich. The output is an oddly readable, often hilarious amalgamation with embedded nuggets of wisdom. New random "speeches" are generated every ten minutes, Clintov on the 0's and Gingov on the 5's.

We strongly suggest that these speeches be read aloud, preferably to a drunken audience of journalists.

Oh, and be sure to copy & paste your favorite bit of "wisdom" into the form at the bottom of the page...

Propaganda Analysis Home Page

http://carmen.artsci.washington.edu/propaganda/home.htm

Politics

Does "propaganda" sound like an outdated, Cold War concept? Not so, according to Aaron Delwiche, who offers his own analysis on this page, based on the Institute for Propaganda Analysis created in 1937. Delwiche starts by identifying some familiar "propaganda devices" like Glittering Generalities (charged concepts like "love" and "freedom" used in a vaguely positive way) and the Testimonial (unqualified persons giving judgments, like "I'm not a doctor, but I play one on TV"). Delwiche goes on to illustrate by citing such noteworthy offenders as Newt Gingrich and the John Birch Society, although an annotated list of propagandisms would make these more enjoyable. This site is as much a rhetorical as a political site, but it's great cerebral reading either way.

propaganda

Propaganda Analysis Home Page

As generally understood, propaganda is opinion expressed for the purpose of influencing actions of individuals or groups... Propaganda thus differs fundamentally from scientific analysis. The propagandist tries to "put something across," good or bad. The scientist does not try to put anything across; he devotes his life to the discovery of new facts and principles. The propagandist seldom wants careful scrutiny and criticism; his object is to bring about a specific action. The scientist, on the other hand, is always prepared for and wants the most careful scrutiny and criticism of his facts and ... criticism. *Dangerous propaganda crumbles before it.*

Refuse & Resist!

http://www.calyx.com/~refuse/
Politics

Sure to warm the hearts of aging hip-pies, this New York-based activist group is vitriolic, opinionated, and pretty effective. "The current war on women... censorship

of the arts, resurgent racism, police state measures, gay bashing, and compulsory patriotism—Refuse & Resist! says NO to the whole package." Yow! The page focuses on charged political issues, such as the Pennsylvania death-row case of African-American journalist Mumia Abu-Jamal. Refuse & Resist! doesn't shrink from inflammatory agitprop, either, with head-lines like "Abortion on Demand and Without Apology!" and "Refuse the 1990s New World Order!" One pro-choice mis-sive began by stating that Hitler was "the Father of the Right to Life Movement." Polite it isn't, but it makes for lively reading.

Right Side of the Web

http://www.clark.net/pub/jeffd/index.html
Politics

The Right Side of the Web is cheerfully one-sided. "Right" means both "con-servative" and "correct" here, where the Democrats are always silly liberals, the president is always Slick Willie, and the *real* president is still The Gipper himself (shown smiling on the first page). Colorful graphics and plenty of photos make it all enticing (have to compete in the free market, after all) and the links to other conservative

pages could keep you on the right track for some time to come. Features the occasionally-updated comic, DeMOCKracy. And what conservative Web site would be complete without its own personal load of Rush Limbaugh links and text files? Few minds will be changed here; conservatives will love it, and liberals will no doubt dis-agree.

The Ronald Reagan Home Page

http://www.erinet.com/bkottman/reagan.html

Politics

Love him or hate him, this one is for the Gipper, here fondly remembered as the leader of "the greatest peace-time expansion in U.S. history." Author Brett Kottmann frequently careens off into kick-the-liberals spasms (declaring that "exposing the liberal lies is... fulfilling"), sometimes invoking Reagan's name only as an afterthought. When the page actually focuses on the 40th president, though, the results are much better. Highlights include a hefty collection of delicious Reagan quotes ("Republicans believe every day is the 4th of July, but Democrats believe every day is April 15th") and speeches that even in print show off that famous Reagan charisma. Also included: a moving "word of thanks" from Reagan regarding his fight with Alzheimer's disease.

State of Nature

http://www.nrdc.org/nrdc/field/state.html

Politics

Saving the environment is the name of the game at the Natural Resources Defense Council, and State of Nature is its watchdog Web site. Included in each issue is Legislative Watch, which hits you right on the front page with updates of Congressional action on various environmental bills such as the Clean Air and Clean Water Acts. The Earth at Stake section presents some scary statistics, including the news that in 1994 one in five Americans drank water contaminated with unsafe levels of pollutants. In fact, this page is loaded with scary and depressing info; despite its usefulness, it can be something of a downer to visit. The page includes a section on NADC milestones, but we were in a deep blue funk by the time we got there.

Town Hall

http://www.townhall.com
Politics

The conservative revolution (or whatever it is) has reached the Net, as exemplified by Town Hall. These remarkably rich pages lead surfers to offices housing The Heritage Foundation, the National Review (W.F. Buckley's columns online!), National Minority Politics, and a dozen or so others. On recent visits, we learned that Arthur Fletcher, a black Republican member of the U.S. Civil Rights Commission, had joined the 1996 presidential race, and read about conferees gathering in San Francisco to celebrate the late Ayn Rand's birthday. And if you'd like to know where exactly your tax dollars are going, there's a list online with just that ($14 billion is going to NASA—and at least half of that must be for production of their Web sites). Will fascinate conservatives, of course, but also politicos of all stripes.

Votelink

http://www.votelink.com
Politics

Proclaiming itself "The Voice of the Net," Votelink is a fantastic virtual polling place, as Net denizens from all over the world vote right here on issues of importance to them. Voting is broken down into "World Vote," "National Votes," "U.S. State Votes," and "U.S. City Votes." The page tends to have a U.S. bias (by virtue of those last two voting areas) but there's still plenty for everyone. A recent World Vote: "Should France withdraw its decision to reopen nuclear testing?" ("Yes" was whipping "No" by 612 to 96). Each question is fleshed out with pro and con points of view. The page favors tight single-screen pages, so Netscape users will squint a lot at the small print. And we'd like to see some archives: what about previous votes? Still, a fun use of the Web.

Health and Medicine

Health and Medicine

Medicine has long been a big player on the Web, with huge databases set up to be accessed by doctors or researchers anytime, anywhere. These databases continue to grow, although they're often impenetrable to anybody without a neurology degree from Johns Hopkins.

Despite all that data, it turns out that the most compelling medical sites are those done by the patients. Check out "Amanda's Home Page," where a young woman in Britain describes her ongoing struggles with cancer. Such pages become a gathering place where anyone with cancer (or diabetes or transplanted organs) can come to ask questions, offer advice, or simply get some friendly support. People who wouldn't dream of asking their doctor an embarrassing question will somehow ask a million strangers on the Internet—and many times, get the answer they need. And the Internet, as the joke goes, makes house calls.

Ask NOAH About Health

http://www.noah.cuny.edu/

Health and Medicine

If NOAH doesn't know everything, he'll at least point you in the right direction for info on AIDS, cancer, pregnancy, sexually transmitted diseases, and tuberculosis. We learn that these are all important health issues in New York City, whose culture flavors this friendly information resource. NOAH has a good-sized database of medical articles, mostly aimed at regular folks, as well as medical professionals. A click on "Nutrition," for example, pops up a library of articles ranging from "A Consumer's Guide to Fats" to a link to an online "Personal Food Analyst." Elsewhere, you'll find a report that shows how a soon-to-be father's behavior—from unhealthy work environments to drug use—may hurt a pregnancy. Serving the "underserved," NOAH speaks Spanish, too. Muy bueno!

Amanda's Home Page

http://www.dircon.co.uk/adastra/amanda/amanda1.html

Health and Medicine

This is a touching, disturbing, and courageous page created by Amanda, a 29-year-old British health care worker suffering from the cancer known as

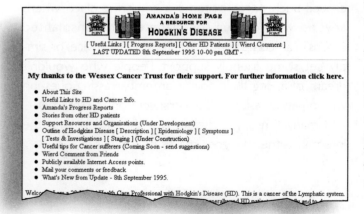

Hodgkin's Disease. Amanda provides extensive, accessible information about Hodgkin's, but it's the personal account of her illness that's the most engaging: "It was the second week of January that I first noticed a swelling on the right side of my neck," Amanda writes. She takes visitors through each step of her battle, from diagnosis to chemotherapy. Other cancer patients like Bill Sterling offer tales of their battles with disease. Sterling writes, "I never thought of myself as a support group type. I changed my mind." All in all, this is a collection of sobering and cathartic tales (and links to related sites)—and a must-see for those affected by cancer.

Balance Fitness Magazine

http://tito.hyperlink.com/balance
Health and Medicine

"If we could give every individual the right amount of nourishment and exercise, not too little and not too much, we would have found the safest way to health." That Hippocratic quote sums up Balance Magazine. (It also sounds nicer than "Flatten that gut!") This is a fine resource for diet and fitness, with back issues well-organized by subject. Graphics are limited. Content is up and down: on past visits, an article on stomach exercises was full of good info, and the "Adventures of Garfield the Glucose Molecule" was funny and educational, but "How to Relax" merely suggested we breathe slowly and take relaxation classes. (If we had time to take classes, we wouldn't need to relax, now would we?) Still, well worth the visit for the fitness-minded.

Biomedical Information Resources

http://www.mic.ki.se/Other.html
Health and Medicine

This overwhelming mountain of links from the Karolinska Institute in Sweden covers just about everything you might want to know about biomedicine, down to the last quark. Sure, you know links like "Molecular Modeling & NMR Spectroscopy" are aimed at the pros, but casual biomedicine fans (you know who you are) will find "Ophthalmology Patient Information" and other friendly links. The "History of Biomedicine" is a particularly interesting read. There's a "Buddhism and Medical Ethics" site, another page where you can look at x-ray films of various broken things, plus chemistry, genetics, anatomy, newfangled "bioinformatics"... and that's just the tip of the ol' stethoscope. Be forewarned: it's dense and it's from Sweden, so it can be slow going at times.

The Body Electric

http://www.surgery.com/body/
Health and Medicine

Given the chance, many people would jump at the opportunity to have at least one part of their anatomy tucked, tightened, or trimmed. This plastic surgery page gives you the lowdown on what they call "body enhancement," including some enhancements you may never have considered. (Implants to increase the size of the calves, for instance, take about an hour per calf.) Sponsored by the California-based Tulip Company ("The Soft Touch for Soft Tissue"), this site shows those interested in taking things one step further how to locate a Tulip-sponsored specialist who practices in their area. What sets this page apart are the many before-and-after photos, which are weirdly fascinating, and the pleasingly frank discussion of prices and procedures. For a commercial site, this has got a lot going for it.

The Canadian Health Network

http://www.hwc.ca/
Health and Medicine

This text-only server in English and French is about the broadest resource we've seen for general and family health info. Although dubbed a Canadian page (and Canada does provide much of the content), the lists and links culled from around the world will interest everyone from Dr. Mom to Dr. Welby. Regular Joes who aren't sick will still find useful items at the general-interest reference desk, which points at reference works, including the "English-Romain Dictionary of Equivalent Proverbs." Leap to sites ranging from the "National Pollutant Database" to the "StressFree Net" to "DEAF Net," an Italian site for the deaf with some *serious* attitude. (But where's the National Apple Council?) Older citizens will enjoy links like the "Seniors Computer Information Project." Note: connect and download times can be extremely slow.

CancerGuide

http://bcn.boulder.co.us/health/cancer/canguide.html
Health and Medicine

This is a hopeful, folksy guide to fighting cancer. Creator Steve Dunn, "a fellow patient" and advocate of extensive research, says he offers "a point of view, not... sanitized by committee!" Dunn starts with a neophyte-friendly essay on cancer fundamentals, and then goes on to show how to plug into the big-time medical databases. Dunn includes useful tools like "Advice on Researching Rare Cancers," the highly-recommended "The Median Isn't the Message" by Stephen Jay Gould, for those with difficult prognoses (four-percent survival is *not* the same as zero, and there are plenty of ways to boost your personal odds), and lots more.

"Steve's Guide to Clinical Trials" includes the observation that "medicine is extremely conservative in nature," and discusses Interleukin-2, the drug that saved his life.

Centers for Disease Control National AIDS Clearinghouse

http://cdcnac.aspensys.com:86/
Health and Medicine

The Centers for Disease Control have set up this central repository for AIDS information, and boy, are they thorough. In addition to offering help on getting into the big databases of AIDS-related information (like the "Culturally-Specific Educational Materials," or the "Resources and Services Database"), the CDC also publishes a daily summary of AIDS articles in major U.S. news publications (like *The Washington Post*). These stories range from treatment reports to personal profiles of those afflicted. On our last visit, we read about a prison inmate in Florida with AIDS who recently had his sentence commuted. News releases from the clearinghouse are

also included, along with the addresses for a mailing list and an FTP site where AIDS-related documents are kept. They also point you to actual *humans* (reference specialists) who can help you get to the data.

Center for Food Safety and Applied Nutrition

http://vm.cfsan.fda.gov/list.html
Health and Medicine

The CFSAN, part of the Food and Drug Administration, offers a huge buffet of data on edibles. The consumer advice is particularly strong, with help on everything from mercury in fish to

handling eggs safely (store below 40 degrees, cook above 140 degrees, don't put all in one basket). A lot of the data is aimed at the food industry, but it's still interesting to sniff around. Why, you may

continued

Center for Food Safety and Applied Nutrition continued

wonder, does the FDA restrict levels of benzene hexachloride to 0.05 parts per million in most foods, but let 0.3 ppm slip by in frog legs and carrots? Are fat substitutes safe? How do they taste? You'll even find flashes of humor: the page on pathogenic bacteria and parasitic protozoa is called the Bad Bug Book. Highly useful guide for both professionals and the general public.

Cyber-Psych

http://www.charm.net/~pandora/psych.html

Health and Medicine

Monika, a graduate student at Loyola College, has created this collection of links to valuable mental health resources. Users can jump to big organizational Web sites (the National Alliance for the Mentally Ill), personal public-service pages (like the one on Chronic Fatigue Syndrome), online magazines (such as *Self-Help*), Usenet support groups (check out alt.support.shyness), and online tools (take the Meyers-Briggs personality test, if you dare). Around one corner is a psychological games page, which poses queries such as "If you were king for a day, what is the *least* pleasurable experience that you would choose to have?" (sounds like a trick question). This quirky listing isn't by any means comprehensive, but it does have interesting and useful links.

Depression

http://www.duke.edu/~ntd/depression.html

Health and Medicine

"Depression is an illness, not a weakness." So opens this uncommon page from the moderators of the alt.support.depression newsgroup. They've extracted the best items from their Frequently Asked Questions files, and distilled it into a "Depression Primer." The site answers questions about dysthymia (a bit more serious than having the blues), and why it is you always feel sad at Christmas (even when Santa *didn't* jerk you over). Are you persistently anxious or having difficulty concentrating? Are you persistently anxious or having difficulty concentrating? (Sorry.) Here you can hunt up newsgroups where you can discuss your concerns with others, or connect to "The Option Institute," a teaching center offering programs to help overcome depression.

The Diabetes Homepage

http://www.nd.edu/~hhowisen/diabetes.html
Health and Medicine

This is the single best spot for diabetes information on the Web. Not only does it have detailed information for the layperson (like a careful explanation of insulin, or what "juvenile onset" means), but it's presented in an entertaining (if jarring) graphical format. The offbeat tone takes a little getting used to (diabetics are initially referred to as "those whose Pancrei have opted for early retirement"), but the well-organized links to the world's major diabetes sites are worth hunting for. (Many of the links are gopher sites.) What's really strange (and interesting) about this site is the Virtual Diabetic game, where you try to get Derwood the Diabetic through one adventure-packed day without ending up in the hospital. (It's *hard!*) This comprehensive site even offers links to data on diabetes in cats.

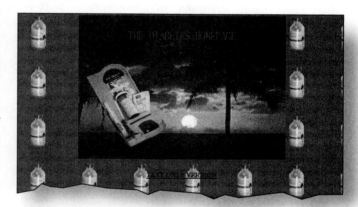

Diseases & Disorders

http://www.mic.ki.se/Diseases/index.html
Health and Medicine

If you think you've got it, chances are this server does too. This page, part of the Karolinska Institute's Biomedical Resources index, is a handy disease guide for doctors *and* patients. It's mostly a collection of links, but what links! The amazing array of Web sites around the world range from a USDA site that helps us "Outsmart E. Coli" (doesn't sound too hard), to a study from Iceland about the "Occupational Hazards of Piano Playing." Suffering from *blepharitis* (chronically infected eyelashes)? You're directed to the State University of N.Y., which instructs you to break out the Q-tips and Johnson's Baby Shampoo. Remember to *always* consult your doctor (or corner one at a cocktail party) before beginning any treatment program.

The Ebola Page

http://ichiban.objarts.com/ebola/ebola.html
Health and Medicine

Claiming to be "the most complete source of information about Ebola on the Net," this amazing site puts its mon(k)ey where its mouth is. Explore viral microbiology and read interviews with (rare) survivors. Or view the exhaustive links to other sites, phenomenal graphics (including detailed maps of Zaire, where Ebola has recently wreaked havoc), and hypotheses about the disease and its origins. All are presented efficiently and even enthusiastically. The revolting description of the effects of Ebola on your insides (reprinted from Richard Preston's book "The Hot Zone") is not for the faint of heart. Especially impressive: the chronology of events related to the ongoing crisis, each linked to a media or governmental source and updated daily. Incredibly strong use of the Net.

Emergency Medical Services

http://www.einet.net/galaxy/Community/Health/
Emergency-Medicine/fritz-nordengren/ems.html
Health and Medicine

Fritz Nordengren, a litigation consultant and volunteer paramedic, created this guide to Web resources on Emergency Medical Services. Trauma is the number-one killer of Americans under age 41, we learn, so you might want to look at the useful "What to do in a medical emergency" section *before* you buy that hang-glider. Visitors can also try, for example, the links to TraumaNet; the Virtual Hospital (a multimedia database); the Los Angeles Fire Department (who point out that it's *always* brush-clearing season); *Good Medicine Magazine*; the Civil Air Patrol; and even fan-pages for TV shows about emergency medicine. Yet, amid so much practical info, the "bizarre medical nature" link leads to some very amusing emergency room stories. All in all, an excellent collection for emergency specialists and the public at large.

Emergency Medicine and Primary Care

http://www.njnet.com/~embbs/
Health and Medicine

What started out as a BBS for doctors has turned into a great online repository for emergency medicine and primary-care medical resources. Many of the features here are photos—x-ray shots from the radiology library, pictures of cases (check out the gross bug bite on some guy's left calf), and other assorted medical phenomena. The x-rays collection has a load of views of normal human parts, too (which helps make sense of the damaged stuff). Or take a look at the Electrocardiogram of the Month (we're not kidding). It's a great place for doctors who like to "talk shop." Warning to non-medicos: prolonged exposure to these photos and stories from the emergency room may induce a severe case of the creeps.

Global Emergency Medicine Archives

http://solaris.ckm.ucsf.edu:8081/
Health and Medicine

The medical community's attempts at putting info on the Internet have varied in quality, but this Net-based medical journal is a superior effort. With contributions from several print journals and government agencies (like the Centers for Disease Control), GEMA has created a valuable Web resource. Visitors can take a look at a report on AIDS Mortality Among Women, or at papers examining how San Francisco's homeless use emergency medical services. On our last visit, we found video clips of a gall bladder (it doesn't do much, after all), an interesting article about cellular phone use during disasters (they might not work as well as you'd hope), and an editorial about the convergence of managed health care and the Internet. The archives of EMED-L, a mailing list for the profession, are also on tap here.

The Global Health Network

http://www.pitt.edu/HOME/GHNet/GHNet.html
Health and Medicine

The Global Health Network is an ambitious attempt to prevent disease by linking health care professionals around the planet. This Web site presents their slightly breathless vision: instantaneous access to massive amounts of medical data, advances ranging from telemedicine (consultations with remote doctors) to disease prediction in large populations (by monitoring and forecasting diseases much the same way we do with weather). Already this site has gathered worldwide health links and resources, from the World Health Organization to BIREME, a Latin American health center, to U.S. State Department Travel Advisories. The number and variety of resources and contacts here is very large. Not to be missed by those seeking the widest range of health information.

Go Ask Alice

http://www.cc.columbia.edu:80/cu/healthwise
Health and Medicine

We can't say enough good things about this general health and wellness site from the Columbia University Health Service. Colleges face a special public health challenge, serving people who are living on their own for the first time and who may suffer from medical ignorance (or bad judgment). Students (and Internauts) can turn to Go Ask Alice, where students can anonymously ask questions about anythingfromsnoring to sex to watchband irritation. Alice's answers are archived, and it's easy to get hooked on browsing these very honest questions and forthright responses, organized into general sections like "Fitness and Nutrition," or "Sexual Health and Relationships." (You're likely to find a few you might have written yourself.) Though aimed at Columbia students, this is a great spot for anyone with a health or nutrition question.

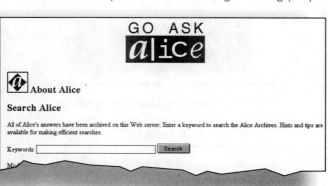

Grohol Mental Health Page

http://www1.mhv.net/~grohol/
Health and Medicine

John Grohol, a clinical psychologist, brings you Psych Central, an index to the latest Net news on mental health and psychology. Is that memory lapse of yours a sign of Dissociative Identity Disorder, or just a bad case of too much red wine (or too much of a bad case of red wine)? Either way, the good news is that your roommate's hyperactivity may be treatable (and you thought she was just... bubbly). When we last visited, the featured Article of the Month was "Flame Wars," which discussed why some otherwise pleasant people act like such jerks online (it's more than just anonymity). There's a load of consumer info here, too, including helpful distinctions between therapists' degrees (a PsyD turns out to be a clinically-oriented PhD). Plenty of links to Usenet newsgroups and other psych hot spots, too.

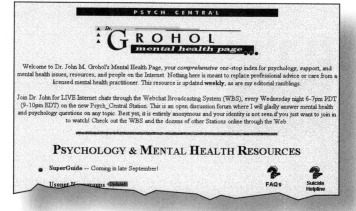

Harvard Medical School Health Publications Group

http://www.med.harvard.edu/publications/
Health_Publications/
Health and Medicine

America's oldest university offers up some health news that even non-Ivy Leaguers can understand. Harvard's med school produces four topical newsletters and other special reports each month, and this site puts the current issue of each online. A recent issue of "Harvard Heart Letter" addressed the components of a risk-reduction program (don't smoke, be active—the usual doctor's speech). It also lamented the fact that while Americans have reduced their fat intake, they're compensating by wolfing down more food. Another newsletter on women's health issues asks and answers the question "How much exercise is enough?" A recent school study showed that high levels of exercise are much better for you than occasional activity. It's not always earth-shaking stuff, but this is solid info from an impeccable source.

Interactive Medical Student Lounge

http://falcon.cc.ukans.edu:80/~nsween/
Health and Medicine

Ward-weary, lab-laboring, pre-M.D.s will be happy to find this virtual student lounge at the University of Kansas, where studying can be mixed with pleasure. Library links include the Vestibular Disorders Association, *Grape Vine*

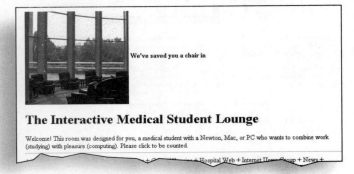

We've saved you a chair in

The Interactive Medical Student Lounge

Welcome! This room was designed for you, a medical student with a Newton, Mac, or PC who wants to combine work (studying) with pleasure (computing). Please click to be counted.

+ Hospital Web + Internet Users Group + News +

Interactive Business magazine, the Time, Inc. medical bulletin board, a cool "interactive patient" site (to practice history-taking and diagnosis), and much more. Agonize over residency selection (always a major med-student issue) or scrounge for summer research jobs with your peers around the world. And for developing that bedside manner, religion and philosophy pointers include "Sufism" and "Christian Apologetics." But enough work. The lounge's recreation area is admittedly still small, but includes fun Star Trek links and sports talk. And we can heartily recommend a downloadable version of the original video game classic "Pong." Delightful place to hang out.

The Interactive Patient

http://medicus.marshall.edu/medicus.htm
Health and Medicine

This teaching tool offers a virtual patient that medical students can examine and diagnose. First we asked, "Does it hurt on your left side?" The patient replied, "My left side feels alright. Although, sometimes the pain will radiate a little." We then asked, "Have you been vomiting?" He replied, "When I vomited this morning, I hardly made it to the

bathroom," and we were treated to a picture of the patient covering his mouth. (That's the limit of medical questions we've gleaned from watching *ER*, but others will no doubt have more to ask.) You may also listen to the heart and lungs, then submit a diagnosis. The program evaluates your opinion and e-mails the results to you.

International Food Information Council Foundation

http://ificinfo.health.org/
Health and Medicine

The nonprofit IFIC Foundation is on a mission to tell the world about healthy eating. It describes this Web site as *"the* source on food-related issues." The text here comes mainly from Foundation brochures, conveniently broken down by area of interest: consumers, reporters, and health professionals are all offered different topic lists. The newsletter, "Food Insight," is also included—one article describes how astronauts can forego the pastes and gelatin cubes of space flights in the past by selecting from a list of specially prepared "regular" foods. Note that this site seems generally slanted toward food manufacturers. The food additive sec-tion, for example, is pretty interesting, but implies that all food additives are completely safe. And the discussion of "Food Biotechnology" is an unrestrained paean to genetically-engineered crops.

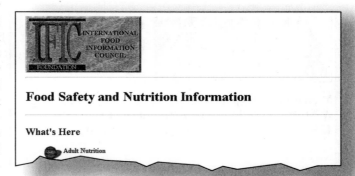

Midwifery, Pregnancy, and Birth-Related Information

http://www.efn.org/~djz/birth/birthindex.html
Health and Medicine

Donna Dolezal Zelzer maintains this online library of articles, reviews, and other information about pregnancy and midwifery. The site is a good introduction to one midwife's outlook on mainstream medicine; Zelzer has strong opinions—*very* strong—about how many doctors handle birthing. The article "Gracious Births" announces that "Birth is not a clinical exercise. It is not a medical procedure. In nearly every instance, it should not be major surgery." (The same article introduced us to the term "birth abuse.") We also found an "Appeal For Indiana Midwife," from the state where it's a felony for any non-M.D. to deliver a baby. Visitors to this page can also explore the "HomeBirth Choice," get information on becoming a midwife themselves, or find out "What midwives want from their clients."

National Library of Medicine: HyperDOC

http://www.nlm.nih.gov/

Health and Medicine

The National Institutes of Health maintains the National Medical Library, reportedly the biggest one-subject library in the world, and this is its home page. There's a wealth of fascinating medical

**Welcome to HyperDOC
A Multimedia/Hypertext Resource of the
U.S. National Library of Medicine (NLM)**

Donald A. B. Lindberg, M.D.
Director

● About This Service (Tips & Warnings, Usage Statistics, Internet Access Information)

information here, like Clinical Guidelines, which tell your doctor how to treat ailments ranging from back pain to urinary incontinence. But you have to dig through yards of bureaucratic bombast to get to it. (Example: instead of a "Go Back" control, you're offered "Parent document within HyperDOC Hierarchy.") This site offers Telnet links to a several large biomedical databases, like MEDLARS, TOXNet, AIDS-LINE, and Grateful Med, though for many you have to establish an account first. Much more interesting: the History of Medicine section, with its 60,000-image database. The online exhibitions on topics like "Cesarean Section: a Brief History" are interesting, and there's also the popular "Visible Human Project."

OncoLink: U. of Pennsylvania Cancer Resource

http://cancer.med.upenn.edu/

Health and Medicine

This online clearinghouse from the University of Pennsylvania Hospital provides excellent education and support resources for cancer patients, professionals, and families. It's a large but well-organized site, and many items are even marked by audience ("Patient Oriented" is the most common notation, although there are loads of articles for health care professionals, too). Meetings are announced, *Neoplasma* and other journals are offered,

there's a keyword search, and items are arranged by medical specialties. Personal essays include "Peter Polishuck: A Normal 28 Year Old's Struggle," "Cancer and Sexuality," and other moving stories. Given the deadly topic, visitors may be pleasantly surprised to find a fine balance between docspeak about items like astrocytoma, and ordinary layman's interests like a gallery of children's art. Updated frequently. A very solid site.

The Parkinson's Web

http://neuro-chief-e.mgh.harvard.edu/
parkinsonsweb/Main/PDmain.html

Health and Medicine

Parkinson's Disease (PD) is a growing national problem, with more than one million victims in the United States alone. This page from Massachusetts General Hospital offers information to people with Parkinson's Disease, their families, and caregivers. If you're just learning about the disease, the online primer provides a thorough, easy-to-understand introduction. Although the actual causes of Parkinson's remains a mystery, these neurologists do understand a lot about how the brain functions, and they patiently explain concepts like neurotransmitters and enzymes. An extensive glossary of medical terms is helpful, too. The directory of support organizations is comprehensive and truly global, and a link to the MGH Neuro-WebForum enables you to post questions to moderated discussion groups. The caregiver's handbook is especially invaluable.

Preview the Heart

http://sln.fi.edu/tfi/preview/heartpreview.html

Health and Medicine

The human heart beats two and a half million times in an average lifetime (more than that for you coffee drinkers). The Franklin Institute's "virtual heart" presentation is a good way to spend a few dozen of those beats. This is real scientific stuff, not a kiddie trip, though it is presented as a tour. Learn about blood types—a person with Type AB blood can receive a blood transfusion from any type donor, for instance—or compare x-rays of a normal-sized and enlarged heart. The whole interactive enchilada is here: movies, audio segments (they call the two heart sounds "lub" and "dub"), and pictures decorated with lavish descriptions and explanations. You can actually watch a movie of the exchange of oxygen and carbon dioxide between the capillaries and arteries. Your fascination here "will lead to understanding and respect."

The Recovery HomePage

http://www.shore.net/~tcfraser/commrec.htm
Health and Medicine

This highly-organized collection of information and links is for anyone who suffers from the maladies addressed by

12-step recovery programs. Tom F. starts off with selections from the AA Big Book, but quickly broadens his scope to include addictions like cocaine, sex, and overeating. You'll also get instructions for using other electronic recovery media, like Usenet, Internet Relay Chat, and BBSs. Commercial recovery organizations (like the "Serenity Shoppe") are also "supplied here as a service to those looking to spend some money." (We also enjoyed the "Dysfunctional Family Robinson" t-shirts.) In addition to the links, Tom F. also shows us some of his own recovery-related artwork (the pink lighthouse is pretty cool). Very strong coverage of a serious subject, without ever becoming preachy or pompous.

Specifica

http://www.realtime.net/~mmjw/
Health and Medicine

Maintained by Texas psychologist Jeanine Wade, this site offers hearty links and info on the medical scene. Try the link to the huge Pharmaceutical Information Associates page. (Is low-dose

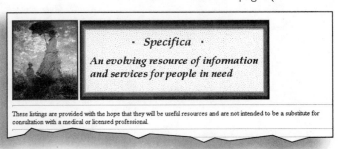

aspirin safe during pregnancy?) For cancer news, connect to "OncoLink" and learn how tobacco and blood pressure are related to kidney cancer. Or discover the eye-opener that a "bad" relationship may in fact be an addictive one. (You may want to cultivate your *own* needs, for starters.) Some of the sites merely *seem* strange, like "Noodles' Panic-Anxiety Page" (it's the unsettling color scheme), but others are actively odd, like the Obsessive-Compulsive Disorder link. Great links to AIDS and HIV resources around the world, too.

TransWeb: Organ Transplantation and Donation

http://www.med.umich.edu:80/trans/transweb

Health and Medicine

ere's another page that makes you wonder how we got by without the Internet. TransWeb offers organ transplant patients and families all kinds of answers and info about transplant issues. Transplant-related press releases range from announcements of new drugs to policy issues (like those raised by Mickey Mantle's liver). Extensive question and answer sections ("How can I find my position on the waiting list?"), plus a great collection of stories about (and by) transplant patients. The University of Michigan has compiled data on pending legislation; visitors will also find old standbys like Medic Alert bracelets.

Doctors should also find this a useful way to keep up with developments. A magnificent use of the Web.

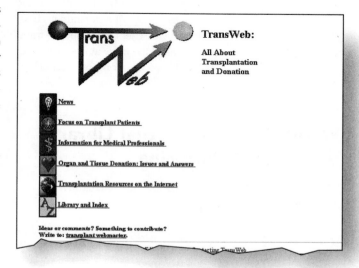

Jonathan Tward's Multimedia Medical Reference Library

http://www.tiac.net/users/jtward/index.html

Health and Medicine

edical student Jonathan Tward (and who knew med students had this kind of time?) manages this collection, which is divided into categories like "Medical Software for Download," "Research Journals," "Hospitals on the Web," and "Medical School Curriculum." The latter seems especially interesting (although some of the sites' URLs need updating). The best part is the

hierarchically-organized medical reference library, which is a large virtual collection of medical texts, images, and videos. You can jump from the Constipation Page, for example, to the fascinating Intern On-Call Handbook from the University of Oregon ("The residents are your friends. We want to help"). The squeamish might want to skip the "Visible Human Project," however. Fine medical school listings, too.

Visible Human Project

```
http://www.nlm.nih.gov/extramural_research.dir/
visible_human.html
```
Health and Medicine

The National Library of Medicine has set out to map the human body in three dimensions in excruciatingly fine detail. Using the body of a 39-year-old convicted murderer who donated his body to science, researchers are collecting transverse images of the body at one-millimeter intervals. There are computer-generated "fresh-cadaver" images made by CAT and MRI scanning machines, plus the ever-popular "frozen-cadaver" (cryosection) images, in revolting, fascinating color. (Cryosection means they deep-freeze the body and then, in essence, run it through an extremely expensive deli slicer.) You can only view samples of the resulting images here; the complete set is so voluminous that you have to register and pay a pile of money to get it. But it's worth the visit just to contemplate the whole idea.

World Wide Web Virtual Library: Biosciences—Medicine

```
http://golgi.harvard.edu/biopages/medicine.html
```
Health and Medicine

If it's a biology or medicine-related Net site, you can get there from here. We're talking *major* medical: schools from the U. of Aberdeen to Yale, the "Web of Addictions," "Rethinking AIDS," and so much more! The pros can really use this online almanac, but sore layfolk (you know who you are) will benefit from the repetitive strain injury primer and its many cousins here. Even old Bowser isn't left out: the Budapest U. of Veterinary Science is here, too. And those with fast computers won't want to miss General Electric's now-legendary multimedia "Colon Fly Through." Getting the picture? This virtual library gives one a sense of the Net's awesome potential, for better or worse, as a huge informational warehouse.

Humanities and Arts

Humanities and Arts

Maybe it's just because artists have a lot of time on their hands (or are always looking for an excuse to avoid the canvas), but the Web is soaked in artwork. The experimental nature of the Internet and the experimental nature of modern art seem to be a natural fit; you'll find museums, galleries, and personal collections galore here. The theater also seems to be a hotbed of experimental Web usage.

History, on the other hand, is underdeveloped. You can find 25 home pages devoted to Jerry Seinfeld, but you won't find 25 for, say, Joe Stalin. Or even for a world-beater like Alexander the Great, who has only a single page (though a mighty friendly one). It's easy to imagine the fabulous learning pages that will someday exist: the complete battle of Marathon, with maps, interactive games, links to Greece and Persia, ancient art, modern tours, the Olympics... what an event! Still, some fine sites exist already, and we present the pick of the litter here.

art

@art

http://gertrude.art.uiuc.edu/@art/gallery.html

Art

Students and contemporary art fans will be drawn to this innovative electronic gallery for multimedia artists, curated by faculty at the University of Illinois at Urbana-Champaign. The images are alluring, even if esoteric and sometimes unsettling: on our last visit, Peter Campus attempted to "show how we sentimentalize nature, and by doing that, erode it." His "Grayscale Fields" of insects had a surreal, almost transparent quality. Jeff Murphy's studies of the human body combined static and organic elements, resulting in "cyber-organic entities never before encountered." Woo! The curators here have done a fine job of bringing the best progressive artistry into the electronic arena. Major works are archived; other exhibitions change regularly.

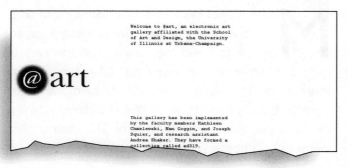

AACME Image Propaganda Server

http://www.tristero.com/~aacme

Art

The members of this arts collective in San Antonio say they "no longer think of themselves as "individual artists." Instead, the group has pooled its creative resources to generate esprit de corps projects like the "San Antonio Bus Project," where they placed questions on the backs of city buses for idling motorists to ponder ("Look around you, what do you feel is vital?") and included a phone number for viewers to call with answers. (Surfers can respond online.) Visual pieces have included "Cage Static," an homage to performance artist and composer John Cage,

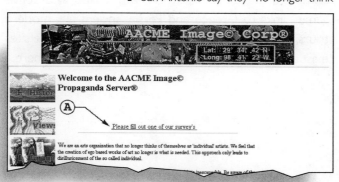

who was "not interested in creating art, but... cultivating the mind." Whatever you say. AACME viewer surveys want to know: "What is there in your life that you don't doubt?" Provide your answer online and become part of a living art project.

Art on the Net

http://www.art.net

Art

Painters, poets, musicians, and performance and video artists maintain and curate their own exhibitions in this free-wheeling, eclectic gallery. There are many halls to explore—this way for a visual poetry exhibition, that way for a New Guinea sculpture garden. On past visits, poet JJ Webb included selections from his recently published volume of poetry, and lamented in "2 A.M. News," "Its God-mother-magistrated/Fairy-legal-legislated /Time /To close all the bars." In the music gallery, check out The House Jacks, a "funky a cappella in your face" ensemble from San Francisco. With the video downloading here, time management is key: you could fold all your laundry by the time there's something to see at some of these spots. But just about every studio looks polished and professional.

Art on the Net

The Voice of Reason in a World of Chaos...

Welcome to Art on the Net! Join fellow artists in sharing works together on the Internet. Enjoy visiting artists studios and roaming the gallery.

● Artists Studios

Artz

http://www.magic.ca/magicmedia/artz.html

Art

This hip, splashy page sponsored by magicmedia (an online 'zine from Toronto) is a collection of galleries, reviews, and news about the arts in Canada. Swing through an electronic photo gallery for a few tubby views from the Florida beaches (by Canadian photographer Stephen Stober), or grab the latest dish on the independent Canadian film world from *The Nightingale Report*. (The *Report* recently whispered the rumor that a jazz documentary series to be produced on BRAVO by Canadian filmmaker Scott Dobson received a pitiful $8,000 per episode budget.) Lee's Cyber Palace has info on alternative music dates at Toronto's Dance Cave, not to mention an impressive (and thoroughly eclectic) array of record company links. Other ports include Artists in Residence, news briefs, concert reviews... in fact, *artz* features so many groovy stops, we just can't mention them all.

Chain Reaction

http://www.nmt.edu:80/~bridge/

Art

A subset of Project New Mexico, this page recounts a 4,000-mile bicycle journey through the state. But it's much

more than a travelogue: the trip is part of an interactive art project designed to "bridge the hi-tech and low-tech worlds" and to "stimulate creativity among its followers." George and Holly, who host the project and this page, send regular updates from the road, describing what and who they see along the way as they organize public art projects using trash and recyclable materials. It's a wonderful mixture of the mundane ("Need to find a bike shop... for new pedals") and the poetic ("[we have] a better understanding of people taking care of people"). A very creative use of the Web that offers a new take on the classic American road trip.

DaliWeb

http://www.highwayone.com/dali/daliweb.html

Art

DaliWeb is the official online counterpart to the Salvador Dali Museum in St. Petersburg, Florida. (The city begged for the facility, coughed up the cash, and voilà! Here it is!) The site is divided into a large main collection and a separate gallery of the Spanish surrealist's early work. Though you won't find *The Persistence of Memory* here (the famous melting watches are

housed in New York's Museum of Modern Art), you'll find the companion piece, *The Disintegration of the Persistence of Memory.* More than 94 oils, 100 watercolors, and 1300 graphics, sculptures, and objets d'art are deftly reproduced here. A special treat for the home Webmaster: groovy downloadable "wallpaper"—and yes, a variation of the melting watches is included.

Infinity City

http://www.tmn.com/Community/arose/infcty.html

Art

Artists Ann Rosenthal and Stephen Moore created this site to commemorate the 50th anniversary of the detonation on July 16, 1945 of "The Gadget," the first atomic bomb at Trinity Site, New Mexico. "At that moment," write the artists, "the future of humanity was irrevocably altered." Here, they focus on projects that examine the collective social effects of living in "the shadow of the bomb." The multimedia exhibit features photos, visual art, and text, and is presented as a travelogue and diary of the artists' journey to places figuring prominently in the development of nuclear weapons. At Trinity Site, "a sign warns to remove any cosmetics before entering" (an oddly unsettling image). This is a fascinating document, beautifully executed.

The Krannert Art Museum

http://www.art.uiuc.edu/kam/

Art

The real-time collection at the Krannert—part of the University of Illinois at Urbana-Champaign—spans over four million years, and curators have supplied a generous selection for this virtual presentation. From antiquities like *Yupa*, an Egyptian stone carving circa 1304 B.C. (long before most of us were born), to Yves Tanguy's 1948 surrealist painting *Suffering Softens Stones*, the Krannert is as good a place as any to start a comprehensive art history lesson. The "Krannert Art Museum Explorer" features hypermedia projects reserved exclusively for Web visitors, like the one for Dutch Master Frans Hals, famed for his casual approach to formal portraiture. (Blue jeans allowed.) The Krannert also posts notices of upcoming real-time exhibitions here, as well as ongoing events and series, like the Visual Learning Initiative. A stellar art site.

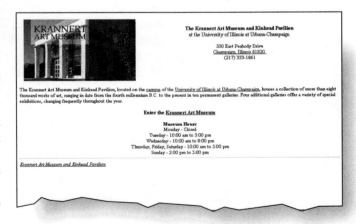

Lin Hsin Hsin Art Museum

http://www.ncb.gov.sg/lhh/lhh.html
Art

Peruse the works of celebrated Singaporean artist, poet, and computer consultant Lin Hsin Hsin at this charming virtual museum. Hsin Hsin exhibits more than 800 pieces of her abstract art here, like *Life in the Fast Lane*, an oil and text piece addressing the paradox of low-tech art in a high-tech medium. The site is full of nifty interactive surprises: start by hopping on the tour bus bound for "cyberspace, Singapore," then relax and enjoy the scenery as the Museum Guide shows you the world's first acid-free papaya paper. The not-so-virtual telephone booth lets you fax or leave a phonemail message for the artist, though more conventional surfers can send feedback via e-mail. And if you think you've seen everything a Web museum has to offer, you haven't visited Hsin Hsin's cyber toilet.

Michael C. Carlos Museum

http://www.cc.emory.edu/CARLOS/carlos.html
Art

This Emory University museum is one of the most lively and multifaceted art sites on the Web. It boasts a permanent collection of more than 15,000 objects, from Valdivian fertility gods to 20th Century Sub-Saharan sculpture. We toured the galleries to ogle a wrapped mummy from ancient Egypt, and found the fine craftsmanship of a Nigerian Helmet Mask beautifully rendered online. Choose from several temporary exhibition galleries, where you might find ancient art from the British Museum or a display of contemporary American prints and drawings. A behind-the-scenes peek at curatorial and conservation activities will especially gratify art historians.

Musée du Louvre

http://www.paris.org:80/Musees/Louvre
Art

Less than two dozen items from the Louvre's 300,000-piece collection of classic artworks can be seen here. But what a group they make: *Winged Victory*, the *Venus de Milo*, a wall from the tomb of King Seti I... these are the 800-pound gorillas of the art world. The Louvre page offers photo displays of individual pieces that you might not get to scrutinize so closely on a full-blown tour of the museum. But plan plenty of time: it takes about four minutes to download the *Mona Lisa* with a 14.4 modem. Of course, it's not the same thrill as a trip to the actual Louvre in Paris. But this way you save 40 francs admission, and you don't get a lot of French guards scowling at you if you lean too close to the screen. What better way to contemplate that famous Mona Lisa smile?

The Museum of Bad Art

http://sashimi.wwa.com/mirror/orgs/moba/moba.htm

Art

Here's a fine collection of work by "talented artists that have gone awry," and "works of exuberant, although crude, execution by artists barely in control of the brush." MOBA's exhibit features such unwieldy entries as "The Athlete," acquired by online curators from a Boston trash bin and described as "a startling work." Or feast your eyes on "The Circus of Despair," another garbage retrieval with an odd Fauve-like appeal. But it would be silly to wax *too* poetical here. The curators promise continued exponential growth, and invite viewers to join the burgeoning legions of "Friends of MOBA," a group of tireless patrons who endeavor to bring "the worst of art to the widest of audiences." This is a welcome respite from the world of artspeak.

Paintings of Vermeer

http://www.ccsf.caltech.edu/~roy/vermeer/

Art

In an unlikely marriage of fascinations, CalTech computer engineer Roy Williams has taken time off from parallel computing to create this homage to Dutch master painter Jan Vermeer. The artist's uncanny understanding and manipulation of light raised his renderings of ordinary people to near-holy heights, none of which is lost on the viewer in this electronic gallery. A perfect example: Vermeer's well-known *Woman With a Water Jug*, an innocuous scene that is made memorable by the master's magic stroke. A splendid clickable map locates other Vermeer classics from Amsterdam to Washington. Excellent selections and reproduction.

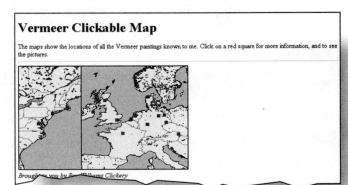

Vermeer Clickable Map

The maps show the locations of all the Vermeer paintings known to me. Click on a red square for more information, and to see the pictures.

Brought to you by Roy Williams Clickery

The Surrealism Server

http://pharmdec.wustl.edu/juju/surr/surrealism.html

Art

This page explores the art (or anti-art) movements of surrealism and its precursor, Dada. Like Dada, this doesn't take itself too seriously: it includes super background and reading lists on Dali (a former Dadaist turned surrealist), Duchamp (a Dadaist who spurned surrealists), Magritte (your basic surrealist), and that whole crowd. Visitors will find Tristan Tzara's classic instructions on how to write a Dadaist poem ("Take a newspaper. Take a pair of scissors...") and new and interactive versions of surrealist standbys, like a digital "exquisite corpse" that lets you produce a randomly generated work of art. The Surrealist Compliment Generator may compare you to "a staircase falling exotically into a sea of spilled macaroni." This is mainly for hard-core fans and the curious.

WebMuseum

http://sunsite.unc.edu/louvre/

Art

The concept is both elegant and populist: take the classics of world art and put them on the Web for all to see. Parisian computer consultant Nicholas

THE WEBMUSEUM NETWORK IS GROWING ! NEW

11 Sep 1995. WebMuseum mirror in Athens, Greece by Hellas On Line (Pipex), thanks to Antonis Giannopoulos!

10 Sep 1995. WebMuseum mirror in Battle Ground, Washington state by Little Red Caboose (thanks to Katie & Mike Randolph)

Mark Harden Presents:
PAUL CEZANNE
The biggest collection of Cézanne paintings ever collected is exclusively on the WebMuseum!

Bienvenue au WebMuseum!

Welcome to our guests from all over the world! The ever-expanding **WebMuseum network** is now welcoming 100,000 visit... document! (PS. remember to *click* on the inlined thumbnail images to enlarge

Pioch originally called this non-commercial site "The Louvre," but after a legal wrangle with the famous museum, he changed the name to "WebMuseum." Now this popular Web site is roaring back with a strong Impressionist collection from painters like Degas, Monet, and Renoir. (Sorry, no Red Skeltons yet.) The museum adds new exhibitions daily: on our last visit, we enjoyed the works of post-Impressionist painter Cezanne, a Cubist exhibit, and selections from Les Tres Riches Heures du Duc de Berry, a classic medieval book of prayers representing the height of 15th century manuscript illumination. The WebMuseum is the next best thing to being there, and no one will kick you out at "closing time."

Whitney Museum of American Art

`http://mosaic.echonyc.com/~whitney/WMAA/INT4.html`

Art

One of the most famous (and contro-versial) venues for modern and contemporary American art, the Whitney shows its usual imagination and aplomb with this Web site. Even the opening page is characteristically "Whitney": the background intermittently changes to reveal works by Hopper, Gottleib, Twombly, and even you—if you send your original (digital) work for display. Online exhibitions have included a recap of the latest biennial exhibition (but alas!, so few images), a superb selection of paintings by Edward Hopper, and the campy, stylized work of Florine Stettheimer. Excellent essays, too. For lively dialogue on contemporary art and literature, telnet to ECHO, a New York City electronic bulletin board and site of a Whitney-sponsored conference on American art. The Whitney is not for all tastes, but the quality of the work comes through clearly here.

World Wide Arts Resources

`http://www.concourse.com/wwar/default.html`

Art

Links to more than 250 museums worldwide (cataloged by country), 560 galleries and exhibitions, 50 publications, and 40 arts-related institutions are, believe it or not, only the tip of the iceberg here. There are also antiques, an "Arts Site of the Day," and much more. Visitors can locate a dealer who can say whether that armchair in grandma's attic is really a Chippendale, or they can mine the index of major artists for links to Ernst, Esher, Picasso, Pollack, Arbus, Bosch... and thousands more. Museums vary in focus and diversity, from the National Wool Museum in Australia to Pittsburgh's newly opened Andy Warhol Museum. A tip of the palette is due to site compiler Markus Kruse. We've yet to find a more comprehensive arts index on the Net.

history

Alexander the Great

http://www.rmplc.co.uk/eduweb/sites/hampscit/alex.html
History

Elvis gets dozens of home pages, so why not Alexander the Great? Who can forget the story of young Alexander taming the wild horse, Bucephalas, by turning its head into the sun? (When did Elvis ever do that?) Who can ignore the stirring story of Alexander driving a symbolic spear into Asian soil on his first arrival there? (Elvis was even in the army, but when did he ever conquer Asia?) All kidding aside, this is a fast, enjoyable rundown on Alexander the Great, one of the few people in history who set out to conquer the world and actually made a go of it. A hearty pat on the back to the delightfully named Thomas Wallop William-Powlett (hint: he's English) for this page.

American and British History Resources

http://info.rutgers.edu/rulib/artshum/amhist.html
History

If it's mentioned in the history books, it's probably here—unabridged. From Jonathan Swift's *A Modest Proposal* to the first inaugural address of Franklin Roosevelt, this heavy-on-the-text site hits all the high points of American and British history. Most of these documents are offered here in their entirety for those who want to work with original sources (a polite way of saying "plain dry text"). The range is extraordinary, from the autobiography of St. Patrick to Karl Marx to Vietnam-era material and contemporary international law documents (NAFTA, for example). Maintained by Rutgers University Libraries, it isn't ALL documents, offering many resources for subject guides and electronic text archives, and a hefty collection of other history home pages, too.

American Memory: Historical Collections for the National Digital Library

http://rs6.loc.gov/amhome.html

History

This is a virtual treasure trove of Americana and historical images from a Library of Congress special collection, containing hundreds of photograph, text, sound, and even motion picture files of American culture from way back when. Civil War photographs and hundreds of early motion pictures from 1897 to 1916 offer a visual slice of life, and outshine the archive of documents, which includes nuggets from the Folklore Project (check out the marvelous "Life Histories"). Many of the "short" films, however, won't seem so short while downloading, even with a high-speed connection. Still, this is a great source, and how many places can visitors travel back to the 1906 San Francisco earthquake or watch the 1901 opening of New York's Pan American Expo in an early film from Thomas Edison?

The Ancient City of Athens

http://www.indiana.edu/~kglowack/Athens/
Athens.html

History

This is almost like making the journey to Athens yourself, though without the earthquakes. This tour through the city is an archive of photos of some of ancient Greece's archaeological and architectural wonders, containing scores of color photographs, each with details from sites like the north or east slope of the Acropolis, the Lysikrates Monument, a side of the Church of the Holy Apostles in the Agora, and (our favorite) the Pynx. It would be nice to see some basic informa-

continued

The Ancient City of Athens *continued*

tion for novices about these places, but as the site is primarily designed for students (it comes from Indiana University), the

photos are almost strictly for study. Still, the beautiful sunny photos had us thinking "let's go there!", and since personal views of some of the world's most famous structures aren't cheap, this site provides a nice service.

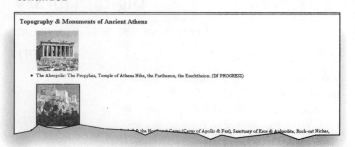

ArchNet

http://www.lib.uconn.edu/ArchNet/

History

There are any number of jokes to be made here about skeletons and Neanderthals, but why stoop so low?

(Oops.) ArchNet is a terrific index to archaeology and anthropology sites on the Web, from Italian museums to rain forest researchers in Central America. Lovely graphics and well-organized categories make this a great help to professionals, students, or anyone who wants to bone up (oops!) on the subject. And it's a broad subject indeed, covering specialties like Ethnohistory, Lithics, and Mapping. Its best-kept secret is an excellent listing of museum sites on the Net, offering fine starting points for amateurs. A firm pat on the back to the U. of Connecticut anthropology department for this top-notch site.

Blooper History of Western Civilization

http://ukanaix.cc.ukans.edu/~medieval/
mar1-14_95/0067.html

History

This hilarious history of western civilization is made up of several student blunders pasted together to form a narrative of sorts. Webmaster Dan Wages claims the material is over 20 years old, but we'd guess students haven't changed *that* much. Socrates, we learn here, died from an "overdose of wedlock." Too bad CNN wasn't around back when "Sir Francis Drake circumcised the world with a 100-foot clipper." In Europe, "victims of the black death grew boobs on their necks," poor souls. Martin Luther didn't have it so good, either, dying "a horrible death being excommunicated by a bull." Things were rougher than we thought! We knew Ben Franklin was an odd duck, but here it says here he "invented electricity by rubbing cats backwards." Sad commentary on education? Yeah, maybe. Funny? Yes!

The Civil War Letters of Capt. Richard W. Burt

http://www.infinet.com/~lstevens/burt/index.html

History

Poems and war songs make up nearly half this fine collection of letters from Burt, a newspaperman from Peoria who fought in the 76th Ohio Volunteer Infantry. A detailed account of the movements of the 76th is good background for Burt's letters, which display his journalistic skills and a knack for wry understatement. His casual remarks reveal the intimacy of a civil war, yet mask the obvious horrors of the battlefield: "When Gen. Sherman learned that the rebels killed all the foragers whom they captured, he informed the rebel Generals that he would have as many rebel prisoners in our hands shot as they killed foragers, and that had the desired effect." We particularly enjoyed the lighter verse, however, including "Jeff Davis in Petticoats" and "Phil on Picket in Dixie," about a pig "that dared to cross the picket line/And never (gave) a countersign."

Captain Richard W. Burt
Civil War Letters From The 76th Ohio Volunteer Infantry

Introduction
Fort Donelson

Civil War Photographs

http://rs6.loc.gov/cwphome.html
History

Over 1000 photographs from one of the bloodiest "modern" wars on record are reproduced here, courtesy of the friendly Webrarians at the Library of Congress. Most of the shots were taken by the private "corps" of photographers under the supervision of Matthew Brady, whose remarkable images of Confederate and Union soldiers set the standard for wartime photography. Some of these were exhibited by Brady in 1862 at a New York gallery; "The Dead of Antietam" was the first time many civilians had actually seen the carnage of war. Although some photos appear oddly cropped (because originally they were for a stereographic format), the image resolution here is first-rate, as is a handy timeline tracing events from 1861 (the Battle of Bull Run) to Lincoln's assassination in 1865.

The Cuban Missile Crisis

http://www.paranoia.com/~az/cuba/
History

"The British Response to the Cuban Missile Crisis" is the subtitle of this site about the 1962 brouhaha that nearly brought the U.S. and the U.S.S.R. to nuclear war. Centering on two figures, Prime Minister Harold Macmillan and Ambassador to Washington Sir David Ormsby-Gore, this page offers a keen analysis of the behind-the-scenes activity of Britain prior to and during the crisis. The crisis is characterized as the last time close, effective diplomatic contact existed between Britain and the U.S. on such a scale (until the Reagan-Thatcher "revival"), and much is said about the personal relationship of Ormsby-Gore and Kennedy. Primary and secondary sources are excellent, including Cabinet memos and minutes—this is a fine, brief introduction to a rarely mentioned aspect of this infamous incident.

The Dead Sea Scrolls

http://sunsite.unc.edu/expo/deadsea.scrolls.
exhibit/intro.html

History

These are the few scraps of disintegrating paper that caused so much controversy among biblical scholars and historians ("I found them first!" "No, I did!"). Actually, a bunch of Bedouin shepherds found them in 1947, stashed away in a cave. Now the Library of Congress traces the scrolls' history and Biblical interpretation on this deep, *deep* Web site. These are the online versions of the original Library exhibit, focusing on the question of authenticity, the "secrets" they reveal, the historical context of their creation, and of course, the tale of their discovery some 2,000 years later. The pictures are unsatisfyingly vague, with only a dozen or so fragments represented, but you'll find no shortage of study guides and other info here about one of the great archaeological finds of the century.

Diotima: Materials for the Study of Women and Gender in the Ancient World

http://www.uky.edu/ArtsSciences/Classics/
gender.html

History

This historical resource focuses on women in antiquity, and provides a wealth of university materials for study. The site is named "Diotima," for the woman who supposedly taught Socrates about love. Featured are college courses from around the U.S., including biographical essays on Hypatia and women of the ancient world, and discussions of gender issues in antiquity, from politics to architecture. Reviews of historical texts and links to ancient history materials make this an admirable example of the usefulness of the Web. From Palestinian Bronze Age figurines to Roman portraits, plenty of images can be found also, and as these come from other sites, much of this information pertains to antiquity in general.

Welcome | Announcements
Courses | Anthology | Essays
Reviews | Bibliography | Images

Miami **CLASSICS** Kentucky

1492: An Ongoing Voyage

http://sunsite.unc.edu/expo/1492.exhibit/Intro.html
History

A well-organized presentation makes this online exhibit from the Library of Congress a breeze for beginners to learn about pre- and post-contact America and the Mediterranean world. A concise outline helps you navigate the exhibit. You'll find mostly social and cultural history here, with several visual treats, but traditionalists should be warned that this is not the "classic" Columbus story. This exhibit reflects a contemporary approach to the European conquest of the Americas: attempts are made to examine the native continental culture prior to and after the visits by Columbus, who, for example, in "Man and Myth," is characterized as being motivated by self-interest and greed, with no mention made of his Christian mission. A very conspicuous omission. Still, a very solid page.

From Revolution to Reconstruction

http://grid.let.rug.nl/~welling/usa/revolution.html
History

This excellent resource for students and devotees of early American history is a conglomeration of data collected by college students and history buffs around the world, focusing on the period from the War for Independence to World War I. The entries are extensive and highly readable, and include such memorable moments as the East India tea scandal (otherwise known as The Boston Tea Party), and full text of the ironically named Maryland Toleration Act, a 1649 sanction for public whippings of anyone suspected of being a heretic or schismatic (those guys were so *uptight!*). Wide-ranging and extremely dense; many of the essays and biographies are written by contributors who aren't exactly Pulitzer material, and the "version" you get is generally non-controversial and pedestrian. For a casual read, this is great.

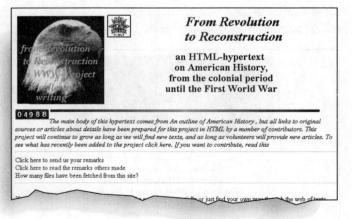

The City of Hiroshima

http://www.city.hiroshima.jp/
History

This site aims to provide information about Hiroshima, "A city that sings the praises of humanity and serves as an inspiration to the world." Let's hope so. The site covers not merely its obvious tragic history, but also city minutia from the amount of raw sewage collected (212,431 kiloliters) to the number of fishery establishments (485, for the record). Naturally, plenty of space is devoted here to anti-nuclear activism and the history of Hiroshima's devastation (186,940 were killed). Stunning color and black-and-white photographs share Web space with two Hiroshima 6th graders' statements that "compassion and kindness toward our friends is of the utmost importance in achieving peace." A "New Century City Vision for Hiroshima" outlines this gallant effort at rebuilding a vital city.

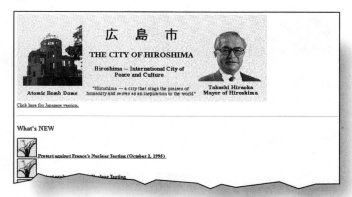

Nixon Audio Archives

http://www.webcorp.com/sounds/nixon.htm
History

Ironic, isn't it? Richard Nixon preserved on tape (or at least on the Net) for future generations. Tricky Dick's Greatest Hits are all here, from the days before he went commercial (the "Checkers" speech) to his later work (the "Resignation" speech). Sadly, there's no evidence of his studio sessions ("Watergate"). Be forewarned: some of these files are downright huge (just as in real life, he takes *forever* to resign), but they are all worth it. This isn't an educational site, mind you; it's more like a satirical swipe at a Commander in Chief who insisted "I am not a crook!" and "You won't have Nixon to kick around anymore!" Includes very brief commentary from the Webmasters at Webcorp, the Net service provider who backs this page.

Romarch

http://www.umich.edu/~pfoss/ROMARCH.html

History

This mostly-text server from Dr. Pedar Foss at the University of Michigan is a terrific (and huge) art and archaeological resource for Italy and Rome, with a focus

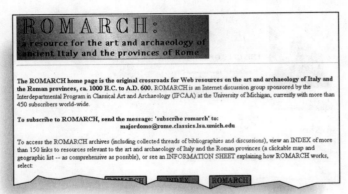

on work from 1000 B.C. to A.D. 600. The Romarch archives house postings from its newsgroup, covering items from the 13th International Bronze Congress to the question, "Are languages necessary?" A clickable map of Imperium Romanum leads browsers to endless resources on ancient Armenia, Hispania, Gallia, Syria, and Asia Minor (just to name a few). Links to contemporary Italian servers include AssoNet, and a variety of sites covering ongoing excavations, including those at Poggio Colla in Tuscany. Super museum pointers for archaeology buffs, and course resources and outlines from universities around the world.

The Titanic Page

http://metro.turnpike.net/T/titanic/titanic.htm

History

This amateur historian's site amasses trivia on the most famous sunken ship of the modern era, covering everything from the Titanic's weight to its list of passengers traveling in First Class (an unfortunate term). A brief history of the ship includes the dimensions and a list of provisions for a transatlantic journey, which included 15,000 bottles of ale and 75,000 pounds of fresh meat (plus the passengers,

of course). Brief biographies of selected survivors include John Jacob Astor's wife, Madeline, and the original "Unsinkable" Molly Brown. A list of "bad omens" records the weird feelings some passengers and crew members had before sailing. Spooky? Yes, and only slightly overeager in its avid coverage of one of history's most compelling disasters.

Tito

http://www.fer.uni-lj.si/tito/tito-eng.html

History

Josip Broz Tito ruled Yugoslavia as President from 1953-80, an independent dictator who did for the eastern bloc what Heather Locklear did for "Melrose Place." Tito is dead, but the cult of personality lives on. Audio samples enable him to speak from beyond the grave, and the host of photos would make a supermodel blush. This is a real rogues' gallery, too, with pictures of Tito and Idi Amin, Yasser Arafat, Nicolau Ceausescu, Kurt Waldheim, Richard Nixon, and Henry Kissinger. More relaxing moments show Tito with his pooch, or working with a router (no foolin'!). Finally, visit his casket with Margaret Thatcher or Saddam Hussein! An inspired fan page for a dead dictator of a country that no longer exists.

Today in History

http://www.whetzel.com/today.html

History

A quick visit here is all it takes to find out what significant event happened in history today (a rather complex concept in itself). Most of the entries are from United States history, although international incidents and catastrophes also make the grade. You can work through the archive to find out when Lynette "Squeaky" Fromme took a shot at President Ford, or refresh your memory with tidbits like the downing of KAL Flight 007 (two years to the day *before* the discovery of the *Titanic*). And if you're looking for a practical use beyond memory-refreshing, today's birthdays are included for both present-day celebrities and historical figures. The next time we send a card to Buddy Hackett, we'll know, "oh yeah, Itzhak Perlman, too!"

The U-Boat War, 1939-1945

http://rvik.ismennt.is/~gummihe/Uboats/u-boats.htm
History

This nicely presented info on hundreds of U-Boats whets the appetite, but doesn't quite fill you up. The site is for sub and U-Boat enthusiasts, and focuses on what happened to the German subs at the end of World War II. Some sections are simply lengthy lists, such as those that describe "Operation Deadlight," the code name for the scuttling of unwanted U-Boats. Other departments offer more for those of us who don't know our Type XBs (minelayers) from the Type XIV "Milch Kuh" ("Milk Cows," big supply boats). The best items here are the historical tidbits, such as the story of the highly decorated U-Boat commander who survived the war, only to be shot by a German sentry on May 14, 1945 for giving an incorrect password. Bis zum *bummer*!

Vatican Library

http://sunsite.unc.edu/expo/vatican.exhibit/Vatican.exhibit.html
History

This handsome site recreates a 1993 Library of Congress exhibition titled "Rome Reborn: the Vatican Library and Renaissance Culture." It's just as brainy as it sounds: you'll meet the amazing old objects in the Vatican library (and we don't mean the Cardinals), with commentary by distinguished, tweedy scholars. Tracing the history of the revitalization of Rome in the fifteenth and sixteenth centuries, the site offers plenty of online museum entries, visual and textual. Photographs of ancient documents are accompanied by brief histories and notations, from Homer's *Iliad* to Henry VIII's love letters to Anne Boleyn (alas, we couldn't find the part where he says "I promise I won't cut your head off, dear"). Not for holiday historians, but a gold mine for serious-minded scholars from college age on up.

The Vincent Voice Library

http://web.msu.edu/vincent/index.html
History

G. Robert Vincent began recording voices for a sound archive in 1912. Now the collection is maintained by Michigan State University, and is open to the public. Voice samples of U.S. presidents from Cleveland to Clinton are the highlight here; most samples are brief, and the focus is not on content, though you can hear JFK's inaugural and Nixon's farewell speeches, the longest bits. Perhaps unintentionally comic is Clinton's entry, a mere eighteen seconds on "the purpose of government." A small collection of the voices of "interesting people from the last 100 years" is an odd assortment indeed: George Washington Carver, Betty Ford, Babe Ruth, and Anwar Sadat, to name a few. The site is primarily a promotion for the actual library, where thousands of sound files preserve American audio history.

MICHIGAN STATE UNIVERSITY

The Vincent Voice Library at Michigan State University

The G. Robert Vincent Voice Library is the largest academic voice library in the nation. It is located on the fourth floor of the West wing of the Library. It houses taped utterances (speeches, performances, lectures, interviews, broadcasts, etc.) by over 50,000 persons from all walks of life recorded over 100 years. Since 1974, the Vincent Voice Library has been headed by Dr. Maurice Crane.

Samples from the Vincent Voice Library

Sound Samples from US Presidents - from Cleveland to Clinton

religion and philosophy

The Big Dummy's Guide to Religion, Philosophy, and Ethics

http://www.industrial.com/~simon/bdintro.html
Religion and Philosophy

Here's a discussion of religion, philosophy, and ethics, geared toward computer people. The title is a spoof on the popular *Dummies* series of computer books, but it works the other way around: this is for computer "technoids" who haven't had time to study anything else. Besides providing an essay on The Essential Vocabulary of Deep Thoughts (what we mean by the terms religion, philosophy—

continued

The Big Dummy's Guide to Religion, Philosophy, and Ethics
continued

religion's "evil twin"—and ethics), Webmaster Orrin R. Onken lists the Seven Deadly Arguments, which are seven arguments to avoid at all costs, lest ye become mired in eternal pointless "discussions" (an academic euphemism for "fights"). The page avoids taking sides, with a few notable exceptions—"The fact is that Creationists are crackpots," for example. Even for dummies, this is an enlightening read from a witty writer.

Bjorn's Guide to Philosophy

http://www-und.ida.liu.se/~y92bjoch/
Religion and Philosophy

" The object of these pages is to establish a platform from which one should be able to explore most aspects of philosophy available on and also off

the Web," writes enthusiast Bjorn Christensson. This elegant and detailed resource will please newcomers and veterans alike! It features slick hypertext profiles of the heavy hitters, from Aristotle to Wittgenstein; with good bits like "In 1889, (Friedrich) Nietzsche collapsed on a street in Turin, unable to bear the sight of a horse being flogged, and for the remaining years of his life was clinically insane" (some would argue he had screws loose before that). Also included are would-be classic electronic texts such as Joe Schiller's "Millennium: Feminism vs. Masculinism," the *Journal of Buddhist Ethics*, and much more. This is great stuff, a "fan page" for mostly western philosophy.

Global Hindu Electronic Network (GHEN)

http://rbhatnagar.csm.uc.edu:8080/hindu_universe.html
Religion and Philosophy

This excellent project of the non-profit Hindu Students Council has a wealth of entries on scripture and practice. For those just starting to navigate the dharma circuit, GHEN offers access to books and treatises from around the world, including the entire text of the *Bhagavad Gita* online. As you get deeper, you'll find that some categories, like that for Jainism, are merely links to other pages (though the other pages tend to be very good). Other sections, like the Swami Vivekananda Study Center, offer more primary source material. Terrific Buddhist and Sikh Dharma pages are also linked here. It's clear that many hours of work (and thousands of years, after all) have gone into these pages.

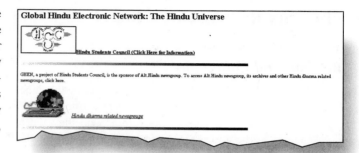

The APS Research Guide

http://www.utoronto.ca/stmikes/theobook.htm

Religion and Philosophy

This is a tremendous search tool for any student of theology, or for that matter, the spiritually curious. The page is sponsored by theology faculty at the University of St. Michael's College in Toronto, Canada, with links divided topically and by religion. Webmasters provide pithy commentary on each entry. Connections to the Sikh Home Page and the Christian Coptic Orthodox Church of Egypt are accompanied by more traditional links, including Vanderbilt University's renowned Divinity Library and the official home page of the U.S. Presbyterian Church. A link to sacred texts from world religions is alone worth the visit: virtual Bibles, the Hyper Quran, and the Tao Teh Ching are just part of a massive list that will have scholars swooning.

Christian Resources

http://www.webcom.com/~nlnnet/xianres.html

Religion and Philosophy

This surprisingly eclectic page offers superb links to Christian Web sites around the world. Dig into your favorite *cantus firmus* at the Gregorian Chant Home Page (sorry, no droning monks yet), or stop by the Amy Grant fan club for something completely different. "Devotional Help" links the pious to e-mail lists for daily guidance and to great practical pages like "Keys for Kids," a changing collection of stories on "life lessons" illustrated by Bible verse. For a bizarre finale, don't miss *Snake Oil: Your Guide to Kooky Kontemporary Kristian Kulture*, an e-zine devoted to exposing the vagaries of certain less-than-savory televangelists. Sponsored by Agape Europe Online, an interdenominational Christian mission organization.

Christus Rex: Sistine Chapel

http://www.christusrex.org/
Religion and Philosophy

It's the next best thing to being the Pope! 325 color images of the Sistine Chapel, more than 800 from around the Vatican, and 400+ from cathedrals around the world highlight this collection from Christus Rex, a non-profit group dedicated to spreading the good word through cathedral art. The pics are gorgeous (even if resolution is sometimes fuzzy), and fans of the Italian Renaissance will find many familiar names here: Giotto, Perugino, da Vinci, Raphael, and of course, Michelangelo. Catholics and disciples of papal politics will enjoy recent Papal Encyclicals that accompany the exhibition, not to mention a generous helping of Pontiff-ications, including the full text of John Paul II's pivotal June 1995 "Letter to Women." Due to the sheer volume of images, download times can be lengthy at times, but expect divine inspiration while you wait.

Engaged Buddhist Dharma Page

http://www.maui.com/~lesslie/
Religion and Philosophy

This enlightening page is for those who would "engage" in (or at least monitor) worldwide human rights struggles via online resources. "Mexico Out of Balance" offers background on the debt crisis, with links pertinent to the resultant "Chiapas rebellion." Nelson Mandela's autobiography "Long Walk to Freedom" is accessible, along with Baby Milk Action, OXFAM, and a host of other grassroots groups. Buddhist action and ethics are then discussed, along with vegetarian recipes, and, of course, you'll hear about Tibet ("the U.N. has banned any references to the Dalai Lama in the 50th anniversary book"—well, you can't expect them to *brag* about their role). This is a bit heady, but a fine-featured call to action, more *thoughtful* than pushy.

**Engaged Buddhist
~Dharma Page**

lesslie@maui.com

"Whatever affects one directly, affects all indirectly. I can never be what I ought to be until you are what you ought to be. This is the interrelated structure of reality."
- Dr. Martin Luther King Jr.

Hyper Philosophy by WWW

http://www.physics.wisc.edu/~shalizi/hyper-weird/
philosophy.html

Religion and Philosophy

This branch of Cosma Rohilla Shalizi's page "Hyper-Weirdness by WWW" appears to be (and is!) a gateway to virtually all the Net's philosophy texts. The special bonus here is the many annotations such as: "Confucius did not write fortune cookies. Few competent scholars today think he wrote anything at all..." or "Daniel Dennett is the late 20th century's answer to William James. Alright, so that's an exaggeration, but they both focus on the mind, both are devout Darwinians...." We can't prove the guy knows what he's talking about, but he sure *sounds* like he does. And he's fun! This is a boon both for serious students of philosophy, and for those who just want to fish for some loose thoughts.

Islamic Server

http://www.usc.edu/dept/MSA/

Religion and Philosophy

Sponsored by the USC Muslim Students Association, this constantly evolving page explores fundamental principles of Islam in precise detail. It covers topics ranging from Allah to pillars of the faith to politics. Also here are frank discussions of the role of women in Islamic culture, and Hijab, the traditional requirement that women cover their bodies in public. A section entitled "What is *not* Islam" tackles misconceptions: followers of Islam believe in only one God (Allah), who is the Creator and *not* a human being; the page also argues that followers of Islam are not racist by belief, and quotes the "true Prophet of Islam" as saying, "All of you belong to one ancestry of Adam and Adam was created out of clay. There is no superiority...." This is a excellent survey of this growing religion.

Jewish Web World Home Page

`http://www.nauticom.net/users/rafie/judaica-world.html`
Religion and Philosophy

This site offers to bring even the most traditional Jews into the 1990s. Visitors can get a daily dose of religion with Torah Fax ("Torah on the spot for people on the go!") and download a Mac program that will remind them to say *sefirah* whenever they start their computer. The Asian Kashrus Page serves up some unusually delightful kosher recipes, like Coconut Loozena and Burmese Gin Xao Xaot (chicken with lemon grass). Amazingly diverse Jewish and Israeli resources connect to *bar mitzvah* lessons, Chabad servers, and a host of Judaica galleries. For the kids, JWW offers space to create and display original interactive artwork, and get feedback from other kids around the globe. This is a very lively religious festival. And for even *more* Judaic resources, link to Jewishnet.

The Monk Page

`http://www.efn.org/~russelln/`
Religion and Philosophy

Even site founder Russell Neville confesses that this may not be the most *accurate* resource on monasticism, but it is certainly resourceful. The story begins with an Italian hermit named Benedict way back in the sixth century (whose memory lives on in a Belgian beer by the same name), a fairly spiritual guy who founded the Christian order of (surprise!) Benedictines. A concise history of the solitary practice reveals that nearly every world religion embraces some form of monasticism, and that it predates the appearance of Christ by nearly ten centuries. If you think only guys are monks, guess again: visit the home page of the Sisters of St. Benedict, who have their own claustral digs in Minnesota. Direct links to other monasteries (there's even one in Macedonia), the Hill Monastic Manuscript Library, and a hodge-podge of "ancient texts and other things" make this a most amusing Web stop. Enjoy this alone or with friends.

Philosophers Page

http://129.101.39.86/Philosophy/default.htm
Religion and Philosophy

Some of history's most prominent philosophers are at your fingertips here. If only understanding them were as easy as retrieving them! Simply search and scroll, click, and you're into "The Doctrine of the Mean." Speaking of mean, Nicolo Machiavelli's *The Prince* is also accessible here. This is mostly an all-male affair (Mary Wollstonecraft is the lone female philosopher), and it's traditional as all get out. The indexing system is a standard word search; searching for "existentialism" yields St. Augustine and Immanuel Kant, which is more than you get for "positivism" (nothing there at all); a search for "zen" somehow only got us Plato. At least "tree fell in woods" garnered dozens of items. Lots of deep info, but be prepared to be unsatisfied if you're looking for anything but the classic old post-Enlightenment crowd.

Su Tzu's Chinese Philosophy Page

http://mars.superlink.net/user/fsu/philo.html
Religion and Philosophy

This page will be a welcome respite to those seeking solace from the confusing world of cyberspace—especially those who read Chinese and have BIG-5 (a Chinese language reader) downloaded on their computer. Those who don't will find more limited choices. In any case, the page offers an alternative to the western philosophers that dominate the Web. Delicate watercolors accompany chapters from the *Tao Te Ching*. Selections from Chuang Tzu's *Inner Chapters* are serene, and a link to the Virtual I Ching has its practical value. On the flip side, read *The Art of War* by Sun Tzu, who says "All warfare is based on deception." (Western philosophers, of course, may say "well, no duh!") One may also say about this page: "Still Web sites run deep."

The White Temple

`http://www2.gol.com/users/claude/shin.html`
Religion and Philosophy

This delightful Japanese server explores the realms of Shin Buddhism, or the way of "the White Path." To know the Path is to know the way of Sakyamuni Buddha, explained here in a parable that warns of straying too far onto the "eastern bank," or the human world of impermanence. Full text of the *Prajna Paramita*—the "Heart" Sutra—is provided in English, Chinese, and Roman Japanese. "Form does not differ from emptiness," the Sutra teaches, "and emptiness does not differ from form." (We're not sure what that means, but we like the sound of it.) A beginner's primer answers general questions about Buddhist beliefs, the practice of spreading "Nembutsu only" and Mahayana principles (as opposed to Hinayana, a more monastic form of Buddhist practice). Other parables and essays cover "The Problem of Death" and "Buddhist Salvation." Excellent info.

The WWW Bible Gateway

`http://www.gospelcom.net/bible`
Religion and Philosophy

Nick Hengeveld says he is "a sinner... saved by grace." He's also a host of the larger Gospel Communications Network and the Webmaster at this unusual Biblical reference site. In any of seven languages (including Tagalog and the Latin Vulgate), browsers can search five different versions of the Bible for a favorite verse or passage. Compare a translation of Genesis 1:1 from the NIV version ("In the beginning, God created the heavens and the earth...") with the Darby version ("In the beginning of God's preparing the heavens and the earth..."). Ah, what a difference a gerund makes. The nifty search engine lets you enter a Biblical citation for instant retrieval. This is a super tool for both theologians and laypersons.

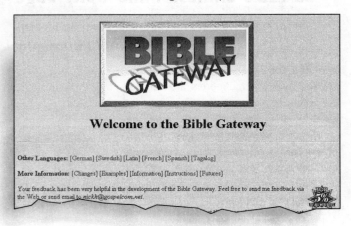

BIBLE GATEWAY

Welcome to the Bible Gateway

Other Languages: [German] [Swedish] [Latin] [French] [Spanish] [Tagalog]

More Information: [Changes] [Examples] [Information] [Instructions] [Futures]

Your feedback has been very helpful in the development of the Bible Gateway. Feel free to send me feedback via the Web or send email to *nickh@gospelcom.net*.

theater and dance

Laurie Anderson's Green Room

http://www.voyagerco.com:80/LA/VgerLa.html

Theater and Dance

This is the next best thing to being on the tour bus with America's premiere performance artist. The "virtual green room" whisks you across North America and Europe and behind the scenes of Laurie Anderson's 1995 multimedia extravaganza, "The Nerve Bible." Techies will drool over the details of Laurie's "drum suit" and "laser tunnel," and hungry vagabonds will want to hunt down her recipe for Hotel Hot Dogs. Most insightful are her road-diary entries, which expose the human side of this techno-artist as she ponders Dollywood, encounters good barbecue, and has an awkward conversation with a childhood friend. The visually dazzling (and gargantuan) site was developed by Voyager Co., the producer of Anderson's recent performance piece on CD-ROM, *Puppet Motel*.

CHAINS

http://found.cs.nyu.edu/andruid/CHAINS.html

Theater and Dance

Coded Messages: CHAINS began as a series of performances in Ghana in 1994. At this vivid site, a "public manifestation" of the work, Ghanaian Francis Kofi collaborates with American artists Andruid Kerne and Melissa Lang to produce the first in what the group hopes will be a succession of multimedia projects. Here, "chains" serve as a metaphor both for physical bondage and the technological bondage wrought by post-modern societies. (Yes, an odd topic for a Web site.) Patrons can enter a cyber-theater to hear the Gadzo song "Kale Nutsuwo," or become a virtual participant in "Adzogbo," one of the oldest and most spiritually powerful dances of the Eve people of Ghana. Reads the introduction: "A creative event... requires that one leaves the realms of the known, and takes oneself there where one does not expect, is not expected to be."

Dancescape

http://wchat.on.ca/dance/pages/dscape.htm

Theater and Dance

Dancescape is "your Internet information center to the world of competitive ballroom dancing," where words like "sport," "battle," "champion," and "challenge" are used in conjunction with Slow Waltz and the Quickstep. It's strictly ballroom, and it delivers a stunning array of sights and services. Disciples can check out photos from the '95 British Open Championships, get a contact number for the Atlantic City Dance-O-Rama, or pick up a hot tip on a pink and lilac ballgown for sale. Our last visit turned up a "Ballroom Tragedy," the story of an aspiring young dancer whose partner "poured petrol over her and turned her into a human torch." Yow! And the site features regular write-in contests, like "Tell Us Why Ballroom Dancing Should be Included in the Olympics."

Ball'room Danc'ing

(bôl'room' dăns-sing)

A competitive sport that requires teamwork between a man and a woman, in a battle against other couples on a dance floor. The champion is the team that has out-maneuvered the others in a challenge of strategy, skill, and determination.

Welcome to the World of Ballroom Dancing and Dance Sport. Welcome to the World of Dancescape™.

DanceSCAPE™

You are Visitor Number since July 17, 1995.

© R.Tang, 1995. All rights reserved. For more information, please send Email to: rtang@wchat.on.ca . Please note that a Text Only option of this Home Page is also ava

The Dramatic Exchange

http://www.cco.caltech.edu/~rknop/dramex.html

Theater and Dance

The Dramatic Exchange gives new meaning to the word "playground." This revue of the undiscovered offers anyone who has written a play the chance to get "published" by posting it here. The plays can be viewed at this Web site in their entirety, along with synopses, playwright background, and production provisos. The selections range from comedies, tragedies, and dramas to audience-participation and experimental plays. The plots, more often than not, fall into the realm of the eclectic: dead bodies recite poetry; a shy dentist finds more than an abscessed tooth with a beautiful construction worker; a Finnish woman is suddenly granted her wish: a tuba! None of these pique your interest? Go write one yourself!

Gilbert and Sullivan Archive

http://diamond.idbsu.edu/gas/GaS.html

Theater and Dance

The Gilbert and Sullivan Archive examines the lives and comic operas of this quarrelsome Victorian team. The stellar site is in good hands, maintained by members of SavoyNet, a hardcore G&S discussion group. The archived librettos alone contain enough words to support two search engines, enabling you to do fun things like see how many times Gilbert wrote the word "lovely" into his operettas. You'll also find information on solo efforts, a photo gallery that's well worth the wait for downloads, and worldwide performance schedules for people with nothing better to do than jet from one production to the next. Several thoughtful links are included to sites whose G&S connection may not be readily apparent, such as used bookstores in which you might find topical out-of-print books.

Les Misérables Home Page

http://www.ot.com/lesmis/lesmis.html

Theater and Dance

Everybody's favorite musical about human suffering gets royal Web treatment at this blockbuster fan-site. Webmaster William Kartalopoulos, a history major at Dartmouth College, has compiled loads of "Miz" information with sounds and images, presented here in a package worthy of Broadway. An impressive transcription of the libretto, complete with action notes ("She dies with a smile"), will make you feel as though you've plunged into the River Seine (or at least trudged through the Parisian sewer). You can also sample the musical's somber sounds, as sung by an assortment of street gangs, beggars, and urchins. If all of this isn't enough, Victor Hugo's 1861 novel (upon which the musical is based) is available for download. It's all about misery, but the site is a delight.

Phantom of the Opera Home Page

`http://vvv.com:80/phantom/`
Theater and Dance

This phantasmagoric phan site focuses on both the Andrew Lloyd Webber musical and the Gaston Leroux novel that inspired it. Webmaster Jason Emery, an aspiring electrical engineer, writes of being "on the fringes of fanship" in the site's early stages. But there's nothing "fringe" about

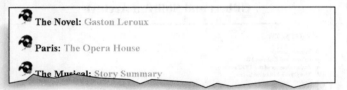

the end result. If you're not up for downloading the novel (which you can do here), a quick historical tour of the Paris Opera House sets the stage nicely for the musical, the libretto of which is also included. (Sound effects are neatly interspersed throughout the text.) Get ticket information for productions from St. Louis to Singapore, or flip through every *Phantom* logo known to mankind. Probably only an excursion under the Opera stage could get you closer to the hideously deformed creature than this.

The Pope Joan Workshop Web

`http://orlok.vs.mcs.net/`
Theater and Dance

From Chicago's Orlok Productions, here's an unusual behind-the-scenes view of what it takes to produce a Broadway musical. The subject: *Pope Joan*,

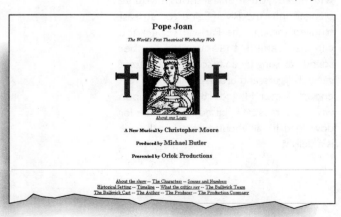

"a love story based on the rise and fall of the only female Pope," in its preliminary Chicago run. Yes, they're serious: "With its use of period and ecclesiastical accents to flavor a pop score (and) set against the backdrop of the pageantry and ritual of the Vatican, *Pope Joan* explores themes both ancient and in today's headlines." Visitors can read selections from the script ("Act One... LOUIS, half-dressed, lounges in the bed, while JOAN, in priestly robes, instructs him. A bell tolls....") or the sometimes near-hysterical production notes ("The deal we've been working on for months appears to be aborting..."). The weekly progress reports are quite fascinating.

Stephen Sondheim Stage

http://www.innocence.com/sondheim

Theater and Dance

The man who revolutionizes the American musical with practically every show he composes is explored here with a passion. Fans can pore over biographical information, download logos and audio excerpts (with bizarre labels like "Bobby" and "Ummm"), and read a CompuServe interview so comprehensive and articulate that you almost stop wondering where the Frequently Asked Questions are. (The FAQs are here too, of course—did you know Sondheim also creates crossword puzzles?) Sondheim's descriptions of the movies he wrote with Tony Perkins, of which only *The Last of Sheila* was produced, will make even the most casual of fans lust for what might have been. Visually, this page is no razzler-dazzler, but it sure has substance.

Steven Berke's Breakin' Home Page

http://rowlf.cc.wwu.edu:8080/~n9344199/bd/bd.html

Theater and Dance

Steven Berke couldn't find anything on the Web about the fading art of break dancing, so he started a "breakin'" page of his own—and he's gathered an entertaining mass of '80s memorabilia. Discover the meaning behind the phrase, "Man, we got on the subway and we were buggin' out." See demonstrations of "popping," "headspins," and the "electric boogie." Or listen to a sample of the classic "Rapper's Delight." Berke even details his personal breakin' history ("My friend Daemon and I always had heated battles on who had the better backspin"), with photographs of his succession of jambox-toting "crews" in full gear. For better or worse, the vernacular and craft of graffiti artists are also explored here, so you can view a handful of colorful names and images sprayed on the sides of subway cars.

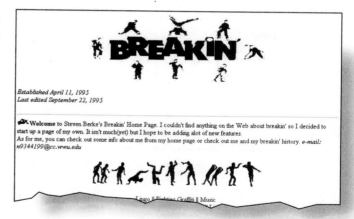

Tap Dance

http://www.hahnemann.edu/tap/
Theater and Dance

With this informative site, Webmaster Paul Corr accomplishes his stated goal of providing "one-stop shopping" on tap dance and related resources—and he does it with toe-tapping cadence. Visitors can learn the difference between a "scuff" and a "shuffle" in the Tap Glossary, and learn to do the "Shim-Sham" at the Tap Steps page. A reference section gives a brief history of tap dance, and profiles "tap patriarchs" King Rastus Brown ("Mr. Tap") and "Juba," who was apparently the first to combine African steps like the shuffle and slide with jig steps. Dancers can listen to an audio clip of Gregory Hines clacking away. This is also the place to go for consumer tips on snappy items like Jiffy Tabs, those removable taps for street shoes.

> TAP
> DANCE
> HOMEPAGE
>
> Quick Index:
>
> [Tap House][Who's Who][Calendar][Specials/Places][Film/Video][Sounds]
> [Glossary][Steps][Books/Ref][Supplies][Musings][NetSites][Clozzing]
>
> • WHAT'S NEW? A list of changes and history.
> • What is the International Tap Association?
> • Comments from the author of the Tap Dance Homepage
>
> Join the Mailing Li

Theatre Central

http://www.mit.edu:8001/people/quijote/
theatre-central.html
Theater and Dance

This exemplary online clearinghouse contains links to theater-related Web and gopher sites from all over the world. Coverage is ALL-inclusive, with connections to professional companies (The Shaw Festival), scholastic groups (Roadkill Buffet), online magazines (*Aisle Say*), and esoteric asides (rec.arts.puppetry, anyone?). You could spend days here rooting through links like computer-aided set design or the Virtual Headbook for casting. Overseer Andrew Kraft is an MIT theater major specializing in technology and the arts, so the site should be in good hands. In fact, the site has "grown dramatically" (his pun) since its inception. Sadly, you won't find cut-rate tickets to *Cats* here. But serious thespians will be seriously rewarded.

> **Table of Contents**
>
> FEATURED SITE:
> Directory of Theatre Professionals on the Net
>
> NOTE TO REGULAR USERS: This page was completely reorganized during the weekend of September 16, 1995. Links may no longer be under the same categories as they were previously.
>
> Keys to Reading This Page
>
> 1. Contact Services
> 2. NEW Unions
> 3. NEW Current & Regional Theatre Listings
> 4. Professional Companies & Calendars
> 5. NEW Amateur Companies & Calendars
> 6. NEW Community & Regional Theatre
> 7. NEW Shakespeare Festivals
> 8. NEW Alternative & Non-Traditional Theatre
> 9. Individual Shows & Performances
> 10. Scholastic-Based Groups
> 11. Academic Programs & Classes (University)
> 12. NEW Other Training Programs & Classes
> 13.

Internet and Computing

Internet and Computing

Anyone could guess that computers would be a hot topic on the Internet, but could anyone guess that there would be so much coopera-tion? The Web has thousands of sites devoted to shar-ing hardware and software tips, or even software itself. Of course, you can't be sure if the tips are coming from a genuine expert or an eight-year-old in Akron (or both), but if you can't find it here, you just aren't looking hard enough.

The category "Web Gadgets" is a fun collection of strange machinery, switches that let you steer a model train halfway across the world, and oddball up-to-the-second shots of freeways, fish, and coffeepots. In one sense, these are some of the "purest" sites on the Web—items that could only exist because the Web itself exists. In another sense, they're a symbol of just how easy and fun it is to waste time in cyberspace.

computer art ─────────────────────────

computer art

(Art)^n Laboratory

`http://www.artn.nwu.edu/`

Computer Art

"Online images do not do justice to PHSColograms," announces this page. "You have to see them in person." Well, yeah, but in the meantime, this virtual gallery of 3D images comes darn close. It's

> "They copied all they could follow but they couldn't copy my mind so I left them sweating and stealing a year and a half behind."
> – Rudyard Kipling

(Art)ⁿ Laboratory

Words   Enter Galleries   Past & Future Shows

Virtual Photography

a showcase for the digital style you may recognize from virtual reality games and scientific modeling, like the ubiquitous DNA chain. This site is huge, and the entries range from "video portraits" to custom computer gaming images created for companies like Nintendo and Hudson Soft ("Virtual Boy"). We were also impressed by the group's commercial projects, particularly images created for a Chinese pipe manufacturing company and a custom logo for IBM. But if you really want to fawn over fractals, the scientific visualization entries come closest to achieving that real-time 3D thrill.

atom

`http://www.atom.co.jp`

Computer Art

You'll find a plateful of visual sushi at "atom," a bilingual and eponymous site created by the Japanese graphic design firm. It's a melding of 'zine (*Virtual MacLife*), Monty Python-esque interactive fun, tortured-artist exhibitions, and Japanese indie

music. You may not understand the uniquely-worded English text any more than the Japanese (you either "agree" or "unagree" to enter the "unsound" page), but that's OK—the toothless smiles and floating body parts that dot this unusual page need no translation. Artist Toshihiro Sakuma attests, "The empathy I feel when imagining the very first movement and the actual instant of the movement of the original form of life is so strong that it is beyond my understanding." Woo! Groove to the sounds of Seance-Room Music as you ponder it all.

Welcome to atom home page!

What's New?   *What's new?*
Information   *Information from atom*
Virtual MACLIFE   *Virtual MACLIFE* NEW

Center for Electronic Art

http://www.cea.edu/
Computer Art

The CEA is a San Francisco non-profit school providing training in electronic media, with a particular edge in the fields of computer graphics and video design. This site exists in part to promote CEA's programs, which are offered both for college credit and certification in desktop publishing, multimedia, and animation. The real grab here is the school's online gallery, where some remarkable work is on display. In the recent past, we've dug the digital playground of artist Michael Rex Booth, whose searing portraits take American Gothic to post-Modern levels. And Su Z Brat's electronic surrealism, Shawn

Cassidy's graceful Matisse-inspired drawings (love those lines!) were evidence enough that the CEA is doing something right.

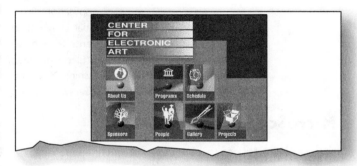

Fluxus Online

http://anansi.panix.com:80/fluxus/
Computer Art

When we first cruised this page sponsored by artist Nam June Paik (the wall-of-televisions guy), we asked, "Are people still *doing* Fluxus?" (It was an offbeat 1960s movement that believed art should reflect the modern world's unpredictably mutating nature.) Doing it they are, and now with more electronic multimedia elements than anyone knew existed 30 years ago. Fluxible flyers can spin Fortuna's cartoonish wheel to experience a 3D video installation "Yuppie Ghetto With Watchdog" or the moving (literally) "Fat Heart Video." The giga-normous JPEG files offer hours of viewing (and waiting for downloads). And in keeping with the

Fluxus mandate, things here change and rearrange in perpetuity. This is mainly for art students still floundering in that "New Genres" department.

Matt's Fractals and Fractalesque Artwork

http://www.wam.umd.edu/~mcarswll/

Computer Art

Matt's Fractals and Fractalesque Artwork is—OK, we'll say it—a site for sore eyes. Maryland's Matt Carswell uses a popular software application called "Fractint" to create the initial image, then adds his own embellishments to achieve striking results. Entries like "Elephant Head Nebula" and "The Evil Washing Machine" are evidence not only of Carswell's sense of humor, but of the painstaking process required to produce these bio sci-fi landscapes. He's not always behind a computer terminal, though—a link to "Mountain Biking Stuff" shows that he makes it into the great outdoors. Naturally, though, the biking photos are fractalized and digitized for other die-hard fractal fanatics.

MicroScapes Gallery

http://www.att.com/microscapes/microscapes.html

Computer Art

This gallery of photographs taken by AT&T researchers displays "the microcosm of inner space" made possible by high-tech thermography, spectroscopy, and interferometry. (Woo!) These unbelievably magnified photos sometimes look like a set from a cheap '50s sci-fi movie, or the lost blueprint of Atlantis, but since they happen to be actual representations of silicon atoms and superconductors, they take on much greater significance. Click on each image to reveal the "hidden" caption, and you may discover the fine line between art and science. At the very least, you'll learn that "Smectic G Liquid Crystal" is an example of non-solid packing "symmetry" in a layered structure, rather than a graffiti slogan from South Central Los Angeles.

Ozone

Computer Art

You have to push a lot of buttons to access this library of computer art and fun. "I just like buttons," says "Doc" Ozone, whose stirring art often has the depth of a hologram. Images range from mossy bark and textural landscapes to global thermonuclear war. Don't let the war thing scare you off, though—Ozone has a good sense of humor. (Try activating his "low-bandwidth option," for example.) When you're finished with the images (and this may take a while), follow links to The Annoying Post Brothers (a couple of greedy "twisted bad boys"), or to a place called Demonweb, which may provide your most horrific experience yet on the Net. The Doc's even got a File Transfer Protocol site, just in case you want to download a few of his images to your own computer. This guy's good.

Paul F. Jones's Tracespace

Computer Art

With Tracespace, Paul F. Jones has created a gallery for displaying his talent in the art of "raytracing," in which computer graphics are used to produce "3D" images. It's quite impressive, especially if you're into the macabre. (Jones admits, he has "a 'thing' for skulls.") Sample piece: "Genetica," a mythical disease that "leads to total bio-genetic disruption of the victim." Other images bring to mind a range of visual metaphors, from pre-historic lava surges to film stills from *Poltergeist*. Jones also provides some not-so-creepy links to his favorite personal home pages, and several valuable resources for computer artists, not the least of which is a cache of graphics and software that even newbies will love. All terrific stuff, but he's kidding himself if he thinks we're even going to *consider* downloading "Deathmask," with its warning that "this image is cursed."

Pixel Pushers

http://www.pixelpushers.wis.net/

Computer Art

What's a pixel pusher? Weeell... it's a digital artist who pushes around little refracted bits of light and eventually makes a picture. If that doesn't quite explain things, this totally interactive icon-driven site from a digital artists' collective will do the job. It will also take care of any sensory deprivation you've been experiencing lately. Click on a 3D globe to access the main menu, then wander through a gallery of first-rate images that run the gambit of taste and genre, from straightforward portraits to questionable manipulations. Canadian artist Louis Fishauf's entry successfully incorporates elements from a Toronto cemetery; and even '60s folk singer and "Sesame Street" star Buffy Sainte-Marie gets into the pixel push with her dreamlike "Pink Village." The politely devious can leave graffiti on the pixel bathroom wall.

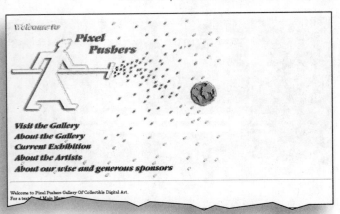

computing
computing

Adobe Systems

http://www.adobe.com

Computing

Graphics designers and desktop publishers may want to jump through their computer screens and live here (although we hear the food is bland). Now that Adobe has swallowed competitors like Aldus and CoSa, this site offers just about every software tool a designer could imagine. Where do you start? We suggest downloading the free Acrobat Reader software; it's becoming useful all over the Web as more sites provide Acrobat documents, which are print-quality files that can be viewed on many platforms. (For example, we happen to know the IRS site has many downloadable tax forms in Acrobat format, which are just as official as the ones you pick up at the post office.) With that in hand, you can download product brochures and support documents until the digitized cows come home.

Alias/Wavefront

http://www.alias.com/

Computing

Alias/Wavefront is a digital software company, the product of a recent merger between Alias Research and Wavefront. Its home page is a collage of computer-generated images and animation meant to knock the socks off of designers everywhere. The graphics pack a punch, and are handled with panache. A student gallery features some impressive amateur work; this site also features work done for corporate clients like Nintendo and Turner Productions. Visitors can select from a batch of artsy "postcards" to e-mail to their friends, or watch clips from a computer-animated movie titled "the end," which creator Chris Landreth calls "a light-hearted, hellish frolic on the buffalo chips of cyber-profundity." The in-jokes and technical info are meant for potential buyers, but everyone can appreciate the looks of this stylish site.

Apple Computer

http://www.apple.com

Computing

Apple, Inc: mild-mannered computer maker or dangerous cult? You decide at this mega-site, where the company with the intensely loyal following has set an admirable standard for Web quality. Discover the quirks of Apple's confusing array of models named with P (Performa, PowerBook, PowerMac, Pippin) and take a journey into the amazingly detailed product support area. Or, check the *What's New* list to get the latest hyperlinks to Apple's myriad software libraries and Quicktime files. Computer industry insiders might be amused at Apple's extensive dissertation on why Macintosh is better than a PC running Windows 95: it's either paranoia bordering on fear, or a sign of Apple's complete assurance in the quality of their product. A must for Apple-philes; a temptation for frustrated PC users.

ArchiText

http://www.atext.com
Computing

This refreshingly fun promo site from a small Silicon Valley company shows off what could be groundbreaking Net search software (for Unix boxes). ArchiText finds information "by concept," in effect making the search more human. Other entertaining human touches here are the Virtual Garage (where six Stanford grads started the company, and where you can click on different objects around the room to get amusing anecdotes about them) and MarketText, a right-on spoof of computer industry marketing gibberish. You can also hit the "Look What We're Wearing Today!" page, to get yet another live picture of their office area. (We still haven't seen what they're wearing, but we can tell you that they leave their office lights on overnight.) Some genuine laughs—a good promo page.

Berkeley OS/2 Users Group

http://warp.eecs.berkeley.edu/os2
Computing

OS/2 cultists, under increasing pressure from Windows 95, will find a friendly oracle at this moderately fun page from Cal-Berkeley. (Shouldn't these kids be out protesting?) The Webmasters are vigilant about posting demos and betas of new commercial releases for OS/2 (like the new OS/2 Web browser), plus the hottest shareware. The support pages range from official IBM (all done up in respectful blue), to a hip section about sound cards. Non-OS/2 computer users can find lots of great stuff, here, too, like bitmap libraries (including Homer Simpson after a doughnut), and the Fun Stuff section, which brings on the latest in Microsoft bashing and other computer-related humor, including "What if people bought cars like computers?" You must know the secret OS/2 handshake to enter.

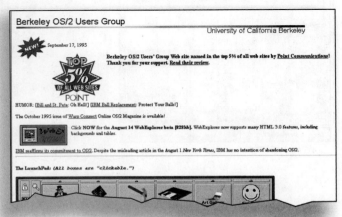

Jim Brain's Commodore Home Page

http://garnet.msen.com/~brain/cbmhome.html

Computing

Some people (and computers) don't know when to quit. Long before the 32-bit computers of today, clunky boxes of the '80s like the Commodore Pet talked in abrupt 8-bit sentences. So host Jim Brain (NOT a stage name) is committed to keeping these relics alive, explaining how they can still do a passable job at stuff like e-mail and simple word processing. And this free-will love offering provides loads of documentation (from operating system instructions to ROM maps and Hidden Secrets), plus instructions on where to get software (FTP sites, Usenet), and even a useless load of monthly Commodore trivia questions that would stump a *Jeopardy*

champion. Still, it's reassuring to know that someday when your Pentium system is worth $20, somebody like Jim Brain will be saying "Don't give up! Your computer's still useful!"

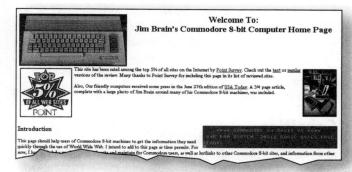

Compaq Computer Corp.

http://www.compaq.com/homepage.graphic.html

Computing

Computer shoppers and support pros will appreciate this no-nonsense archive from one of the world's top PC makers. Compaq promotes its latest line of fast PCs while also delivering one of the best online computer support services we've seen. And thanks to a cuddly relationship with Microsoft, you'll find plenty of information on Windows 95 and its heralded "Plug and Play" technology. (Contrary to popular opinion, "Plug and Play" has nothing to do with taking a bath.) And if it plugs but doesn't play, you download diagnostic software or check a list of common questions to ease your computer

headache. We'd like to see more zany activities here, since great customer support only goes so far.

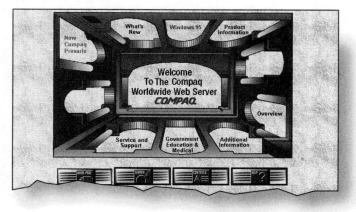

Computer Hardware and Software Phone Numbers

http://mtmis1.mis.semi.harris.com/comp_ph1.html

Computing

Until we have total global online Yellow Pages, this site will have to do. Harris Semiconductor faithfully maintains this current list of phone numbers and other electronic addresses for vendors of computer hardware and software. Sounds dull, but could be a lifesaver if you're trying to find obscure software, or if your software vendor has deftly hidden its phone number in your manual (a common practice in the fly-by-night computer industry). As a bonus, you'll find those elusive BBS numbers, since many software and hardware vendors are noticeably absent from the Net. Actually, it's kind of funny to see the silly 800-numbers that the gear-heads come up with (e.g., 800-TINY-RAM). Of course, once you get these numbers, you'll still have to spend hours listening to muzak after the electronic operator says "Your call is very important to us."

CorelNet

http://www.corelnet.com/

Computing

This independent users group for Corel's graphics software has become an overnight Net phenomenon, thanks to loyal "Corelians." It's so popular, in fact, that Corel itself has decided to join the site, adding the official company line to this already rich collection of files and discussion groups. Users here are enthusiastic to share secrets about Corel's graphic arts and desktop publishing software, and they discuss them at length in the several Hypertext messaging forums available. There are also occasional live, moderated chat sessions (which requires downloading some software and a little configuring) with official voices from Corel. Clips from The Cartoonist, a syndicated comic strip, are sprinkled throughout—created using (surprise!) CorelDRAW.

Cray Research Inc.

http://www.cray.com/

Computing

You may think you have a super computer, but for Pete's sake don't call it a "supercomputer." This lofty term belongs to the likes of Cray Research, makers of computers powerful enough to do even Bill Gates' taxes. Propellerheads can gaze longingly at the Massively Parallel Cray T3D system, which you can order with staggering 2048 processors. Interesting application notes show people using Crays for tasks ranging from quantum mechanics to car crash simulation and fast rendering and animation of large datasets (sounds like the game DOOM, actually). The Cray folks also make a convincing case for using their big iron in business, although you still pay a premium for the Cray name. If nothing else, a visit here will show you how fast a Web server should be.

Digital Equipment Corporation

http://www.digital.com:80/info/home.html

Computing

Make no mistake: the folks at Digital want you to know their lightning-fast computers can wow even NASA rocket scientists. This catch-all site touts the new 200-plus megahertz Alpha systems (souped-up rivals to the Pentium), yet still provides support for older ("honored citizen") mainframe systems. We found loads of information on Digital's corporate strategy, emphasizing "connectivity" after the "wrenching transition" from vertical to horizontal computing. (In English: they're tired of selling those messy room-filling computers and want to make money connecting smaller ones.) The pages load briskly, and they'd better: after all, NASA uses Digital computers to launch the Space Shuttle.

Global Village Communication

http://www.globalvillage.com/
Computing

This modem company comes across with a site that is "warm" (in Marshall McLuhan-speak), since it welcomes new Net users with cute small town graphics and invites them to tour the Net. You'll find plenty of information on Global Village's broad range of modem models, and extra perks include a library of Internet software to help beginners get launched on the Net. The Customer Support Center goes to great lengths to support both the hardware and software dilemmas that can often make users feel like the Village Idiot. In a world where some computer hardware vendors have adopted the approach of Orwell's *1984*, this village is indeed a pleasant escape.

THE VILLAGE
FROM GLOBAL VILLAGE COMMUNICATION

Welcome to The Village, Global Village Communication's presence on the World Wide Web. Global Village develops and markets communication products for personal computer users. Visit the different areas in The Village to learn more about communicating from your computer, including faxing, accessing on-line services and the Internet, and connecting to remote networks.

Come explore our village:

- Visitor's Center
- Newsstand
- Solution Center
- Internet Depot

...or click directory for an alphabetical listing of key topic areas.

Hewlett-Packard

http://www.hp.com/
Computing

One would expect an excellent Web site from electronics whiz-kids HP, and yet they've still outdone themselves. Their state-of-the-art, icon-rich interface is a delight to navigate. Consumers will appreciate the index of product documents and catalogs (including a Windows 95 support page). Business-folk will enjoy the company briefs, news releases, and HP's Worldwide Contacts. Job-seekers can search the database of HP employment opportunities by entering the state, department, and kind of job they prefer. And everyone can check out the Palo Alto garage where Bill Hewlett and Dave Packard got started. Garages, garages... hasn't anyone ever started a high-tech company in their kitchen? Well, no matter: this is a top-notch corporate page.

Hewlett-Packard at Telecom 95

Access HP

HEWLETT PACKARD

IBM

http://www.ibm.com
Computing

Chances are that nearly any computer user can find something of interest at IBM's Web site, since these people have their fingers (sometimes up to their wrists) in every pie. Clicking around here is one of the best ways to get support on IBM software or hardware, and Big Blue will tell you what's new in the computer industry while you're looking. The company news here is conspicuously global—you can access an IBM server in the country of your choice by clicking on a list at the bottom of the home page. The IBM ad campaigns get a workout here, too; on our last visit the question was, "Would three Greek divers really need IBM's Global Net?" Make sure to check out IBM's Digital Library, a sweet new info search technology. No zany fun here, but at least you can skip the blue suit.

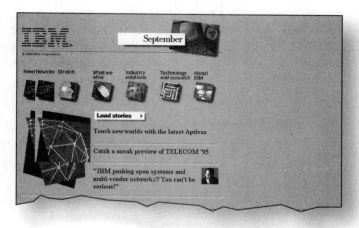

The Info-Mac HyperArchive

http://hyperarchive.lcs.mit.edu/HyperArchive.html
Computing

This is a Web interface to the Mac software archives at Stanford University, probably the biggest single collection of Macintosh freeware and shareware in the world. (The archive is mirrored in many machines across the Internet.) The HyperArchive isn't the first to provide a Web interface, but it's the most advanced: in addition to downloading files directly through your Web browser, you're able to sort in different ways, check for recent changes, and view the abstracts of specific files (as opposed to the old way, which was to load the abstract for all the files in a given directory). It still takes some study to use it well, and beginning users may have trouble with it, but the alternative is to get involved in FTP transfer arcana. Trust us, this is easier. A great concept that can only get better.

Kai's Power Tips and Tricks for Adobe Photoshop

`http://the-tech.mit.edu/KPT/`
Computing

Kai Krause, a Photoshop whiz, publishes his magical tricks on America Online. (Photoshop is a popular software package from Adobe.) This site gives the Internet public a chance to read them, and *thank goodness!* You can learn more cool tricks in a single Power Tip than several days messing around with the program would get you. If you've ever needed to put drop shadows in weird objects, or if you have no idea what "channel operations" are, this is a must-read. Most tips come with screen shots of the procedures in progress; all are explained in detail. Some are hard to grasp, some are surprisingly simple, but all are guaranteed to make your graphics more exciting. The site also sports a HyperNews messaging system to discuss Photoshop issues with other users.

Kaleida Labs

`http://www.kaleida.com`
Computing

Kaleida, the historic joint venture between longtime rivals Apple and IBM, struts its multimedia stuff on this Web site. The company only has two products, but you can download one of them—the cross-platform Media Player—right here. If you have the time and the patience (and a Mac or Windows 3.1), you can download the Media Player and configure it to run with your browser. As you click on their sample links, the Media Player performs animation, which demonstrates its powerful potential in the Web context. Most commendably, the corporate milestone category doesn't shrink away from the hard facts: layoff numbers and executive shuffles are listed with all the gory details. On the bright side, you can visit quirky employee sites, like a link to yummy recipes featuring crickets and beetles. Developers are a strange breed.

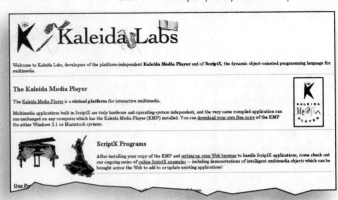

Lotus Development Corp.

http://www.lotus.com/
Computing

Even though Lotus is now part of IBM (Big Blue paid $3.5 billion for it), you still have time to get Lotus's opinion at this site devoted to products like the critically acclaimed *Notes*. Meanwhile, Lotus proves it's still knocking heads together by offering an excellent online support area, with extensive FAQs and file updates to calm nervous customers, plus industry-specific tips on using *Notes* (for banking, pharmaceuticals, telecommunications). The View From Lotus injects a little corporate culture and fun; it lists lots of Boston-related links in case you wanted to drop by the headquarters for a visit (how 'bout those Red Sox?). Don't miss the exemplary Lotus Selects product catalog for Lotus upgrades and paraphernalia. Highly recommended for business PC users.

Macromedia, Inc.

http://www.macromedia.com/
Computing

Visitors to this classy site from the multimedia software giant will find some of the finest graphics on the Web, backed up with a healthy library of articles and multimedia clips for both hobbyists and seasoned professionals. Beyond the usual support and product info for its Mac and PC software like *Director* and *Freehand*, Macromedia creates a "virtual community" for the entire multimedia industry by offering news, a file library, and even a "chat" area. Highlights include the Industry Pulse, a collection of daily industry news updates, and Free Toys, a solid collection of multimedia utilities and clips. What will probably most interest the Web community is the company's efforts in making Director, their popular animation/presentation program. Highly recommended; a site worth emulating.

Microsoft

http://www.microsoft.com
Computing

Some genuflect and some gag at the mention of Microsoft, but nearly everyone can use this site. Microsoft asks

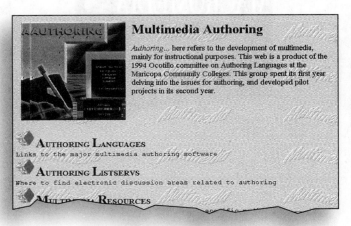

"Where do you want to go today?" then lets you get software updates, patches, and help files for its many products. A lightning-fast database lets you search by key words. (Searching for the word "bug" quickly gets you a document explaining how to become a beta tester, a sort of crash-test dummy for new software.) And a Top Ten list features the most common questions site visitors have and the pages that answer them. The massive library is likely to answer 95 percent of your questions. This is a marvelous substitute for long hours spent on hold for Microsoft's telephone technical support! Highly recommended.

Multimedia Authoring Web

http://www.mcli.dist.maricopa.edu/authoring/
Computing

Most of this site is a collection of links, but it's such a *useful* set of links that

multimedia authors ignore it at their own risk. You'll find lists of multimedia language resources, mailing lists that will get you in contact with other like-minded authoring professionals, and more. The page also contains plenty of information on Macromedia Director (the popular animation/presentation software), with searchable databases. Even if you don't author multimedia applications, the list of Centers of Multimedia Development ("Places that are at the cutting/bleeding edge") are enjoyable to view, since they're created by people who whip up dynamic presentations for a living.

PC/Computing Online

http://www.ziff.com/~pccomp/
Computing

PC/Computing is a great resource for Internet beginners, avoiding nerdy computer talk and aiming squarely at home computer users. Features include the perennial "101 Tips" on various subjects and one-minute guides to "impress your friends and confound your enemies." We like the uncluttered interface, clearing your mind to concentrate on tips like

"hold down the Alt key and click on the right mouse button to view an item's properties" (a recent Windows tip). The site changes monthly, so it's worth a check if you're dead-set on becoming a computer whiz. But this is no *Wired*; it presumes you worship the information highway and want to jam your computer with perky little utilities. And who doesn't?

Quantum

http://www.quantum.com/
Computing

Hard disk users who eat 10 to 20 megabytes a day will feast on this "information buffet" from Quantum Corp. If your wimpy hard drive is under 500 megabytes, you'll quickly feel like you're in the Dark Ages while browsing through detailed brochures on drives now measured in gigabytes (of which you use about 25 megabytes). Or if you only dream

about that much real estate, you can enter a weekly drawing for a free hard drive. Techies will be all over the guides to jumper settings and drive specs, saving those annoying tech support phone calls. Don't miss the info on new solid state drives that could someday make hard drives measured in megabytes as outdated as trilobites.

The Father of Shareware

http://www.halcyon.com/knopf/jim
Computing

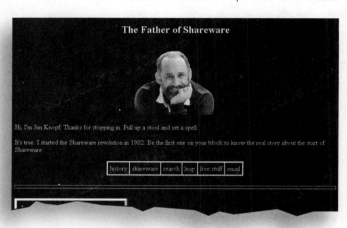

You'll find plenty of links to shareware resources here—this site tends not to waste its time on specific shareware programs, but points you to all the right places to find them. The site is split into useful divisions such as links for users from creators, links for creators themselves, and the like. Jim Knopf, the maintainer of this site, calls himself The Father of Shareware and takes credit for the shareware concept. You'll have to take his word for it, but in any case, it's interesting to read how his company began its shareware trek wayyyyy back in 1981, in the early PC era. And, since this is Jim's site, he also showcases his collection of freeware—some of it pretty impressive, like a multimedia player for Windows that can handle ten different popular formats. At this price (free!), you can't beat it.

Scanning FAQ

http://www.dopig.uab.edu/dopigpages/FAQ/The-Scan-FAQ.html
Computing

No relation to the cult movie *Scanners*, this is an informative guide to the world of computer scanners and scanning techniques. Created by a knowledgeable techie at the U. of Alabama-Birmingham, this site breaks scanning issues into four types—line art, halftones, grayscale, and color scans—and walks you through concerns and techniques for each. For example, in some cases (like reductions) it's actually better to scan at a lower resolution, because high-resolution "data overkill" won't make a difference in the final piece, and will only cause costly delays at the final image processing step. The site also includes tips on common scanning mistakes, cropping and sharpening, and much more. Nice use of photo examples. Includes a great essay on legal issues and copyright infringement.

Silicon Graphics

http://www.sgi.com

Computing

Forget for a minute that you can't afford a Silicon Graphics computer, and proceed immediately to this site. It's worth the trip. SGI makes high-end Unix graphics workstations, which turn out to be ideal Web servers, among other things, and so they put up one heck of a sharp-looking Web page. Despite its overuse of hackneyed surfing and information highway metaphors, the stunning graphics will have you saying "Kewl!" like a UCLA freshman. Skip the product info and go straight to the Serious Fun area, where you'll get to try out WebSpace, their 3D Web browser. SGI also provides a stunning gallery of computer-generated images. Check out the GRAFICA Obscura section for out-there concepts like synthetic lighting.

Software Net

http://software.net

Computing

Software addicts will need therapy after visiting this convenient online store. Just a few clicks can have you ordering from their massive software library; most are shipped to you the old-fashioned way, but a few can be downloaded immediately for a quick fix. With over 8,000 products listed, it's an excellent source for hard-to-find software—made easy to find here, with a simple search engine. Online *PC World* articles are provided for reference, and some products come with full online brochures (which are often just as detailed as the information you could get from the back of the box). The server is fast, the interface sleek, and the free demos are worth a look. Note: if you catch yourself ordering software before noon, seek professional help.

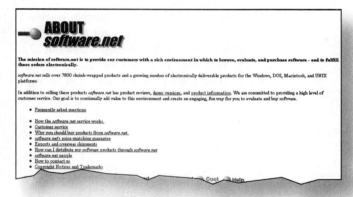

Sun Microsystems

http://www.sun.com
Computing

Sun workstation computers and software used to be the best-kept secret of brainy engineers. But in the world of the Web, Sun is as prominent as its namesake. This site's snazzy interface leads you through its treatises on tools that can connect you to the rest of the blue planet. Graphics are slick and crisp, with good use of interactivity and well-organized, incredibly comprehensive data. Sun even offers a chronology of office pranks, including the assembly of a 1966 Volkswagen in the president's office. Customers, job-seekers, and investors can all benefit from this site, but don't expect modesty. This cocky 12-year old company proclaims itself (with Macaulay Culkin-like charm) to have had the most successful start in the history of American business. But among corporate Web sites, they've earned a right to brag.

Virtual World Entertainment

http://www.virtualworld.com/
Computing

As flashy as this site appears, don't think you'll be able to experience "The World's First Digital Theme Park" from the Web—this is merely a promotional tool for interactive gaming centers located in several big cities around the world. At these centers, we learn, you shell out $7 to $9 a pop on games like "BattleTech" and "Red Planet," which are wars or races against other human players. You play from within your virtual reality pod (like a flight simulator), with as many as 100 different controller knobs and pedals (and you thought operating a mouse took motor skills). Highlights include the "Journals of the Virtual Geographic League," and a collection of Nose Art (for virtual spacecraft, not your proboscus). If your town's not VR accessible, then it's at least a fun stop for the looking.

Virtual Software Library

http://vsl.cnet.com/
Computing

This is the mother of all software archives on the Net. And we're talking the kind of mother that holds your hand, shows you the way, and bakes you cookies when you get home. This mind-blowing shareware server uses shase, a brilliant indexing system (created by Dr. Ziga Turk of the University of Ljubljana, Slovenia, if you must know). Merely click on an icon for your computer type, enter a few search words, and a list of relevant shareware from servers around the world pops up nearly instantly. Or, if you want to know what's hot, you can get a list of the top 30 requested files. (Note to developers: the number of people who've requested the files would be a neat thing to know.) For users who've dawdled away hours trying to find software on a BBS or online service, this is staggeringly simple.

VRML World

http://www.mecklerweb.com/vrml/current/vrml.htm
Computing

The basic problem with reading a virtual reality magazine is this: halfway through you think, "How do I know my whole life isn't just a particularly believable VR simulation, and I'm actually going to turn out to be a nerdy 10-year-old from Detroit who's been playing it?" Once you get past this profound concern, you'll enjoy VRML World, a newsletter about a new tool called Virtual Reality Modeling Language. VRML World's new-frontier topics are often fascinating: the world's first cyberwedding, 3D glasses that can distract squeamish dental patients, and our current favorite: "Drag 'n' Drop World Builders." They're starting with 3D Internet browsers, but these slightly geeky visionaries have their sights set on cyberspace for the masses. And it reads well for both techies and amateurs.

The Well Connected Mac

http://www.macfaq.com/
Computing

This aptly-named site serves as a starting point for many things Macintosh. Ever since Apple split their single unofficial FTP site into several official ones, it's been a bit confusing—but links to each, with descriptions, are provided here. It also contains a list of nearly 1,400 Mac vendors, over 200 of which have Web sites, and extensive product reviews of several Mac apps. The site could use indexes for the bigger pages, but the What's New section promises the pages will be more

continued

The Well Connected Mac continued

manageable in the near future. When that happens, The Well Connected Mac could become a formidable Macintosh resource.

It's all courtesy of Elliotte Rusty Harold, a New York Mac freak who does a great job of sharing his cheerful obsession here.

Windows NT Internet FAQ

http://www.mcs.com/~thomas/www/ntfaq/
Computing

So you want to use Windows NT as a Net workstation or server? Get step-by-step help from this meticulously organized question-and-answer list. Questions like "Does 3.5's RAS support dynamic ip addressing?" are collected from news groups and answered by NT experts in academia. It's pretty complete, and probably can answer even your more obscure questions: under subsection 4B, you'll find the answer to the question, "If I use WFWG V3.11 RAS to connect to a NTAS V3.5 server, can I use telnet and FTP?" Sure, you laugh now, but if you're up at 3 a.m. and have that question, you'll be thankful someone asked it for you. This is all on one gigantic page, which takes a while to load, but the careful organization makes up for its size. And it does beat long-distance calls to Microsoft.

Zenith Data Systems

http://www.zds.com
Computing

Zenith Data Systems (the computer wing of a company known for its TVs and electronics) serves up product

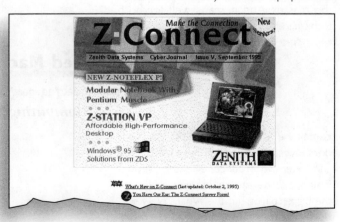

support and info for its desktop and laptop computers here. But instead of the typical cold-looking company site, you'll find a refreshing "cyber-journal" with frequently updated feature stories. Expect lots of chip this, Windows that, but there's no heavy reading here unless you're thinking about buying a Zenith or already own one. Beyond the front page, Professor Zed's Service and Support adds a human touch to enliven tedious fact-finding. A pleasant alternative to the hard sell for megahertz and gigabytes; you'll wish other computer manufacturers would follow their lead.

the internet
the internet

Addicted to Stuff

http://www.mindspring.com/~labrams/a2stuff.htm
The Internet

This odd-by-design site is a clearing-house for people who are irresistibly drawn to certain kinds of "stuff." Stuff like words, for example. Words you hate and words you like can be submitted to the already large lists, or you can find out the loves and peeves of previous visitors. You'll find links to a few Net sites for collectors, or post unique addictions by visiting a collectors' bulletin board, where we found requests for *Happy Meal* toys and for soda tabs and barf bags. (One addict collects "Inspected By" tags from clothing.) Other sections include cars, quotes, and cheesy TV talk shows, and a wonderful list of worries (are you addicted to worrying, or even addicted to worrying about your paper clip collecting addiction?). Even the dreaded addiction to the Web is addressed, with instructions on starting your own page.

The Advertising Media Internet Center

http://www.amic.com/
The Internet

This site, run by Telmar, a Net-savvy company that makes advertising media planning software, has created a clever virtual community for its customers. You have to register to visit, but if you're in the advertising or media fields, it's well worth the extra trouble. Advertising industry news and a chat area will make you feel at home, and the Industry Forums are useful for any potential advertiser. The AMIC site is also home to the Advertising Research Foundation, a non-profit organization dedicated to improving advertising, marketing, and media research in pursuit of more effective marketing and advertising communications. (Yes, these people really know what they're doing.) Behind the scenes, Telmar is gently promoting its array of software and database services. An excellent example of how a page can be both promotional and useful.

Atomic Vision: dex

http://www.atomicvision.com/dex_now/index.html

The Internet

Prepare to enter a different dimension at this stimulating minimalist site from a Web design firm. Called "dex," this e-zine may lose you for a while, but stick with it.

Once you understand its purpose as a gentle promotion for the font design and Web consulting services of Atomic Vision (cool name!), you'll appreciate the fresh approach. We suggest you start by reading about the man behind the mysterious curtain, Matthew Butterick (a font designer turned Web consultant). Then explore the collection of illustrations and essays. The digital artwork is crisp in an understated way; the opinions on interface design and user behavior are thought-provoking. Expect some debunking of the Web's design myths, and perhaps even some ideas on what NOT to do with your Web site.

Beverly Hills Internet

http://www.bhi90210.com/

The Internet

This enterprising "interactive advertising" site from Beverly Hills has combined creativity with a little Hollywood glitz to offer one of the Web's most useful virtual communities (here they call them GeoCities). If you register, you can create your own personal Web page, with an address resembling an actual Beverly Hills street address, like 1049 Rodeo Drive (don't forget to tip the valet). Many of the personal home pages we previewed were still "under construction," and were quite slow to load, so there's still a lot of work to be done here. But *BHI90210*, as it's called, hopes to make money by hosting company Web sites and selling ads. Fun features include the live pictures of the intersection of Hollywood and Vine and a bus bench on Wilshire Boulevard. (Is that De Niro sitting there?) Applause for the free Web pages; the graphics are appropriately chic.

BrowserWatch

http://www.ski.mskcc.org/browserwatch/
The Internet

If you think Netscape and Mosaic are the only two flavors of Web browsing software, you'll get a shock when you visit this info clearing house. Sort of a fan page for browsers, BrowserWatch lovingly describes all the details, and encourages users to report new browsing software when they find it. (People who work for the browser-producing companies are invited to spill secrets, too, but somehow they don't seem too eager.) If you enter a new tidbit that hasn't been given by anyone else, the author gives you "net.fame" in return—your name and e-mail posted for everyone to see. (Not much, but it's cool anyway.) Check the browser stats and you'll discover surprising diversity among Web users.

CommerceNet

http://www.commerce.net/
The Internet

CommerceNet is a non-profit consortium that provides "the first large-scale trial to support electronic commerce via the Internet." The point, in other words, is to help make the Internet an easy-to-use and secure tool for businesses. Here you can explore this new business frontier and even join a subscription program to get your business up on the Web with an electronic storefront. For most users, the best resources here are the directories of companies providing internet services; the "Getting Started" Web design tutorial is also quite helpful. You'll find plenty of menus before you get to the main course; we'd like to see a search engine to make it easier to get around. Still, it's a valuable service if you're looking for examples of the Net's commercial sites.

Communications Archive

http://sunsite.unc.edu/dbarberi/communications.html
The Internet

Thanks to this repository, some of the Net's most wild and memorable moments have been saved for all eternity (that's about two weeks in cyberspace time). You'll find the intense transcripts of the first reports of the Los Angeles earthquake on an Internet Relay Chat, or happier moments like online weddings (the happy couples *had* also met in person). The archive also covers MUDs (Multi-User Domains) and MOOs (MUD, Object Oriented), complete with academic papers on their social significance. (Doesn't everyone wish they'd written "Aesthetic Approaches to the Design and Study of MUDs in English and Performance Studies: Interface, Realism, and the Dialectic of Interacting"?) For fun, stop by the April Fool's page for archives of some of the Net's famous hoaxes.

Computer Professionals for Social Responsibility

http://cpsr.org/home
The Internet

Those wary of the effects of computers on society gather at this information and discussion clearinghouse. The CPSR chats up a storm on several major topics, and you'll find lots of info on each topic here. For instance, on the topic of "Caller ID" (equipment which enables you to see the phone number of a caller before you answer the phone), you can read the testimony of Jeff Johnson, Chair of CPSR, who outlines a disturbing lack of understanding of privacy issues in the California State Assembly. For non-technical users, we recommend the workplace issues archive, which offers warnings about use of computers on the job. These are heavy issues and this is heavy reading, but it's also an excellent look into the controversies of the future.

The Cool Site of the Day

http://cool.infi.net/
The Internet

The wonderfully simple concept of picking an entertaining new site each day has built Glenn Davis's creation into one of the most compelling on the Web. Granted, it's just one man's opinion, but it's often quite reliable. And the idea has built thousands of followers—creating a guaranteed flood of visitors to a site when it makes the list. For proof, you need only check the credible list of previous Cool Sites from the list's beginnings in August, 1994, when the Web was an obscure novelty. The site has many imitators (the *Fool Site of the Day*, for example). But the page now has advertising and Davis has gone pro, so look for this site to be one of the Web's kingmakers for a long time to come.

CRAYON

http://sun.bucknell.edu/~boulter/crayon/
The Internet

This creation by two Bucknell University students lets you check off news sites of interest, and within seconds, automatically generates a sort of "newspaper" that hyperlinks you to the latest news, sports, weather, and comics on the Net. You can even name your paper by entering a title on the form; the "whatever" Times. To test, we named our sample paper the "They Were the Best of Times, They Were The Worst of" Times, and included news from *Time* magazine, the *San Francisco Chronicle*, ESPN SportsZone, and the Intellicast weather site. Once created, you can save the file to your computer and use the page as often as you like. Or, you can print it out and wrap fish. This could use more news site choices, but for a volunteer effort, it's a great service.

Cyber-Rights

http://jasper.ora.com/andyo/cyber-rights/
cyber-rights.html

The Internet

"**G**ive me cheap Net access or give me death," may be your cry after visiting this manifesto on Web privacy and security. Organizers of this citizen campaign want the U.S. government to guarantee that rights to basic Net services won't be taken away or made too pricey. Man the barricades! One of the documents in their exhaustive online library is the ongoing story of the Wish Book BBS, a dial-in computer system in Arizona, which has been charged with carrying illegal material. The systems operator maintains that he is innocent, but his defense is costing several thousand dollars, and Cyber-Rights is distributing his message in the hopes of getting financial support for his cause. A great starting place for researchers or activists on this touchy topic.

Cybersight

http://www.cybersight.com/

The Internet

This virtual marketing team hopes you'll be sufficiently impressed by their interactive promotional pages to ask them to develop one for you. While you're deciding, you can Web-shop at the online bazaar and sample some of CyberSight's handiwork: they've created sites for Molson Beer and Stolichnaya Vodka, as well as popular (?) groups like Ned's Atomic Dustbin and Korn. Navigational and communications applications ("The Phlogistician's Corner") aim to offer users more chances to interact with companies promoting products and services on the Web, something we'd like to see. In some cases, you'll probably find "more sizzle than steak," but then again, isn't the Web all about frittering away time on less than substantial things?

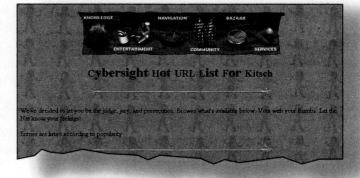

Culture Shock

http://www.cultureshock.com/
The Internet

It's often confusing, but this is a good place to find the latest innovations in Web visual design. Culture Shock is a gang of young designers and Net experts who hope you'll hire them to design your Web page. ("Basking in the nexus of commerce, art, culture, and technology," is how they describe the company.) Watch your mouse as you navigate this page; just about every dot or doodle you see (and some you don't) is a link. On past visits we wandered through a maze of nonsensical equations, dividing E=MC squared over Andy Warhol and ending up at the poetry of Robert Frost. (And we shudder to think what *he'd* have to say about the Web.) The content is garbled but amusing, just about perfect for a coffee-break stop.

E-Law

http://www.leepfrog.com/E-Law/
The Internet

Reading these academic papers on the legal liabilities of online services is enough to scare you away from writing e-mail to your Mom. (She probably prefers cards and letters anyway.) Chicago attorney David Loundy (this is also his home page) contributes these articles not as legal advice, but to raise issues about gaps in technology law. His online paper, "E-Law: Computer Information Systems Law and Systems Operator Liability in 1995," is an extensive work on everything that can make service providers nervous: for instance, what is the legal situation when someone uses a computer system for illegal actions without the owner's knowledge? You'll also find the latest on cases like *Stratton Oakmonth vs. Prodigy* and *Cubby vs. CompuServe* (really!). This is aimed at online publishers, but of interest to anyone who uses an online service.

eWorld on the Web

http://www.eworld.com

The Internet

Instead of just an ad for Apple's *eWorld* commercial online service, you'll find a good sampling of the actual town-like eWorld environment here. This site caters to teachers who have eWorld accounts at home, but want to access Apple's educational resources from the Internet at school. Included are full details about the Apple Classrooms of Tomorrow (ACOT) program, a decade-long research project on the immediate benefits of bringing technology to the classroom, with several reports describing different aspects and the effectiveness of the program. In general, Apple succeeds in presenting a down-to-earth, user-friendly visage for this site, which is what they seem to intend eWorld to be about. And, if you're suitably impressed, you can order a free 30-day trial online. Fine for teachers and kids, or Apple users shopping for a friendly online service.

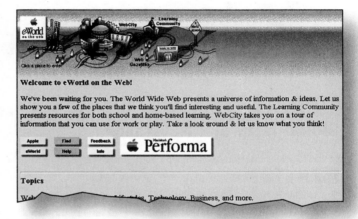

First Virtual Holdings Incorporated

http://www.fv.com/

The Internet

First Virtual is another "money across the Internet" company—those who join up can buy and sell information among other account holders, without worrying about credit card security issues. Your credit card is never sent over the Internet (you have to call an 800 number to enter your credit card number, and FV insists that the numbers are never Internet-accessible). All transactions go through FV's main computers and are checked at your mail address for verification. In other words, you join a "virtual community" of people with whom you can buy and sell freely. On our most recent visits, First Virtual was only for U.S. residents, but was promising worldwide service in the near future.

Galaxy

http://www.einet.net
The Internet

Seldom hyped, this Internet search engine quietly collects thousands of visitors every day, in direct competition with Yahoo (see our review). Its greatest power is its flexibility to work as both a directory (like a phone book) and a Web search robot. You can take the approach of browsing different categories, or you can take the direct approach of finding text relating to a "keyword." Our whimsical search for My Funny Valentine netted a direct hit, calling up all the facts on the song from a Miles Davis discography. Great speed and accuracy, but the interface isn't always clear (beginners may discover they have more choices than they can handle). The advertiser-supported site is offered free of charge by TradeWave (formerly Einet), the publishers of the lesser-known WinWeb and MacWeb browsing software.

Global Network Navigator

http://gnn.com/gnn/gnn.html
The Internet

If the Internet were an airline, this would be O'Hare Airport. (There are tons of gates, it's easy to get lost, and like it or not you'll probably spend a lot of time here.) The Global Network Navigator (owned by America Online) has something for nearly everyone, offering guides to new sites, business listings, and the well-known "Whole Internet Catalog." It will also be the centerpiece of America Online's new Internet service, featuring its unique GNNWorks software. For what it does, it does a great job—giving you directions, moving you around efficiently, and reminding you just how vast the Internet can be. It even has some useful online magazines covering sports, finance, and travel.

The List

http://thelist.com/
The Internet

The List is a database of more than 1,000 Internet access providers around the globe. Almost all the listings have delightful piles of information: connection fees, customer service numbers, e-mail addresses, and the like. You can pull listings by area code or by country, and you can also search by the provider's business name. The majority of the sites are in the U.S., but more than 60 other countries are listed—so if you're in Belarus, Kazakhstan, or Zambia, you might not be totally out of luck. Neat feature: if your provider is listed (and it probably is), you can rate its service and provide notes. And if it isn't listed, submit the doggone thing! User support is one reason why these listings are so extensive and reliable—the Internet community knows the benefit of finding a good provider.

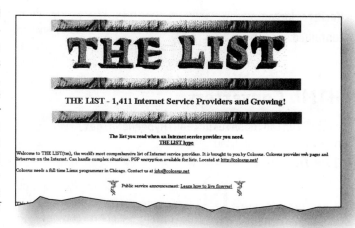

THE LIST

THE LIST - 1,411 Internet Service Providers and Growing!

The list you read when an Internet service provider you need.
THE LIST hype

Welcome to THE LIST(tm), the world's most comprehensive list of Internet service providers. It is brought to you by Colossus. Colossus provides web pages and listservers on the Internet. Can handle complex situations. PGP encryption available for lists. Located at http://colossus.net/

Colossus needs a full time Linux programmer in Chicago. Contact us at jobs@colossus.net

Public service announcement: Learn how to live forever!

Prodigy

http://www.prodigy.com
The Internet

Don't fool yourself: Prodigy is no kid's toy anymore (although this commercial online service still caters to kids). In a short time, Prodigy has evolved into a mature Net access provider, and you get a taste of the new space-age look at this promotional site. Sure, this site exists so they can sell you on their service, but it certainly seems interesting: the graphics-based path is a large, colorful, clickable image, while the text-only path is written as if you were taking a tour of the Prodigy building. Prodigy also does something few other services do: they provide a schematic overview of their whole network, so technically-minded people can see how well they're configured. You'll dig the stunning graphics, but don't expect actual samples of Prodigy information without signing up. Mostly for Net access shoppers.

Hacker's Jargon

http://hyperg.tu-graz.ac.at:80/C404E11E/Cjargon
The Internet

Are you a "card walloper?" Have you ever "kluged" a problem? This glimpse of the hacker subculture (brought to you by the Graz University of Technology) helps you learn its obscure language by listing of words and phrases supposedly used by savvy computer nerds. Despite the tarnished image of hackers as evildoers trying to destroy Western (and Eastern) civilization as we know it, this is really quite harmless stuff. You may even learn useful ways to describe daily tasks: re-booting a

continued

computer is known on PCs as the "three fingered salute" (Ctrl+Alt+Delete) and on all computers as the "Vulcan Nerve Pinch" (from *Star Trek* lore). Despite the characteristically cold interface (hackers don't need pretty pictures), this dictionary-style site may give you a taste of what you've been missing.

HTML Converters

http://union.ncsa.uiuc.edu/HyperNews/get/www/
html/converters.html

The Internet

Nothing fancy here: just a straight-up list of more than 100 sites that will help you convert HTML (HyperText Markup Language, the language of Web file creation) into ICADD, build tables of contents automatically, and perform dozens of other tricks of the Web publishing trade. Sure, you don't know what ICADD is now... but there are plenty of obscure formats and requirements Out There, and if you suddenly feel the need to convert your Web documents, this is a swell place to start. These are utilities you don't know you need until you read about them; and then you can't live without 'em. And who can resist names like the World Wide Web Wonder Widget? A fine public service.

HTML Design Notebook

http://www.w3.org/hypertext/WWW/People/
Connolly/drafts/html-design.html

The Internet

The title may make this sound like a guide to writing HTML, but its true purpose is to explain everything about the workings of the Web, and how it got where it is today. These pages lay out, in great detail, the origins of the Web and the story of its continued development. And it's right from the horse's mouth, as it were: these pages are maintained by the World Wide Web Consortium, a group of people who determine specifications and standards for how data is transmitted via the Web. You'll find everything from conference dates (September finds you in Wagga Wagga, Australia) to personal histories of the chief Web brainiacs. Like the Web itself, this site is full of fascinating information.

HTML Tutorial

http://www.cwru.edu/help/introHTML/toc.html

The Internet

This hypertext help guide from Case Western Reserve University is a sort of "HTML for freshmen" course. (HTML is the code generally used to write Web pages.) It's structured like a term paper, but uses plain English and practices the carefully structured HTML code it preaches. No fancy stuff; just the basics that every college student or Net beginner will need to prepare a first Web page. It's well-organized, and the outline format is handy for quick reference. For example, it explains the difference between logical and physical styles—you should be using <em> and <strong> instead of <I> and <B>. (Got it?) Sure, you can buy a book or an HTML authoring program, but why pay the money when this is free for the reading?

Imagiware

http://imagiware.com

The Internet

Imagiware, a Web publishing company, created this site to advertise their abilities—but it's so fun and useful, you'd never know it was an advertisement. Web versions of standards like Mastermind and Mancala are provided, but there's also some unique tidbits, like Nowwwhere, a 3D first-person puzzle where you can see other players, and the Virtual Image Archive, which has links to thousands of image sites, organized by subject. And since they're here for the business (see, you forgot already, right?), they give details on how you can get them to create such cool toys for you, too. For now, Web games may be far from the excitement of typical computer games (after all, all that stuff has to go over a modem), but these folks are taking a credible shot at it.

InfoSeek

http://www.infoseek.com/
The Internet

If you aren't happy with other Web search sites (too slow, out of date, not reliable), try the free version of this subscription-based site. Casual users may not want to pay to find Web sites, but this service is geared to professionals who want the latest and most in-depth information. InfoSeek's search "robot" regularly grabs text from sites across the Web, and puts them in a precise index. (The down side? Sometimes the descriptions of sites don't make any sense.) The index isn't always perfect: we tried a whimsical search for "Neil Diamond Live at the Hollywood Bowl" and got 16 listings, among them an LA dance club, two references to Monty Python, and the inexplicable "Brief History of the Oregon Bach Festival." (We *thought* "Song Sung Blue" had baroque overtones.) Serious searches bring more luck, but even playing around can yield many hours of fun.

Internet Advertising Resource Guide

http://www.missouri.edu/internet-advertising-guide.html
The Internet

Advertising is obviously becoming a bigger part of the Internet, and the IARG (sounds like "yeaargh!") is a terrific index to this touchy topic. This page doesn't take sides, but brings you everything there is to know. Business people new to the Net will find much to learn here, especially in links like Acceptable Advertising Practices on the Internet. Pay particular attention to this area if you represent a business seeking online revenue for the first time: applying traditional practices to the Net "can result in retaliation through flaming, hate mail, and other acts of hostility." Also helpful: a list of exemplary storefronts. The Web has no Speedy Alka Seltzer figure yet, but can he be far away? Kudos to Hairong Li of the Missouri School of Journalism for managing this fine page.

The Internet Public Library

http://ipl.sils.umich.edu/
The Internet

This thoughtful service from the University of Michigan is a fine starting point for students and educators as they discover the Web's amazing resources. You'll find links to loads of online texts and Web guides, all with a familiar library inter-face (a picture of a library reference desk). High school and college students will appreciate the science and humanities indexes, and even the ability to query an on-duty desk librarian. The Youth Division includes "Molly Whuppie" (an English fairy tale) in Story Hour, along with the chance to go exploring with Dr. Internet. (Real librarians can explore their "spinsterish, bespectacled, shy" image, as portrayed in the movies with resources available here.)

These friendly cyber-librarians have even provided a MOO room for interactive chat—whispered, of course.

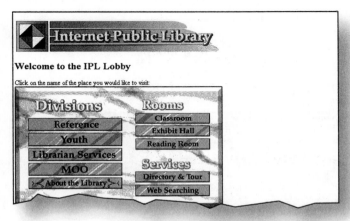

Internet Sleuth

http://www.intbc.com/sleuth/
The Internet

This researcher's fantasy-land is the best we've found of many sites that collect databases and let you search them from simple forms. Subject headings like "Entertainment" lead you to the colossal Musical CD Database, or the wacky Light Bulb Joke Collection. Then you type in a few keywords and search each of them and gather your findings. For more serious research, you can peruse dozens of cate-gories to find more than 200 databases. Instead of jumping across the Web to find just the right database, you can save a lot of time by searching from here. Some of the commercial search sites may not be thrilled with this short-cut, but for now, it's a valuable service.

Internet Society

http://info.isoc.org
The Internet

The *Internet Society* exists to maintain and extend the development and availability of the Net. Since nobody owns the Internet, nobody dictates order; the

WELCOME TO THE INTERNET SOCIETY, Internauts!

The Internet Society is a non-governmental International Organization for global cooperation and coordination for the Internet and its internetworking technologies and applications.

A NSF Press Release on the new implementation of the new NIC Domain Registration Fee Policy is available here.

Society hopes to keep the anarchy organized through discussion and consensus. One of their biggest concerns is standards: you can read their lengthy discussion called "What's In A Standard?," which covers their thinking on how data is passed back and forth, all the way down to how your e-mail address is written on your business cards. You'll find information about ethics, yearly conferences, and more; you'll also learn about the secret handshake and the special decoder ring. (Just kidding.) Some Web experience and technical knowledge will be helpful here.

Dan Kegel's ISDN Page

http://alumni.caltech.edu/~dank/isdn/
The Internet

ISDN (Integrated Services Digital Network) is an all-digital telecommunications service that allows (among other things) voice and data calls on the same phone line. And Dan Kegel is wild about ISDN, faithfully gathering every scrap of information he can find to promote its development as a worldwide standard. Judging by the volumes of material Kegel has gathered, it's safe to say ISDN has

reached prime time. As if the FAQ provided weren't already a wealth of information, the site also provides specifics, such as how to get an ISDN connection in your area, and what software/hardware you need (an ISDN "terminal adapter," for one). Still, we recommend a modicum of computer expertise to understand all of that phone company gibberish.

Lycos: the Catalog of the Internet

http://www.lycos.com/
The Internet

When you're ready to experience this colossal search server, block out a few hours: Lycos can be addictive. Few other Internet search tools are as likely to create such a hypnotizing stream of cyberspace consciousness. Every word that every Web author writes has a chance of showing up in this catalog, no matter the context. For a test, we chose the name of a vice president who also knew a lot of big words: "Spiro Agnew" dredged up 726 hits, including Agnew's famous description of the media as "nattering nabobs of negativism," and the news that you can rearrange the letters of his name to read "A Power Sign." Lycos's depth and pinpoint accuracy is unmatched, and though it may intimidate some beginners, it's truly a "launch pad into the unknown."

Minitel

http://www.minitel.fr
The Internet

If you think Internet commerce is still a twinkle in Al Gore's eye, visit the French online network that's flourished since George Bush played second fiddle. Minitel offers a staggering 25,000 online services (mostly databases) that each cost a few francs to access. At our last visit, Net users could demo the service for free, and we discovered a slow, clumsy telnet (text-only) interface with loads of information in several languages. (If you don't already have a telnet program on your computer, you can download a free one here.) On our last visit, our search for "hamburger" under business services struck out (no ugly Americans allowed here!); we did successfully browse through the French telephone directory. The antiquated interface makes it awkward for sophisticated Web users, but surfing Paris has its charms nonetheless.

NCSA Mosaic

http://www.ncsa.uiuc.edu/SDG/
Software/Mosaic/NCSAMosaicHome.html
The Internet

There's a chance you've checked into the Mosaic for Windows home page to get software or find help, but have you really explored it? A more thorough browse will find useful FAQs on nagging messages like "Failed DNS Lookup" and "Socket Connection Refused." The most useful hidden nuggets are the links to

continued

NCSA Mosaic
continued

other software, which enable you to view formats like Quicktime, PostScript, and MPEG. If you've ever spent 15 minutes downloading an audio or video file only to have it crash, you'll probably find relief here. Another hidden gold mine is the "What's New" page, a great way of finding out about brand new sites. Mosaic may have faded a bit now that Netscape and company have come along to take the browser market by storm, but don't forget that the whole Web revolution started here.

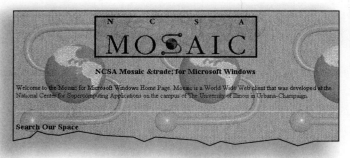

Netiquette Home Page

http://rs6000.adm.fau.edu/rinaldi/netiquette.html

The Internet

If you're new to the Net, you know how grouchy old-timers can be. And if you're one of those grouchy old-timers, you know how quickly newbies can turn cyberspace into cybersnarl. Both sides will be glad to see Arlene Rinaldi's Netiquette Home Page (subtitled "I'm NOT the Miss Manners of the Net"). She offers complete, accurate, good advice on the niceties of everything from e-mail to newsgroups. (For instance: read the list of frequently asked questions, or FAQs, before posting a question yourself.) Most helpful to new users is the World Wide Web section, which provides tips for the conscientious Web site creator. If everyone followed the advice provided here, the Internet would be a much happier place indeed.

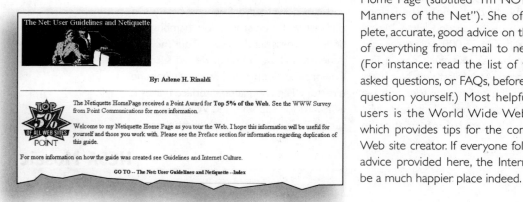

NetPhone

http://www.emagic.com/netphone
The Internet

Your Macintosh could soon be "ringing off the hook" with this software in hand. *NetPhone* enables most Mac users with a microphone and a Net connection to place calls to other NetPhone users across the world, and talk as long as they like for no extra cost (beyond the cost of your Net account). You can get a free online demo of the software to believe it for yourself. Audio quality varies; you probably won't hear a pin drop (sometimes it's more like a faraway AM radio station). For fun, you can visit "NetPubs," where NetPhone users gather to shoot the breeze. In our travels so far, this is the best effort we've found to creatively integrate Web sites with the Internet phone calling concept. Of course, several others are in the works.

Netscape Communications

http://www.netscape.com/
The Internet

Netscape *Communications* may be the future 800-pound gorilla of Internet browsing software. This fast-changing page tells you about the latest improvements to the software, lets you download a free version, and offers help on how to use it. Netscape's developers are also leading the charge toward secure credit card transactions on the Net, so expect to find out the latest on Web-based buying and selling. Even if you don't use Netscape, you'll discover useful resources like the terse What's New page (not to be confused with competitor NCSA Mosaic's page of the same name) and the popular What's Cool list of sites favored by Netscape staffers. Also useful is the Internet White Pages listing, which offers help in tracking down the e-mail address of "that special someone." Well worth the visit.

Newbie No More

`http://www.ccnet.com/~lva`

The Internet

This basic guide designed for "newbies" answers basic questions by linking you to the Web's definitive help resources. (If you don't know what a "newbie" is, you're probably one yourself: it's a mildly

Web Page

*Charles Seiter defines a newbie as...
A faintly derogatory term for users in their first months on the internet, employed freely by people who have been on the system one week longer.

derogatory nickname for users who are brand new to the Internet.) Questions like "What are some good browsers and how do I obtain them?" will take you to the popular W3 Clients Page, which lists browsers you can try. Topics are organized by subject, from e-mail to listservs, and the page includes a glossary of Internet terms such as IRC (internet relay chat). Despite the crisp organization, the greenest of users may still wish for more layman's language here; it may not fully erase the specter of "newbieness."

NeWWW

`http://grafton.dartmouth.edu:8023/`

The Internet

Even if your SATs didn't get you into the Ivy league, you can still get the Dartmouth view of the Net. NeWWW is a useful bi-weekly Web guide offering reviews of about 30 selected sites, plus feature articles on topics like the perils of e-mail or Web pornography. This is only published during the school year, so don't expect any guidance for your summer Net

browsing. Articles and descriptions of sites are student-written; who else has time to fritter away hours on the Web? We like their choices; it's a useful resource for those in and out of ivory towers. If nothing else, you can impress fellow surfers with lines like "My friends at Dartmouth suggested I scrutinize this Net locality."

O'Reilly and Associates

`http://www.ora.com`

The Internet

The people who created the Global Network Navigator offer this site for beginning Web publishers. Even though O'Reilly and Associates is now a part of America Online, you still get support for their popular *WebSite* software and helpful ideas for Web publishing. You can even get *WebSite* for a 60-day free evaluation to help decide if you're up to the task. For other technical tips, *Ora.com* magazine offers excerpts from books they've published, covering topics like "Clickable Image Maps" and "PGP: The Privacy Wars." The site isn't updated very often, so don't expect a steady stream of new information showing up here. But if you're just interested in getting started at creating a new site or setting up your own server, this is a useful place to scout around.

PC Lube and Tune

`http://pclt.cis.yale.edu/pclt/`

The Internet

Finally, a palatable use of the "Information Highway" metaphor: a virtual service station on the Web, which offers repairs, maps, and gas from a wise computer scientist at Yale. Howard Gilbert warns he "does not speak for Yale University... and has yet to find anyone else who does." But he reflects well on his employer with sage advice in articles like "The Storm before the COM," explaining how to avoid the pitfalls of COM ports on PCs (where you plug in your mouse or modem). No glitzy graphics here—after all, this is a pit stop. And Howard is a busy guy, so don't expect this thing to get updated every week. But clear language and charm make it a recommended stop for PC users seeking some friendly advice.

Qualcomm Eudora

`http://www.qualcomm.com/quest/QuestMain.html`

The Internet

You may already have tried the free version of Qualcomm's popular *Eudora* mail program for Mac or PC (it's known as the hands-down market leader in Internet mail software). And surprisingly, a basic version of this time-tested software can still be had for free. But a visit here will tickle your conscience (or your envy) to pay for Eudora Pro, a full-featured package targeted for business users. If you haven't tried Eudora Light (the freeware version), you can download it here and get surprisingly clear, cheerful resources (100-page manual, mailing list, online feedback). If you send e-mail—and honestly, who on the Net doesn't?—this is a sensible stop.

RealAudio

```
http://www.RealAudio.com
```
The Internet

Web users weary of waiting four minutes to download a ten-second sound clip will be all ears for this promo site. The ground-breaking *Real Audio* software lets PC or Mac users play sounds in real time, just like playing a radio (almost). A free sample version of the software is available here, and you can try it right away by listening to ABC or NPR radio reports. We're particularly fascinated with the software's flexibility; you can jump from the start of a one-hour broadcast to any point in the file with a single click, with only a slight delay (great for the State of the Union address). The implications of non-linear Net broadcasting are mind-boggling, to say the least. And why say the least?

The Smiley Dictionary

```
http://olympe.polytechnique.fr/~violet/Smileys/
```
The Internet

The :-) has become an international symbol for the "smiley," as it's called. (Such symbols are also known as "emoticons.") Frenchman Pierre Violet is an expert on this most complicated subject, and has compiled a useful dictionary that should clear up any confusion. According to Violet, :-) is "your basic smiley," while :-x is a "kiss-kiss." (The French no doubt use this one a lot.) Then there are "Celebrity Smileys," like the ever-popular "Uncle Sam." =) :-) Granted, it makes the rest of your punctuation a nightmare, but it can also help you avoid those feared "flames" (a nasty, insulting message) when your online jokes are taken the wrong way. With the disarming smiley in your bag of tricks, nobody's likely to take offense. A fun site, especially for kids.

Specter: WebWatch

```
http://www.xensei.com/users/janos/specter/
```
The Internet

Windows users who are serious about the Web will love the clever utility offered here: give it a list of your favorite sites, and it automatically checks them to see if there's anything new. (This site lets you download this small Windows utility for a free evaluation.) For a test, we fed a two-month old NCSA "What's New" list to the program, and it quickly scanned all the sites and created a list of sites to re-visit. Put it to work for you, and you're more likely to find fresh information in your precious cruising time. The online documentation is brief, but that's not really an oversight on their part: the program is just easy to use. And, if you have any trouble, a list of frequently asked questions and known bugs (with fixes) is available. One of the best Web utilities we've seen.

Talker

http://www2.infi.net/talker/

The Internet

*T*alker is a Web-based chat system, bypassing the need for any special software other than your Web browser. Co-created by Web guru Glenn Davis (of Cool Site of the Day fame), it enables you to chat with other people, represented by interesting or silly icons (animals, cartoon characters, and so on) that they select on entry. Don't expect discussions on heady topics like the federal budget deficit. You're more likely to find incessant messages like "Where are you, Poppy?" from people simply seeking online interaction. We'd love to see these types of sites overcome the inherent linearity of chat rooms, in which responses to your messages come only after a stream of responses from unrelated conversations. Still, the ability for savvy users to enter HTML commands (the language of the Web which allows use of pictures and variable text) makes this site a technical achievement of note.

Texture Land

http://www.europa.com/~yyz/textures/textures.html

The Internet

*T*exture Land donates free background images to art-starved Web creators. (It's the equivalent of "public domain" writing or music clips.) And my, what a feast! Chris Pearce's page offers over 100 "normal textures"—such as rock, weed, and brick backgrounds. And that doesn't count the oddball textures available, all free for a click of a mouse. The wildest? A hypnotic, mind-bending, blue swirl. Woo! Don't expect tons of state-of-the-art stuff here—it's free, after all. And don't forget, textured backgrounds are only useful for browsers that can read them. But don't limit yourself to Web creation, either—a lot of these textures would be great for any art project.

Texture Land!

Where do you want to go today?

Normal Textures *Lite*
One page from the six that make up the normal textures section. Visit a mirror to see them all!

Trace Online

http://trace.guinet.com/

The Internet

This unique service from the U.K. lets users register possessions with their serial numbers or "tags," so they can be traced in the event they're lost or stolen. So, in this brave new online world, you can: 1) check to see if something you're buying is "hot"; 2) search for your own lost items; or 3) post public notices of missing items. You can search the database by tag ID or by keyword, or you can search by e-mail address (in case you lost track of everything you registered). Your cost? Zilcho. The site's advertisers pay your way. To test the service, we successfully registered an autographed Bill Russell basketball lost in 1969. (True story! We cried for days!) This may or may not catch on as a service, but it's another fascinating use of the Web.

Trojan Room Coffee Machine

http://www.cl.cam.ac.uk/coffee/coffee.html

The Internet

This is simply 24-hour, 365-day-per-year video coverage of the coffee pot in the University of Cambridge Computer Lab in England. The shot is updated once per second for instant transmission around the world. If you have to ask why, you're just not getting into the spirit of the Web. To be honest, the original intent was to let the building's denizens check the pot before climbing two flights of stairs to the coffee room. Once the local computers were hooked up, the site leaked onto the Net, and the coffee pot became a celebrity in its own right. (No movie deals so far, however.) This was one of the earliest of the silly Web cams, and somehow it's still compelling.

WAIS, Inc.

http://www.wais.com/

The Internet

Tour the company that "pioneered online publishing" with its popular search software called WAIS (rhymes with "chase"). The company now belongs to America Online, but its WAISserver software for Web searches will keep its name and live on as a major player in Net publishing. As you might expect, you use the search software to find information on the site. As a bonus, the database links you to WAIS databases across the Web, giving you a shot at searching for reams of valuable information on a broad range of topics. For example, by entering the keyword "congress," you get a list of WAIS database covering the latest bills in Congress. And for potential Web publishers (especially those considering using a WAIS database), this is one of the richest archives of technical information we've found.

The Well

http://www.well.com/

The Internet

The Well is the best-known small online community in America, a pioneer service based in Sausalito and stocked with California's famed free-thinkers. (The Well's home page calls it an evolving experiment in virtual community.) This site gives very limited access to outside Web surfers, including info on discussion groups and other home pages by Well members. (For full access, you can become a subscriber). For example, you get a little taste of their Mirrorshades conference, a discussion dedicated to tracking culture of the Net and media coverage thereof: "If it's in Mirrorshades, it'll be science fiction in a year... in three years teenage girls will be wearing it... in five years it'll be 'discovered.'" It's unfortunate you can't see any of the actual discussion (which is the hook to get you to subscribe, of course). Regardless, this is worth a look-see; zero hard news and an infinite flood of ideas.

Worlds Chat

http://www.worlds.net

The Internet

Worlds Chat wants you to select a 3D character (or "avatar"), walk it around in a virtual space station, and chat with other users who are doing the same. Sound too good to be true? It's still in a testing phase, and has glitches, but it's a wild idea that's bound to catch on mostly with 3D enlightened teenagers. Worlds, Inc. gives PC users the software freely here, but plans to charge other Web providers to set up Worlds Chat servers. Block out some time to download the software (3 megabytes) and configure your "avatar," and don't try it without a pretty powerful computer. Since it's pushing the envelope on the Web, this can be tricky to use. Still, if you're adventurous and patient, you can try your hand at becoming a handsome stud, a fish, or a toaster oven in this alternate universe.

WWW Viewer Test Page

`http://www-dsed.llnl.gov/documents/WWWtest.html`
The Internet

This page helps you make sure you have the viewers you need to use all the WWW has to offer. For example, you need a viewer to be able to listen to sound files (maybe they should call it a hearer). Here you can push the "Test"

WWW VIEWER TEST PAGE

Select the TEST buttons on the **right** to test your viewers. If you do not have a viewer, or if it is installed incorrectly, then you need to go to the appropriate subsections. Select the text on the **left** to go to the appropriate subsections and download a viewer. The objects closer to the top of the list are more generic than those near the bottom. There are discussions and viewers for U~~~~~~~~~~~PCs in each subsection:

button next to AU audio. If you hear the sound, you have the viewer and it's installed properly. If not, you then click on the AU audio link and get info on how to get the viewer you need (and download it immediately, in most cases). The test files are mostly mercifully short (the MPEG video clip, for example, is only 100 KB). You can test the capabilities of your e-mail reader, too, by having the robot send you mail. An excellent, and helpful, Web gadget from the kids at Lawrence Livermore labs.

World Wide Web Worm

`http://www.cs.colorado.edu/home/mcbryan/WWWW.html`
The Internet

The Web is one of the few human endeavors (other than fishing) in which a worm is a good thing. The World Wide Web Worm (WWWW) is good enough to handle a staggering 2 million searches a month. The stark interface asks for keywords, a limit on the number of matches you want to see, and lets you choose slower or faster search methods. Compared to other Web search software,

you might get fewer hits because WWWW only indexes hypertext references, the highlighted references to other pages or sites in Web documents. You may not get the most organized list from this type of search, but it's fast and does some things other searches won't. For a particular kind of search, this is one of the best tools available, and (as of our last visit) is still non-commercial.

Yahoo

http://www.yahoo.com/

The Internet

Yahoo has become the accepted authority on the size and breadth of the Web. This terrific index lists tens of thousands of Internet sites in categories ranging from African Art to Animal Rights; users can stroll category by category (kind of like reading the dictionary cover to cover), or search the database by key words. The lists feature short classifications of the sites, and are generally dependable despite a few outdated references from time to time. Many of the sites listed are less than stellar, but if it's on the Net somewhere, there's a good chance it's listed here. Started by two Stanford whiz kids, Yahoo has grown into a commercial enterprise with considerable financial backing, so look for it to remain a top player on the Web.

The Year 2000 Information Center

http://arganet.tenagra.com/cgi-bin/clock.cgi

The Internet

The arrival of the millennium is expected to give fits to many computers and software programs, as the "chickens come home to roost" for short-sighted programmers who calculated years based on two digits instead of four. Many people expect problems with the obvious software, like spreadsheet applications or payroll databases, but the Information Center wants everyone to know the trouble will be deeper than that. Using software that simulates the turn of the year 1999, they've found that few system-level programs "know" that the year 2000 is a leap year (and hey, probably 85 percent of data processing officials don't know this, either). And consider financial projection software that gives estimates for sales five years in the future: it's already in trouble! This is good reading for gurus, futurists, and accountants.

The current time is: 20:01:22 GMT Friday, September 29, 1995

Time remaining until Jan. 1, 2000 (GMT):
4 years, 93 days, 3 hours, 58 minutes, 38 seconds.

The Year 2000 Information Center

The date change to the year 2000 is less than 1700 days away! For many computer and software systems, the year 2000 will bring a host of problems related to software programs that record the year using only the last two digits.

In his September 6, 1993 ComputerWorld article DOOMSDAY 2000, Peter de Jager describes how this problem can trigger fatal errors in mission-critical systems. This web site has been created to provide a forum for making information available about the year 2000 problem and for the discussion

web gadgets

The Amazing Fish Cam!

http://www.netscape.com/fishcam/fishcam.html
Web Gadgets

The Amazing Fish Cam is a camera (two cameras, actually) trained on a very nice tropical aquarium. Every five minutes a fresh (or maybe saltwater) image is posted for access by Internauts everywhere; if you want, you can get fast-loading 10 KB versions, updated every 30 seconds. For Netscape users, there's the continuously-refreshing fish cam, a great example of "server-push animation," which is explained in gleeful detail here. Netscape users can also explore the secret Ctrl+Alt+F key combination. Even the stodgy *Economist* likes it: "In its audacious uselessness—and that of thousands of ego trips like it—lie the seeds of the Internet revolution." If you're lucky, you'll spot the green moray eel or the (no kidding) tomato clown fish. If not, well, you've still had a relaxing Internet moment.

The Amazing Parrot-Cam

http://www.can.net/parrotcam.html
Web Gadgets

You just can't get enough of real-time cameras connected to the Web—which is good, since there seem to be so many. This one is pointed at Webster, the pet parrot of Consolidated Access and Networks in Canada (yes, it sounds a lot like the famous Fish Cam, which is acknowledged). He may not be in view—an "about" file explains that, while the cage is Webster's home, the door is left open. Webster likes to climb on top of his cage (out of camera view), fly over to people's desks, and chew papers and things to pieces, so you might not see him. The office even provides a number to call if you think Webster is ill (since thousands of people viewing the page might notice first). But he likes to hang upside down sometimes, so don't be alarmed.

Bat House
Temperature Plot

http://nyx10.cs.du.edu:8001/~jbuzbee/
bat_house.html

Web Gadgets

Yes, this site actually plots the current temperature inside the Buzbee Bat House—even though Buzbee's Bat House is batless. Perhaps we should start at the beginning. Our hero, Jim Buzbee, "was crossing the Nile... and was fascinated by the sight of bats skimming the surface of the river, snatching up the insects." Upon his return to Denver, Buzbee thought it would be cool to have some bats of his own, and so erected a bat house in his backyard, assuming that the bats would move right in. Well, they didn't, and the book that Jim's wife bought him said that temperature was important to home-shopping bats. So Jim set his computer up to sample the temperature, and now it's published for the world, on a 30-minute-interval plot. Jim has a *very* patient family.

The Electric Postcard

http://postcards.www.media.mit.edu/Postcards/

Web Gadgets

The Electric Postcard enables you to send "postcards" via e-mail and the Web. You choose from a variety of cute, amusing, and strange postcard graphics, ranging from Claude Monet to Vietnam images to one that uses current Boston weather. Then you write a message on the card, which can include text, images, and even links to other Web sites. Preview the final product, and then send it to an unsuspecting friend or co-worker. (They're notified by e-mail, and must have Web access to receive and claim the postcard.) When this site was created, there must have been several other Webmasters around the globe muttering "Now why didn't *I* think of that?!" to themselves. A simple idea that's a lot of fun.

Electric Postcards@SIGGRAPH

To **send** a postcard go to the SIGGRAPH Postcard Rack.

To **pickup** a postcard go to the **Pick-up Window**.

The **SIGGRAPH Postcard Rack** has a huge collection of fresh computer images from the SIGGRAPH 95 program. You pick the card you like, write your message, and send it off. The recipient will be notified by email that a card has been sent and to claim it at the **Pick-up Window**.

Cards are held at the **Pick-up Window** for three weeks after they are sent. In addition, they are held for two weeks after they are claimed (if they are viewed additional times, they are held longer).

E-minder

http://www.netmind.com/e-minder/e-minder.html
Web Gadgets

Users with porous minds will appreciate this free service: fill out a form here now, and get an e-mail reminder on the date you specify. Remember birthdays and anniversaries with ease; or if you have no shame, use it to remind other people of *your* birthday. The system lets you enter the day of the event, and how many days early you want the reminder (so you'll have plenty of time to buy that present). You can even have it keep the notification permanently, so that long after you've lost track of this site, it'll still send you a cheerful reminder message every year. Simple, safe, and effective. Good fun, but you still have to go out and buy the present yourself.

feet cam

http://www.dcs.qmw.ac.uk/~nickbk/web_camera/
Web Gadgets

This is one of those goofball experimental video sites, like the Trojan Room Coffee Machine. (And what *is* it with the British, anyway?) In this case, a doctoral student named Nick at Queen

Mary and Westfield College in London has pointed a video camera at the feet of passersby in the QMW lounge. Every five minutes you get a new set of "arch" rivals. If there's nothing interesting on view from the live feed, take a look in the extensive galleries. They include images from the feet cam, like Geekay (size 7.5) and Mike (a whopping 11 in green sneakers), as well as contributions of interesting foot art from visitors. Some frightening British food (called "fairy cake") got left on the floor at one point, and there's a scary picture of that, too. Extra-long downloads, but an amusing result.

Figlet Service

http://www.inf.utfsm.cl/cgi-bin/figlet
Web Gadgets

This page takes any text you give it and converts it into a cartoony ASCII graphics font. What this means is letters (three to ten lines tall) are drawn up out of basic keyboard characters, like # or *. This is useful mostly for putting BIG text (like signatures) into computer media that don't normally support graphics (like e-mail). Traditionally, this process is extremely tedious, but with this page, you type your text, choose a style from the 100+ fonts available, and press a button. Your graphics are displayed faster than you can say "cool signature, dude." This sounds simplistic, but check out the font library, where you'll be astounded by the ingenious variety. (It helps to squint with some of them.)

The Great Web Canadianizer

http://www.io.org/~themaxx/canada/can.html

Web Gadgets

Many Canadians are concerned about American cultural dominance. This silly site takes direct action against the "hosers" (that's Canadian parlance for "Americans," it seems) by taking the average "hosehead" page and "Canadianizing" it. Beauty, eh? You just enter the URL of your favorite site, and this gadget "translates" the page by adding well-placed burps and back bacon references. For example, a visit to the White House now begins with "G'day, eh, and welcome to the House of Commons." Then you can link to "The Hosehead's Cabinet." Beauty, eh?

Some of the funniest results can be obtained by aiming the translator at serious Canadian sites, like the Molson brewery ("carin' for your brewski BURRRP! Scuse me eh?").

Interactive Model Railroad

http://rr-vs.informatik.uni-ulm.de/rr/

Web Gadgets

Who better to make the trains run on time than a German? This site actually enables surfers anywhere to control and operate a model train set (in a funny Bavarian model village) at Germany's University of Ulm. You watch the results in real-time video. "The railroad waits for your command. You can drive a train from one platform to another. Unless somebody else is faster than you. In that case,

continued

The Great Web Canadianizer continued

your command is lost and you have to try again." Like most Web gadgets, this process turns out to be something of a technical challenge, and propeller-heads will enjoy the description and diagram of how it's done. Mostly we tried (unsuccessfully) to engineer a train wreck. Still in development: visitors remote-control an actual New York subway car.

Paul's Hot Tub Status

http://hamjudo.com/cgi-bin/hottub
Web Gadgets

When we last checked in to this site, the hot tub was "nice and warm at about 98 degrees Fahrenheit." The tub—an "Esther Williams Spa" to be exact—belongs to Paul Haas of Ypsilanti, Michigan, and the temperature reading that you will see here is programmed automatically via a complicated electronic system that we, frankly, don't understand. But, this spa is so packed with gadgets (like the ozone generator that Paul uses instead of chlorine) that we just couldn't resist. While Paul sounds a little geeky (he programmed all this stuff himself, from scratch, using software like a "finger server"), he also sounds like a bit of a party animal: his "octagonal whirlpool spa" can "hold eight people comfortably, although it has held many more people than that in the past."

PhoNETic

http://www.soc.qc.edu:80/phonetic
Web Gadgets

This amusing engine converts your phone number into letters, which you can scan to see if they happen to spell a catchy phrase. So if your phone number is, for example, 244-5375, you can proudly tell your friends to "call me at BIG-JERK." (Do *not* call this number; we made it up by typing it into the words-to-numbers translator.) Or you can use the handy new dictionary-checking module, so that the gadget filters out nonsense words (warning: a lot of numbers don't translate into real words, but that's OK: you can shut off the spell-checker). Shakespeare it ain't, but it's hard not to like. We also enjoyed the historical explanation for why Q and Z are missing, and why the numbers one and zero don't correspond to letters.

San Diego BayCam

http://live.net/sandiego/

Web Gadgets

ho needs a window in your office? This site is connected to a TV camera pointing out at San Diego Bay, which is generally jammed with picturesque watercraft ranging from sailboats to aircraft carriers. This is one of those useless sites, but it's a nice relaxing one. It's particularly scenic at sunset, when the camera and the digitizer do a creditable job of capturing the subtle reds and pinks, and the new "server-push" animation puts the harbor traffic into motion (sort of). You can even get the current weather conditions, which are usually monotonously perfect. This site also offers various San Diego information links (a lot of yachting), and links to other video feeds (like the much less restful I-5 JamCam), but the real attraction is the view.

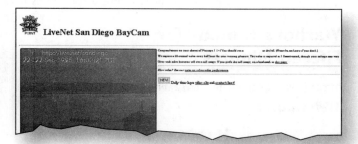

Talk to my Cat

http://queer.slip.cs.cmu.edu/cgi-bin/talktocat

Web Gadgets

ittsburgh computer engineer Michael Witbrock hopes you'll talk to his cat long-distance. He has a voice synthesizer hooked up to his computer; type in your message, and the computer (apparently) says it aloud. There's no guarantee the cat will be awake, of course, or even in the room. But if he's alert and attentive, you might amuse him. What's really interesting about this site, besides that fact that it's kind of fun to think up something clever for your long-distance oration, is the list of the last 30 messages to the cat from previous visitors. When we visited, the public had just made statements ranging from "Here Kitty kitty" to "Putty wanna beer?" to "I like fat women," all at a rate of 15 messages per hour. Poor cat.

URouLette

http://kuhttp.cc.ukans.edu/cwis/organizations/
kucia/uroulette/uroulette.html
Web Gadgets

Hate to make decisions? Play URouLette. One click on the floating roulette wheel and you're spun off to a Web site chosen at random by the URouLette program. (URL—get it?) Don't like the result? Go back and spin again. On our last visit, our first spin led us to the photo of a generic New York research scientist. His collar was open, but that was about it for thrills. The next spin led us to the Harvard-Smithsonian Theoretical Astrophysics Group home page, a star-crossed selection at best. Next was the Willie Nelson fan page. You see what we mean by "random." But as the URouLette home page cheerfully notes, sometimes you spin to a defunct server, sometimes you hit pay dirt. In other words, welcome to the Web. Please, no wagering.

Warhol's Famous for Fifteen Minutes

http://www.grapevine.com/warhol/warhol.htm
Web Gadgets

It seems as if every 15 minutes we're reminded that Andy Warhol predicted that someday everyone would be famous for 15 minutes. This site chips away at the pile of billions who have yet to have their moment of fame, by offering up a new personal home page every—you guessed it—15 minutes. The site couldn't be simpler: just a few lines and a head shot of Andy, looking (as always) as if he's answering the door after being awakened from a late-afternoon nap. Click on Andy's face and you're automatically zapped off to the page of the moment. Naturally, not all these pages are winners, a fact of which Warhol would no doubt be proud.

Wearable Wireless Webcam

http://www-white.media.mit.edu/~steve/netcam.html

Web Gadgets

This page shows us Steve Mann's *exact* view of the world, thanks to the helmet that covers his eyes, but has cameras mounted on the front. The added bonus is that he also carries a transmitter that sends the pictures to his Web server. We see what he sees. This isn't Virtual Reality—it's, well, Actual Reality. For those times the Webcam isn't active (to rest Steve's aching neck, presumably), you can view the last few images he captured, or see some sequences from previous days (like the campus fire on the day he was chosen for Cool Site of the Day—which was *dismissed as chance*). This is a truly odd site, sort of cinema verité crossed with William Gibson. As Steve puts it, "It's fun being a cyborg!"

Wearable Wireless Webcam

Number of computers watching Wearable Wireless Webcam to date: **0047808**

Put yourself in my shoes and see the world from my perspective. Pictured above is an old communications antenna array on copper [...] used. Now I use the "visualfilter". Through the VisualFilter, I perceive my surroundings by [...] the world [...]

Web Voyeur

http://www.eskimo.com/%7Eirving/web-voyeur/

Web Gadgets

The Web-Cam sites that are popping up in cyberspace these days offer a funny kind of satisfaction. Even though these video feeds rarely show anything of the slightest use or interest (unlike, say, *Baywatch*), they're strangely fascinating in a way that normal television can never be: it's cool to be able, on a whim, to see what's happening *right now* at some remote location. This Web site offers no fancy-schmancy page graphics, just links to live video from an enormous variety of places around the world. From Hollywood and Vine to Germany, from Norway to Stockholm to Hawaii, this monster collection of links includes a "page put together by a fellow who claims to be so concerned about ghosts that he's set up FIVE cameras under his bed to take pictures at regular intervals."

What Miles Is Watching On TV!

http://www.csua.berkeley.edu/~milesm/ontv.html
Web Gadgets

Why on earth would we care what a slightly demented-looking engineering student at U.C. Berkeley is currently watching on TV (instead of studying)? Hmm. Is he getting better reception than we are? In fact, this site actually just offers a sequence of stills from Miles's TV, which can get confusing when Miles channel-surfs (which he does habitually), or even a little disturbing, like when images from denture commercials are taken out of context. Nor does Miles advertise himself as some kind of arbiter of TV taste (he doesn't seem to care if we like what he watches or not). So why *do* we care? Well, it's just interesting. Even mildly habit-forming. Perhaps it has something to do with the Jungian collective unconscious... well, let's not go overboard. We just like TV, that's all.

WorldCam

http://www.ovd.com/
Web Gadgets

"The Planet's Moving Picture Show," is an online collection of video clips, server-push images, and live feeds. It all looks and feels sort of like a very hip art house movie theater. WorldCam has created a theater for viewing live feeds from a whole world of Web cams and other online video in their "CamCorner," and a cool handful of viewer-submitted movies stock the "Screening Room." The "Video Assist" page provides links to film festivals, schools, and studios. This site puts designer school gloss on such diamonds-in-the-rough as "Car Wash Cam" and, of course, "The Amazing Fishcam." Take a break from that darn coffee pot and see what the rest of the Net is doing with *their* cameras, or upload what you've done with yours.

Kids

Let's be honest: what other generation of six-year-olds has been able to write poems and have them published to an audience of millions worldwide? Quite a number of pages for kids are based on writing stories for the Web, or hooking up with "pixel pals" around the world. Science is popular, too: sites like "Nye Labs" and "You Can With Beakman and Jax" put the test tubes right in kids' hands—virtually speaking, of course. We've put parenting sites in this chapter, too, because sites like the "Family Surfboard" can be shared by the whole family. And of course, this way parents can sneak a look at all the fun kid sites.

kids and teens
kids and teens

Aunt Annie's Craft Page

`http://mineral.galleries.com/annie/auntannie.htm`
Kids and Teens

Reviving that most typical of summer camp activities, Aunt Annie drums up a new project each week. On our last visit, she was making flexagons—brightly

colored, folded-paper polygons that change faces as they're flexed. One moment, three faces; the next, six! After rating the project's hardship ("average to difficult"), ol' Annie lays out her recipe: "Computer paper, scissors, ruler, and glue," and the ability to follow step-by-step directions. Other projects have included home-made stamps, stencils, and paper appliqués. Annie also has a shareware program, available here, that promises more cutting, coloring, and pasting enjoyment. Hey, you can nearly taste the Elmer's Glue!

The Canadian Kids Page

`http://www.onramp.ca/~lowens/107kids.htm`
Kids and Teens

This page provides all kinds of great links to cool Canadian sites for kids (and some non-Canadian sites, too! Look for the maple-leaf flag icon to find out which is which). When we visited, we took some cartooning lessons and learned how to draw Yo on his bicycle. Or, visitors can link to The Noodlehead Network to find out about videos made by and about kids. Good topical lists on subjects like computer camps and Internet chatting for kids. Updated and rearranged regularly, with new lists displayed on the home page and old lists stored at the Canadian Kids Page Archives. A great resource for parents and educators, too.

Crayola

http://www.crayola.com/crayola/
Kids and Teens

This colorful corporate site will stir a lot of memories for baby-boomers. The "How Are Crayons Made?" puts it this way: "We start with the basic crayon ingredients: color pigment and paraffin wax. The wax is heated in a large kettle to 240 degrees Fahrenheit." (Isn't that the same recipe for lipstick?) In "Crayola History," we learned that Binney and Smith made paint pigments, slate pencils, and "dustless chalk" before plunging into the bright world of wax crayons—their first box of eight crayons sold for a nickel in 1903. Some of the old favorite colors like bittersweet and periwinkle make cameos here, amid other fantastic trivia: in 1962, Crayola changed the name of its crayon color "flesh" to "peach," "recognizing that not everyone's skin is the same shade." Also includes stain removal tips!

CyberKids

http://www.mtlake.com/cyberkids/
Kids and Teens

CyberKids is a quarterly online magazine by kids and for kids. It offers fiction, art, and news articles, like "The First African-American Woman in Space," by correspondents aged 7 to 16. The writing and art, both impressive, are the products of a series of contests sponsored by Mountain Lake Software and Turner Home Entertainment; on our last visit, we found a story about a time-traveler who accidentally altered history by preventing the attack on skater Nancy Kerrigan. Besides the thrill of being published on the Web, contest entrants can vie for software, books, and cash prizes. CyberKids is put together with wit and what seems like very little adult meddling. (The comments section is full of every possible variation on the words "this page is cool.") This should be a popular destination for preteens and early adolescents.

CyberKids is a cool place for kids to learn and have fun. Our free online magazine contains stories and artwork created by kids. Have fun doing puzzles, playing games, and more. Tell the world about yourself and find keypals from around the globe in CyberKids Interactive.

1995 Writing & Art Contest

The Exploratorium

http://www.exploratorium.edu/

Kids and Teens

This innovative San Francisco museum had interactive media while most of us were still in our interknickers. In this virtual Exploratorium, visitors can discover

The Exploratorium is located in the Palace Of Fine Arts in the Marina district of San Francisco.

Welcome to ExploraNet!

The Exploratorium's World Wide Web server

A collection of electronic exhibits and resources for teachers, students and science enthusiasts!

Click here to visit The Learning Studio

A photographic journey and discussion of issues on the 50th anniversary of the bombing of Nagasaki
CLICK HERE TO VISIT... REMEMBERING NAGASAKI

the wonder of genetics and DNA coding first-hand from a throng of mutant fruit flies. Or try our personal, vibrating favorite, the Bronx Cheer Bulb (must be experienced to be fully appreciated). The museum also sponsors such ambitious projects as an internet video conference between NASA's Kuiper Airborne Observatory and students and teachers "on the ground." And site visitors will find plenty of suggestions for putting together their own experiments and exhibits at home with excerpts from two Exploratorium books, "Hands-On Science" and "The Science Snackbook." Your kids (not to mention the kid in you) will love this imaginative and well-executed site.

The Field Museum

http://www.bvis.uic.edu/museum/Home.html

Kids and Teens

Chicago's Field Museum of Natural History here presents a sight-and-sound-filled tour of some of its educational exhibits. You'll see a lot of dinosaurs, of course, but the timeline also reaches back to pelycosaurs, the first land animals, and forward to early humans, the first insurance salesmen. (Just kidding!) Check out some bizarre-looking early mammals at Teeth, Tusks, and Tarpits. Along the way,

you'll be invited to visit the "lab" for in-depth information on fossils and evolution. Another online exhibit here is the museum's fantastic collection of Javanese Masks, "among the oldest and most beautiful Indonesian masks in the United States." A teacher's guide facilitates classroom use of the site, which has good stuff for children of any age.

The Froggy Page

http://www.cs.yale.edu/homes/sjl/froggy.html.

Kids and Teens

This is a wonderful pondful of links to "froggy things" on the Net. (And by "frogs" we don't mean the French.) Did you know the East Texas frog croak is very different than your average "ribbit"? You can hear it here, along with a selection of other croaks, ka-blurps, and peeps. You can also read "The Frogs" by Aristophanes, sing "I'm In Love With A Big Blue Frog," view frogs being dissected, or glance at a list of famous frogs (yep, Kermit's there). Frogs may not be the smartest creatures around ("they'll attempt to mate with anything that moves, including other males and floating leaves," according to the Frequently Asked Frog Questions), but site creator Sandra Loosemore identifies with them anyway: "On the Internet," she says, "nobody knows you're a frog."

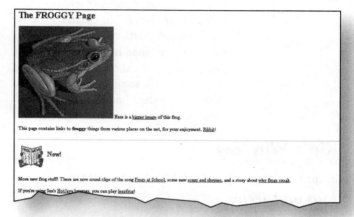

Fuzzy Logic's Home Page

http://www.digi-net.com/Fuzzy/Home.html

Kids and Teens

This educational cartoon space adventure gives students and teachers a sampling of the endless possibilities of the Net. Fuzzy Logic is a kid-friendly interlocutor who, while conducting an experiment with frogs in space, hits some snags and turns to the Internet for help. Help includes an Internet advisor who counts "flipping pogs" among her favorite hobbies, and a coffee grower in Costa Rica ("Hola!"). These situations smartly segue into areas of educational merit: teachers can link up with the InterNet Training Resources Network or the InterLinks Internet Access Navigator, while students get a history of the blues, scope out the Search for Extraterrestrial Intelligence, or take a trip to "a fairly normal sized neutron star."

KIDDING Around

http://alexia.lis.uiuc.edu/~watts/kiddin.html
Kids and Teens

At last, here's a list of kids' links that leaves out Barney and Thomas the Tank Engine and concentrates on the more sophisticated tastes of middle-school kids and teenagers. Site creator Heather McCammond-Watts covers a lot of territory with her "road map," with categories like music, movies, comics, sports, and museums, plus some offbeat stuff like "Weird Wonders" and "Spooky Sites." Heather also includes links especially for teens, like the Grouchy Cafe's Favorite Teenage Angst Books. Some categories included a "bookshelf" of recommended reading, so visitors can take a trip to the library after their journey through cyberspace. Even if you're not quite old enough for your own driver's license, this site invites you to cruise the info highway with "windows rolled down, cool song on the radio, and the freedom to go anywhere you'd like."

Kid's Window

http://jw.stanford.edu/KIDS/kids_home.html
Kids and Teens

Learn Japanese here using clickable pictures and sounds! Visit the Kid's Restaurant and start your day with a Japanese breakfast—rice, soup, pickles, and raw eggs. (No Froot Loops?) Next, it's time for language class: "oomu" means "parrot" in Hiragana. You'll also learn how to write Kanji characters for words like "sun" and "child." At the Library, read a story called "Momotaro" ("Peach Boy"), with text and audio narration in both Japanese and English. Finish your day with a lesson in origami, a cool way to make birds and animals just by folding sheets of colored paper. This terrific page is part of the Japan Window Project at Stanford University.

Kidlink

http://www.kidlink.org/

Kids and Teens

Kidlink is a sort of global pen-pal system for the 1990s. Kidlink subscribers answer questions about where they live and how they'd like to make the world a better place, and the service (it's free) hooks them up with other kids through electronic mailing lists. These "personal introductions" are archived at this site, as are postings to KidForum, part of the Kidlink service that lets kids respond to topics specified in advance, like their "Global Address" (latitude and longitude of the city they live in). The service claims participants from 69 countries so far, writing in Japanese, Spanish, Portuguese, and Nordic languages, as well as English. Kidlink is especially designed for classroom use, but anyone between the ages of 10 and 15 who can follow the very wordy step-by-step instructions will get a kick out of going global here.

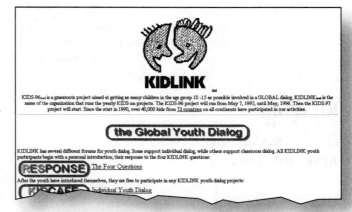

Kids Web

http://www.infomall.org/kidsweb/

Kids and Teens

Frustrated because mom and dad's encyclopedias were last updated in 1972? Relax! Kids Web, a digital library for school research, is here! This tremendous list of links takes you to educational resources all over the world. For that assignment on the *Mona Lisa* (what's she smiling about, anyway?), click on the WebMuseum. Or if you're trying to untangle the evolutionary web, point to the Biology and Life Sciences page, where you'll find a Primer on Molecular Genetics. And not only can you access the complete works of Shakespeare, you can also link to a Shakespearean Insult Service and "experience the wrath of the Bard." Sports, history, literature, and government are just a few of the other offerings.

Kids' Space

http://www.interport.net/kids_space
Kids and Teens

This totally cool interactive site is home page to thousands of kids around the world. In the Kids' Gallery, you can see artwork from Kaitong Ariel in Hong Kong or Nicholas in New York ("Spaceships!"). Make new cyberfriends online—on our last visit, kids from Russia, Israel, and Italy were looking for pen pals (so were *lots* of American kids). Groove to music at the On Air Concert, or read some flights of literary fancy at the Story Book (cookie jars and rubber duckies were some common motifs on our last visit). Best of all, you can share your own artwork, music, stories, and personal home pages with other kids on the Net! If you need inspiration, the Beanstalk project lets you write a story for someone else's drawing, or draw a picture from someone else's story. Great fun!

KidsCom

http://www.kidscom.com/
Kids and Teens

This Internet playground features the wit and imagination of the middle-school set. Read stories written by other kids (vote on the one you like best!), leave messages on the Graffiti Wall, or visit the Pet Arena and swap tales of heroic puppy dogs and errant bunny rabbits. (We read about a cat named Honey who "affectionately rips your eyeballs out in the morning. Who needs an alarm clock?") What Do Ya Think? opens up the floor for a discussion of questions like "What kind of 'chores' do you do around your house?" ("Cleaning, cooking, entertaining family with outrageous sense of humor," writes Alexander Miller). KidsCom also offers games and prizes (sponsored by SpectraCom, a marketing survey group), but the neat thing about this site is that so much of the material is provided by the kids themselves.

Please Click on one of the buttons below:

I'm a kid that needs to register

Play Now! I'm A Registered Kid

Parent's & Adult's Place

You can Preview KidsCom at the Parent's and Adult's Place

To get the most up-to-date web browser to fully enjoy this site, download

the 63???nd person to access this site!

MidLink Magazine

http://longwood.cs.ucf.edu:80/~MidLink

Kids and Teens

Billed as the electronic magazine for kids in the middle grades, MidLink has enough humor and insight to snag a few curious adults as well. The page tries to teach and entertain: we spent time following a research ship through the Indian Ocean (though we passed up the chance to send it a message via satellite) and investigated a dangerous raptor (which turned out to be a stuffed bald eagle). The legendary, elusive jackalope makes an appearance here as well. Kids are invited to discuss people they admire, review books they like, and share jokes they've written ("How do you catch a rabbit? With a 'hare' net!"). Middle-schoolers have also put together a useful list of their favorite Web pages. Solid, educational fun.

Nye Labs

http://www.seanet.com/vendors/billnye/nyelabs.html

Kids and Teens

This online home of Bill Nye, the Science Guy, contains "a whole cosmos of information" about his wacky fun-with-science TV programs. The show is made by a Seattle production company and runs on both public and syndicated television. Each episode here has a listing that includes a show synopsis, related links, and an at-home experiment, like how to make a fire extinguisher out of a peanut butter jar. Bill's favorite science books are listed here, with more information on topics like "Fossils," "Soap," and "UFOs and Things." This site also tells of the Science Guy's humble beginnings as an engineer for Boeing who did stand-up routines on the side. Fans can preview upcoming shows, download a copy of the theme song, and listen to Bill's mantra: "Science rules!"

Questacon

http://actein.edu.au/Questacon/
Kids and Teens

Questacon bills itself as a real-time interactive learning experience, and it carries that philosophy right into cyberspace. The site—an official online version of "Australia's premier hands-on science and technology centre"—includes a virtual tour of the physical building, and a dandy array of exhibits, like "Good Vibes," described by curators as "a festival of light and sound."

Eyeball a giant dung beetle at "Gargantuans from the Garden," then jog over to "Puzzlequest," a short section full of brain teasers that should send you scrambling for pencil and paper. Perhaps the most frustrating aspect of this site is that it makes you want to go to Questacon, which could be tricky for non-Australians. Great fun!

Rollercoaster!

http://www.echonyc.com/~dne/Rollercoaster!
Kids and Teens

This paean to "primal scream therapy at 60 miles an hour" is nearly as much fun to ride as the coasters themselves. Terrific design: you start off perched atop a huge incline, grab your ticket, and go. Check out "the most terrifying coaster" (the now-defunct Crystal Beach Cyclone in Canada) or "the least terrifying coaster" (the Sky Princess). Lovingly written by coasterholic Bob Coker, the lively site has giddy essays on "The Need for Speed" and "Why We Ride." Coker's "Quest for the Ultimate Ride" is a discussion of the different merits a coaster can have—beyond "its top speed, its highest hill, its fastest drop," he considers such factors as aesthetics and drama (no mention of nausea, though). Some pictures of classic rides, too. The graphics load fast—appropriate for describing these 80-mph steel behemoths.

Safari Touch Tank

http://oberon.educ.sfu.ca/splash/tank.htm
Kids and Teens

If you can't make it to your local tide pool (or if you live in Nebraska), try the Safari Touch Tank. It's a colorful sort of cyber-saltwater fishbowl; use your mouse to "touch" the Purple Sea Star, and you'll learn the disgusting facts of how it extrudes its own stomach to slowly devour an oyster. (This is why we lock the car doors whenever we drive near the beach.) Even the plants have stories to tell—the eelgrass may be hiding a school of young fish. Many interesting photos and even movie clips here. This undersea world provides just a sample of the sort of things a team of scientists, divers, archaeologists, and kids got to see during Safari '94, a project sponsored by the Royal B.C. Museum.

The School House Rock Page

http://hera.life.uiuc.edu/rock.html

Kids and Teens

In the '70s, School House Rock treated Saturday-morning TV viewers to some infectious tunes between 'toons. If the phrase "Conjunction Junction, what's your function" conjures up good memories—or if you're currently enjoying the instructive interludes in reruns—this site is for you. It revives the School House Rock classics and lets you read along as the song plays. Get a history fix with "Sufferin' 'til Suffrage"

("Those pilgrim women who braved the boat/Could cook the turkey, but they could not vote"), travel the solar system with Interplanet Janet, get your adverbs at Lolly's, or learn about human anatomy ("Minus bones you're just a blob!").You can even find out where to order a CD of "Multiplication Rock." Appropriate interjection: wow!

Sports Illustrated for Kids Online

http://www.pathfinder.com/@@BNs3NDBqlQMAQPUm/SIFK/

Kids and Teens

Yet another part of Time Warner's Pathfinder pages, the online version of *Sports Illustrated for Kids* includes articles from the magazine and special features like a search form to find out which famous athletes share your birthday. On our last visit, we picked up tips on becoming a great BMX bike racer from Gary Ellis, the world champ, and read a kids' discussion of the question "Which is Better: Real Sports or Video Games?" Readers are invited to submit their own sports-related artwork or stories to the Webmaster for possible inclusion on the site. One poetic youngster even wrote an ode to baseball: "The

object of the game is to hit a run/But more important than that is to have lots of fun." Tell that to the pros, kid!

Come on in! Here are the features you can visit at SI For Kids on Pathfinder (and don't forget: Send us e-mail!):

SUPER TIPS: ROLLERHOCKEY - Goalie Manon Rheaume of the ... you tips on how to ... hottest

Street Cents Online

http://www.screen.com/streetcents.html

Kids and Teens

"Street Cents" is a Canadian consumer awareness TV show for kids—sort of Ralph Nader meets 21 Jump Street. Each show has a different focus; on one recent visit, four football players were testing light fast food by shoveling down burgers and salads and voting for the tastiest. Other topics have included hair (make sure you're not ripped off at the salon) and sports (how much can you expect to pay for a good-quality badminton racquet?). One fun feature compares what the hosts are like in real life to their on-screen personas. (Two-Bit, the show's mascot, describes "what it's like to be an African Pygmy Hedgehog on TV.") Also entertaining is the "Whining" forum, where young consumers can vent their own frustrations. Despite the mainly Canada-centric info, the themes cross borders very well.

Theodore Tugboat Online Activity Center

http://www.cochran.com/TT.html

Kids and Teens

Theodore Tugboat Online brings this popular 3D animated character from Canadian TV to the Web. Targeted at young browsers and their parents, the page features happy color graphics and chuggin'-fast downloads. Read about the show's elaborate cast of characters (Gregor the Fishing Trawler, Owan the Oil Rig, and Rebecca the Research Vessel), then check out some cute, cozy story synopses. A special highlight is Theodore's Surprise Friend, an interactive story that lets you choose the action. (Will you send Theo to befriend a freighter or out to sea?) The downloadable coloring book lets you zip pages onto your hard drive, and you can register to receive a postcard with Theo's picture on it. A very charming page indeed!

WELCOME TO OUR ONLINE ACTIVITY CENTER for Theodore Tugboat, the Canadian TV series about a cheerful tugboat who likes to be friends with everyone. Life in his playful Big Harbour community is always changing, and whatever each new day brings, Theodore likes to do the things that friendly tugboats do.

There's lots to do and see here about Theodore and his many floating friends. (last updated Monday, September 18, 1995)

CHILDREN can help Theodore decide what to do next in an illustrated, interactive story created especially for the Internet. You can also download a page from our online coloring book or receive a postcard with Theodore's picture.

PARENTS and TEACHERS can review a synopsis of some episodes, find a description of our characters (we have more than 30 of them) or read about how The Big Harbour works. You can also participate in our email discussion list or reserve a Theodore Tugboat T-shirt. With any other thoughts, questions, or suggestions, please send email anytime to theodore@cochran.com.

PEOPLE WHO WORK IN TV ALL THE TIME (and anyone else who's interested) can find more information about the production. We also maintain a list of links to other sites of interest to TV professionals.

FROM HERE you can also find over 100 links to other sites for children, researched and rated by our own Online Librarian, Berit E_____ _____ake this a consistently reliable starting point to help you find children's activities on the Internet.

Uncle Bob's Kids' Page

http://gagme.wwa.com/~boba/kids.html

Kids and Teens

This is "a treasure chest of links, which have been cleaned, checked, and annotated" by Bob Allison, a.k.a. Uncle Bob. The silly rave reviews at the beginning may make you think this is just an ego trip for ol' Uncle Bob, but don't be dismayed: the links are terrific for kids of all ages. Seven site-filled sections include links to pages on sports, games, museums, toys, science, and more; a description of each site lets you know a bit about it before you plunge in. Bob also "spotlights" special categories of links like animal pictures, reference materials, and Star Trek sites. After you spend a day or two here (and you easily can), you may be ready to send U.B. a rave review yourself. (There's a link for that, too.)

You Can With Beakman and Jax

http://www.nbn.com:80/youcan/

Kids and Teens

"You Can With Beakman and Jax" leaps from the Sunday comics to the Web in this impressive compendium of facts. This official page is basically an archive of the "You Can" strip, in which author Jok Church answers kids' questions about science. "A good question is a powerful thing" is his motto, and you can visit here for the answers to queries like "What are fingernails made out of?" and "Where does Jell-O really come from?" "You can" learn a lot, including how to make your own fake mucus. (In fact, much of this site comes from the gross-but-true domain of scientific endeavor.) Regular followers of "You Can" or TV's "Beakman's World" may have seen much of this material before; the Web site also includes a few mildly controversial pieces some newspapers wouldn't run.

parenting
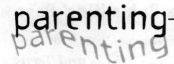

Adolescence Directory On-Line

http://education.indiana.edu/cas/adol/adol.html

Parenting

Indiana University's Center for Adolescent Studies offers online support for educators, parents, and those actually negotiating the hormone-frenzied years. The *Teacher Talk* archives include "Female Fighting and the 'Male Dance.'" ("I would rather deal with ten male fights than anything that has to do with females," said Chuck Hibbert.) On our last visit, we found a photo documentary titled "Closer Look at Teen Pregnancy," and an article about a lifelike, computerized doll that's meant to teach teenagers about the reality of infant care. A list of "Mental Health Risk Factors for Adolescents" provides links to educational resources about such potential adolescent traumas as eating disorders and depression. On the lighter side, "For Teens" featured a pubescent film critic, who gave this assessment of *Reality Bites*: "All it shows is you can rebel against your Dad by overspending on his gas card."

Children's Literature Web Guide

http://www.ucalgary.ca/~dkbrown/index.html

Parenting

Put together by a specialist at U. of Calgary, this site is an incredibly deep archive of WWW pages about children's literature. Teachers and parents can find great books for kids here, and there are eye-opening lists: Little Red Riding Hood made the list of Most Frequently Banned Books in U.S. from 1990-1992, for instance. (Must be the cruelty to grannies angle.) Check out a list of Favorite Teenage Angst Books, find out what authors like John Updike and Joyce Carol Oates would recommend as literature for teens, and uncover Brave, Active, and Resourceful Females in Picture Books. This page also has links to children's literature that you can read online, from "Alice in Wonderland" to "Politically Correct Bedtime Stories." A field day for any kid-lit freak.

Cute Kids Page

http://www.prgone.com/cutekids/index.html
Parenting

Here's your Recommended Daily Allowance of juvenile cuteness. These pages offer a collection of stories written by parents about, yes, cute things their children have said or done. Some of the kiddie quotes have the familiarity of classics (to a pregnant woman, on being told she had a baby in her tummy: "You ate a baby?"); many are, like the kids, one of a kind. Computer humor even creeps in: the parent of a seven-year old writes that the child "looked at the MSDOS box and said 'Why isn't there a Mr. DOS?'" To submit stories about your own adorable moppets, just fill in the form—though "the only compensation you will receive is the great feeling that comes with knowing your kid is cute in the eyes of the Netizens that visit this site." Fun mostly for parents, but kids may enjoy the silly laughs, too.

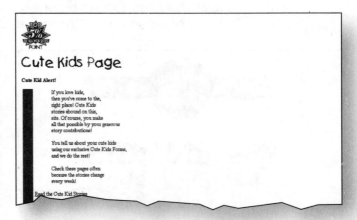

Divorce Home Page

http://www.primenet.com/~dean/
Parenting

Dean Hughson, a divorced dad, has created this page to help others going through a painful separation. Whether you started the split or were an unwilling participant, you'll probably find a resource here. Hughson's own "Steps Toward Recovery" include links to pages that provide help on sleeping well, eating well, and regaining a sense of humor. (A page called Dumping Your Lover Electronically "makes me laugh even though it didn't sound so funny when I was dumped," he notes.) This site provides a broad array of self-help guides like *The Newly Divorced Book of Protocol: How to be Civil When You Hate Their Guts*, as well as info on support groups and other organizations. Most of Hughson's own advice is anecdotal; he offers a telephone hotlist for professional help.

Family World

`http://family.com/indexGX.html`
Parenting

"Taking a Backpack of Fears to Middle School" and "Bonding Made Simple" are two typical articles from this newsy site, a collaboration by a number of publishers of parenting magazines. The huge list of articles also includes plenty of how-tos, like how to help a stagestruck child get involved in the theater or how to keep naming a new baby from becoming a family feud (the sibs like "Charles" or "Michael" while their folks like "Kaleo" or "Skylar." What's a New Age parent to do?) Parents can also post questions, advice, or funny stories about raising children, check out some book and software ads, and read about family-oriented events going on across the U.S. Deep and informative; new editions monthly. Now, if they could only tell us how to get rid of the Power Rangers...

Family Planet

`http://family.starwave.com`
Parenting

This "online service for moms and dads" offers fun, well-packaged advice on coping with snobbish PTA presidents, hypercritical grandparents, and kids who won't make their beds. If you want advice on a particular topic, just e-mail one of the site's resident experts—they're on rotation. Each answers questions on a different day of the week. In addition to providing family-oriented Web links (with plenty of background on each recommended site), Family Planet reviews books and movies (rated in categories like "The Fidget Factor"), and includes some books for parents right online. The Penny Whistle Traveling With Kids Book, for example, has tons of suggestions on preventing bored young travelers from tearing up the back seat during trips. This is another slick production from the prolific folks at the Starwave Corporation.

Family Surfboard

http://www.sjbennett.com/users/sjb/surf.html

Parenting

This online guide to family Web surfing is put together by parenting authors Steve and Ruth Bennett; their mission is to help parents and kids get the most out of technology, while "preserving childhood" in its low-tech and no-tech forms. In the "Bennetts' Best" annotated list of kids' links, each site description includes a related (nonelectronic!) family activity to engage in "when you return from cyberspace." Steve and Ruth also share some ideas for introducing kids to computers, like making a spreadsheet of family members' favorite ice cream toppings. On our last visit, an Internet "scavenger hunt" started youngsters on a search of U.S. cities for a famous monument. Visitors can help out with some of the Bennetts' projects by responding to surveys that might be included in an article or book (one they've done is "Kids' Answers to Life's Big Questions"). Plenty of general information on parenting, but especially worthwhile for parents spooked by the electronic media.

Kid Safety on the Internet

http://www.uoknor.edu/oupd/kidsafe/start.htm

Parenting

This site opens with an innocent cartoon kid sitting in front of a PC terminal, while on the next page he gets zapped via the computer line by a dirty old man. The message is clear: "If anyone uses nasty language or mentions things that make you uncomfortable, don't respond and log off." This is a helpful, if somewhat limited, page from the Oklahoma University Department of Public Safety; kids will find a "What Should You Do When a Bully Picks on You?" primer, sound advice on dealing with friends who use drugs, and what-to-dos for emergencies like fires, accidents, and getting lost. The advice and cartoon illustrations are easy to understand; though parents may not learn anything new from this site, they may want their kids to visit.

Thomas Clark King's CyberNursery

http://www.xmission.com/~gastown/cking/tommy.htm

Parenting

Young Thomas Clark King's parents devote this page to him not only because they're proud of him, but because

Thomas Clark King's CyberNursery

"Look at me Mommy!"

Thomas is 14 months old, 10-1/2 months corrected. Thomas was born 3-1/2 months early and cared for by the Neonatal Intensive Care Unit (NICU) at William Beaumont Hospital in Royal Oak, Michigan. Today he behaves like a perfect little 10-1/2 month old, which in his case is age appropriate!

As a "perfect little 10 month old", he is into all the trouble a 10 month old gets into (including reaching for the reset button... Daddy's... ......). He crawls and cruises everywhere, only getting away with his mischief because he

they want to share their experience with Tommy's very premature birth (he was born at 25 weeks gestation instead of the usual 40 weeks, and weighed only 1 pound 10 ounces). Clark King narrates the painful story of his son's long hospitalization in a Neonatal Intensive Care Unit, and Tommy's slow progression from what King calls "the smallest and most sickly baby I had seen in my life" to "a perfect little ten month old" (last we checked). The site also includes links to other sites with information about premature babies, and lots of general parenting info as well. An excellent resource for parents of preemies.

ParentsPlace.com

http://www.parentsplace.com/index.html

Parenting

This "Parenting Resource Center on the Web" offers interactive shopping for "Tushie's Diapers" (really!) and other such merchandise, plus info, resource lists, and chat forums for parents. When the "Live Chat" is hosted (check the schedule), topics include single parenting and rearing twins; when it isn't, parenting may or may not be the topic of conversation. The Reading Room is the main attraction; offers scads of online texts on topics that you may have trouble finding elsewhere on the Web: "Full-Time Dads," "Single Parenting in the Nineties," and "The Stepfamily Association of Illinois" are all newsletters that have gone online courtesy of ParentsPlace.com. A search engine is available for the site if you want to check for info on a particular topic. Voluminous and valuable offerings.

SurfWatch

This seems like a great idea at the right time: SurfWatch software lets parents and schools (and employers!) prevent access to sexually explicit Internet sites. You buy the initial software, then pay a small monthly fee for updated lists of naughty places. The idea is that rather than censor information all across the Internet (and what a ruckus that idea has caused lately), users can simply filter it out as it comes into the house. (The authors say it causes no problems with your browser, either.) No demos here, but you can order the software online. To look at it another way, you'll have no more late nights trying to find all the sites the kids shouldn't be seeing.

Leisure Activities

Leisure Activities

The World Wide Web is perfect for hobbyists, who can join endless discussions about model rocketry, needlepoint, or stuffed-pig collecting. Some pet owners now automatically go online when Booper turns up with a funny cough—they know there is *somebody* out there whose pet has had the same problem and knows what to do about it. Dog lovers are one of the few groups who will paste "I Love My Great Dane" bumper stickers on their computers. And then there are the beekeepers, the hang gliders, the coin collectors...

Meanwhile, for some of the most intimate spots on the Web, visit our selection of Personal Home Pages—those done by surfers just for the pleasure of their own creativity. You may be baffled or startled here, but you won't be bored.

food and cooking

Bubba's Collection of BBQ Potato Chips

http://sage.cc.purdue.edu/~bubba/bbqchips.htm

Food and Cooking

Gary Beason's quest for the ultimate barbecue chip is simple and straightforward: let's face it, this is merely an address list of chip manufacturers. Ah, but no Lay's or Eagle Brand here, folks. And no corn. Only regional potato chips need apply. Like Gibble's Home Style Bar-B-Q Flavored Potato Chips, located six miles south of Chambersburg, Pennsylvania. Or Beason's Holy Grail of chips: Bob's Texas Style Potato Chips Mesquite Bar-B-Que Seasoned, located in Brookshire, Texas. "Perhaps I've read too many Greek myths and too many issues of *Thor*, but I think that quests are necessary to ensure the quality of life, that desire is good and that obstacles reaffirm what is good," Beason reasons. Ah, the wealth of the Web.

CheeseNet

http://www.efn.org/~kpw/cheesenet95/index.html

Food and Cooking

From the tame ricotta to the fearsome Limburger, CheeseNet provides a pungent connoisseur's guide to cheese types, textures, and flavors. Sponsored by Foamation, manufacturer of weird cheese-shaped products for Green Bay Packer fans ("Cheeseheads"), these pages are surprisingly broad in scope. "The Wide, Wide World of Cheese" delves into the annals of cheese history, then explains the alchemy of cheese making. And a "Cheese Glossary" covers the language of cheese, which "can be surrounded by as much mystique, nonsense, and pretension as that of wine." Much of the humor at this site is derived from the fact that ordinary phrases sound funny with the word "cheese" in them (like "Ask Dr. Cheese"); it's not endlessly amusing, but it's fun for a while.

CyberCafe

http://www.bid.com/bid/cybercafe/

Food and Cooking

At the CyberCafe, you can "get wired" amid all the features one expects from a real coffeehouse—except real coffee, of course. This informative site is loaded with enough facts and tips on beans and brewing to make even the most hopeless java junkie jitter. Links are offered to an amazing number of coffee (and tea) retailers and wholesalers, enabling visitors to shop online for vanilla nut, Ethiopian Moka Harrar, or a Grindmaster espresso-cappuccino machine. And you can spread out the pages of the *San Francisco Chronicle*, or check out Seattle coffee-houses in *MotherCity Espresso*. Don't miss the site's mythical account of the discovery of coffee, which involves a goatherd named Kaldi, an imam from the local monastery, and a chorus of dancing goats.

Dining Out on the Web

http://www.ird.net/diningout.html

Food and Cooking

The intro to Dining Out on the Web says it best: "This is a list of restaurant guides. No recipes, no wine, no beer, no brewpubs, no cafes. Focus is the key to success." And this site definitely delivers the goods with its selective links to restaurant listings and menus around the world. The heart of the site is an index by state or country, enabling visitors to chase down the restaurant with choicest red-chili sauce in Santa Fe, or the fattest, juiciest sirloin in Kansas City. And a tasty selection of links to comprehensive pages pretty much runs the gamut, from a kosher restaurant database to the World Wide Sushi Restaurant Reference. The page's pappy, John Troyer, says, "I made this list because I am insane." He should know—but he's a gastronomical success in our book.

The Dinner Co-Op

http://gs216.sp.cs.cmu.edu/dinnercoop/
home-page.html

Food and Cooking

More than 1,500 links to gastronomic delights await at the Dinner Co-Op, hosted by 15 funny folks in the Pittsburgh area who simply love food. Start with the

Welcome to the Dinner Co-op!

This is a page for lovers of food... folks who enjoy cooking and/or eating... We have nearly 1500 links to restaurants, shops, recipes and food information pages. Enjoy!

★ ★ Please complete our survey so we can improve our service to you! ★ ★

The Dinner Co-op

We're a group of about 15 people in the Pittsburgh area who love food, cooking & eating. Most of us are CMU CS & Robotics grad students, but there's a few professionals and random others too -- right now we have a doctor, a chiropractor, and an electrical engineer (and looking for more non-CS types :).

- ▶ General Introduction
- FAQ
- A Brief History
- Cooking Schedule Information

group's mind-boggling assembly of favorite recipes, like "Sweet Noodle Kugel" and "Mango Rum Cake." The site features an excellent search engine. Our query for listings with "peanut butter" turned up a page full of links to yummy recipes, including a mousse, a pie, and a curious sauce with instructions to "Place the peanut butter together with tomatoes, garlic, and water... and blend." Links go to places like a culinary 'zine called *Electronic Gourmet Guide*, which features, among other things, a hopping good piece on homebrewing. And serious kitcheners can shop the nearly 200 online gourmet outlets.

Don't Panic Eat Organic

http://www.rain.org/~sals/my.html

Food and Cooking

This "home page of an organic farmer" provides truckloads of fresh information for the (soil) rich and fa(r)mous. Organic farmers and home gardeners can dig deep into this info-garden for facts and updates on subjects like earthworms, Edaphon soil composition, and friendly (to your garden), rodent-eating raptors. Order "nature's best all-around predator" and pest-controller, the Green Lacewing. Or

read up on the barn owl (a.k.a. the "flying cat"). If it's food you're after, learn the secrets of organic Cherimoya (fruit of the Incas) and whip up one of Aunt Lucy's Cherimoya custard pies. Added plus: many links to other related sites, like a source for market and postharvest information on tropical fruits, and publications from the Consolidated Farm Service. For organic agriculture fans, this is a pure delight.

Fatfree: The Low Fat Vegetarian Archive

http://www.fatfree.com
Food and Cooking

The only thing "fat" here is the list of recipes: more than 2,000 of them at your disposal. These vegetarian entrees are collected from submissions to an e-mail list, and it's all done just for the love of fat-free cooking. To prove the vegetarian claim, we searched for "steak," "lard," and "pork" and found no cheaters throwing meat or fat into their recipes. However, when we looked for "barbecue," we came up with almost 30 recipes for veggie cook-outs, including "Tofu Steaks" and the ever-popular "BBQ Sweet Potatoes" (plump when you cook 'em?). The site also lets you search the USDA Nutrient Database, which helps to answer burning questions like "Does broccoli have fat?" and "Is quinoa a good source of iron and zinc?" Naturally, you'll find no bloated graphics here.

The FOODplex!

http://www.gigaplex.com/wow/food/index.htm
Food and Cooking

"There are lots of sites on the Web that tell you where to eat," opens this page from food critic Merrill Shindler. "This one tells you why you love to eat." (The site is part of the gargantuan Gigaplex entertainment complex.) Seen here holding a mystery bun aloft with obvious glee, Shindler does indeed love to eat. He starts off slowly, pondering the imponderables (there are apparently 14 *H*s in a typical bowl of alphabet soup), then moves through Noshes and Nuggets to Mouthwatering Morsels. Savor Shindler's recipe for meatloaf ("that most wondrous of all Couch Potato dishes"), or ponder the results of his dog biscuit taste test: "as far as I can tell, [they taste] like overly thick Rye Crisps." If you just can't get enough of this guy, check out Shindler's Scrapbook for photos of the mega-muncher in action with cutlines like "seen here praying to the garlic god for packages of Breath Assure." Highly amusing and artfully written (and don't discount the serious food info).

The Garlic Page

http://broadcast.com/garlic/garlic.htm
Food and Cooking

This Web resource devoted to the "stinking rose" provides garlic recipes, information on its medicinal uses, and tips on growing it at home. Site creator Roger Corydell even advocates garlic as a mood-altering drug: you go into a pizza joint, order a pizza with "enough garlic to choke a horse (make the waiter write it on the check)," and "voila... all is well with the world." Read about "Garlic's Role in Preventing and Treating Cancer" in the health section. Or learn how to pull together a mess of broiled garlic oysters, garlic potatoes, and a "garlicky" carrot-yogurt salad—all to be washed down with many mugs of "Gak and Laurel's Garlic Beer." As a past visitor has noted, "Great page... I can smell it from here."

Godiva Online

http://www.godiva.com
Food and Cooking

Godiva is the Victoria's Secret of chocolate makers: sensual, aristo-cratic, and slightly sinful. Godiva and *Chocolatier* magazine have teamed up for this online explosion of chocolate. Dark, deep chocolate. Chocolate rich and creamy and sweet and delicious and... ah, where were we? You'll find some nice recipes here, and a clickable map that will help you locate a Godiva boutique in the Congo, but the site's real goal is to make you want to place an order. (With such a luscious subject, who can hold that against them?) Explore temptations for every occasion in the online catalog—like the chocolate Tom Turkey ("gobble up one for each place setting"). The site even extends a "gift reminder service," which will prompt you via e-mail to dispatch a truffle assort-ment for Mother's Day.

Godiva and Design of Woman on the Horse are trademarks of Godiva Chocolatier, Inc. Copyright 1995.

La Comida Mexicana

http://www.udg.mx/Cocina/menu.html

Food and Cooking

This zesty page, presented in both Spanish and English, cooks up some of the best Mexican food on the Web. A voice from the cocina welcomes you to the resource ("buen provecho!"), while a rousing mariachi band wails in the background. The site includes a well-organized history of Mexican cuisine (don't miss the entry on "Turkeys and Dogs"), but mostly it's a tantalizing collection of recipes. Open the clickable cookbook and try your hand at creating a big bowl of Sopa de Albondiguitas (meatball soup), a plate of authentic Huevos Rancheros, or a skillet of crispy Pescado Panadera (pan-fried fish).

And while you're at it, why not blend a pitcher of Rompope to wash it all down? Nearly a dozen salsa recipes, too!

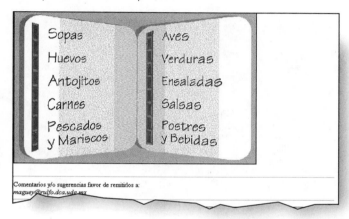

Lucidcafé

http://www.lucidcafe.com/lucidcafe/

Food and Cooking

This online promo for the Calistoga Coffee Company features a cafe full of famous figures, with pictures and bios on each and a new set of characters each month. On our last visit, the rather motley crew included Lyndon Johnson, Mother Theresa, and Napoleon (java fans all, we're sure). The product catalogue offers java paraphernalia (mugs, books) and a nice selection of coffee blends, from decaf Colombian to Tanzanian Peaberry. A Forum schedule lets you in on the upcoming "web-talkshows" the site hosts, the topics of which range anywhere from "Coffees of Mexico and Central America" to "What

is Philosophy?" Some of this is rather pseudo-intellectual fare for coffee-drinkers, but that in itself has a certain appeal.

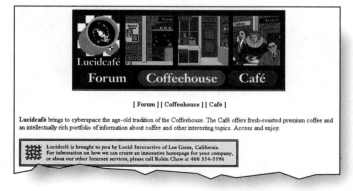

Mycelium

http://www.igc.apc.org/mushroom/welco.html
Food and Cooking

Here's your Web connection to "the fascinating world of mushrooms." (A "mycelium" is the web of fibers at a mush-room's base—get it?) The fruit of enthusiast Wayne Harrison's efforts, this is a great resource for fungophiles (and it's not one bit dank or smelly). Experienced munchers will find tips on stalking mushrooms in the wild; tales from the front include a squabble between two mushroomers over who first spotted some roadside Agaricus. If you're hunting for storebought 'shrooms, you can check out a few wild varieties available in supermarkets, and anyone with a fondness for fungi will appreciate the list of recipes offered here (Shiitake-Leek Quiche, Cajun Glazed Mushrooms). For kicks, don't miss "Wayne's Wacky Mushroom Glossary."

Welcome to Mycelium

Mycelium is your WWW connection to the fascinating world of mushrooms. Like the World Wide Web, mycelium is also a web - but one that weaves its way underneath a mushroom. Clever connection, huh? A standard disclaimer here; Mycelium is not associated with any mycological society or group.

You don't have to be a mycologist to explore here. Beginning mushroomers are more than welcome. To find out what's available on Mycelium, go the Index, or just page through and browse using the direction arrows at the bottom of each page. Here you'll find information on where to find and how to identify mushrooms, how to preserve mushrooms, and delicious recipes for cooking mushrooms.

Over The Coffee

http://www.gryffin.com/coffee/
Food and Cooking

Inspired by the coffee newsgroups on Usenet, this site is for members of what creator Tim Nemec calls "the Internet coffee community"—a serious bunch, judging from the intensity of the debates about whether to use a burr grinder with a French press. Some of the participants in this java free-for-all even wax poetic: "What makes my love of coffee grow? What picks me up when I feel low?" runs one ode to caffeine. Addicts can also browse retail listings or leave comments on the "Wall of Java." Tucked away in a corner of this site is an autographed picture of Juan Valdez (okay, it's autographed by the actor who plays Juan—still, coffee lovers may want to stop by and pay tribute to the Great Colombian One).

About Over The Coffee!
What's New?
Coffee Reference Desk
Business Section
Other Ports Of Call
The Wall Of Java!

Over The Coffee
has been rated among the top 5%
of all sites on the web by Point Survey.

Over The Coffee is enhanced for Netscape Navigator.

Ragú Presents: Mama's Cucina

`http://www.eat.com/index.html`
Food and Cooking

Ragú is an enlightened Web advertiser: long on fun and short on sales pitch. And if you happen to get hungry for a certain brand of Old World Style Spaghetti Sauce, so much the better. Mama, the Ragú hostess, offers stories of the Old Country (even if the Old Country happens to be Hoboken), plus Ragú-drenched recipes like Spicy Apricot Chicken and Veal Cutlet Parmesan. We particularly enjoyed the art lesson on a recent visit: the story of Michelangelo's David. Besides, Ragú will also teach you to say in Italian, "Has anyone ever told you that you have a head like an eggplant?" OK, so it won't change your life, but why can't more Web advertisers come across with entertaining sites like these, if only for their own good? We admit it, Mama—you're a charming gal.

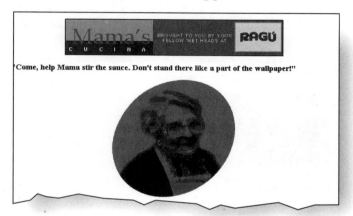

"Come, help Mama stir the sauce. Don't stand there like a part of the wallpaper!"

Real Beer Page

`http://realbeer.com/rbp/`
Food and Cooking

You've gotta love a site with a section titled "Burp Me" (yes, these are audio files—not for the delicately inclined). The Real Beer Page has a smooth, rich interface and barrels of detail, all presented with obvious affection for the topic. The site gives detailed information (history, beers, brew processes) on a handful of microbreweries, and a search engine will help you locate one close to you. A particular highlight is the Games entry, outlining beer game etiquette, and rules for contests with names like "Beer Bungee," "One Big Chicken," and "Jerry Lewis Telethons" (three drinks required whenever Jerry sings "You'll Never Walk Alone"). The game descriptions alone give this site a high fun factor. A guide to public transportation is also thoughtfully provided.

Scotch.com

http://Scotch.com/
Food and Cooking

Scotch.com is a serious scotch-lover's paradise, with an emphasis on the history and production of single-malts. When the boys at the Classic Malts Society say a

whisky has character, they mean it. Talisker scotch, for instance, is "a strong, rugged dram big enough for warriors and poets, for fighting and contemplation." Visitors can also watch a video of the essential sniff test (nothing has proven as effective in discovering what's going on inside a cask). Several distilleries have their own pages here; some take a while to load, since they're accompanied by pictures of the surrounding countryside. This sort of background seems very important to the creators of Scotch.com, because "within every bottle of Classic Malt whisky is a distillation of the Scottish people and the spirit of the place."

Vegetarian Pages

http://catless.ncl.ac.uk/vegetarian/
Food and Cooking

The amount of water used in production of the average American cow is sufficient to float a destroyer—at least, so say the Vegetarian Pages, a feisty guide to meatless living on the Internet. Vegetarians and vegans will enjoy leafing through these pages, which are loaded with links and practical information. Visitors can flip through "The Hare Krishna Book of Eggless Cakes" for recipes, or get the

details on the Vegan Camp in North Wales. You can also read the latest vegetarian news ("Lisa Simpson Goes Vegetarian") and read reports on such topics as vegetarian diets for dogs and cats. For inspiration, browse a list of famous vegetarians and vegans, from Buddha to Brooke Shields. And activists will enjoy "How to Win an Argument With a Meat Eater" (source of the cow/destroyer factoid).

Virtual Vineyards

http://www.virtualvin.com/

Food and Cooking

If God is in the details, He (or She) probably spends time at Virtual Vineyards. Founder Peter Granoff, an experienced enologist (look it up), gives great advice on wines produced by small, well-respected wineries and makes it easy to order a case of Chardonnay to match your tastebuds. An interactive "tasting chart" of a wine's seven perceptions (oak, complexity, and so on) helps you get the perfect vintage. You can also read a feature article from *Wine & Spirits* magazine ("How to Buy Wine in the Cellars of Burgundy"), or track down recipes for exotic food counterparts like "Indonesian Hot and Sweet Fruit Salad." If phrases like "light, young, zippy acidity and

a snap of residual sugar" excite you, then don't hesitate to visit. Extra points for the Q&A title: "Ask the Cork Dork."

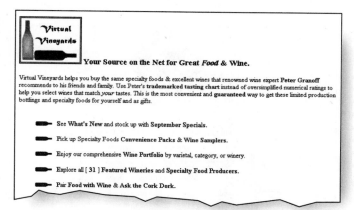

Your Source on the Net for Great *Food* & Wine.

Virtual Vineyards helps you buy the same specialty foods & excellent wines that renowned wine expert Peter Granoff recommends to his friends and family. Use Peter's **trademarked tasting chart** instead of oversimplified numerical ratings to help you select wines that match *your* tastes. This is the most convenient and **guaranteed** way to get these limited production bottlings and specialty foods for yourself and as *gifts*.

- See What's New and stock up with September Specials.
- Pick up Specialty Foods Convenience Packs & Wine Samplers.
- Enjoy our comprehensive Wine Portfolio by varietal, category, or winery.
- Explore all [31] Featured Wineries and Specialty Food Producers.
- Pair Food with Wine & Ask the Cork Dork.

hobbies
hobbies

Balloon Modeling on the Net

http://grampy.ent.rochester.edu/pub/balloon/

Hobbies

Hundreds of balloon modelers (people who twist long rubber balloons into the shapes of dogs and airplanes) have contributed to this archive of how-to messages and pictures on their unique art. It's a whirlwind trip: in the FAQ, we searched for the word "poodle," and up popped a diagram explaining how to make a French poodle's head. A photo of Woody Woodpecker as balloon appears here

(watch that beak!), as do the addresses and phone numbers of Net-using balloon sculptors (Spatz the Clown has an e-mail address!). Larry Moss compiled this formidable library from contributions to an e-mail list. And as you might expect, he's a "a former street performer, now suffering the fate of a 'real' job as a computer programmer."

Burlingame Online's PEZ Exhibit

http://www.spectrumnet.com/pez/

Hobbies

With its cult following, PEZ candy has invaded the Web here with an exhibit of roughly 175 dispensers. Before entering the exhibit, we learned that PEZ

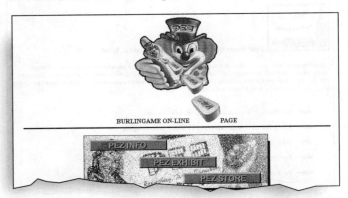

is an abbreviation of the German word for peppermint, and that the seemingly addictive little bricks were created by Austrian Eduard Haas in 1927 as a cure for smoking, no less. At that time, they were marketed for adults in plain, characterless dispensers known to collectors as "regulars." The page includes a diagram showing how to properly insert the pellets into the dispensers, and ads for PEZ collectibles like the out-of-production Smurf dispenser. The collection includes the usual suspects—Miss Piggy, Foghorn Leghorn, and Daffy Duck—along with stranger entries like Mr. Ugly, Wounded Soldier, and Diabolic. Sorry, no Marie Antoinette.

Collector's Coin Universe

http://www.coin-universe.com/index.html

Hobbies

Numismatists of every denomination will want to put a bookmark in this excellent home page for coin and currency collecting. Among the offerings at this

online collector's 'zine are news of upcoming coin shows, dealer ads, a U.S. Coin Directory, and a "Coin Dealer Newsletter." At the catalog for Heritage Rare Coin Galleries, we found quite a selection, including an American coin from 1793 selling for more than $50,000! Links and searchable indexes will put you in touch with the "Israeli Government Coins and Medals Corp.," "Frank Chlebana's Coins Page," "Scott Travers' Rare Coin Consumer Protection," and lots more. There's even (inevitably) coin software. Enjoyable "Coin Market Slang" file includes the meanings of "bellybutton dollar," "onepapa," and "whizzing."

Cyberspace World Railroad Home Page

http://www.mcs.com/~dsdawdy/cyberoad.html
Hobbies

Whew! (Or, woo-woooooo!) This roundhouse is stuffed with steel wheels, club cars, and timetables. Don't expect toy choo-choos: it's a serious train site for serious train buffs. (And don't call it the home page—it's the "main manifest.") Handsome photos (including "Things I Photograph Along the Rails That Most People *Don't!*") and graphics accompany a wide range of articles and newsletters: on our last visit, we found a huge article on the opening of the Steamtown National Historic Site in Pennsylvania, a copy of the Conrail Transportation newsletter, and an essay on traveling by steam train in China. Site creator Daniel Dawdy includes online schedules for Amtrak, Via, and Chicago's Metra lines. Looks like a lot of old brakemen hang out here.

Daylilies Online

http://www.assumption.edu/HTML/daylilies/about.html
Hobbies

This virtual garden of daylilies is lovingly tended by Nick Chase, who maintains that this site is "the Internet's most extensive collection of high-resolution daylily photos." It's hard to argue with the sheer volume of images here, not to mention with a guy who sets forth such explicit instructions on getting the best results out of your color monitor. Adjust your color viewing levels to "thousands" or "millions," then blast into the glorious petals of regal blooms like Ceremonial Dance, an early-midseason semi-evergreen diploid. The article "Triploids Are Fertile" advises that nothing is known for sure about the fertility of triploids when crossed with tetraploids. A frightening thought, isn't it? Superb links to other daylily connections and commercial nurseries.

GardenNet

`http://www.olympus.net/gardens/welcome.html`
Hobbies

Gardennet is a super gardening and botanical reference with real eye

appeal. With pointers to gardening associations, online catalogs, and even a virtual "visitors' center," it's hard to imagine anything that GardenNet hasn't thought of first. Take a stroll through a Rhododendron paradise, or use "Gardens On-line" to order specialized brochures and browse a list of English country gardens across America. Knot gardens, herb gardens, maze gardens, children's gardens, even gardens with wheelchair access—if they're out there, GardenNet points them out. Also includes the latest horticultural news and reviews, and a huge list of links to societies for everything from bamboo to Siberian irises. (In fact, it's rather amazing how many floral associations are out there.) You'll find that this garden is beautifully tended.

The Garden Patch

`http://mirror.wwa.com/mirror/garden/patch.htm`
Hobbies

This terrific gardening page (part of the online magazine *The Virtual Mirror*) will turn even the blackest thumb a shade greener. Gardener Barry Glick bring visitors up-to-date on the latest horticultural news, fielding the tough questions on *Pachysandra procumbens* and dwarf conifers. When you're through with Barry, grab some hot turf tips or post a request

for that oddball tiger lily seed in the Garden Exchange, where you can also explore ways to combat those troublesome garden pests. The *Southern Perennials & Herbs* catalog offers deals galore. If you *still* don't see what you want, link to the Garden Spider's Web for pointers to botanical pages around the world.

Hang Gliding Site Guide

http://www.poweropen.org/hang/Sites.html

Hobbies

Far-flung, wing-clad cliff jumpers will appreciate this guide to our planet's best hang-gliding sites. Click on the continent of your choice and the "sensitive" world map (from Arizonan Gill Couto) directs you to steep relief everywhere from Ed Levin Park to Baba Dogi. Details include elevation, seasonal restrictions, permit requirements, the nearest (yikes!) emergency facilities. We learned that there are wells scattered around the pasture at Shiotsuka Kogen in Japan: "You would be well advised to avoid landing in one." (A little hang-gliding humor, there.) A list of frequently asked questions ("What is a static line?" "What is a payout winch?") is included here, and hang-gliding clubs and businesses are also listed. It makes a fine resource for thrill-seekers everywhere.

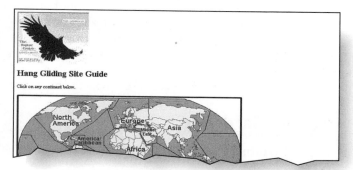

The Sky is a Big Island in Your Mind

http://www.well.com/user/winslow/index.html

Hobbies

Winslow Colwell's colorful kite pages may cause you to leave your job and go fly a kite. Just his opening image—a kite tail of falling pink men, floating in a blue sky—is cause for jubilation. In real life, Colwell is a graphic artist for the Whole Earth Review, but in these pages you'll find images of his ripstop-nylon kites (plus a little story on Renee Magritte to read while downloading them), a review of kite resources, and several links to other pages. This site is really more about the philosophy than the business of kites, though, and the author's personal memories and musings provide much of the material. For instance, he admits that he really doesn't "get gravity" and calls kiting the art of "applied haiku." It's hard not to catch his excitement here.

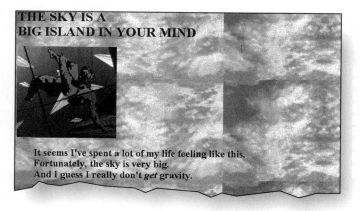

THE SKY IS A BIG ISLAND IN YOUR MIND

It seems I've spent a lot of my life feeling like this.
Fortunately, the sky is very big.
And I guess I really don't *get* gravity.

Kew Gardens

`http://www.rbgkew.org.uk/`

Hobbies

Kew Gardens are London's landmark royal botanic gardens. This page offers a great introduction to Kew's famous aquatic and conservation gardens, though it lacks the visuals one might hope for from a group which reports that it's making 3D pictures of its "hardy woody" collection. But we did find scads of info on Kew research, like that being done in the Living Collections Department, where scientists are assembling what they hope will be the world's largest and most diverse collection of plant life. Kew's work in biodiversity and plant ecology makes fascinating reading for both student and scientist. An aerial map plotting the layout of the gardens gives the viewer an idea of the massive London presence of these gardens—they cover nearly 300 acres from the River Thames to the Kew Road.

Master Gardener

`http://leviathan.tamu.edu/lls/mg`

Hobbies

The Master Gardener has a fountain of advice for the troubled garden. Appearing here courtesy of the Texas Agricultural Extension Service, this is a sort of "Dear Abby" for your bean patch. Spots on your tomatoes? The solution could be as simple as discontinuing overhead watering and removing debris from the plant base. And if those darned curcurbits (squash and melons) are misshapen or bitter, the problem may be poor soil fertility. (If *you're* misshapen or bitter, the problem lies elsewhere.) We searched the database for "all trees" and turned up more than a dozen common problems, along with possible causes and solutions for all of them. From lettuce and onions, mangos and papayas to zoysia and boxwood, the Master Gardener seems to cover all the bases.

Model Horse Gallery

`http://www.ecst.csuchico.edu/~rebecca/mh/`

Hobbies

Model-horse collector Janet Piercy is passionate about miniature horses and the artists behind them. Her site leads you to photo gallery after photo gallery—more than 1,000 images all told. You'll see model horses artfully made over to look more real, with additions like lifelike manes and tails and miniature saddles of tooled leather. Visit the Carol Williams room and you'll discover a series of the artist's blanket-and-varnish Appaloosas—many of which are photographed in fields outdoors, against a blue sky. (Surrealism at its finest!) Elsewhere, Piercy leads you to "The Model Horse Manufacturers Encyclopedia," which she's drafted herself. Pictures of a few other animal species are included, too, though you may wonder why anyone would make a model hog. And as a kicker, she throws in pictures of kittens for free!

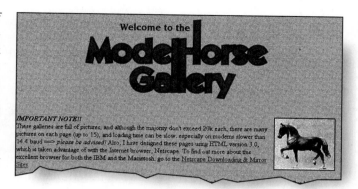

Welcome to the
ModelHorse Gallery

IMPORTANT NOTE!!
These galleries are full of pictures, and although the majority don't exceed 20k each, there are many pictures on each page (up to 15), and loading time can be slow, especially on modems slower than 14.4 baud ==> *please be advised!* Also, I have designed these pages using HTML version 3.0, which is taken advantage of with the Internet browser, Netscape. To find out more about this excellent browser for both the IBM and the Macintosh, go to the Netscape Downloading & Mirror Sites.

Classic Mustang Page

http://www.dwx.com/~bob/topics/mustang/

Hobbies

Fans of the Shelby GT-350 Fastback, Convertible, Mach 1, and other classic Mustang models will be revved by this fine page. Photos from the Central Iowa Mustang Club show are slow-loading, but worth the wait. The trivia page provides a history of the age of Shelby, listing what new cars and options appeared each year between "1964 1/2" and 1973. And don't miss the account of site creator Bob Dooley's 1965 Fastback restoration project, in which he overcame "delusions of grandeur" and doled out a "butt-load of cash, but man is it fun to drive around." (You can see and hear Bob's fixed-up Mustang "being naughty.") Virtual community is also encouraged here, with classifieds, clubs, and the chance to submit your entry to "Mustangs of the Net."

The Orchid House

http://sciserv2.uwaterloo.ca/orchids.html

Hobbies

"In the world of flowers," boasts this lovely site, "orchids are the undisputed champions." (And we have to admit, they are beautiful.) Here's a mammoth guide to the much-loved blossom, complete with species-by-species breakdowns of color, size, ideal temperature, humidity... even appropriate fertilizers. Orchid myths are exploded right and left: they don't need a greenhouse to get started, not all blooms come from the jungle, and they're no longer just "a rich man's hobby." Once you feel secure in your orchid expertise, you can check the index of show regulations to prepare your handiwork for judging by the pros. Aimed at the orchid hobbyist, the Orchid House also includes a nifty H.G. Wells story, "Flowering of the Strange Orchid."

The Plastic Princess Collector's Page

http://deepthought.armory.com/~zenugirl/barbie.html

Hobbies

You can't help but love this monument to Barbie, Ken, and the rainbow of other plastic fashion dolls. Here, you learn that a couple of Santa Cruz lifeguards once fitted Ken with a pair of cement boots and shoved him from the city's wharf. (There's photographic proof.) Or, if your Barbie feels like being politically incorrect, you can contact a woman who makes miniature mink stoles. The smattering of photos on the home page includes Barbie in a fantastic Bob Mackie gown; keep exploring and you'll find more photos and more dolls, including Francies, Caseys, Staceys, and Julias. (We also met "Billy, The World's First Out and Proud Gay Doll," manufactured by a company in England.) Site-mistress Zoli Nazaari-Uebele, an engineer in real life, even reveals her dream item: a DKNY Barbie (brunette, please).

The Rose Gallery

http://www.halcyon.com/cirsium/rosegal/welcome.htm

Hobbies

The scent is lacking, but the roses sure look swell in this virtual gallery. This is

THE ROSE GALLERY

A Collection of Old and Old-Fashioned Roses

Last Updated: September 18, 1995

heaven for flower children, offering an exhaustive collection of varietals classed by color, height, and aroma. Viewers will delight in the blooms of Bourbons, Teas, Noisettes, and Ramblers, and find super indexes of hardy roses for cooler climates (including one named for actor James Mason) and of roses with exceptional disease-resistant toughness (we hereby nominate Bette Davis). Charming names like Mermaid, Moonsprite, and Awakening give way to bright bursts of color, and may make you wish there really *was* a scratch 'n' sniff button for your computer screen. Cultivation tips, history, and more, all expertly tended by Washington state rose gardener Andrew Schulman.

SailNet

http://www.sailnet.com/
Hobbies

From Hallberg-Rassi custom-rafted boat specifications to the "Bacardi Bayview Port Huron to Mackinac Race," here is a virtual community for recreational sailors. Visitors can ponder the problem-of-the-month in *Ocean Navigator* ("the most serious magazine in the recreational marine field"), visit the U.S. Coast Guard's new server, or link to online class associations like the Snipe Sailing Server. SailNet provides news and commercial services; on our last visit, we learned how Seabreeze Yacht Charters in the British Virgin Islands weathered Hurricane Luis by tying their 30+ yachts in a mangrove swamp, and we browsed a collection of Yager Sails.

Order Omega "Reef Runner" amphibious footwear, read how all the medals won by MIT varsity sailing coach Fran Charles would probably sink a boat, and enjoy surfing the expansive links from here.

SEDS High Power Rocketry Page

http://seds.lpl.arizona.edu/rocket/rocket.html
Hobbies

Part of the University of Arizona Students for the Exploration and Development of Space Web site, these pages describe all you'll ever need to send those powerful, not-quite-toy rockets sky-high. That includes how to get an FAA waiver for your high power rocket launch and where to find radio controls, engines, and even Super-8 rocket movie cameras. You can download plans, read up on frequently asked questions, contact related clubs and organizations, or learn where to buy a model of the space shuttle *Endeavor*. In the glossary, you'll discover that "kitbash" refers to a contest in which teams must

combine two model kits into a new, workable design. (And we thought it was just a hobbyist's angry outburst.)

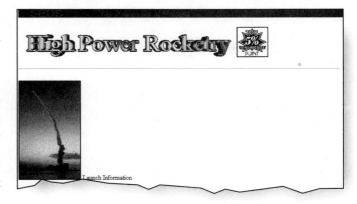

Virtual Flyshop

http://www.flyshop.com/

Hobbies

The Virtual Flyshop is home to what it calls "The First Internet Journal of Flyfishing," featuring articles such as "If I Only Had One Fly," offering tactics for fishing the Woolly Bugger. Another onsite feature, "Riverkeeper," tracks fishing conditions from Florida to California and Alberta to New Mexico. This page also offers the "finest in quality flyfishing merchandise" from a variety of vendors, plus classifieds by and for its readers. The Forum combines, say, expert backcasting advice with a chance to brag about your Deschutes River catch, share photos, solicit suggestions for fishing in Switzerland, and so on. "The Internet is a community," this site insists, "and as a community, we need to have a Flyshop." It can certainly carry those big ol' fish stories to new heights (or rather, lengths).

The Virtual Garden

http://www.pathfinder.com/@@u0fpgKDYIQAKAPPe/vg/Welcome/welcome.html

Hobbies

This first-class home gardening resource from Time-Life looks great *and* offers up some of the best online info around.

Reference materials include a terrific book list (complete with lengthy excerpts), and a superb interactive plant encyclopedia. And if your thumb is only green indoors, consult the House Plant Pavilion for advice on choosing the best plants for your home. Fun, easy how-to projects take you step-by-step through building a rock garden or digging a lily pond. Nice botanical tours are included, too. Of course, the folks at Time-Life hope you'll buy a book or two while you're here, but it's hard to hold that against them, considering the quality of the material they offer here. This is one of the sunniest garden spots on the Web.

Wonderful Stitches

http://www.webcom.com/~stitch/
Hobbies

Few navigate the no-man's-land between folk art and technology better than The Needlepoint Gazette (a publisher of stitch collection books). With meaningful links at every turn, its site offers needlepoint and cross-stitch patterns, as well as a very politely presented selection of books for sale. The craft is easy to learn: "One only need know that each stitch begins in a specific hole and ends in a specific hole." Once you've mastered the basics, a "Decorative Stitch of the Month" lets you try techniques like the Scotch Check and Corn on the Cob. Well-organized and photographed (including close-ups), the patterns run the gamut of styles and patterns, but our favorite was a mix of old and new—Cybersampler I depicts numbers, the alphabet, and a sampling of designs based on pixel patterns in MacPaint. How techno-retro-homespun-chic!

pets and animals

All You Ever Wanted To Know About Hedgehogs!

http://www.primenet.com/~khyri/hedgehog
Pets and Animals

In truth, you'll probably still have questions after you see this, but at least you'll be on that hedgehog superhighway we keep hearing about. This short grocery list of links will tell you how to get one of the U.K.'s most promising exports, and then what to do with the furry little thing once it has captured your heart. Brian MacNamara, whose pet's name is Velcro, tells how to pick up a hedgehog (carefully,

continued

All You Ever Wanted To Know About Hedgehogs continued

of course!) and warns that "a free roaming hedgehog will climb anything it can get its claws hooked into," while site creator Liz Bartlett answers the question, "Can you draw a hedgehog in ASCII?" If you're just browsing, our advice is to go directly to the "hedgehog flavored crisps" aisle and gain an appreciation for the *seriousness* of the subject for some.

Ask Mr. Puddy

http://www.sils.umich.edu/~nscherer/AskPuddy.html

Pets and Animals

A funny and lively take-off on Dear Abby-type columnists, Ask Mr. Puddy is for kitties and their owners (or "slaves," as the kitties call them here) who need a helping hand with life's little traumas. Questions range from "Why does my cat chew on my toes at three a.m. every morning?" to "I'm not a good watch cat, so they're getting another one. Do I have to like him?" One feline correspondent, wanting to know why her owner was behaving strangely, was advised to "call the nearest State Mental Health Facility and have her institutionalized for her own good. Make sure you get her ATM p.i.n. number before they drag her off." A light-hearted romp through the kitty and human psyche, Ask Mr. Puddy also carries a disclaimer, lest you think he's a certified puddytherapist. He's only an amateur.

The Beekeeping Home Page

http://weber.u.washington.edu/~jlks/bee.html

Pets and Animals

This is a beekeeping clearinghouse, with links to university archives and bee-related newsgroups. Honeybees are emphasized (they're the ones that make money, after all), but other bees get their due, like the so-called "killer" bees (now traveling under the more delicate, less threatening title of "Africanized"). You'll find online apiaries, articles like "Protecting Beehives From Bear Damage," plans for building a honey extractor, and even a link to some literary quotations ("How doth the little busy bee..."). Our favorite stop here is the B-EYE page, an interactive program that enables you to view and manipulate a series of patterns and images, then click to see how a bee views the same image.

A Breed Apart

http://www.pcix.com/abap/index.html

Pets and Animals

This top-notch greyhound page is what an online magazine ought to be. Fans and owners of the speedy pups should race here to see pinups of handsome dogs, learn about breed history, or submit their own stories. Retired greyhounds are available nationwide for adoption, and the terrific resources provided here can help you find your next pet (perhaps an old racer who didn't quite make the Hall of Fame in Abilene, Kansas). Articles generally focus on greyhounds as pets rather than as athletes, though on our last visit we read about some hounds who were working on second careers as "therapy dogs." Lovers of other breeds can still find useful information here (like an elaborate recipe for "liver cake"), but they may wish the producers of "A Breed Apart" had a magazine for every breed.

Canine Web

http://snapple.cs.washington.edu:600/canine/canine.html

Pets and Animals

Malamutes, Rottweilers... Tibetan Mastiffs? Yup, they're all here, and then some. This is a darn fine index to dog info across the Web, compiled by grad student (and apparent canine fiend) Terri Watson. Scroll down the long list of links to find sites on individual breeds; there's excellent information available on quite a lot of dogs, from the Dalmatian to the Hungarian Viszla. This page will also take you to canine-friendly sites like obedience school, the Iditarod sled races, even the dog genome project at Berkeley; you'll also find lists of frequently asked questions and advice from owners and breeders.

Cat Fanciers' Home Page

`http://www.ai.mit.edu/fanciers/fanciers.html`
Pets and Animals

Breeding notes, veterinary questions, and other feline fetishes await you here. (But why so few kitty photos?) The frequently asked questions on cat colors cover such varietal favorites as tabbies and "solids and smokes" (but we want more kitty photos!). The essay "Are Owned Cats Causing an Overpopulation Crisis?" offers a mindbending mathematical defense of cat ownership. The in-depth breed descriptions are full of facts and speculation, like the theory that the Maine Coon "sprang from the six pet cats which Marie Antoinette sent to Wiccasset, Maine, when she was planning to escape from France during the French Revolution." We especially enjoyed the Japanese Bobtail and Siamese entries. (They have kitty photos!) This site has excellent links to cat shows and organizations like The Happy Household Pet Cat Club.

Cat Fanciers' Home Page

Madchen mit Katze II, Franz Marc, 1912

Welcome to the Fanciers home page! We are a group of cat breeders, exhibitors and other ailurophiles brought together by an Internet mailing list called Fanciers.

Cat Map

`http://www.timis.ac.jp/tcat/catmap/www_cat_map.html`
Pets and Animals

This handsome map shows you Web cats around the world! The virtual tour of pussycat home pages takes you from Tokyo to Toronto as you circumnavigate the globe the Calico way. Visit the Pet Port in Holland for some information about boarding cats at their "kattenpension," or drop in on the purrsonal pages of critters with names like Basil and Megahertz. You can even breeze past those wordy White House intros with a link that takes you right to pictures of the Clintons' cat, Socks. We especially enjoyed hangin' loose with Mr. Puddy; we suggest you ask his sage advice on matters of the heart. And yes, you can put your cat on this map as well.

Cows Caught in the Web

`http://www.brandonu.ca/~ennsnr/Cows/Welcome.html`

Pets and Animals

Cow jokes. Cow sounds. Cow trivia. The alt.cows.moo.moo.moo newsgroup. You get the idea. A visit here is a day in the pasture: slow and relaxed, plenty of time to hang with the herd and chew the ol' cud. Check out the car dealer-style Cow Price List, which includes "options" like "two-tone exterior" and "four spigot, high-output drain system." And where else will you find this announcement: "Tomorrow is the anniversary, in 1930, of the first flight by a cow in an airplane. Elm Farm Ollie, while watched by reporters, produced milk that was put into containers and parachuted over St. Louis, Mo." Most heifer surfers will find this a nice break from routine. Call us when it's time to head in for the barn.

Dog FAQs

`http://www.zmall.com/pet_talk/dog-faqs/homepage.html`

Pets and Animals

For the complete dope on dogs, you can't do better than this page written by the members of the Usenet group rec.pet.dogs (and compiled by Cindy Tittle Moore). There's nothing new under the sun, as the saying goes, and whatever you might wonder about your dog has probably already been wondered aloud here. Under "Your New Puppy," for instance, you'll find categories like "Crying at Night" and "Don't Be Surprised When..." Puppies are, of course, just the start. Dogs in the trash? Try slicing up jalapeno peppers and wrapping them in Kleenex, then tossing them in the garbage: "A few days of this should convince your dog that trash cans are not fun." Plenty of info on specific breeds, too.

Electronic Zoo

http://netvet.wustl.edu/e-zoo.htm
Pets and Animals

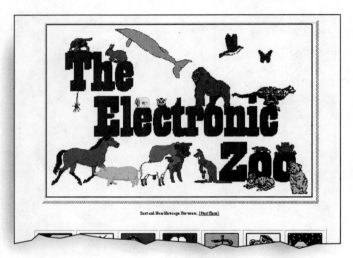

Washington University veterinarian Ken Boschert, who maintains the informative NetVet page, also provides surfers with this site that's a bit less scientific and a lot more fun. This directory of animal images on the Net is a delight: hepcats can dig shots of fossils, cartoon animals, bugs, and birds, in addition to practically every kind of domestic beast. Even fictional animals have their own quarters. Just click on the animal of your choice for lists of places to go (and who can resist a page on the Dismal Swamp Shrew?). For mad-scientist types, check out the "3D Rendering of a Dog Heart." That title alone is a hard act to follow. In short, this is a fine place to start your hunt for animals on the Web.

FINS: Fish Information Service

http://www.actwin.com/fish/index.html
Pets and Animals

From freshwater to salty brine, tropic to temperate climes, find the fish you love using this clever reference tool. If you're not sure what you're looking for and you just want to do a little underwater surfing, try the freshwater or marine fish catalogs. For info on a particular subject, go to the huge Usenet archives and search by subject; you'll find specifics on mantis shrimps, medusa worms, and marine salt. If you prefer to be an armchair aquarian, you'll enjoy the Smithsonian's underwater pictures, not to mention the swell minnow... er, *mini*-movies. If you get hooked, online pet stores are there to help you stock your home aquarium.

The Freddie Street Cats Home Page

http://www.ftech.net/~imagine/home.htm

Pets and Animals

These five felines from Freddie Street (in London) have created their *own* strictly-for-kitties site. ("Don't get distracted by pens and other goodies on the desk," they advise.) Each has a home page; Sass, for instance, is also known as "The Incredible Vomiting Cat," and visitors can learn how he came to acquire this unsettling moniker. Tips for tabbies here include a "Cat's Restaurant Guide" (don't give up on that rabbit hutch: "Perhaps the resident human will make a mistake and leave the door open") and a "Cat's Guide to Sex" ("It is important to remember at all times that girls are armed and dangerous!").

When you've had your fill, follow the territorial markings to other recommended puss sites. Purrrrfect.

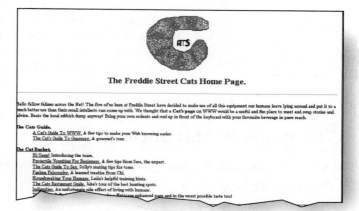

Goats!

http://www.ics.uci.edu/~pazzani/4H/Goats.html

Pets and Animals

The Irvine (California) Mesa Charros 4-H Club wants you to know how much fun goats can be. This friendly guide gives you tips on everything from finding the "favorite scratchy part" to common diseases and goat-raising costs. Tip number one: "We primarily raise does because they are easier to manage, they don't have an offensive odor (unlike bucks), and there are more shows for does." Offensive odors aside, we had *fun* here. We filled up on goat stats, watched a LaMancha "grow" ears, then pondered the big question, "Artificial Insemination vs. Natural Breeding," with its beefcake photos of a buff buck and an alluring aluminum cylinder. It's a simple page, really, but it's nice to see the kids get into the act like this.

Hamster Page

http://www.tela.bc.ca/hamster/
Pets and Animals

"Hamsters are honest, fun-loving, and trustworthy rodents that are deserving of more respect!" announces this page. The authors admit that their page began as "something of a joke," but the little varmints seem to have grown on them. Perhaps you'll feel the same way after visiting the "Useful Hamster-Related Resources," "Useless Hamster-Related Resources," and "Not Really Hamster-Related Resources." Where else will you find links to *Svenska Hamsterforeningen*, the "national club for Swedish hamster fans"? You'll find no pictures here, but you can link to Helen the Hamster's Homepage for a view of Helen taking a ride in a pint-sized air balloon and nibbling on some sweet and sour sauce. We admit it: they're cute!

The House Rabbit Society

http://www.psg.lcs.mit.edu/~carl/paige/HRS-home.html
Pets and Animals

This all-volunteer non-profit wants to enlighten you to the joys of rabbit ownership. Why would you want a

Welcome to the House Rabbit Society WWW Server!

The House Rabbit Society is an all-volunteer, non-profit organization with two primary goals:

1. To rescue abandoned rabbits and find permanent homes for them and
2. To educate the public and assist humane societies, through publications on rabbit care, phone consultation, and classes upon request.

Since 1988 over 2,800 rabbits have been rescued through House Rabbit Society foster homes across the country. The House Rabbit Society has been granted a tax-exempt status under the Internal Revenue code for prevention of cruelty to animals.

Thumper in the house? Well, they're social, curious animals, and they can be trained to use a litter box. (It's a weird image, we admit.) They even *purr* when they're happy! The Society places abused and abandoned domestic rabbits in loving homes regardless of breed or temperament. (Of the rabbits, not the owners.) You can look for rabbits in your own locale via the online adoption roster here, with pictures and bunny bios. New owners will find plenty of advice on food, exercise, and vet care, including a list of rabbit toys: try a "soft drink can with a pebble inside it for noise."

LlamaWeb

http://www.webcom.com/~degraham/welcome.html

Pets and Animals

Llama gurus Dale Graham and Tom Reichert have years of experience with llama love: "When breeding llamas, the *first* time they breed is a great time to trim toenails on both male and female llama. This is one of the only times that they will not notice their feet being handled." (Same with us.) Pictures of these charming camelids abound, and readers can submit their own photos to an ongoing "Cute Baby Llama Contest." This site has plenty of suggestions on the routine maintenance of llamas, plus some Fun Things To Do with them. Whether your llamas are hiking companions or sweater sources, you may well agree that this is "the single most informative source" for llama lore on the Web.

Mike's Herpetocultural Home Page

http://gto.ncsa.uiuc.edu/pingleto/herp.html

Pets and Animals

Herpetology is the study of amphibians and reptiles, so this page is chock full of fun critter names like Day Gecko, Western Worm Snake, and Rosebelly Lizard. Mike Pingleton is an amateur herp-lover who recounts his snake-crazy background and current breeding projects: "I wasn't the only seventh-grader out tramping around the woods and grabbing garter snakes and box turtles, but I'm the only one left who still does." Look at his photo gallery of strange frogs and you can start to see why he's mesmerized. You can also read Mike's Herpetofaunal Life List, in which he recounts all the species he's observed in their natural habitats, including the Keeled Earless Lizard. (Lizards have ears?) Nice collection of links to other herpetology fans, too.

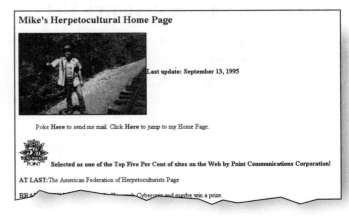

NetVet

http://netvet.wustl.edu/
Pets and Animals

NetVet marks out its territory here with a colorful list of veterinary home pages. Vets and zoologists will frolic amidst these fields of links to colleges, labs, and animal-rights groups. The site features a Pick of the Litter (the best animal page of the week), and it's also the Web home of the USDA's Animal Welfare Information Center, which covers topics like "ruminant anesthesia problems." Pet owners who just want to know how much to feed a two-headed calf will have more trouble. Finding ANYthing can be hard here, since the links are piled up behind complex categories like Informatics and Virtual Library. Still, veterinarian Dr. Ken Boschert deserves a scratch behind the ears for his hard work in compiling this site. Good boy!

Wolf Society Home Page

http://www.edu.isy.liu.se/~z93joala/wolf/
Pets and Animals

This beautiful page from the Wolf Society of Sweden is devoted to dispelling myths and fears about the Canis Lupus. "If humans were more like wolves," the Society avers, "we should have a better world." We'd all drool a lot more, too, but why quibble? Stunning photos accompany the history and folklore; a bit of an anatomy lesson is accompanied by instructions on how to tell wolf tracks from those of a lynx or dog. (If you find it all a bit *too* compelling, the site can send you to "100 Ways to Tell if You're Becoming/Have Become a Werewolf.") The page reprints some stories and poems—though "Howl," we found, is not a reading from Alan Ginsburg, but a haunting wolf call. Great page.

The World Equine Resource List

http://www.abdn.ac.uk/~src011/equine.html
Pets and Animals

A horse is a horse, of course, of course. Unless, of course, you're a member of Scotland's Aberdeen University Riding Club—then you might want to make some distinctions among your equestrian friends. This page lists over 200 resources, from the mundane (bridles and tack) to the exotic (the frozen horse heads of Australia's Murdoch University). Those still reluctant to saddle up can amble over to the Model Horse Web Page to share news on expos and trading with other hobbyists. And if you really want to sing "A horse is a horse of course, of course," check out the complete lyrics to the famous Mr. Ed theme song, which are here too.

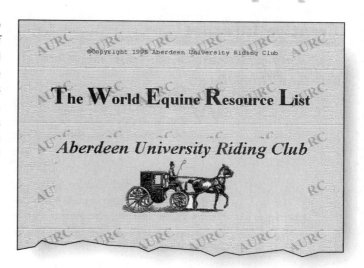

©Copyright 1995 Aberdeen University Riding Club

The World Equine Resource List

Aberdeen University Riding Club

personal home pages

personal home pages

Carolyn Burke's Diary

http://carolyn.org/~clburke/
Personal Home Pages

This is, quite simply, the ongoing diary of a real woman named Carolyn Burke. Carolyn is a Canadian resident, and she used to live with a guy named Peter. They broke up, but she still loves him, which occasionally reduces her to tears. Seem too personal? Well, it is her *diary*, and it's filled with happy, tense, exasperated, and sobering moments (kind of like actual life). For added thrills, imagine being one of the Net-connected friends whom she discusses, and not always in the nicest of terms. Much of it is meaningless to the casual reader, but if you have the patience to catch up on all the days you've missed so far, you'll wonder again how anybody could bear to lay out so much of their guts for public perusal.

Creative Internet

http://www.galcit.caltech.edu/~ta/creative.html

Personal Home Pages

What happens when you give two grad students in aeronautical engineering some space to play with on a Net server? Nutty fun, judging by Creative Internet, which emanates from CalTech. Links include the Pop Culture Scavenger Hunt, a trivia tour of the Web; the WWW Dating Game, a lighthearted interactive matchmaking service borrowing the TV format; and the politically incorrect Asylum, which is stuffed with enough strangeness to be a site in itself. And, if you're lucky enough to have your own Web site and some programming knowledge, they cheerfully provide scripts you can use to create your own wizardry. Far too many activities to list here, but rest assured it's a fine way to blow a perfectly good evening. With wacky aeronautical engineers like this, you may think twice about boarding your next plane.

Crime Scene Evidence File

http://odin.cbu.edu/~vaskin/crime/crime.html

Personal Home Pages

"True Crime" meets the Web at this site from "Yoknapatawpha County" (the imaginary setting of many of William Faulkner's stories). This fascinating scene purports to provide details of two unsolved but connected murders. "The badly beaten body of William Giblin was found in a Miami motel room. Evidence at the crime scene links Greg Giblin, the victim's brother, to the killing." Visitors can explore the scene, examine evidence, and even suggest solutions. Eerie and elaborate, with gruesome evidence photos and video clips from "surveillance cameras." The creators go out of their way to cover their tracks and present this as a realistic investigation; it's quite a production. Even as a put-on, it's stark and dramatic. Gripping use of the Web.

Cybergrrl

http://www.cybergrrl.com/

Personal Home Pages

Who says there aren't women on the Web? Cybergrrl (yup, it's spelled that way—it's a Net thang) dishes up a potpourri of information, mostly having to do with cool places by, for, and about women on the Net and beyond. We especially like Webgrrls!, and yes, the site is mostly just full of links, but the links are useful, well organized, and presented in such a personal way that they're hard to resist. Cybergrrl's got a classic Web addiction: she offers hot links, speaks her mind (especially on domestic violence), plugs her favorite movies, even introduces her personal trainer. There's also a collection of articles published by the site's creator. But the big strength of this site is its surfability: anyone who suggests visits to both the CIA and the Indigo Girls is OK by us.

The Cybergrrl Original

For those of you who are used to the original Cybergrrl, here are some of the areas featured there.

Some Things I've Written

Various articles and a story or two.

My Favorite Things

Some things that I like - if I like 'em, I'll plug 'em.

Dave's Web of Lies

http://www.cs.man.ac.uk/~hancockd/lies.htm

Personal Home Pages

"Humphrey Bogart's real name was Bumphrey Hogart." "Egg yolks are placed inside eggs using a special tool called a Stimpson's Wrangler." The Web of Lies ("Since 1873") takes the guesswork out of the Internet—you *know* everything here is false. The page is happily devoted to avoiding the truth. Visitors can contribute their own lies to be listed along with other whoppers, such as "The pogo stick was originally invented by the Pope as a convenient mode of transport inside the Vatican." Even the Web details are lies, including the following error message: "The database server cannot be accessed due to a severe ant infestation."

The Faherty Web

http://www.ultranet.com/~faherty/
Personal Home Pages

C'mon over to the Fahertys' place for a little supper. Ring the doorbell, wipe your feet, and buzz the intercom. Host John will welcome you into his delightful

Welcome to the Faherty Web Home Page

domain, where you can meet the whole family, or just hang with the Faherty cat, Felix, at his CyberScratchingPost. This is honest-to-goodness, cyber-fashion family entertainment, where everyone gets into the act: even third-grader Joey has a home page (though we suspect Dad, a technology consultant for DEC, had something to do with it). Keep your headphones handy: half the fun here is finding surprise audio clips around every corner. Speaking of sounds, you can also flip through the "Meet the Fahertys" section, with recorded messages for each family member is available (yes, that includes Felix). The graphics are super, and the "virtual house" motif works very well.

The Garden of Eden

http://www.ugcs.caltech.edu/~eveander/
Personal Home Pages

Eve Astrid Andersson, the CalTech student who creates this page, is something of a Web celeb for her fascination with the mathematical concept of pi. (The antennae that sometimes sprout from her head also make her somewhat memorable.) Andersson has a swell imagination and a sense of humor to match: she tells stories, shows off pictures of her dog, and

pretty much chats up a storm; she's the kid you loved sitting across the table from in study hall. She's also one of America's few mechanical engineers with a passion for cows and the "pulsating red sea squirt." And she's so enthusiastic about pi, you may even wish you'd memorized its first 200 digits yourself.

George H. Goble

http://ghg.ecn.purdue.edu/
Personal Home Pages

Purdue University engineer George Goble (*not* the comedian of *Hollywood Squares* semi-fame) has found the quickest way to light a barbecue: simply take a standard grill, get a small fire going, and dump on several gallons of liquid oxygen. This page provides photos and (huge) video clips of the ensuing firestorm. Goble provides us with the age-old warning, "don't try this at home," because liquid oxygen (LOX) is serious stuff: the grill is reduced to slag and almost completely vaporized. (Goble would look like a Greek god of fire wielding hot death, if it weren't for the T-shirt and jeans.) Dave Barry once wrote about this page in his newspaper column, which gives it a certain cachet along with sometimes-heavy traffic. It's quite funny and well worth the trip.

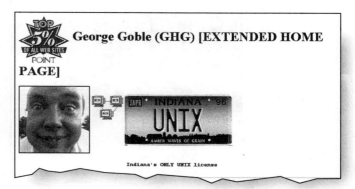

George Goble (GHG) [EXTENDED HOME PAGE]

Indiana's ONLY UNIX license

The Stephen Kings' Page

http://www.isisw3.com/sking/
Personal Home Pages

As its title suggests, this site is not about THE Stephen King, it's about Stephen Kings in general. The Webmaster, whose name coincides with that of the very famous author, shares some of the trials of his daily life. He gets questions like "Are you the real one?" ("How would you like being asked 'are you the real you' on a daily basis by complete strangers?") and "Are you related?" ("Yes, we're brothers. Think about it."). Similar tales of woe have been submitted to the site by Stephen Kings around the world (and there *is* an entry from the one who writes books in Bangor, Maine); even if your name isn't Stephen King, anyone suffering from "Famous Name Syndrome" is offered help with "setting up your own therapeutic home page."

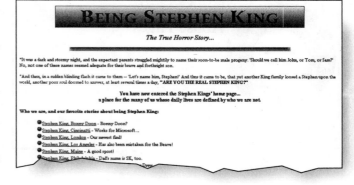

BEING STEPHEN KING

The True Horror Story...

Blake Kritzbergs's Liquid Bistro

`http://ucsub.colorado.edu/~kritzber/Home.html`

Personal Home Pages

Blake Kritzberg's site is most well-known for the "Babes On The Web II" exhibit, a tongue-in-cheek listing of the "babes" on the Web. It's not what you may expect—Blake is female, and the babes are men. (You have to imagine there are a lot of annoyed males using search tools to hunt for "babes" and getting this.) The page is a response to "Babes On The Web," a site by another author, which IS exactly what you'd expect. Less well-known is Kritzberg's personal writing collection, including "The Semi-interactive True Romance Page." That page includes winning lines like, "It wasn't merely Rogaine's e-mail eloquence that made Olivia's spine tingle. It was the self-portrait GIF he'd asked her to FTP from his account." An interesting read.

Blain Nelson's Abuse Pages

`http://www.az.com:80/~blainn/dv/index.html`

Personal Home Pages

Not until his wife left him did Blain Nelson know the degree of his abuse of her. Now the world knows, via the Net. In text form, Nelson offers two frank testimonials, and includes a half dozen or so from other contributors, including victims. The notes are sometimes weirdly personal: a week after his wife's departure, Nelson reports, he "returned to my house kinda cold and having discovered a plantar wart I hadn't known existed." He also lists about 40 questions to help readers identify themselves as an abuser or a victim, and emphasizes that just because a person can say "I didn't hit him/her" doesn't necessarily mean there isn't an emotionally abusive relationship (as Nelson's personal account illustrates). An unsettling and highly personal site.

Nomadic Research Labs

http://microship.ucsd.edu
Personal Home Pages

At first he may seem like a wandering Gump on wheels, but spend time here with '90s nomad Steven Roberts and his computerized recumbent bike, Behemoth, and you'll get drawn into an amazing travel adventure. Roberts is a technomad—he pedals around North America on a modified bike packed with electronic gadgetry that lets him file reports from wherever he happens to be.

You may think you've surfed into a Monty Python sketch, but there is a real and valuable discourse going on. (And great technical information about the Microship, a technomadic boat in development.) When you find yourself asking why he does it, check out the view from his office—116 KB of majestic mountains and valleys that may make you question your day job.

Pigeon Kickers of America Home Page

http://www.pitt.edu/~haast2/Pigeon/
Personal Home Pages

This site is about the (fictitious) sport of Pigeon Kicking. It's a nasty little page, but it's about a nasty little animal—the pigeon. With these winged irritants taking over the world's cities, a few hardy souls have decided to take matters into their own... feet. Visitors can browse letters from other sympathetic pigeon-kicker-wannabes, or read unflattering and strange

poems about pigeons ("Seven young pigeons/bang bang bang bang bang bang bang/make for a nice soup"). A suggestion for the Lazy Pigeon Kicker's Trap is also included: set up a large pane of glass and wait until a confused pigeon flies into it and renders itself paralyzed, and you kick it. This is not serious, exactly, but it is fairly funny—unless you're a pigeon.

Ram's Psychedelic Home Page

http://www.ram.org
Personal Home Pages

By day, Ram Samudrala worries about the protein folding problem (and after all, who doesn't?) at the Center for

Ram Samudrala

I'm a graduate fellow, doing my research on the protein folding problem, at the Centre for Advanced Research in Biotechnology in Rockville, MD. Click on the imagemap to explore some facet of me (be gentle!).

My interests are varied. First and foremost, I'm a computing nerd. I love music; I play the guitar, write, and record music as well, and publish stuff under the name of TWISTED HELICES. I am also the maintainer of the Primus band page (which was voted the best www band page). I just got myself a new set of rollerblades. I read a lot of comic books and goto the movies often. I am ordained as a Reverend in the Universal Life Church (even though I'm a staunch atheist) and we have started the Church of the Almighty Revealed in Biotechnology which explains my religion.

- My in-depth review of Woodstock '94, complete with pictures
- Cool pictures (and art done by me)

Advanced Research in Biotechnology. In his spare time, he stocks this crowded studio apartment of a site, which contains a list of links to places you don't see too often (no "NCSA What's New" or "Yahoo" here). Not only is Samudrala an atheist, but he's co-founder of the Church of the Almighty Revealed in Biotechnology (which is, in part, based on the protein folding problem). He's also a guitarist in the band Twisted Helices, a movie reviewer, and maintainer of the Primus home page. And he's funny to boot! A name like Ram must draw plenty of computer-geek jokes, but he doesn't seem to mind.

George Rarey's Cartoon Journals

http://www.nbn.com/home/rareybird/
Personal Home Pages

George Rarey was a fighter pilot in World War II, and he kept a cartoon

George Rarey's Journals of the 379th Fighter Squadron

In 1942 my father, George Rarey, a young cartoonist and commercial artist, was drafted into the Army Air Corps. He flew a P-47 before he drove a car. During his service he kept a cartoon journal of the daily life of the fighter pilots. A few weeks after D-Day he was killed in combat over France.

journal of his experiences. Sadly, he was killed in combat over France a few weeks after D-Day, but his son, Damon, shares portions of his journals on this Web site. Impressive enough, but it's particularly poignant when you discover the elder Rarey died without ever having seen his son, which makes this site not only a tribute, but a son's reflections on a father he never knew. To give a more personal side to the pilot and the times he lived in, Bob McKee, Rarey's wing man on his last mission, provides background notes to some illustrations. Rarey was a talented artist, and his drawings show a personal side of a very rugged situation.

Scott's Page of Evil

http://rampages.onramp.net/~scottgl/index.htm
Personal Home Pages

Scott's Page of Evil welcomes "all seekers of refuge from the banal recesses of home pages promoting goodness and light." Scott Glazer has pulled a switch on the usual cool bands/cool people/cool links idea and filled his personal page with things he hates—like Andie MacDowell ("Lucifer's actress"), Piers Anthony ("foul scribe of Hades"), and the French ("a whole nation of distilled evil"). He has a bit to say about organized religion, too (what page about evil would be complete without it?), and even he suggests that anyone easily offended should avoid it at all costs.

Visitors can leave their own evil ideas in a suggestion box, though Glazer admits that suggestion boxes may be evil in themselves. Funny and delightfully twisted.

Dave Siegel's Home Page

http://www.dsiegel.com/
Personal Home Pages

Dave Siegel's an expert on fonts and typography, Web site design, *and* the creation of screenplays for successful movies. He isn't shy about saying so, either. He says he can help screenwriters develop blockbusters with his "Nine-Act Structure" theory, simply by analyzing the plot structures of top-grossing movies. He'll tell you how to design a Web site the way it *ought* to be. He'll even tell you how to tie your shoes a better way, how much money *Pulp Fiction* has grossed to date, and how to kiss a woman. Whew! He makes no excuses for his arrogance, and at least in the realm of Web design, his attitude is justified.

Beyond that, Dave's soapbox is as big as it is beautiful, a vault of useful information for Web site designers and budding screenwriters.

Bob Sokol and Amyl on Stupid Pet Tricks

http://www.io.com/~twobit/spt/spt.html
Personal Home Pages

This is the personal narrative of Bob Sokol, whose dog, Amyl, appeared on Letterman's Stupid Pet Tricks back in the show's early days. Bob gives a behind-the-

Bob Sokol and Amyl on Stupid Pet Tricks

scenes rundown on his brush with fame from the time he answered the classified ad ("Have you taught your pet to do something good?") to Amyl's well-received performance. If you're really interested, you can download an entire movie of the appearance; what we liked, though, were descriptions like this one of Chris Elliot: "a very nice fellow who welcomed me with more enthusiasm than you would have expected from a guy who was spending his day interviewing little old ladies with parrots." (This was 1985, mind, so now you know what Chris had to wade through to become famous.) Pop-trivia buffs will appreciate this page.

Solid Space

http://www.teleport.com/~shojo/Solid.html
Personal Home Pages

A campy collection of oddments, this site offers diversions about music and pop culture artifacts. The Fabio Page

serves up typical pictures of the male model, replete with hokey romance-novel-inspired audio clips spoken by Fabio himself: "Your caress is my command," "I listen to a solo, and I think of a duet." Learn of the sinister trimmings surrounding PEZ candy dispensers, or visit a mini-museum on ViewMaster slide viewers. There's also a monthly offering called "Awful Music"; on our last visit it lambasted an album called "Switched-On Bacharach." ("Every song on this album should have 'in outer space' added to the end of the title," says the Webmaster.) Even with the insults, this is much more amusing than offensive.

Spinnwebe

http://www.thoughtport.com/spinnwebe/

Personal Home Pages

Spinnwebe is Greg Galcik's personal sideshow of peeves, funny contests, and odd exhibits like The Dysfunctional Family Circus, where Bil Keane's popular cartoon gets reworked by twisted visitors. A commercial enterprise called "Confusion Wear" (which is, in fact, pretty confusing) plays second banana to comical rants about misplaced apostrophes and those signs that "emphasize" a word with quotation marks. (Also included are photos of blunders like the retail pitch, "Uncle Alan has infants and children's clothing.") Spinnwebe also offers occasional funny contests, like the chance to rearrange the letters on an actual signboard in rural Pennsylvania. Galcik's wordy broadsides at whatever gets on his nerves are usually fun reading.

The Stupid Homepage

http://metro.turnpike.net/S/spatula/

Personal Home Pages

Also known as Spatch's Homepage ("Spatch" is short for spatula), this is a collection of amusing oddments, including some spoofs on the "things that do useless stuff" craze so prevalent on the Web these days: the Page That Tells You Where It Is tells you the site is still at metro.turnpike.net ("Reload this page after a few moments and find out where it is then!") and the VCR Clock page, which Spatch has painstakingly programmed so you can see exactly what time his VCR clock says it is (which reveals a blinking "12:00"—*groan*). There's also a collection of text files (mostly culled from alt.stupidity, appropriately enough). The content may be stupid, but it's a smart site, if you know what we mean.

photography
photography

All Pictures

http://www.cse.unsw.edu.au/~s2156495/pics/
Photography

A beachworthy Claudia Schiffer (sans David Copperfield, guys!) greets you at this Australian site that is, as the name implies, a massive collection of pictures. The links are heavy on pretty girls, natch—expect a dozen listings for Alicia Silverstone and not a single one for, say, Margaret Thatcher. Still, All Pictures does include an impressive bunch of links to places like the "Kodak Home Page," "Aerospace Images," and "Sydney Bush Fires." And there are guys, too: the "Kevin Bacon Game," anyone? Still the real attractions here are the girls, girls, girls. From "The Spew Presents Linda Evangelista" to a gold mine of Anna Nicole Smith JPEGS, the biggies are all represented. And if All Pictures doesn't include your favorite celeb, you can make a request.

Ansel Adams: Fiat Lux

http://bookweb.cwis.uci.edu:8042/AdamsHome.html
Photography

In 1968, the University of California commissioned Ansel Adams to produce a "current portrait" of the university for that its centennial celebration. Three decades later, this fascinating site presents the Web premiere of the exhibition, *Ansel Adams: Fiat Lux*. You can read essays or interviews about the project here—even hear audio clips of the artist talking about how he set up some of the shots—but the real joy comes in exploring Adams' characteristically eloquent images, which capture the life and landscapes surrounding University of California campuses. Visitors will find page after page of crystalline images of subjects, such as a stockpile of sugar beets and "segregating pupae" in a lab. And rarely has California looked as strangely beautiful as it does in Adams' black-and-white landscapes.

Hear Ansel Adams discuss this photo: [399Kb Ulaw Soundfile]
Ansel Adams: Fiat Lux

California Museum of Photography

Watch greater Los Angeles develop before your eyes, or visit Ellis Island in 1900, via the exceptional photos at this Web gallery for the University of California at Riverside Museum of Photography. Some famous images can be seen here, like "Emigrants Starting for America" (in stereo-vision!) and "Air View of Ellis Island." An experimental section "enlivens" historical photographs ("Los Angeles Olympics, 1932") by treating them as navigable QuickTime movies. The site also includes images and text from the museum's temporary installations, like "Garden of Earthly Delights," a side-by-side comparison of the works of Edward Weston and Robert Mapplethorpe. For more whimsical fare, check out the Net Work Shop's collection of experimental Web-art projects, including an artist's interactive letter to a long-lost friend and a virtual tour of Riverside. It's a warehouse of eye candy.

Fixing Shadows

Fixing Shadows is a collection of mostly black-and-white, mostly historical, and mostly unmanipulated photographs. Especially intriguing is the page devoted to "found" images, a sort of virtual lost-and-found for photographers. See if you can identify a mysterious 5x7 plate of "Maude," found in New Hampshire; or create a story for a picture of a young woman in turn-of-the-century South Carolina. Old tintypes (of children, babies, and dogs) are on display here. And the site's creator, J. David Sapir, seizes this opportunity to display some fascinating photos shot while doing anthropological and linguistic work in West Africa throughout the '60s. These photos depict chaotic scenes of ceremonial rites and mock warfare, as well as somber moments, like "Girl taps her iron clacker and sings for her brothers." Fascinating photos.

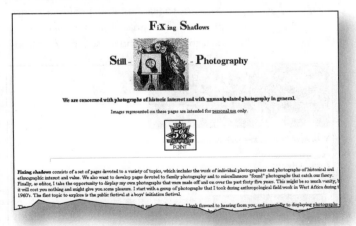

Keith's Second Sight

http://www.access.digex.net/~keithj/2Sight.html
Photography

This very personal page presents the favorite photographs of a professional photojournalist. (Keith has a day job "working for a not-so-quaint metropolitan newspaper.") The images here are often out-takes, but, as the photographer explains, they are often more telling than the stuff that's put to print. A presentation titled "Cuba Rising" is especially gratifying: it tours the island and its people, from an inside shot of Castro's former prison cell to a haunting view through barbed wire of downtown Havana. Another recent feature, "Postcards from Washington," shows off a grinning Newt Gingrich. From "praying for salvation" in North Carolina to "body builder" in Salem, Massachusetts, these sights are superb.

Kite Aerial Photography

http://www.ced.berkeley.edu/~cris/kap/
Photography

Charles Benton, a Berkeley, California, photographer and professed neophyte to kite aerial photography ("KAP"), built this page to showcase a growing body of work while sharpening his HTML skills. So far, so good on both counts. KAP, he says, is "the ideal Sunday afternoon pursuit." It works like this: you get a kite, you build a "rig" using a remote-control radio, and you attach a lightweight camera. Benton links up with plenty of technical info for those inclined to follow in his kite-steps (links to *Into the Wind* catalog, and the West Coast-kite-flying-essential "Recent Wind Data from the Bay Area"). But armchair KAP-ers will be more than content with the panoramic scenes from this stunning online gallery, which includes shots of the artist gazing up into his eye in the sky, and up-and-away views of places like the campus at Berkeley's Pacific School of Religion.

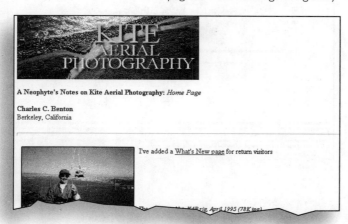

Photo Manipulation

http://aleph0.clarku.edu/~bmarcus/home.html
Photography

Photo manipulation is the process of digitally altering a "straight" image (perhaps to fit the tastes of tabloid publishers). While most people can spot an obvious phony—like Nixon landing on Mars to receive a diplomatic award—more subtle manipulations are harder to detect. Brandon Marcus, a photo illustrator, gives the browser a few sleuthing lessons here for spotting a doctored photograph. (For instance, pay attention to perspective.) He also shows how to create your own photomontage. An example shows a swooning Marilyn Monroe cuddling Abe Lincoln (and our newfound perception skills had us irritated by the fact that her skirt was blowing up without a fan or air-duct in sight). Practical jokesters may want to consider placing an order with Marcus's custom-photomontage service. As he jokes, "A picture of your friend and a NAKED stranger would make for interesting conversation."

PHOTONet Index

http://www.scotborders.co.uk/photon/netindex.html
Photography

This invaluable index for photo buffs and pros is an offshoot of *Photon* magazine. Here, editor David Kilpatrick "points you painlessly and slightly personally" to sites of interest. With its reviews and direct links, the index can make for one of the most aesthetically pleasing experiences on the Web. (These reviews don't muck about, either: "Rock music photo sites are rarely of great photographic merit, and this is no exception," begins one entry.) The index is vast, but visitors may also want to flip through the current issue of *Photon*. Professionals can shop for a silk parachute backdrop, and those who just want to look at pretty pictures can browse installations in the *Photon* image galleries.

PHOTONet Index

Welcome to PHOTONet Index, the page of Icon Publications Ltd's **PHOTON** WWW photo magazine where editor David Kilpatrick points you painlessly and slightly personally to Internet sites of photographic interest. You are PHOTONet Index access number 186943

PHOTON World Wide Web Photo Magazine

Down the Line '95 – Internet photo exhibition, London

In conjunction with **Photon**, Covent Garden, London, imaging lab and bureau Visualeyes plan a public exhibition of prints by

The PHOTOplex!

http://www.gigaplex.com/wow/photo/index.htm
Photography

This is one of the most professional (and professionally presented) photo sites on the Web. (It's part of the huge Gigaplex entertainment complex.) Top-notch photographers are represented here, like Robert Landau, Ken Kobre, Eric Estrin, and Annie Leibovitz. Superb selections from Landau's "Billboard Art" exhibit include the familiar "Superman" and "Oasis" images. And celebrity watchers will get a big kick out of the site's interview with Leibovitz. Also available are Kobre's insightful essays on photojournalism, like "Positive/Negative," which examines the media's propensity for "doctoring" images. A "Funny Pictures" page includes some timeless feature shots that "make people smile." Good stuff.

Time Life Photo Gallery

http://www.pathfinder.com/@@cDK5vHCmgQEAQPIh/
pathfinder/photo/sighthome.html
Photography

Yanked from the files of *Time*, *Life*, *People*, and *Sports Illustrated*, this extraordinary collection of photographs spans more than a century of global history. Early photos from the American Civil War include a shot of President Lincoln (in that crazy stovepipe hat) at Antietam. A gallery of photos from the '50s includes—what else?—hula hoops, rock and roll, and a bomb shelter. And Elizabeth Taylor has never looked as fetching as she does in this site's celebrity wing. "Your Picks" is a virtual request line, and a photo links page will take you to a *Sports Illustrated* baseball photo gallery or to a "Full Moon Rave" with *Life*. The page is halfway commercial; you can order calendars, prints, and posters from the collection, but there's plenty to look at even if you don't.

Photo Gallery | Photo Essay | Photo Links
Your Picks | Photo Shopper | Feedback

Welcome to Time Life Photo Sight on Time Warner's Pathfinder.

The Time Life Photo Sight focuses on photography. We'll draw from the extraordinary resources of the Time Inc. Picture Collection which houses ... gathered or taken on assignment for Time

Toy Camera Page

http://www.concom.com/~winters/toy_home.htm

Photography

Don't laugh—more and more photographers are using toy cameras to get unusual images, and it's all documented right here by Jonathan Winters, a toy camera devotee. Winters claims that using these plastic contraptions helps the photographer better express himself, and moves away from current high-tech trends to a simpler style of image-making. He'll even tell you where to buy a choice Holga 120S (or two—there's a bulk discount). These cameras really do produce beautiful pictures: the evidence appears in Winters' warm "Maternal Protection" and chilly "Preacher and the Damned." Shutterbugs can submit their own toy shots, too. For fun, don't miss the site's toy camera poetry. ("I am having a love affair with holga / she is plastic / easy to take everywhere...")

Toy Camera Photographers Unite!

Welcome to the toy camera home page.

romance

Cupid's Network, Inc.

http://www.cupidnet.com/cupid/

Romance

Cupid's Network, Inc. beats old Cupid and his arrows to the target here. This site contains links to lots of singles services, magazines, travel organizations, and personal ad services, from the Carolina Singles Network ("singles from the Carolinas and some other states") to the Bay Area Single Parents Club. While browsing in Cupid's Bookstore, you can download a copy of *How to Find a Lasting Relationship* (3rd Edition!) or get the lowdown on titles like *Cruising Solo* and *A Good Man is Easy to Find in Southern California.* The Cupid News link includes the CISS Alert, with news items like the one about a fraudulent dating service that had to refund millions. We're psyched for the "Flirting Convention" in Clayton, Missouri (winners receive the title of Mr. or Ms. St. Louis Flirt).

Cyrano Server

http://www.nando.net/toys/cyrano.html
Romance

Every romantic should visit the Cyrano server, which writes love letters on command. You answer a few questions about your beloved, select a style from poetic to steamy, and let Cyrano do the romantic heavy lifting. Check your results before sending: our trial run included the winning phrase, "I can imagine myself kissing your Episcopalian body and slathering you with various oils and sushi." On the flip side, Cyrano will also compose a Dear John letter, which runs more to lines like, "It is time for you to remove your pathetic clogs from my closet and to detach your annoying pet ferret from my leg." (If that doesn't do the trick, your love life may be beyond help.) Cyrano is all silly fun, courtesy of the NandO Net of Raleigh, North Carolina.

Gard's Laws on Love

http://www.hials.no/~ga/love/laws.html
Romance

The subtitle of this site is "...or things that make you go Aaaaaaaaaargh!!!" At times witty and wise, Gard has a unique view of that crazy thing called love. He

...or things that make you go... Aaaaaaaaaaargh!!!

1. If you meet a woman, and you like her, then she...
   - has a boyfriend
   - is lesbian
   - has many friends she prefers to you
   - doesn't notice you're there
2. If a girl likes you, then you won't know before she has lost her interest in you and it is impossible to get her back.
3. If you meet a girl who likes you, and you like her, and she doesn't have a boyfriend, then she will have one within the week, and it isn't you.
4. The only way to win a girl is to take her love for granted (if you keep questioning it, she'll get tired of you).
5. If you take love for granted, everything will just go to hell.
6. If you don't have a girlfriend, there's always someone to remind you about it.
7. If you know a girl, date her, etc. etc. and in the end tell her that you love her, you won't hear from her again for the rest of your life.
8. About who picks you up:
   - If you're heterosexual, then homosexuals will try to pick you up.
   - If you're homosexual, then heterosexuals will try to pick you up.
   - If you're bi-sexual, then noone will try to pick you up.
9. If you have a friend who knows a girl who is desperately looking for a boy, he'll splice her with someone else.
10. About finding lo...

devotes an entire section to pondering whether it's true that women are suckers for men with blue eyes. (Gard, of course, has blue eyes.) The only drawback to his wildly funny reflections is that Sir Gard is Norwegian, so some of the English isn't perfect. But you get the point. He also includes hundreds of translations for "I love you," from Chicksaw to Esperanto to Javanese (for you coffee drinkers). This may be useful as a time-killer with that special someone. Then again, if you have one and you're still killing time on the Net, how special can that someone be?

Joe's Amazing Relationship Problem Solver

`http://studsys.mscs.mu.edu./~carpent1/probsolv/rltprob0.html`

Romance

Had enough of trying to figure out your romantic life on your own? Try Joe's Amazing Relationship Problem Solver. You just answer a series of simple questions until you reach The Truth about your relationships. For example: "Does this involve another person/significant other/boyfriend/girlfriend/neuterfriend?" Answer no and Joe 's response is "Trust me, it's much better this way." Answer yes and he asks, "Are you dating this person?" (Your answer choices are "no," "yes," "maybe," or "not for long.") A disclaimer warns that Joe's page is for entertainment purposes only. "I am not a professional, I have no training, I'm not even particularly good at handling my own relationships." Joe may not be able to solve your problems, but you may laugh enough here to forget them.

Lucy Lipps

`http://www.cybersim.com/lucylips/`

Romance

Lucy Lipps ("the siren of style") is a radio "love doctor" and advice columnist who calls herself a "cyberbabe" for the '90s. (She's not shy about self-promotion.) Advice to the lovelorn, and suggestions for how to avoid becoming that way, are two of Lucy Lipps' specialties; her advice is serious, but given with a touch of humor. Besides an archive of questions and answers, Lucy also offers peeks into her little black book, photo album, and a schedule of personal appearances. (She's coming to a mall near you.) We especially enjoyed Lucy's Celebrity Scoop, which contains the "hottest and latest news on the stars." (Christie Brinkley has been spotted at an L.A. discount store with a cart full of half-price children's clothes!) Need direct advice? Lucy accepts e-mail queries, too.

The Love Blender

http://www.cs.tufts.edu:80/~kisrael/romance/
index.html
Romance

With stories and tales, poetry and pictures, the Love Blender is devoted to thoughts of *l'amour*. Hopeless romantic Kirk Logan Israel offers up everything from the last lines of Woody Allen's *Annie Hall* (which somehow lose their luster with the whole Soon-Yi thing) to a real 1928 love letter from a 70-year romance. You'll find dozens of touching, funny, and thought-provoking snippets and stories about romance, including "Theory," a not-so-mushy poem from Dorothy Parker: "Into love and out again / Thus I went and thus I go... All the songs were ever sung / All the words were ever said / Could it be when I was young / Someone dropped me on my head?" The page also contains a shot of perhaps the ultimate 20th-century romantic moment: the final scene from *Casablanca*.

Match.com

http://www.match.com/?twlncsanew
Romance

This fun personals site asks you to "just leave your bags behind," along with "those blind dates, bar scenes, hang-ups, put-downs..." (What a life you must lead!) First you have to register (it's free). Then you can either browse categories ranging from "All" to "Women Seeking Women" to "Men Seeking Women," or you can enter a specific member's name. Sadly, neither Tom Cruise nor Sharon Stone had a profile available on our last visit. Not to worry, though: there are lots of other singles available, like the California woman who likes "candlelight dinners and music (everything from Snoop Doggy Dogg to Pavarotti)." The site's coolest feature measures the distance between you and each person whose ad you peruse. That way you'll know you're just 313 miles from that mystery date in Pittsburgh.

The Romance Web

http://www.public.com/romance/
Romance

The Romance Web bills itself as a "sanctuary for hope and love as a human condition." Cherubs and angels adorn this site, which offers humorous reflections on romance, a personal quiz (is naked Twister really appropriate on a first date?), and a dissertation titled "Every Man Can Be A Romeo." And if you don't like the suggested titles on list of romantic poetry ("Sonnets from the Portuguese: #43" and "She Walks In Beauty," to name a few), there's a link to the Random Love Poem Server, which will "choose a love poem from around" the Web. This site also includes links to personal ads with about 17,000 potential mates. Brought to you by the folks at L&L Information Services, who are also quite willing to deliver a pitch on their other ventures.

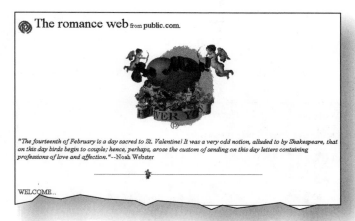

The romance web from public.com.

"The fourteenth of February is a day sacred to St. Valentine! It was a very odd notion, alluded to by Shakespeare, that on this day birds begin to couple; hence, perhaps, arose the custom of sending on this day letters containing professions of love and affection." --Noah Webster

WELCOME...

WEB Personals

http://www.webpersonals.com/
Romance

WEB Personals is a user-friendly site for anyone seeking love or just heavy friendship. Date seekers and seekees are categorized in the appropriate straight or gay directory—you'll even find a guide to what the initials mean when DWM seeks DDFW (there's an abbreviation for cross-dressers, too). The site enables you to browse or submit your ad, and the Love Hound will notify you of any suitable matches in case you don't have the time to check for yourself. (Anyone who's worried about good, clean dating fun on the Internet will be interested to learn that this site's Open Forum was taken offline because "it had evolved to a point where the discussions offended too many people who prefer a more professional experience.")

sports and fitness

sports and fitness

The Daily Rockies Web

`http://rainbow.rmii.com:80/~rlewis/rockies.html`

Sports and Fitness

Trust us, the fellow who created this site is a big fan—of both the Colorado Rockies and the Denver Broncos. "Home of the world's greatest fans" is the Rockies' boast, and the fans must be great to soak up everything this site has to offer. Baseball's most successful expansion team (now there's a résumé item) gets the star treatment here, from player profiles to well-reported stories from a cadre of freelance writers. Brand-new Coors Field looks pretty good in cyberspace, too. Over at the Broncos Web ("home of the AFC West's premier team," says Robert Lewis, the site's creator), take a look at the (big surprise here) John Elway Photo Page and official NFL stats. An added bonus: the salaries of every player!

ESPNET SportsZone

`http://espnet.sportszone.com/`

Sports and Fitness

Dah duh DOM! Dah duh DOM! Okay, there's still no catchy theme music, but cable sports colossus ESPN (in cahoots with Starwave Communications) has tossed up a state-of-the-art complement to your daily sports page. Sure, it used to be free, but as they added extra stuff (like more columnists, AP photos, and better NFL previews), the word "subscription" started popping up for complete access. Still, most of the stuff sports fans want is still free: photos of Steffi Graf jumping into her serve at Wimbledon, late-breaking hockey stories, boxscores, and more. The page also offers regular columns from anchor Keith Olbermann, sports nut Frank Deford, and others. As announcer Dan Patrick says of a swished jump shot, SportsZone is... Good!

Fish Page

http://www.inetmkt.com/fishpage/index.html

Sports and Fitness

Granted, most people aren't going to sit down at their computers to plan a fishing trip. Maybe more should start. Whether you're shopping for a bamboo fly rod, hoping to "hook up" with the Iceland Angling Club, or just want to know if 10-inch largemouths are legal keepers on Maryland's Clopper Lake (they are), this site is a strike. Among the featured items are fishing reports from the Sierra Nevadas to the Georgia coast that tell you what lures are working best and what fish are lying in wait. Links to outfitters include D&D Camps on Saskatchewan's Wollaston Lake, offering northern pike, walleye, lake trout, and arctic grayling fishing along hundreds of miles of shoreline. Or explore the Muskie Homepage, where "every lure tells a story."

Footbag WorldWide

http://www.footbag.org/
Sports and Fitness

Footbaggers will love this "global source of information" on their sport, which is also known by the product name "Hacky Sack." These kids take their play seriously; the official rules note that freestyle routines are to be "judged by fellow competitors because of the high level of expertise required to make an evaluation." This page (from the Bay Area Footbag Foundation) also includes club and league news and a link to the home page of current world champion Julie Symons and other footbag players. The World Footbag Championships—the "Super Bowl of Footbag"—are covered in grand detail, as are the rules of the sport. In line with the footbag's friendly image, the sixth "general goal" of the sport is "peace through play."

GolfWeb

http://www.golfweb.com
Sports and Fitness

Having joined forces with *Gold Digest*, this site promises to be "the most comprehensive and entertaining World Wide Web golf resource." And we wouldn't argue. It's beautifully presented with photo-links to a Chicago golf guide, Eye Cue putter manufacturers, the winning scorecard from John Daly's final round at the 1995 British Open, and much more. And the coverage of major events like the Ryder Cup includes daily notebooks and photographs, making this site a must for fans frustrated by chintzy television coverage. A great feature is OnCourse, an index of more than 14,000 golf courses throughout the United States that includes comments from other players.

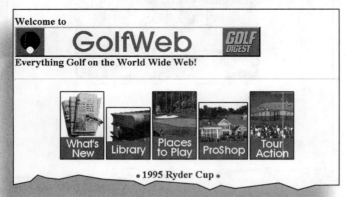

Guide to the 1996
Olympic Games (official)

http://www.atlanta.olympic.org/index.html

Sports and Fitness

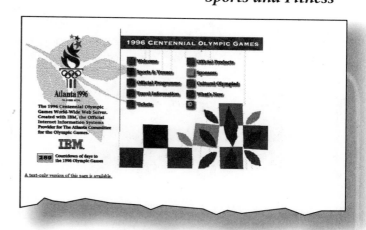

The Atlanta Olympic Committee created this server "to provide up-to-date, official information about the 1996 Olympic Games." This is the *official* site, in other words, so you won't find scalpers hawking tickets here (if you do, you might want to notify the Olympic Committee). The only hawking you'll find is the legalized type, from T-shirts to membership in the Olympic Games Club (only $21.50!). Sports from archery to yachting are here, with images of Olympic Stadium and that bizarre mascot, IZZY, who is generously referred to as "the popular children's character." And once the games end, you'll find results and comment here as well. Ticket news, sponsor info, and a "Cultural Olympiad" link round out this fine site.

Juggling Information Service

http://www.hal.com/services/juggle

Sports and Fitness

Juggling (*de Jonglage* to you Francophiles) takes center stage at this mesmerizing site. Who knew there was so much juggling on the Internet? For that matter, who new that juggling was so complicated? Browse through some back issues of *Juggler's World* or maybe step into the picture gallery, where you'll see a shot of Felix the Cat juggling four mice. You'll also find links to the home pages of jugglers around the world. One can even buy juggling software with features like per-hand dwell ratio control and pattern change control with history browser. Woo! We're still just trying to keep from dropping the oranges. This breezy page delivers the goods without losing a sense of fun; don't be surprised if your mood is altered. And pass the oranges.

Jump

http://infoweb.magi.com/~rwatt

Sports and Fitness

Ski jumpers and fans will enjoy long flights and stylish landings at this fine page from Canadian National team member Rennie Watt. Scoring is explained,

MAJOR COMPETITIONS

along with the jump phases—*inrun, take-off,* and varied forms of *flight.* Of course, every sport has its controversies: "The 'V' style is not as new a development as the media would have us believe. It's originator, Jan Bokloev of Sweden, could be seen doing it as early as 1984!" Links to competition sites include the Hollmenkollen Skifestival, the Olympic Games, and the World Nordic Ski Championships. And you can look up national ski-jumping teams from more than a dozen nations (even Kazakhstan) and find out who's who. Beautiful photographs—great action shots.

Mountain Biking

http://xenon.stanford.edu/~rsf/mtn-bike.html

Sports and Fitness

For "Fat Tire Fotos," racing tips, club links, and the like, this is the place. Read trip reports from places like the Ho Chi Minh

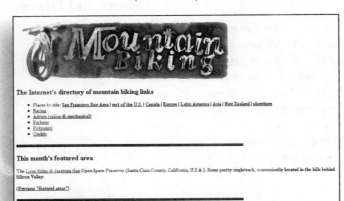

The Internet's directory of mountain biking links

- Places to ride: San Francisco Bay Area | rest of the U.S. | Canada | Europe | Latin America | Asia | New Zealand | elsewhere
- Racing
- Advice (riding & mechanical)
- Pictures
- Potpourri
- Credits

This month's featured area

The Long Ridge & Saratoga Gap Open Space Preserves (Santa Clara County, California, U.S.A.). Some pretty singletrack, conveniently located in the hills behind Silicon Valley.

(Previous "featured areas")

Trail, where, "As an American in lycra shorts and bright shirt on a fancy bike, you are constantly the center of attention." No doubt. Every month, this site features a different bike trail that includes riding directions and the kind of wildlife you'll see along the way (this is *mountain* biking, after all). The emphasis is on riding in the San Francisco Bay area, but you're not out of luck if you live in, for instance, Costa Rica. And those needing mechanical advice can "Ask Uncle Knobby" online. Be sure to check out "101 Tips That Don't Suck."

The NandO Sports Server

http://www.nando.net/SportServer/
Sports and Fitness

For a look at today's starting pitchers, "baseline to baseline coverage of the pro tennis circuit," Indonesian Open semi-final badminton results, and oh so much more, explore this mega-hyper-sportspage from the *Raleigh News and Observer*. Though you'll have to register for access to some links, if it happened on the field, court, or rink, you'll find at least a recap here. "Ghosts of Basketball Server Past" revealed to us, among other brilliant images, a photo of Randolph Childress stealing the rock from North Carolina A & T's Phillips Allen during the 1995 NCAA Tournament. Other cool stuff: great *Associated Press* stories and pictures, and "In the Press Box," a collection of columns and reader e-mail. This page is a bona fide contender for ESPNET SportZone's heavyweight belt!

The 19th Hole

http://www.sport.net/golf/
Sports and Fitness

Here's some consolation if you're stuck at a computer terminal, but long to be teeing it up. With pin placement by Texas golf enthusiast "Jimbo" Odom IV, the site offers complete tournament updates, player profiles, "Sandy Bunker's Golf Tips," and so on. We like "The Golfers Wake Up Call," a comic strip created by a late-night person "inspired by my ability to get up at any hour to play golf and my inability to get up early to go to work." Sound familiar? Get golf updates during the big events and check out some of the golf jokes (gee, only a million or so) in the lounge. Southpaws may link to the National Association of Left-Handed Golfers, too. Unusual scorecard collection; good links to other "cool golf sites."

RaceNet

http://www.primenet.com/~bobwest/index.html

Sports and Fitness

Motorsport fans will appreciate this fan site's full field of auto racing features. It begins with a photo archive, including

the "Damn Yankee 'Cuda Funnycar'" and "Start of the 1966 Le Mans 24 Hours." We went right to the "Racing Freebies" section, where we learned that some of the stuff required a toll call (geez!). If you're ears are a little too sensitive for the raceway, you can sample the "awesome" sound of Bobby Unser's Hotel Tropicana Special Novi during qualifying for a past Indy 500. There's trivia (John Surtees was the first Can-Am Champion) and retrospectives on classic drivers like Juan Manuel Fangio and A.J. Foyt. An exhaustive list of related links include "FerrariNet" and "Formula One On-Line." Fresh rubber all around.

Mark Rosenstein's Sailing Page

http://community.bellcore.com/mbr/sailing-page.html

Sports and Fitness

Mark Rosenstein produces this premier example of a maritime page, the ultimate nautical site for sailing information. It's mostly a list of hypertext links to sites having anything remotely to do with ships and sailing. When Rosenstein can't find resources elsewhere on the Net, he archives it himself, storing everything from maritime history documents to boat design and online sailing texts. You'll even find resources on "land yachting" for users prone to seasickness. News of current and upcoming sailing races keeps it all fresh. Even if you don't sail, you can have some fun: visit the signal flags guide and make up your messages, like "My vessel is a dangerous source of radiation; you may approach from the left."

Ski Web

http://www.sierra.net/SkiWeb/

Sports and Fitness

This page "for skiers by skiers" is a fine worldwide guide. You can peruse the e-version of *Alpine World Magazine*, get rental info on a Tyrolian Village cabin, plan runs on a map of Kittlefjall in Sweden, or order a discount lift ticket card electronically... and that's just among the first four menu items! Can't figure out what to do during the summer months in Europe and the United States? A link reminds you that when it's summer north of the equator, it's winter in places like South Africa, where you'll find Tiffindell Ski and Mountain Resort. We also found links to the Mount Hood Academy for racers, Chile's Villarica-Pucon resort, and even Buck Hill, featuring a 309-foot vertical drop just a few miles south of Minneapolis! It's, well, cool.

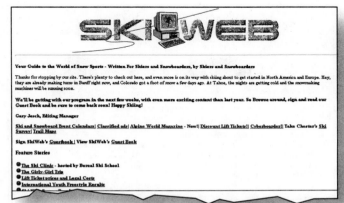

Skilton's Baseball Links

http://ssnet.com/~skilton/baseball.html

Sports and Fitness

Baseball fans will bookmark this page, created by fan John Skilton (holder of season tickets to the Wilmington Blue Rocks). The page itself is, of course, pinstriped. It's a solid collection of links to the national pastime on the Web: from ESPNET SportsZone to the Northern California Minor League Guide, to the Negro League Baseball Archive, to the Minnesota Twins and other individual franchises. Basically, if you don't want to bother with other sports, this is the place to come. This also is, mitts down, the best site for information on amateur baseball teams like the world-renowned Saugerties (N.Y.) Dutchmen. Merchandise, collectibles, and newsgroups round out the lineup. Grab a mouse and step up to the plate.

Sports Illustrated

http://www.timeinc.com/si/

Sports and Fitness

This is your ticket to the best—and most highfalutin?—sports journalism on the Net. You get good seats, too, to

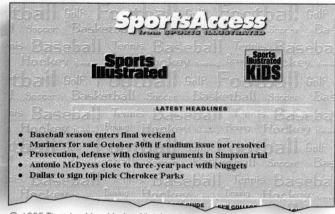

each issue's cover story, to "Classics from the *SI* Archives" (we read vintage articles on O.J. Simpson, Jimmy Connors, and Muhammad Ali), and to the best of "They Said It." (Ex-NFL coach Bum Phillips on how he's spending his retirement: "I ain't doing a damn thing, and I don't start until noon.") You don't get the full content of the actual magazine, but the folks at *SI* do update this page regularly with the latest sports news. You'll also find the opportunity to join "the most exciting fantasy football game on the Web." And, of course, *great* photos.

Mark Wheeler's U.S. Soccer Page

http://www.cs.cmu.edu/~mdwheel/us-soccer/

Sports and Fitness

This page "for soccer fans by soccer fans" is excellent! You'll find data on Americans playing abroad, the Women's World Cup, a "way cool" *U.S. Soccer Fanzine*, and many other links. Covers various levels of play, too. Did you know that six professional soccer leagues operate in the United States? No? Then we'll list them... just kidding. Among the great links is a list of the top male and female high school players and what colleges they chose to attend. The unofficial fan club of the U.S. team, called "Sam's Army," can tell you what hotels the team stays at when it travels. Other fans will appreciate the list of "Pubs in U.S. and Canada which show LIVE English soccer." Use of hands *is* permitted to applaud this fine site.

Stadiums and Arenas

http://www.wwcd.com/stadiums.html

Sports and Fitness

Here's what you need to be sure that ticket will land you at courtside, just like the scalper says. This page provides seating maps and photographs for tons of major sporting venues in the U.S. and Canada. For instance, the hockey blue line appears to fall between sections Y and Z in Calgary's Olympic Saddledome. Or, if you want to be like Spike and talk trash with Reggie Miller, we'd recommend a Q-section seat at Market Square Arena. What's the use of this? If you have to ask, you probably aren't a sports fan, although this collection could be useful for anyone building a stadium in their own backyard. Raceways are beginning to pop up here, and most of the listings include the requisite phone numbers for tickets and other info.

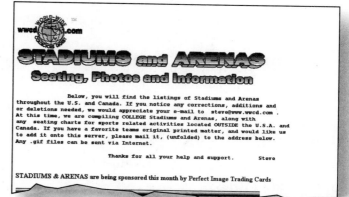

Tennis Worldwide

http://www.xmission.com/~gastown/tennis/index.html

Sports and Fitness

Here's an online tennis magazine "for and by 'netters' around the world." Players and fans will appreciate the events calendar, player profiles, serving tips, and glam photos of Boris, Pete, Conchita, and friends. Submissions are welcome. Did you ever wonder if it's a let when your opponent's hat falls off during a rally? Read "On the Line," a Q&A session with certified umpire Kevin J. Howell. Or plan your couch time with a tennis television schedule that covers up to four months ahead. Serious fans will enjoy the extensive player biographies here (and will probably wish more were included). A bagful of links to newsgroups, classified ads, weather info, and other "smashing" Web sites gives *Tennis Worldwide* all the interest of a five-set match with tiebreakers.

The Triathlete's Web

http://www.iac.net/~miller/triweb.html
Sports and Fitness

As an intellectual property attorney by day, and part-time professional triathlete by night, when did Marty Miller find time to create such a fine Web site? Plenty of triathlete sites exist out there, but this one is also a personal journal. Despite Miller's disclaimers to readers ("You must really be bored"), his training log reveals the work and hurt of training for one of sport's biggest challenges. Visit the "World's Largest Race Listing (or soon to be)" to check out when the next race will be in your area. Speaking of competitions, under Ironman Qualifying—1995, we noted that a few lucky (or flabby) competitors get in by lottery. The dream lives! Or it did, until *The Endurance Training Journal* gave us a primer on "Iliotibial Band Syndrome." Ouch!

The Weightlifting Page

http://www.cs.unc.edu/~wilsonk/weights.html
Sports and Fitness

Who could ignore references from Benjamin Franklin and Thomas Jefferson? These American luminaries both, in their own way, promoted a "strong body." This particular page is a cross between a fanzine and a how-to guide. For the novice, we recommend "Zen and the Art of Weightlifting," which explains that lifting weights *won't* automatically make you a Greek god or goddess. That takes "years of training, gallons of chemical aids, and dietary arrangements that would make most normal humans blanch," Kyle Wilson writes. The results can be impressive, as seen in the many photos here. And instead of strictly weightlifting links, the site includes fitness, nutrition, and general health. Those sculpted figures on the cover of *Flex* aren't that unfamiliar; with a little work, you could be there, too. (OK, a *lot* of work.)

The
Weightlifting Page
Recreational Lifting   Related Links
Powerlifting
Competitive bodybuilding   FAQs

"I live temperately, drink no wine, and use daily the exercise of the dumbbell...."

Benjamin Franklin

"A strong body makes the mind strong."

Thomas Jefferson

WOMBATS on the Web

http://www.wombats.org/
Sports and Fitness

This WOMBAT is not a critter; it stands for WOmen's Mountain Bike And Tea Society. (Guess that sounded better than just WOMBS.) As the authors put it, "women have more obstacles than men to overcome when taking up the sport of cycling." Since 1984, this nationwide group (based in Fairfax, California) has been hitting the rugged trails; now they ride in cyberspace, too. Both informative and inspirational, this site provides plenty of know-how and support for women riders. Check the newsletter to see what's new with WOMBATS or visit a number of other links relating to women and cycling. This site has lots of great artwork (with speedy transfers), plus well-written think-pieces. And heck, the name WOMBATS itself is worth the visit.

WELCOME TO THE WOMBART GALLERY

The Newly Established WOMBArt gallery welcomes you. Thank you for your patronage. Please sign in before you view the collections.

To the left, we have a gallery of Pre-Historic and Early Wombat Art.

To the right, we have a gallery of Classical and Modern Wombat Art.

Ahead of you, we have a gallery of Wombats on Film - A Photographic Retrospective.

In the Foyer, we are serving wine and cheese in celebration of stuffy conversation and deconstructionist theories. please enjoy the refreshments as you browse the gallery.

If you would like to browse elsewhere, here's a gallery of non-wombat bike images.

Women's Sports Page

http://fiat.gslis.utexas.edu/~lewisa/womsprt.html
Sports and Fitness

This no-frills index offers a terrific collection of links to everything from women's soccer to gender equity discussions to track and field. You'll also find plenty of rugby, karate, weightlifting, and other formerly "unladylike" sports. Women's hockey alone has eight different links and women's volleyball has more than a dozen. Compiled by citizen Amy Lewis (a self-proclaimed "philosopher, athlete, subvert, aesthete, student, and gadfly on the Internet"), this is a great resource for anyone excited to know that team handball isn't just for men anymore—and probably never was. Perhaps the greatest thing about this list is that it contains so many things we didn't know existed in the first place.

Jerry Yang's Sumo Information Page

http://akebono.stanford.edu/users/jerry/sumo/
Sports and Fitness

Ah, sumo wrestling. You may think of it as the dignified national sport of Japan, or you may think of it as humongous guys colliding while wearing strange bathing suits. Either way this is interesting stuff, especially the list of frequently asked questions, which reveals that suspicion of fixing matches in Japan exists (just like our pro "wrestling"). To guard against it, "there is a rule that wrestlers from the same heya (stable) do not wrestle each other." You'll definitely also want to view the photos of these amazingly large gentlemen, such as yokozuna (grand champion) Akebono; he looks plenty mean in some of these shots. And Jerry Yang has added movies, too! Also includes tournament results and amusing commentary: "Musoyama... fights like an old lady."

The Adventure Shop

http://www.ashop.com
Travel

This interactive travel-package store from Mountain View, California, links directly to what it considers the best in adventures by land, water, and air. Visitors can learn how to ski Kiwi, peddle off to the Mammoth Mountain Bike Center (a full-service resort area devoted to Alpine cycling), or if the sky's the limit, zap over to Chandelle Hang Gliding and Paragliding, where representatives are standing by to send people sailing over Pacific cliffs. Besides peddling travel packages, though, the Adventure Shop works in some amusing feature stories. Read about "The Wild Side of Switzerland" (or the feral side of the land of fondue), where puffy white blouses and *The Sound of Music* take a back seat to "the world's highest fixed bungy jumping" and excursions into some very scary ice crevasses.

Bali: The Online Travel Guide

http://werple.mira.net.au/~wreid/bali_p1a.html

Travel

The "jewel of Indonesia" gets glorious coverage at this nonprofit page sponsored by big Bali fan Wayne Reid of Australia. Budget traveling is the name of the game here, especially for the hearty who don't mind squat toilets and cold water (ask for a room with a Western toilet if you're a non-squatter). Learn when to avoid the rainy season, and plot your Bali adventure on loads of useful maps. Food-lovers can bone up on Balinese cuisine like "gado gado," a salad served with spicy peanut sauce and shrimp crackers. The site also offers advice on health and safety, some of which is rather obvious ("stay clear of Cholera outbreak areas") and some of which is plain unsettling (hookworm is "best prevented by wearing shoes"). If that doesn't put you off, you'll like this page.

Biztravel.com

http://www.biztravel.com/guide/

Travel

Targeting the true globetrotter, this electronic magazine offers practical info for international business travel. Feature articles (written by "the biggest names in the industry," they say) touch on topics like the hidden costs of airline phones. A piece on airline commission caps, "To Fee or Not to Fee," even evokes the Immortal Bard ("No doubt about it, any Shakespearean tragedy would most certainly give voice to the fact that this is, indeed, the question facing just about every travel agency today"). A virtual tour of Cleveland, Ohio—once called the "mistake on the lake"—suggests that your next business trip there could be cause for celebration. And anecdotal stories from "road warriors" recount the best (and worst) of travel times.

The Bureau of Atomic Tourism

http://www.oz.net/~chrisp/atomic.html
Travel

The Bureau of Atomic Tourism exists, oddly enough, to "promote tourist locations around the world that have either been the site of atomic explosions, display exhibits on the development of atomic devices, or contain vehicles that were designed to deliver atomic weapons." To this end, this slightly nutty (but pointedly serious) page describes places as diverse as the Titan Missile Museum ("The World's Only Public Underground Missile Complex") and the Nevada Test Site ("Land of a Thousand Nuclear Tests"). It's not exactly a vacation wonderland, but you do get a little curious after reading descriptions of Nuclear Age artifacts like 6,000-pound blast doors and still-radioactive Trinitite. Pictures of the attractions are noticeably scarce; bring a geiger counter and enter at your own risk.

CaribWeb

http://www.caribweb.com/caribweb/
Travel

This great-looking interactive site from the U.K. claims to be "the source" for travelers and explorers in the Caribbean. The "electronic beach bar," CaribTalk, is an island-hopping bulletin board where "Caribophiles" can get first-hand info on Barbados rum distilleries (the oldest in the world) or nude beaches at St. Maarten ("Visit the Orient Beach to see all of the bad bodies of others exposed"). CaribSearch combs an extensive database of hotels, restaurants, and yacht charters in the British Virgin Islands. And an Island Guide section links to specific destinations, like the Bahamas and Barbados. What really gives this site a unique edge, though, is CaribMoon, a wedding planner for the Caribbean, which lists all the legal mumbo-jumbo required for tying the knot in the islands.

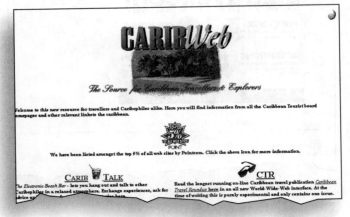

Castles on the Web

http://fox.nstn.ca/~tmonk/castle/castle.html

Travel

Canadian castle freak Ted Monk has built a fortress of royal links to places like Buckingham Palace and the legendary Hearst Castle in California. A "castle of the week" feature invites visitors to "sit back, curl up, and enjoy" a sightseeing tour. Scale the walls of Peel Castle on St. Patrick's Isle in the Irish Sea: climb the tower and go to the castle toilet. ("Judging from the width, it was probably a three-seater. These were very popular in the middle ages.") And despite Queen Elizabeth's recent *annus horribilus*, the House of Windsor's country estate is in fine virtual shape, judging from these views of the state apartments and St. George's Chapel. Bonus: those hungry for their own castles can link to a list of German citadels currently on the market.

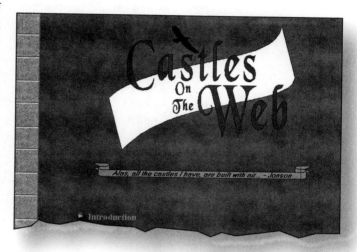

Club Med

http://www.clubmed.com/cm/pages/homepage

Travel

Club Med hopes to seduce you with scenes from their resorts in Mexico, the Caribbean, and the United States— and unless you're an Inuit, we don't think they'll have much trouble. (The perky audio "Welcome" sounds a lot like those annoying kids from The Gap, though, so skip it and get to the good stuff.) These all-in-one resorts with exotic names like Eleuthera and Turkoise will lure even the most hardened snowbunny. Enchanting club descriptions may have you longing to "glide cheek to cheek on the outdoor dance floor, and boogie until the wee hours in the high-tech disco." And the beach scenes alone will have you dragging out your *Bali Hai* soundtrack. Nice, effective, online advertising.

Conde Nast Traveler

http://www.cntraveler.com/
Travel

" The insider's guide to the outside world" comes to the Web—and it's teeming with the same sumptuous photographs and well-penned articles that make the print version of *Conde Nast Traveler* a jet-set essential. An interactive atlas (and searchable database) will have globetrotters clicking for hours while one vacation paradise after another appears on-screen. "Readers' Choice" ranks each destination according to environment, accommodations, activities, and people. And an on-site "Arcade" houses diversions like a "Seven Characters in Search of an Island" game, by which visitors are dispatched to the most appropriate island locale based on personality type. (Sophisticates should beach it on Necker Island, while the young and disco-inclined should stick to St. Barts.) This is a good-time site for good-time travelers.

Essential Guides to NY and LA at Night

http://mosaic.echonyc.com/~voice/
Travel

The singular most powerful judges of "hipness" in New York City and Los Angeles are arguably the *Village Voice* and *LA Weekly*. Now, these chroniclers of cool cut you in on where to go for fun in the Big Apple and Tinseltown after dark. The various tips are presented with the panache and grace of the terminally hip: the *Voice* calls them "basic activities to keep that crucial 8 p.m. to 8 a.m. time slot filled in." Both papers provide detailed info on hot spots for food, drinks, gay life, and body piercing. The only difference seems to be that the L.A. guide suggests cool drives to take (the Century Freeway east carpool lane is "easily the best view of the entire Los Angeles Basin").

Foreign Languages for Travelers

http://insti.physics.sunysb.edu/~mmartin/
languages/languages.html

Travel

Sprechen sie Deutsch? Yeah, we know: "Just a little." If you've already booked that flight to Frankfurt or Budapest, this page offers a quick lesson in the language of your choice. The site is adorned with foreign words and national flags—click on the one that corresponds with the language you want to practice, and you're on your way. Maintained by physicist Michael Martin of Long Island, NY, the site helps shaky travelers learn to check into their room, find the toilet ("Gde zdes tualet?" in Russian), and avoid embarrassment when ordering dinner ("Aceptati credit cards?" is a useful Romanian phrase). Sound bytes accompany many lessons, so you can actually hear how bad your pronunciation is. Pointers to other pages of topical information are also included, from a Japanes-English dictionary to the Serbian Language Page.

The Grand Tour

http://turnpike.net/metro/H/hud/CANYON.HTM

Travel

Immersion in the mile-deep Grand Canyon is the aim of these self-proclaimed "fissure junkies" from Colorado. (The canyon is still in Arizona.) This site aims to be the next best thing to getting the "red dirt under your fingernails, in your eyes, on your teeth, and in your veins." (Come to think of it, the site may be better!) Your companion "backpackers" spot the trails on the virtual hike and sing the praises of two-billion-year-old rock along the way. Plenty of great photos and notes on tourist routes like the Bright Angel trail and the South Bass-Royal Arch ("Pray that it hasn't rained up top during your stay, because the road through Pasture Wash can swallow up jeeps when it's muddy"). A hiker's conditioning guide and canyon permit info are included.

Holiday Inn

http://www.holiday-inn.com

Travel

" We make your trip easy," boasts this innovative service from one of the world's largest lodging chains. Easy and fun,

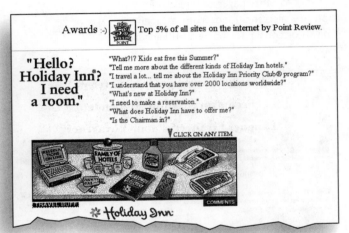

too. A nifty search function invites visitors to pick a tourist site, then locates the closest Holiday Inn. Choosing Colorado from the U.S. map, we selected Buffalo Bill's Grave from the list of attractions, and found the address and phone of a location in Lakewood, just 16 miles away. The site also lets you check room availability and make a reservation, provided you have a credit card. As if that's not enough, we were informed of the Colorado hotel's proximity to the Coors Brewery and the Colorado School of Mines. Graves, mines, and beer: the perfect American vacation, thanks to this cheerful guide and its fast-loading graphics. Free in-room coffee, too.

Welcome to Iceland

http://arctic.msg.net/MainSquare/MS.html

Travel

This page from Reykjavik covers everything from Icelandic driving and road conditions (watch out for that loose gravel) to the local apotek, or pharmacy. The site is garnished with cutesy cartoon icons, and you can let an adorable "traffic puffin" be your guide. A calendar of events in Reykajavik offers an introduction to Nordic music, historical tours, or a seat at "glima," an Icelandic wrestling match. You can also get details on popular outdoor activities like bird-watching (Labtrabjarg, in the West Fjords, is home to the largest razorbill colony in the world). And you'll discover eclectic accommodation options, from bring-your-bedroll "farm holidays" to the Iceland Tourist Bureau-operated chain of "EDDA Hotels." Plenty of information on tour operators and travel agencies, too.

The Internati
Exchange

http://www.ho

Want to stay in an apartment over-looking the Seine on your next trip to Paris... for free? A home exchange could be the answer. This server acts as a clearinghouse for listings all over the world. Options include a direct exchange of homes between residents of different countries, a "hospitality" exchange (home-owners act as mutual hosts), or paid rentals of private homes. We found listings from places as varied as Oslo, San Francisco, Tel Aviv, Amsterdam, and the West Indies. You can trade your beach house on Bald Head Island, North Carolina, for a rustic 17th century home in the South of France (even trade cars to save on rental-car fees). You pay a small yearly fee to participate in the program—and of course, it helps if you have an exotic house to exchange.

The Internet Gui
Bed & Breakfast

http://www.ultranet.com/bi

Heralding its service as "the Internet's most complete bed and breakfast guide," TravelData has compiled a list of literally thousands of Bed and Breakfasts across the United States. (More than 100 in Alaska alone!) A searchable database lets the browser find that perfect homey stopover by city, region, or theme. We found that the fewer keywords used, the better the results: a search using "California," "wine," and "biking" turned up nothing, while eliminating the bicycle yielded eight selections. One drawback: the service is limited to inns in the U.S., so this may not actually be the "most complete" guide ever. Still—from Lady Goldenrod Inn of Boonville, Missouri to Europa Inn in Loxley, Alabama—it's an excellent resource for funky bunking.

Welcome to
The Internet Guide to Bed & Breakfast Inns

ie De Vivre Hotels

p://www.quiknet.com/~cdi/415/hotels/joiedev.html

avel

This page lists some of San Francisco's more intimate (and less costly) hotels and inns. The Commodore Hotel, for instance, is a hot spot for hip and trendy travelers, housed in an Art Deco building with decor that would make even the most avid flea market browser happy. The Phoenix, a remodeled 1950s motor lodge, is reportedly "the favorite amongst the art and entertainment industries." And, for old-world charm, this page recommends the Abigail Hotel near SF's Opera Plaza (a gourmet vegetarian restaurant occupies the first floor). Listings are bang-bang to-the-point, well-researched, and on the money, with simple, clear photos. Besides, you've got to love a name like Joie De Vivre. It's all sponsored by Conceptual Dynamics International, a California-based marketing firm.

Mediabridge

http://www.mediabridge.com/

Travel

If you're bolting to the Big Apple for a weekend fling (or planning to make a life there), this online pit-stop could help you

take the Big Bite. Mediabridge Infosystems uses digital media to promote commerce in New York City by offering headline news, articles, community resource contacts, and a host of entertainment listings. Visitors can use the site to find the address of a sci-fi specialty store (The Forbidden Planet) and track down the pancake house of the moment ("Goooood Morning!"). They can also go sightseeing by neighborhood—from Franklin Furnace in TriBeCa to Bloomingdale's on the Upper East Side—with the "Graphical Picker of Manhattan Island." The site also plays host to "New York's first virtual art gallery." A casual approach with offbeat details.

The National Park Service

http://www.nps.gov/
Travel

A smiling Ranger greets you at this stop devoted to America's 80.7 million acres of national parks and recreation areas. (And whatever happened to Smokey Bear?) Say you've forgotten where Old Faithful belches out her famous greeting. Don't get steamed: search for "geysers" here. Or click on a U.S. map to find out which parks exist in Vermont. In addition to extensive tourist info, the park service offers tips on various park resources ("Parks as Classrooms") and gives hard-hitting lessons on topics like "Biological Diversity: The Eroding Foundation of Life." The site also explains how you can be a better visitor when hiking through forest preserves. And since it's all virtual, you won't need to pack out your Snickers bar wrappers or watch for ticks.

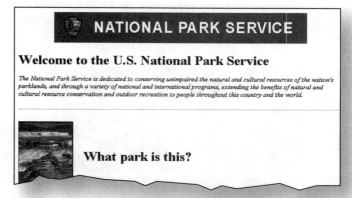

PC Travel—Airline Ticketing

http://www.pctravel.com
Travel

PC Travel turns out to be a "Pretty Convenient" way to book an airline reservation. No matter where you are, no matter where you want to go, this online travel agency (a service of American Travel Corporation) is just the ticket. After creating your user profile (which must include a Netscape browser and a major credit card), you can choose your favorite airline and your favorite bulkhead seat, put in your request for a vegetarian lunch—even reserve a rental car. Tickets are then shipped via overnight mail. A nice tutorial for new users is included here, too. This isn't the only spot on the Web offering airline tickets—and surely dozens more are coming—but it's one of the smoothest.

Relais & Chateaux

http://www.calvacom.fr/relais/accueil.html
Travel

Those seeking a year in Provence (or the Loire valley, Brittany, or even Badgastein, Austria) need look no further than this delightful server hosted by CalvaNet, a French Web design company.

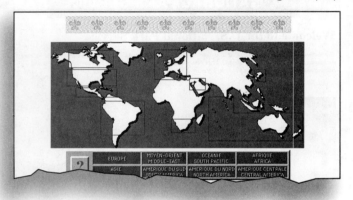

Relais & Chateaux highlights more than 400 chateaux, country houses, and restaurants. The best (and most unusual) pastoral getaways are compiled here by country and theme, and they literally circle the world (through French entries dominate). Provincial cooking lessons, for instance, are featured at the Abbaye de Sainte Croix in (where else?) Provence. And, at La Bourgogne in Punta Del Este, Uruguay, "Jean-Paul Bondoux... raises and feeds the ducks that are used in the preparation of his foie gras, cutlets, and confits." Clickable maps make navigation a snap, and an online form lets you check availability and rates, and even book a reservation for one of these delightful vacation ideas.

Route 66

http://www.cs.kuleuven.ac.be/~swa/route66/
Travel

Take a little trip along the road immortalized by both Steinbeck and Kerouac (and don't forget Nat King Cole). Belgian traveler Swa Frantzen began assembling this online exploration of the legendary drive from Chicago to Santa Monica when

ROUTE 66

planning to "take that California trip" himself. "Current maps do not include the old Route 66," he notes, and Belgian bookstores aren't much help either. So Frantzen gathered facts ("the route is 2448 miles long") and put together a travelogue of his own. Visitors navigate by clicking cities along the map for detailed travel instructions, not-to-be-missed road stops (Exotic World—the Museum of Burlesque), and snapshots to show friends. As the song says, you'll see Flagstaff, Arizona (don't forget Winona), Kingman, Barstow, San Bernardino... and without a doubt, you WILL get some kicks on Route 66.

Shoestring Travel E-Zine

http://metro.turnpike.net/eadler/shoe1.html

Travel

"**A**lternative and offbeat" world travelers will appreciate the resources generously assembled in Eric Adler's 'zine for "shoestringers." ("If you have a cool Bed and Breakfast for $20 a night, I'll probably put it in," Adler explains to link-hungry landlords. "If it's $100, I won't.") Click on Bolivia and you'll see advice on dealing with altitude sickness (walk slowly and chew coca leaves), or select Iceland, where budget accommodations are "almost impossible to find." "Trip on" the Top Ten Obscure Road Trips and Excursions in America here, or consult the excellent "Traveler's Diary" for searchable, date-specific European events. Lots of thoughtful links are included for those in the anywhere-is-better-than-here state of mind. And remember, don't drink the tap water in Hong Kong.

TravelASSIST Magazine

http://travelassist.com/mag/mag_home.html

Travel

This monthly 'zine has helpful tips and vivid reports by and from world travelers. Past issues have invited readers to explore the backroads of "Vivacious Virginia," offered a photo essay on the beautiful beaches of Mexico, and planned an excursion to "A Monastery East of Eden" (Utah, that is) where "33 Catholic monks... find the perfect seclusion and natural beauty conducive to their simple life of prayer and manual labor." (Until the news crews and tourists began circling, anyway.) Among the site's many services, online travel agents are listed under specific categories like "Himalaya" and "Scuba Diving." Stimulating copy ("Death Valley, heat waves shimmering surrealistically under a deep blue sky...") and lots of nice color photos make this a great travel read.

Travel Weekly Home Page

http://www.novalink.com/travel/
Travel

This info-page is sponsored by *Travel Weekly*, an industry newsletter for agents and tour operators. If you're just a traveler, don't let that put you off—here you'll find one of the most extensive collections around of links to other travel sites on the Web. With nearly 500 links from which to choose, you'll tire before the connections do. Whether you're looking to book a flight over the Grand Canyon or locate the frequently asked questions on Disney World, you're in the right place. News features from *TW* are also included, so you can read articles like "Battered Caribbean Islands are Showing Signs of Life," and "Passengers Protest After Cruise is Disrupted by Storm." Like friendly flight attendants, the newsletter staff scatter comments throughout to guide and amuse.

TravelWeb

http://www.travelweb.com
Travel

TravelWeb aims to give you staying power with this online hotel brochure, search engine, and booking service. Whether shopping for mints on your pillow or just complimentary powdered coffee (what kind of compliment IS that, anyway?), you'll find hotels across the U.S. and Canada and in a variety of sunny spots around the world. For your Malaysian travel needs, try the Best Western Berjaya Langkawi Beach Resort. Or get the poop on the so-called "number one destination of America's privileged travelers," John Gardiner's Tennis Ranch in Scottsdale, Arizona. In many cases, you won't find online booking (just the 800 numbers), but slick electronic brochures give a hint of things to come. The smartly designed site also includes links to other resources (like the Worldwide Timeshare Mall) and travel-related news.

Webfoot's Guide to France

http://www.webfoot.com/travel/guides/france/

Travel

This is one of a series of friendly country guides put together by Kaitlin Duck Sherwood (hence the "Webfoot" name); we just happen to like the France guide the best. It offers tons of links with up-to-date information like geography, exchange rates, car rental info, even a satellite map of current European weather. The heart of the site, though, is the fun first-person travelogues and essays. One free-lancing Parisian shares "My Worst Deceptions in Well Known Restaurants," exposing "over-arrogant service, high prices, and sometimes bizarre stuff like 'tomatoes filled with fruits, nuts, and sugar.'" You'll also find plenty of paths to more specific subjects here, from student housing referrals to fabulous luxury hotels. Some of the information is presented in French (although the site includes dictionaries for translation).

Canada's Yukon

http://parallel.ca/yukon/

Travel

Tall tales, travel tips, and dollops of dazzling detail are all part of this top-knotch site from Yukon Tourism. It's "a good excuse to pour a shot of rotgut, bite off a piece of snoose, and tell baldfaced lies about the good old days," among other things. Discover the joys of dog mushing and canoeing, or camping by an open fire while gazing up at the aurora borealis. Take a virtual drive on any of the Yukon's highways, with mileage and time and pit-stops included. The site's historical detail is a hoot, too. Trivial bits give the chilly details on what a "cheechako" (Yukon greenhorn) must endure to become an old-timer, or "sourdough." Six caribou per person and a grizzly bear for every family of five: it's the Yukon, jack!

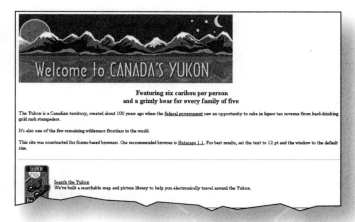

Money

Money

Commerce, which so often drives the bus of life, has been late climbing aboard the Internet. After a predictably rocky arrival, however, business seems to have found a home in cyberspace. Some enlightened companies have created entertaining "playgrounds" for surfers, and others have come up with excellent online customer support. Still, simple information is perhaps the hottest commodity going: annual reports and stock market quotes can now flow freely into any office or home. Are we heading for a future filled with financial giants who swap trillion-dollar empires while wearing bathrobes and those silly open-toed slippers? It seems possible, if slightly embarrassing.

business and investing

business and investing

American Stock Exchange

http://www.amex.com/
Business and Investing

This blue chip site from the American Stock Exchange offers wonderful returns on your investment. Check out the funky pyramid graphic on the image map and click on the other top-notch graphics, fleshed out with impressive information: a listing of all exchange companies, an impressive news database of chronological AMEX events, and the "Information Exchange," a forum offering "insights from influential business leaders" on topics like shareholder litigation reform. You'll also find market summaries and a gallery with photos of the famous exchange and trading in action. AMEX claims to be "The Smarter Place To Be"; for now, it has the Internet edge over its competitors.

Asia Online

http://www.asia-online.com/
Business and Investing

Asia Online is a group of sites about Asia—some informative, some just advertising, but all quite snazzy to look at. And what a great idea, given the Net's opportunities for opening world trade! This Westernized guide offers features like "Asia Business News" from Asia TV network and presents "live" headlines from the newsroom (updated a couple of times a day). You'll also find the unabashedly hip "BigO," an online version of "Asia's most respected rock magazine"—no *Rolling Stone*, but fun anyway. But its greatest strength is its directory of links to Asian sites, often difficult to reach elsewhere on the Web. U.S. and European users can expect to do some waiting while zipping across the digital globe, but you've got it all over Marco Polo.

Better Business Bureau

http://www.econet.apc.org/cbbb

Business and Investing

After consumer disaster strikes, this guide helps users find a nearby Better Business Bureau to call and complain to their heart's content. But its greatest strength is prevention, offering online publications on smarter shopping and advisories on the most common shady sales practices. It's basic information nearly anyone can use, and it's updated regularly. Make sure to check the latest scam alerts to protect Grandma from buying gold futures from that nice young man on the phone. The site's a little too institutional for our tastes, with drab graphics and stiff writing, but there's no denying it's a wonderfully practical use of the Web.

THE BETTER BUSINESS BUREAU®
WORLD WIDE WEB SERVER
brought to you by the Council of Better Business Bureaus, Inc.

About the Council of Better Business Bureaus
What is a Better Business Bureau

Frequently Asked Questions About the Better Business Bureau

Better Business Bureau System Services

- Advertising Self-Regulation
- Alternative Dispute Resolution (ADR)
- Charity Monitoring and Donor Education
- Consumer & Business Education
- Reliability Reports on Businesses
- Marketplace Complaints and Inquiries
- Scam Alerts and Advisories (as of September 3, 1995)

Important Notice Regarding Companies That Advertise Their BBB Membership

Also Available on This Server

Employment Opportunities and Job Resources

http://www.wpi.edu/~mfriley/jobguide.html

Business and Investing

Whew! If you STILL can't find a job after using this home page, something may be wrong. (Have you checked your breath?) Help-wanted servers, recruiter links, professional societies, government job listings... they're all here. Margaret Riley (this is also called "The Riley Guide") maintains this employment resource out of the Worcester Polytechnic Institute. A fine introduction explains how to use the Net to find an employee or a job; this is also a mini-course on Internet usage in general. From government and business through the arts and humanities, this guide tries to cover all the bases, with special emphasis on high-tech and computer employment. It used to take days in the library to dig this kind of stuff up.

Experimental Stock Market Data

`http://www.ai.mit.edu/stocks.html`

Business and Investing

Note the word *experimental* in the name of this site: this impressive collection of stock market quotes and historical graphs is not intended for investors who put fortunes on the line every day. But this project from an MIT student seems destined for the Web's big-time, since it offers easy-to-read charts of popular U.S. stocks and updates them automatically. The pictures here speak louder than words: if you see a graph showing share prices spiraling downward, you don't need a Harvard MBA to know you should start screaming "SELL!" at your broker, husband, or dog. Fine for class projects and market hobbyists; prices are "deemed reliable, but not guaranteed," so don't come crying to this non-commercial service if you lose a few Gs.

Finance Wat.ch

`http://finance.wat.ch/`

Business and Investing

If you can't put your money in a Swiss bank, you can at least put some time into this treasure trove of world financial information from Switzerland. (Do not adjust your set: they *do* spell it "wat.ch." "Ch" is the Net's country code for Switzerland.) Visitors can find exchange rates, stock market data, and even an online training course in futures and options. (The Web was pioneered in Switzerland, after all.) The regularly updated hotlist brings you the newest financial sites, from the Philadelphia Stock Exchange to global market predictions from Perception Knowledge Systems, Inc. A superbly designed site that brings into reach everything from derivatives to a financial glossary. Sure, some of these investments are risky. But what are you going to do, keep it under a mattress?

Fortune

http://www.pathfinder.com/fortune/fortune.html

Business and Investing

This gold mine includes some excellent articles from *Fortune* magazine, but the mainstay items are its Fortune 500 and Global 500 profiles of the largest corporations in U.S. and world, respectively. The "500" lists are far more useful here than they ever were in print, enabling you to search the database and view rankings by different criteria. (Bean counters: you can even get it in a spreadsheet format!) A history of the famous Fortune 500, now in its 40th year, runs through some interesting trends and facts. ("If you had bought $1,000 of Philip Morris stock at the end of 1954 and reinvested all dividends, your stake at the end of 1994 would have been $1,561,100.") For the first time, the list is expanded to include manufacturers, retailers, and financial services. At the risk of sounding like shills, we have to agree, it's "the most important, analytical, one-stop corporate scorebook available anywhere."

FORTUNE

Fortune Business Report: Hear the latest financial and business news of the day in Real Audio.

The Global 500: The world's largest industrial and service corporations.

Fortune 500: A retooled set of rankings for the new U.S. economy.

Freerange Media

http://www.freerange.com/

Business and Investing

Freerange Media, Web consultant/creator to the stars (Time-Warner's *Pathfinder*, for one), shares some of its secrets here. While you can amuse yourself for hours in its games or promotional sections, don't miss the "How To" section. There, documents illustrate all aspects of publishing on the Internet, often with examples. In one section, every HTML code is described and demonstrated. In another, Web tricks are explained. And to get an idea of this company's clout on the Net, check the list of power clients like *CBS Eye on the Net*. Even though you probably can't afford to hire them for your personal home page, these folks are worth emulating.

Douglas Gerlach's Investorama

http://www.users.interport.net/~gerlach/invest.html
Business and Investing

If you had a dime for every Web link on Douglas Gerlach's Investorama, you wouldn't have to worry about money. But for careful investors shaking the trees for

greater returns, this artful "link to links" is a fine place to start. The page is well divided into useful subheadings such as "Quotes," "Brokers," and "Funds" so you can easily find what you need. Choose "Funds," for instance, and you'll find links to mutual fund big dogs like Fidelity, Scudder, and Dreyfus. Throw in a tasty morsel of economic wisdom at the bottom of each page (Confucius said, "When prosperity comes, do not use all of it"), and you have a comfortable little investment neighborhood. Gerlach hands out a little over-the-fence advice, but beyond that you're on your own.

HomeOwners Finance Center

http://www.internet-is.com/homeowners/in-yahoo.html
Business and Investing

If you're clueless about covenants, appurtenances, and ARMS, this page can help you unravel the mysteries of the

mortgage. First-time buyers will get a kick out of the "mortgage calculator," a clever device that instantly computes monthly outlay using the interest rate of your (or more likely, your lender's) choice. You even get daily updates on economic factors affecting home loan rates, including the latest juicy rumors from the Fed. (Did Alan Greenspan just sneeze? And if so, what does it mean?) Even pros will appreciate the loads of useful tips on buying and refinancing. These folks do a nice job of promoting their services, available in 24 states across the U.S., but don't forget to shop around.

Hoover's Online

http://www.pathfinder.com/money/invest/hoover/Hoovers_Home.html

Business and Investing

Hoover's (no relation to Herbert) is a product of *Money* magazine's Personal Finance Center, offering popular blue-ribbon profiles on some 400 of America's best-known companies. Updated as needed, they include specifics like key personnel, competitors, and financial performance—and they're written in a surprisingly punchy style. Ted Turner, for example, is introduced as "former America's Cup sailor and braggadocious character, now rancher (bison in Montana and New Mexico), family man (married to actress Jane Fonda), and philanthropist (donor of $75 million to 2 colleges and a prep school)." Our only beef: companies are listed alphabetically, so Abbott Laboratories and Ace Hardware get a little undue exposure. (We suggest using the search features of your browser—Control+F with Netscape, for example.) Once you find what you're looking for, it's simple, concise, and fun to read for potential investors.

The Hoover's Online database on the MONEY Personal Finance Center provides profiles of about 400 of the America's best-known companies. Company profiles are updated annually and revised when major events affect their content.

- Abbott Laboratories
- Ace Hardware Corporation
- Aetna Life and Casualty Company
- AFLAC Incorporated
- Agway Inc.
- Albertson's, Inc.

IntelliMatch Online Career Services

http://www.intellimatch.com/index.html

Business and Investing

IntelliMatch offers perhaps the most extensive resume and employer match-ups on the Net. Job-seekers fill out lengthy forms—25 or so Web pages worth—to create a specific skills inventory. IntelliMatch then compares those details with the specific qualifications of individual jobs listed by employers. The idea is to create a "structured resume" that becomes part of Intellimatch's database, from which employers can get your address and contact you to say, "We'll pay you a million dollars to watch your feet." The jobs are mostly technical ones, and though you can browse easily through the current postings, it naturally takes quite a bit of time to fill out the forms. The whole process effectively removes any *personality* from the process, of course—but hey, you don't have to dress up!

InterQuote

`http://www.interquote.com/`
Business and Investing

This flexible online stock quote service sells a gateway to its subscription-based services here. You choose from five different packages, ranging from real-time up-to-the-second quotes (for about 700 clams a year) to a simple end-of-day service ($45 a year). The real-time service is unique on the Net, using special software that lets you watch stocks rising and falling on your computer screen (a hypnotic experience). The software is free, and you can register for a 15-day trial to see how it works. The complicated instructions on opening an account may scare away the casual Web user. But for the hard-core investors who can't waste a second, this is an innovative use of the Net.

Koblas Currency Converter

`http://bin.gnn.com/cgi-bin/gnn/currency`
Business and Investing

World travelers will drool over this currency conversion site, written by physics whiz David Koblas for the Global Network Navigator. It's as easy as spending 5000 drachmas for lunch—just access the site and look at the list. (Make sure to select the right currency as your reference point—we'd hate to have you jumping out of 25th story windows.) For instance, at our last visit, one Russian ruble was worth .00030772 Canadian dollars (and it may very well take a week's salary to buy a bowl of borscht in Winnipeg). The list is only updated weekly (sometimes not even that often), but even if you aren't traveling this is a great educational tool. Did you know that Brazil's currency is called the "Real"? (Perhaps to convince citizens it's not "play" money?)

Lombard Institutional Brokerage

http://www.lombard.com/
Business and Investing

Few sites have ventured into the Brave New World of online stock trading. But when you're ready to jump in, the Lombard Institutional Brokerage and its real-time trading and research information center seems a likely candidate. Traders have to register first (it's free), and can then buy and sell stocks, options, and mutual funds, as well as retrieve 15 minute delayed stock and option quotes, graphs, and details that could make Peter Lynch dizzy. Skeptical? The firm is a member of the NASD and MSRB (which should mean they won't run off with your money), and it's running a Netscape SSL server (which means your transactions are secure). All in all, it's a bold venture, but keep in mind those numbers you type represent real money.

Lombard
INSTITUTIONAL **BROKERAGE** INC.

Real-Time Trading and Research Information

Welcome to the Lombard Institutional Brokerage Real-Time Trading and Research Information Center. Our philosophy is simple: 'Through the use of cutting edge technology, we are dedicated to providing our customers in the Internet community with a wide variety of investment options, enhanced investment tools and an unparalleled commitment to customer service...'

Here is a brief demonstration of some of the features of the site...

 Free Registration Desk

First time users must Register here to use this system. If you have already registered, you may proceed directly to ...r Public Access Center.

Money and Investing Update

http://update.wsj.com/
Business and Investing

It may lack the grit of the *Wall Street Journal*, but this site created by the legendary financial newspaper has a leg up on its tree-based parent. Money and Investing Update bills itself as the Net's premier source of financial news and analysis, and it doesn't disappoint. At any time during the business day, you can log into this service and get articles analyzing the latest swings of today's trading, beating tomorrow's *Wall Street Journal* by a mile. You also get material from *The Asian Wall Street Journal, The Wall Street Journal Europe*, and Dow Jones news wires sprinkled in for valuable international connections. What's the catch? You have to subscribe. But for the moment, subscribing is free and relatively painless (if you can remember still another password). We only wish it would allow instant stock quotes, but given the resources of the Journal, this is probably just a matter of time. If you must, you can even print the pages and tuck them under your arm for old times' sake.

The Monster Board

http://www.monster.com/
Business and Investing

This page has nothing to do with horror—unless it's work you're afraid of. The Monster Board is an interactive database of current job openings that you can search in several ways: by locale, by industry, by job title, and by discipline. Bunches of different employers stock the database—from biochemistry to retail sales, from Burger King to Walt Disney Imagineering—and the service is free for job hunters. You'll also find online job fairs and other news in a cute-but-curious presentation. It can be confusing, with almost *too* much data and too little direction. If you know *exactly* what job you're looking for, use the Career Keyword Search (we searched "astronaut," "brain surgeon," and "prime minister," but struck out). Otherwise, we suggest going immediately to Virtual Help for a procedural rundown.

National Materials Exchange

http://www.earthcycle.com/g/p/earthcycle//index.html
Business and Investing

Businesses may do the environment a good turn by using this nonprofit international recycling database. Companies can either buy recycled materials from firms listed here or post recyclables of their own. And we aren't talking bottles and cans—everything from industrial acids and solvents to tires and construction equipment can be posted here. We searched for "storage tanks" and found eight listings in locations across the world (you want to get the tank *before* buying that 500 gallons of used sulfuric acid). The idea is to reduce the nation's clutter of industrial waste. You have to fill out a free subscription form to get access to the database, but once you're in, searching is relatively painless. (Except for that sulfuric acid.)

NETworth

http://networth.galt.com/
Business and Investing

This slick site seems destined to become a top financial presence on the Web. It already offers sophisticated mutual fund information and a delayed stock quote server (to use any of these services, you must fill out the free registration form). The *Mutual Fund Market Manager* lets users search a database of more than 5,000 mutual fund profiles. For further research, you can look at a prospectus for a selected fund. We particularly like "The Insider," an excellent searchable guide to the Net's financial resources. The downside: you can't do anything unless you enter your registration number and password, an annoyance at best. If you don't mind that hang-up, it's a fine resource, particularly for mutual fund investors.

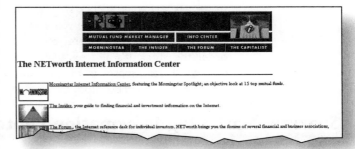

Quote.Com

http://www.quote.com/
Business and Investing

Whether it's pork bellies or mutual funds, Quote.Com is among the broadest financial Web services we've found yet. Investors can check PR Newswire or BusinessWire Report for company press releases by industry, finding out if financial results are better or worse than expected (of monumental importance to some investors). Many services are free, but require registration; others are available only by subscription. The site shines brightly when it comes to volume of information (commodities speculators can even get a global weather forecast), but it lacks graphical polish and needs a better interface. Still, because this site was one of the first of its kind, expect it to remain a major player.

Security APL Stock Quote Server

http://www.secapl.com:83/cgi-bin/qs
Business and Investing

Forget the Italian suits—now you can stop shaving and do all your stock trading at home in your boxer shorts. This amazingly slick service provides stock quotes on a 15-minute delay. The quote server lets you enter a stock symbol, calls up the latest price, and gives you links to other spots on the Net where you could order the stock. It's all free, thanks to Security APL, a company that hopes you'll buy its impressive online stock trading and portfolio management service. We recommend you avoid loading the graphics here—they take too long, even on fast Net connections. Still, the quotes are free and (at least so far) don't require the annoying password registration now catching on elsewhere on the Web. So even if your portfolio is only large enough for tomorrow's lunch, watching the rise and fall of investors' fortunes can bring entertainment in the best Web tradition.

Sharrow Marketing Information Center

http://www.dnai.com/~sharrow
Business and Investing

Say you've invented an underwater toaster, but need help with marketing. (That may not be all the help you need.) Here's a lively collection of ruminations on marketing and the Web—always a popular topic. This San Francisco marketing company mixes fun with useful info; they've created an innovative "Idea Factory" that enables marketers to promote their new products or ask for marketing help. For laughs, don't miss the "Advertising Parody" section, where users can make fun of the ads they love to hate. We appreciate the site's relaxed atmosphere and sense of humor, but found it's easy to get bogged down in its wordy rambling. Bizarre bonus: a listing of 20,000 mail-order catalogs. (Just what the world needs!)

companies on the web
companies on the web

American Airlines: On Board

http://www.amrcorp.com/aa_home/aa_home.htm
Companies on the Web

The owners of "the world's largest, privately owned, real-time computer network" bring you American Airlines schedules online here. American's parent company, AMR Corp., developed the *Sabre* system now used by most of the world's airlines, but this online schedule only offers a taste of what it can do. We checked on flights from Aruba to Atlanta, and found a daily flight at 2:52 p.m. with a stop in Miami and a snack. You can also choose overseas destinations or departure points to find out what movie will be playing on your flight! Online booking still wasn't available on our last visit, but it's likely to arrive soon. For corporate information, check out the AMR Corporation page.

AT&T

http://www.att.com
Companies on the Web

If you had a share of AT&T stock for every time the word "true" is used at this site, you'd have a handsome portfolio. True Voice, True Rewards, True Savings... and it is true that AT&T has amassed a formidable Web site: hundreds of pages about phones, online services, and (of course) long distance. We searched the 800-number directory for "pet supplies" and netted 278 numbers to call. AT&T also features its public service efforts here, like the cookbook put together by the employee Hispanic Association to help raise money for a scholarship fund. Unless you want to browse helplessly, we suggest you go directly to the Site Search page to find what you're looking for (try the keyword "true").

Chiat/Day Idea Factory

http://www.chiatday.com/web/
Companies on the Web

Chiat/Day is a hugely successful international ad agency with more than $800 million in billings, but that doesn't mean they gloat about it. In fact, a fancy client list is nowhere to be found on this artsy, brainy Web page. Chiat/Day invites you to join an "online focus group," or read thinkpieces with "idea chunks" about

continued

Chiat/Day Idea Factory
continued

evolution, invention, and vision. The company even has its own manifesto, "Quotations from Chairman Jay," with zingers like "There are only two reasons to call in sick. Death in the family. And I can't remember the other one." What's it like working at Chiat/Day? "I feel like a kid in Willy Wonka's Chocolate Factory dressed in Bobby Brady's striped T-shirt," says one employee. (Hmmm.) You can tour their cubicle-free office by clicking on a collage of photos, too. Glossy!

Deutsche Bank

http://www.deutsche-bank.de/index_e.htm
Companies on the Web

With total assets of DM 632 billion, Deutsche Bank ranks as one of the largest banks in the world. Their home page can be viewed in English or German (it is interesting to note that the English-language button has a British flag next to it), and it includes several tasty morsels, such as a listing every afternoon of the current share prices of 60 large German companies. Check out financial stats and company news with the annual and interim reports of the bank's performance, published here (on our last visit, Deutsche Bank had just opened a branch in Guangzhou). Also worth checking out are the company history tour—the Prussian government first granted its banking license in 1870—and the slick company Quicktime video.

Erin/Edwards Advertising

http://www.webcom.com/~milcom/eehomepage.html
Companies on the Web

This new-generation "digital advertising agency" promotes tools like CD-ROM and sales videos as a way to reach media-savvy markets. We found hip graphics pushing the concept of "digital recycling," the re-use of the same designs for both print and multimedia projects. The graphic delights continue with a link to Millennium Communications, Erin/Edwards' interactive division, with its electronic animation and 3D images. But the real fun comes from the "Homer Homepage," where you can ask a mythical Net guru (with a personalized license plate proudly displaying GEEK) for general Net advice, from how much to pay for SLIP access to how to work with color palettes on the Web. Homer's responses are helpful and entertaining; don't miss his geeky picks for Cool Sites of the Week.

FedEx

http://www.fedex.com/

Companies on the Web

What has 220,000 feet, 942 wings, and can lift 12.8 million pounds? The answer, of course, is Federal Express. The absolutely, positively overnight courier (which now wants to be called simply FedEx) lets you actually track your packages here online—is this a great country, or what? You may find yourself sending an empty package just to see when it leaves your airport, when it reaches the delivery truck, and so on. You can also download special shipping and tracking software for your personal computer—no more filling out airbills by hand, the company promises. There's other info here, too, but the tracking is the real kick. It's a simple page that gives the straight facts with a minimum of hype.

Frito-Lay

http://www.fritolay.com/index.html

Companies on the Web

Frito Lay's official site offers fun, interactive advertising. Get a "dream analysis" by a virtual Viennese doctor, or have a cartoon "dream date" drawn to your specifications (sense a theme?). You can also read about the adventures of "Pretzel Boy," the Rold Gold fanatic portrayed on TV commercials by Jason Alexander. And if opening a bag of chips seems too easy, you can cook up dishes the Frito-Lay folks have jazzed up with corn chips, like Crunchy Broccoli and Cheese Lasagna. (We can't vouch for these.) And did you know: "The antiquity of the pretzel can be established from the oldest known picture of one in a Fifth Century illuminated manuscript in the Vatican." Papal pretzels? These pages are good grazing for hungry surfers.

GTE Laboratories

http://info.gte.com/
Companies on the Web

GTE Laboratories is out to prove that scientists know how to have fun. The coolest part of their Web site is "Fun Stuff," which includes a Web version of the popular game MineSweeper and a 3D maze for Web surfers to navigate through, both created by a system administrator at GTE Labs. (Do not get caught playing these at work.) You will also find information about the five sections that make up GTE Labs, including the Computer and Intelligent Systems Laboratory, and some special programs like the Knowledge Discovery Mine, which discusses "the nontrivial extraction of implicit, previously unknown, and potentially useful information from data." Whatever happened to test tubes and beakers, anyway?

The Joe Boxer WWW Playground

http://www.joeboxer.com/
Companies on the Web

These picture-packed pages from the Joe Boxer Corporation reflect the company's belief that Web surfing is most fun when you have no idea what you're doing. What happens when you click on the fly? The smiley face? You won't know until you try. Clever visuals include a White House-style form visitors can use to contact "President Nick" for a briefing on boxer shorts. "Who Are We?" and "Stuff We Make" will give you the usual corporate info, but by and large, sheer goofiness rules at this site. Check out "The Weird Site" for instructions like "Press the eyeball and you will return to the baby." (It works!) This is advertising genius that borders on insanity.

Karakas VanSickle Ouellette Advertising and Public Relations

http://www.kvo.com
Companies on the Web

It's generally hard to enjoy a purely commercial site, but this Portland, Oregon advertising agency makes it easy to do so. Visitors can casually join a fictional, nosy outsider on a meandering tour of the firm and its portfolio, employees, and clients. Watch out, though: you could get caught up in the enthusiasm and end up deciding you need your own personal PR firm. (Check out the "Yo, Taxi" ad, in which a Powerbook powers the big Times Square video screen.) The highlight here is really the comical "Where's Pierre" game, where you can win a T-shirt by discovering the whereabouts of Pierre Oullette, KVO's "creative big cheese."

The Land of Snapple

http://www.snapple.com/
Companies on the Web

The best parts of this official Snapple site are those letters from, yes, REAL people about their favorite fruit-juice and iced tea beverages. An outlet for the hordes of people trying to get on TV by writing to the company is the Letter of the Week, selected by the company's staff of letter-readers. Site visitors can also read a little bit about all the Snapple correspondents who have been featured in the TV commercials, and can meet Wendy, the Snapple Lady. One weird feature: the Lunchroom, which lets Snappleholics swap stories about the sugary stuff or even meet that special Snapple-drinking someone—Bali Blast seeks Mango Madness for candlelight dinners and walks on the beach?

MCI

http://www.mci.com/
Companies on the Web

This MCI Net-fommercial covers much of what you've seen on TV: endless info on the "Friends and Family" program, "MCI Proof of Savings," and so forth. And the corporate information folder offers press releases like "1-800-Collect Announces Ad Campaign Featuring Sawyer Brown." But the inspired feature here is the continuing saga of "Gramercy Press," the goofy corporate soap opera launched in MCI TV commercials. (It's described here as a "tale that brings together timeless feelings of love, power, survival, and betrayal.") This is interactive fun—visit a character's office, then check out her shtick and explore her personal belongings. As long as you can put up with the clumsy sales pitches ("...And with all the stuff networkMCI lets us offer our authors, I think Marcus is just the beginning for us!"), this is fun.

Pizza Hut

http://www.pizzahut.com/
Companies on the Web

Pizza online! That's right, the Pizza Hut Server in Wichita, Kansas, actually serves up piping hot pies to Internet customers at selected cities around the U.S. The "electronic storefront," as they have dubbed it, lets diners choose toppings, size, etc., and leave an address for home delivery. (Type in your phone number to find out if the service is available in your area.) Check out the Sample Menu to see what's available—not only can diners select from an array of sizes, toppings, and kinds of crust, they can issue such directions as "no cheese" or "extra sauce." Not sure what you're in the mood for? A few pictures of their specialty pizzas are included at this site, although it isn't as glossy as the menus you get when you actually go to Pizza Hut. We recommend pepperoni with mushrooms—but make sure they hold the gopher.

Planet Reebok

http://planetreebok.com
Companies on the Web

Planet Reebok is the sports shoemaker's high-tech trek into interactive advertising. On occasion, for instance, visitors with videoconferencing software can join in live interviews with Reebok's featured athletes (check the schedule). Or, check out the company financial reports and history, which explains that the name Reebok comes from an African gazelle. The Sports & Fitness pages have a lot to offer; on our last visit, we found a promo for a new all-fitness cable channel that Reebok sponsors. A clever innovation is the interactive personal trainer, in which you e-mail Ronnie from the Wellness Center for free personal help. (Hey, they say it worked for Oprah.) Expect long load times for graphics and video clips. But you can always work those glutes while you wait.

Qantas Airways Ltd.

http://www.anzac.com/qantas/qantas.htm
Companies on the Web

This exceptional corporate page offers much more than pillows and peanuts. Visitors will find everything from the customs and immigration info to in-flight movie listings, and can also check out gracious links to other airlines, a photo archive with a picture of Qantas' first plane, and fare information (including whatever special offers are currently available). A cool history of the "world's second oldest airline" showcases the airline's perfect safety record—"never lost a passenger"—and even has excerpts from the memoirs of a former navigator for Qantas. Also, get the inside scoop about the stars of one of "the world's most successful advertising campaigns," the Qantas koalas. (For the record, the grumpy little koala who hates Qantas made his TV debut in 1967.) A fun, well-handled site.

Rubin, Postaer & Associates

http://www.rpa.com/
Companies on the Web

This prosperous California ad agency does its best to create an entertaining portfolio here. Called "RPA-O-Matic," the site adopts a retro '50s cartoon-style pitch, encouraging lots of button-pushing as you explore company info. Navigating through buttons like "Ad-E-Licious" and "Client-O-Rama" brings you samples of their work for major players like Honda and Disney; "Insta-Facts" provides info on the company (where "ideas are the whole idea") and on Messrs. Rubin and Postaer; there's even a vague connection between one of their ad designs and O.J. Simpson (read about it in "O.J. Pulp"). Chances are you'll fall for the "Don't Push This Button" gag (we did, and lived to tell about it). There's not much to read, but the pictures are neato-keen and make this a fun browse.

Sony Online

http://www.sony.com/
Companies on the Web

This Web site is beautiful to look at (though if you don't have a whiz-bang computer, the graphics take forever to load). We're talking slick Sony self-promotion in five categories: music (reviewed elsewhere in this book), pictures, electronics, electronic publishing, and radio. Movie-goers will enjoy visiting the "Theater du Monde" for behind-the-scenes peeks at upcoming Sony films; we got a "special message" from Jerry Seinfeld on our last visit. A long list of Sony paraphernalia available to consumers here includes T-shirts of such cultural icons as Godzilla, Mr. Potato Head, and Ricki Lake (sadly, not all on the same shirt). Sony's publishing catalog includes "The Haldeman Diaries"—the perfect choice for an audio electronics firm. We recommend a visit... and we hope a "text only" option arrives soon.

Southwest Airlines

http://www.iflyswa.com/
Companies on the Web

Southwest's "home gate" comes complete with lobby chairs and a waiting airplane in the window (but minus the milling crowds). Flight schedules and price lists are fast and easy to use; visitors can also check out a national flag football competition, or read about Southwest's intensely chipper employees. You get pretty much total airline info here, though you can't order tickets online yet. Our favorite spot: the archive of Southwest Airlines ads dating back to 1972 ("In this lighthearted spot, fun-loving Southwest Airlines customers sing and dance their way onto the plane"). Even with the excellent content, the "virtual airport" interface is what really makes this page stand out. We found ourselves wanting to board the plane or wander down the concourse to explore even further.

Sprint's World of Communication

http://www.sprint.com/
Companies on the Web

This site proves that getting your long-distance advertising through the Web is a lot more fun than getting it from telemarketers. You'll find games, phone facts, *and* a secured server that lets consumers check their account balances right over the Internet. A big part of the advertising here is aimed at students, who are invited to meet a fictional "dean of college knowledge" named Druper—a perpetual student who "had two undergraduate degrees before you were even born" and shares advice on roommates, classes, and of course, long-distance calling. Also prominent at this site is "Sprint Stop," a "service station on the information highway." Corny metaphors aside, Sprint has a big stake in the Net already (many online services use their dial-up network), so this Internet guide promotes Sprint as a full-service communications company.

Stoli Central

http://www.stoli.com/
Companies on the Web

No low-minded bar-hopping here: this richly interactive site from importers of the popular Russian vodka attempts to turn libation into liberation. A freedom theme, inspired by the new Russia, brings you activities like the "Freedom of Expression" interactive art page and the "Freedom of Adventure" list of recommended Web sites (in order of their popularity with Stoli Central visitors). And more directly to the point, you're offered "Freedom of Vodka," in which you can create your own cocktail and have other surfers vote on it. (Sadly, many of the submitted recipes deteriorate into typical bar-room bad taste.) If you'd rather have your drinks mixed by the pros, a list of "the best bars and restaurants throughout the U.S.," recommends lots of cafes and clubs in twelve cities and regions.

World of Otis

http://www.otis.utc.com:80/Index.html
Companies on the Web

This earnest, often unintentionally funny site includes an escalator-safety page, which recommends extra caution for bifocal wearers (huh?). But the History of the Elevator is kind of fun, reminding us that without elevators there'd be no such thing as skyscrapers (or, for that matter, the opportunity to stand around and make new friends waiting for the elevator). The information here about the Otis Company reveals that it manufactures not just elevators and escalators themselves, but something it calls Modernization Products, like a system of infrared beams to detect passengers entering and exiting the elevator (so that the doors won't close on latecomers). We also found out that its elevators service 60 of the world's 100 tallest buildings, and read an intriguing discussion about how the elevoids use the elevator to install the elevator.

Ziff-Davis Net

`http://www.ziff.com`

Companies on the Web

Computer magazine publisher Ziff-Davis built an empire on *Computer Shopper*, a magazine that let enthusiastic computer buyers spend hours leafing at random. Now the publishing giant has led its flock of 12 magazines to the Net, where it offers a refreshingly organized twist on the maddeningly scattered info of old. Hesitant to freely give away the helpful tips of PC Magazine and Mac User, Ziff-Davis delivers smaller, fresher Web editions that sell you on the magazine without stealing away all-important subscriptions. You get chronological lists of back issues here, including an easy keyword search function. Other plusses include feedback forms that you can use to e-mail the authors of online articles, and a neatly organized list of links to computing resources (divided into categories like "Games," "Utilities," and "Multimedia").

Zima

`http://www.zima.com`

Companies on the Web

The temptation to use Z words here is almost irresistible. But that would be zilly. (Oops.) Zima's home page is relaxed and refreshingly frank about selling its product. A list of FAQs explains a bit about it: "Contrary to the ol' rumor mill, there is no vodka or grain alcohol in Zima. Likewise, there is no Zima in vodka or grain alcohol." If you're 21 or over and willing to fill out a demographic survey, you can join "Tribe Z" and visit the Loft, where a hanging light bulb distributes deep thoughts, like "Rice Krispie treats actually came from another planet." Our favorite spot: the Zima Fridge, a virtual icebox stocked with what Zima calls cold links (and they don't mean kielbasa). If you're part of Zima's target audience—you know who you are—you'll get a kick out of this zite. Er, site.

News and Information

News and Information

Information, more than you can handle, instantly and 24 hours a day. That's one of the joys (and the irritants) of the Internet. And the electronic age makes for strange bedfellows. In this section's collection of magazines, for instance, you'll find electronic versions of *Wired*, one of the most switched-on and modern magazines around, and of , an esteemed literary periodical old enough to have published original stories by Ernest Hemingway and Ezra Pound. And both fit beautifully. For a complete listing, check the Newspaper and Current Periodical Room, which lists hundreds of periodicals worldwide.

magazines

magazines

Buzz Online

http://www.buzzmag.com/

Magazines

Readers yearning for that L.A. state of mind will find it at Buzz Online. This Web version of the pop culture print magazine doesn't capture all the glitz of the paper version (after all, they want you to subscribe), but still offers more substance than a drive-in juice bar. Some of L.A.'s best journalists cover trends like Hollywood's love affair with male bimbos ("himbos") and to-die-for camp events like the Academy Awards and the Emmys. You're also treated to top-notch fiction pieces and the fascinating Buzz 100 list of the coolest celebrities in the Buzz universe. You won't make the list just by reading Buzz, but you can start practicing Hollywood hipness by reading about "Oliver Stone's Shiksa Goddess Thing" or "New Line's Casting Chemistry." Top-notch entertainment fun.

Computer Life Online

http://www.complife.ziff.com/~complife/

Magazines

This online version of *Computer Life* magazine tries to make your computer life livable. No nerdy dissertations on megahertz and nanoseconds—this is for the typical American family with 1.5 children and 2.3 computers Dad bought "for the kids." So expect wacky fun here, with regular features like "Upgrading PC Memory is a Snap" and "Online Life Savers" to keep you hanging on through this roller-coaster ride we call the computer age. We're impressed by the weekly updates, and the "2 Cool 2 Wait 4 Print" (thankfully, they didn't spell Cool with a K) late-breaking news stories on new sites, software, and games. Don't miss "Go Wild on the Web," a guide to strange and often useless Web time-wasters for "mouse potatoes."

Discover Magazine

http://www.enews.com/magazines/discover/

Magazines

You'll find science both accessible and fun in this abridged electronic version of *Discover* magazine. The well-rounded publication covers everything from a newly discovered "brain glue" to visits to Angkor Wat, all in easy-to-chew language. On our last visit, we read a fascinating story about a doctor whose relentless detective work saved a man from arsenic poisoning. Then exopaleontologist (don't feel bad if you can't pronounce it) Jack Farmer talked about his unusual profession: finding fossil microbes. *Discover* also hosts a nifty science room for educators, with lesson plans, quizzes, and a host of science-related class-room activities. The only downer: no photos. For that, you'll have to go to your newsstand.

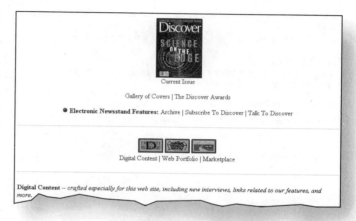

Elle

http://www.ELLEMag.com/

Magazines

The latest fashions, runway images, and "a touch of spiritual direction" are featured in *Elle* magazine's elegant online entry. If you can get past the incredible hype ("Vibrant and visceral, passionate and provocative, diverse and distinctly innovative..."), you'll find the likes of Christy Turlington wearing industrial-strength latex, or Isabella Rossellini in a "menagerie of animal prints just tame enough for city life."

Many photos come with shopping links for those who dare to try such apparel themselves. The interface is stylish, the photos are slick, and rather than endless subscription appeals, this site concentrates on delivering the goods. Because of the many photos, you'll enjoy this most if your modem is as powerful as your fashion sense.

Entertainment Weekly

http://www.pathfinder.com/ew
Magazines

This Net-savvy version of *Entertainment Weekly* is far more than a subscription promo. It's one of the Net's best sites for movie reviews, and a good place to read about the latest on-and-off screen antics of the cast of *Friends* (could they get a little MORE exposure?). Make sure to click on the Hot Sheet to discover the latest of Hollywood's steamy properties, and "Hot List," the best of entertainment links for Net types. Beyond the middle-of-the-road TV coverage, you get volumes of high-quality news coverage of the entertainment industry (including even CD-ROMs), and detailed movie reviews in a freshly updated database. Some features require registration on Time-Warner's Pathfinder service (this site is part of Pathfinder).

ER
CAN TV'S PULSE-POUNDING HIT KEEP UP THE PACE?

'I AM SPOCK'
AN EXCLUSIVE EXCERPT FROM LEONARD NIMOY'S NEW MIND-MELDING MEMOIR

SPECIAL: 'Melrose Place' Issue

SPECIAL: George Lange TV Preview Photo Gallery

Jim Mullen's HOT SHEET

New Movie Reviews:

Fashion Net

http://www.fashion.net/
Magazines

Fashion Net is a non-profit "global meeting point" for amateur and professional style seekers. One half of the page is aimed at the general public, offering an index of magazines such as *Beauty Online*, a link to the Supermodel Homepage, shopping at 3 Suisses (in French), and lots, lots more. The second half of the site is dedicated to business-to-business communications: makeup artist want ads, online portfolios, press releases ("Spain's Spring/Summer '96 International Collections"), and industry bulletin boards. This site can't offer all the flash bulbs and excitement of a seat beside the runway, but it's a stylish attempt to create an online home for an entire industry.

HotWired

http://www.hotwired.com
Magazines

More than just an electronic version of *Wired* magazine, this outpost is the product of a full-time staff dedicated to keeping it fresh. The effort shows in slick neon graphics and intentionally unpredictable content: instead of assigning typical section names, *Wired* divides itself into categories like Signal (news of the wired) and World Beat (travel). HotWired adds flavor from its remarkably thoughtful discussion areas, and variety with plenty of pictures and sounds in its Renaissance (Art and Entertainment) section. There's more than a little self-serving digital snobbery here; the editors have no patience with those who don't share their Utopian visions of a wired world. But stirring up discussion and controversy is precisely what *Wired* does best, and for that, it shouldn't be missed.

Interactive Age

http://techweb.cmp.com/techweb/ia/current/
Magazines

Interactive Age makes online business *its* business. Once published in paper form, it's now a digital magazine, featuring daily trade stories like "Bug Hits AOL Chat Room" and "Tying Networks to Cable Modems." Its strength is coverage of trends in the hot new Web business, making it a good read for gold-rush types. There's no sports section, but we found golf, tennis, and commercial links, plus a column titled, "Tabloid Webism: A Penny a Peek." Includes a terrific library of Web sites of the top 1000 North American companies, as well as the magazine's choices for the top 25 commercial sites on the Net. On the horizon, look for more opportunities to hobnob with industry leaders like Bill Gates in discussion groups and chat sessions here. An authoritative source, and useful every day.

Mother Jones Interactive

http://www.mojones.com

Magazines

Mother Jones magazine (known in Netspeak as MOJOwire) is an online magazine for unabashed leftists and card-carrying liberals (who probably don't believe in carrying cards). Expect plenty of Newt and Rush-bashing here; the bread and butter is stories like "Robbin' the Hood," which accused Wall Street companies of fleecing the poor. (For a wicked case of vertigo, try switching from *Mother Jones* directly to the *Right Side of the Web*.) High marks go to *Mother Jones* for offering a true online magazine with extra features like an updated newswire and the ability to search for articles. If you're itching to debate gun control and socialism, you can join the LiveWire chat system (where you can only talk dirty about toxic waste). And in case you're worrying about the CIA watching, *MOJO* doesn't require you to register.

Phil Gramm's Alibi

The Paris Review

http://www.voyagerco.com/PR/p.toc.html

Magazines

This Manhattan-based international literary quarterly, which first published the likes of Jack Kerouac and Phillip Roth, enters its fifth decade with a stylish edition. Though founded in Paris by '50s American expatriates, this high-minded publication is distinctly American. On our last visit, editor George Plimpton welcomed readers in a short video clip, and Gay Talese's "Looking For Hemingway" ("about the early *Paris Review* crowd's repatriation") shared space with poetry and criticism. Look for more literary reviews to follow this lead; Web users' high education level and intellectual curiosity provide an instant readership, and may eventually replace costly editions printed on paper. It would be great to see even more interactivity and experimentation from *Paris Review*'s gifted staff.

Pathfinder

http://www.pathfinder.com
Magazines

Time Warner makes brilliant use of the Web with this online content machine, combining the best in information from the growing conglomerate's varied sources. You can read a review of new CD-ROMs, check the quotes on the New York Stock Exchange, or visit a "virtual garden" for tips on choosing the right perennials. This is both huge and continuously freshened; it's really about 50 to 100 Web sites in one, yet enables you to move between its sub-sites seamlessly. Why such a web within the Web? Pathfinder wants to become the advertising-sponsored heartbeat of the Web, and to build revenues, bigger is better. For now, Web consumers are the real winners, since they can get essentially all of the articles from magazines like *Sports Illustrated*, *Time*, and *People* in fresh daily editions.

PC Magazine on the Web

http://www.zdnet.com/~pcmag/
Magazines

From the self-proclaimed "best lab-based [computer] publication in the world," here's a generous Net helping of articles evaluating computer hardware and software. Look for the latest on the operating system wars between OS/2, Windows 95, and Windows NT, along with the inside news on Intel's processor one-upsmanship. And now that it's on the Net, throw in some coverage of Web browsers and leading Web sites. So far, you won't find the flood of ads for new computer products that some readers absorb enthusiastically, but for serious lab-coat and pocket-protector-toting computer buyers, the product reviews are all you need. The articles are a little too jargon-laden for many beginners, but *PC Magazine* has a loyal following that will keep it a popular Web destination.

People Magazine

http://www.pathfinder.com/people
Magazines

It may be tawdry or banal, but let's just admit we all enjoy reading *People* in grocery store lines. And now you can read about hairdos for the cast of *Friends* from

the privacy of your computer! We last gobbled up a "Where Are They Now?" for '60s, '70s, and '80s TV stars, featuring a vampy photo of Charo, who retired when her son turned 5. (She didn't want him ever to write a "Cuchi-Cuchi Dearest" biography.) Our archive search for Steffi Graf articles returned 27, including a *Time* recap of her '94 first-round Wimbledon loss to Lori McNeil. And overheard in "Chatter" was Tom Hanks saying of his growing a beard, "I was trying to look dangerous." This often-trivial information adapts beautifully for Web time-wasting.

Popular Mechanics: PM Zone

http://popularmechanics.com/
Magazines

Here's a hands-on-line edition of "a magazine that for 93 years has documented the dreams and deeds of those who believe technology will transform the world for the better." (In other words, it's

for serious gadget lovers.) The regular "Time Machine" feature offers cover photos and synopses of issues dating back to 1902, when *U.S.S. Maine* recovery efforts spurred the invention of the arc lamp. You'll also find the magazine's full-length articles on topics like jukebox history and "The World's Highest-Flying Kite" (Synergy and company hope to get one up to 15,000 feet and beyond). And the ultimate gadget of all, your home computer, gets ample coverage with "under the hood" advice. Particularly impressive are the daily technology updates and "Movie of the Week" video clip library.

The Progressive Review

http://emporium.turnpike.net/P/ProRev/index.html

Magazines

This "longest-running act on the off-Broadway of Washington journalism" offers an online mouthpiece for those disenchanted with the U.S. political status quo (which seems to be nearly everyone). But this isn't a bastion of "we hate the gub-ment" Democrats or Republicans or even independents. It defies classification, denouncing political parties and advocating increased liberty and public accountability.

Among the articles we found was "The Crash of America: How the country's elite wrecked its own empire, ruined the economy, fouled the environment and left Newt Gingrich in charge." This low-budget operation comes in a plain-vanilla text package, so don't expect glitzy lampoons of top political figures. But in the '90s anti-government climate, this alternative view may find a solid Web audience.

Technology Review

http://www.mit.edu:8001/afs/athena/org/t/
techreview/www/tr.html

Magazines

Technology Review is a mainstream (print) magazine from MIT, and you'll find a sampling of its articles here. On a recent visit, we found pieces ranging from a report on a massive civil-engineering project to restore the Everglades, to a set of fascinating articles on the Bomb. No gear-head "fix your hard drive" stuff here; the broader events and issues of research science are covered with outstanding writing from a wide variety of disciplines and viewpoints. As you may know, MIT's scientists helped pioneer the Web, so expect credible use of the new medium (although we found the site a little slow to access at times because of MIT's clogged servers).

And refreshingly, you won't find "gee-whiz" cheerleading for every scientific development—this magazine has a conscience.

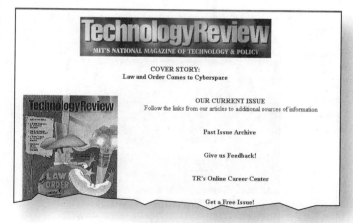

Time Out

http://www.timeout.co.uk/

Magazines

Brit Tony Elliott started *Time Out* magazine as a university student in 1968, using a few pounds his aunt gave him for a birthday present. Now his stable of worldwide city guides tells Web travelers what's up in London, Prague, Madrid, Paris, Berlin, Amsterdam, and New York. Prague diners can head for the Akropolis, a "hangout for the young, terminally hip set," and Berlin club-goers can visit the former Nazi bunker (called, with Teutonic efficiency, Bunker), which "houses all manner of throbbing, decadent nightlife." Worldwide readers can post news about their towns, too. Talk about an ideal candidate for the Web! It's as if *Time Out* were created with global networking in mind and just had to wait a quarter-century for technology to catch up.

Time World Wide

http://www.pathfinder.com/time

Magazines

The *Time* logo is nearly as familiar as your watch, so no introduction is needed here. But this is a better *Time* than most readers have ever seen, offering daily updates, and the combined editions of the magazine's worldwide operation (hence the name Time World Wide). Editors have also overcome the magazine's biggest problem: publishing a cover story only to find it outdated by the time it hits the newsstands. You also get a dizzying array of back issues, search engines, and talk-back boards to make it a formidable research tool. *Time*'s computer-savvy staff has made a bold effort to pioneer a new way of delivering news. The next step is audio and video, and with Time-Warner's merger with Turner Broadcasting (and CNN), you're likely to see rich multimedia elements soon.

Utne Lens

http://www.utne.com/
Magazines

The folks at *Utne Reader* magazine call this excellent online edition a "field guide to the emerging culture" and a "filter for the Infowhelmed." That's a tall order, but this thoughtful digest of social commentary does an admirable job of creating a distinct voice on the Web. Articles gathered from the alternative press don't hesitate to question spin doctors and medical doctors or shoot down the latest popular craze (including the Net). On a more constructive note, community-building is the order of the day in "Cafe Utne." The forward-thinking editors at *Utne* have recognized that the Net's easy access to information isn't enough, providing a guided discussion without resorting to advocacy. A fine addition to the Web spectrum.

VOWWorld: Voices of Women

http://www.voiceofwomen.com/
Magazines

This is the online version of VOW, a Chesapeake Bay area women's magazine and, according to this page, "the most comprehensive women's resource on the Internet." Using what they describe as "intermedia synergy," the editors hope electronic communications will put "a new set of power tools" into the hands of women. Some of these tools include articles like "Talkin' About a Girl Revolution" and "The State vs. Midwives: A Battle for Body and Soul," which challenges the notion that the only "safe" birth is a "technological" birth. VOW is compelling reading, but the page offers more than journalism: it also sponsors an annual women's conference and expo, details of which are available here, and a directory of "woman-owned," "woman-friendly" businesses, from accounting and acupuncture to writing workshops and yoga.

The most comprehensive women's resource on the Internet!

Voices of Women Home Page

news

AP Wire Search

`http://www1.trib.com/NEWS/APwire.html`

News

Much of the news you read in newspapers or hear on radio or TV comes from the Associated Press, a cooperative that links news organizations around the world. And this unlikely contribution from a newspaper in Casper, Wyoming lets you search their archive of AP news stories freely as long as you sign up for a user name and password (for copyright reasons). The interface is a little wobbly in places, with headlines cut short after 30 or so characters, creating headlines like "Clinton proposes linking all S," leaving you to guess the rest of the headlines. (We decided it must have been "Clinton proposes linking all Senators with handcuffs.") Once you get used to this flaw (and start having fun with it), you'll enjoy the steady stream of national (and Wyoming) news available here.

China News Digest

`http://www.cnd.org`

News

Some say the greatest wall around communist China is the one blocking free flow of information. And the China News Digest admirably keeps the news flowing against all odds with help from the Web. Chinese scholars from around the world voluntarily contribute to this frequently updated news service, delivering what is meant to be impartial news coverage of world trade issues, immigration, and cultural affairs in both English and Chinese. The site contains mostly text documents, but a new picture library and Chinese literature archive add interesting resources for those wanting a taste of Chinese culture. The files could use better formatting; you'll often have to search awhile just to find the latest issue. But this is an all-volunteer project, so the technology gap is explainable. A one-of-a-kind resource.

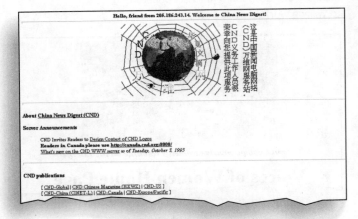

CNN Interactive

http://www.cnn.com/

News

It took a while for CNN to burst onto the Web scene, but this picture-rich site makes the wait worthwhile. CNN's home page covers breaking news, sports, health, and showbiz stories, each nearly always including pictures grabbed from CNN's video cameras. It also offers a few limited video clips, still too time-consuming for most users to download, but clearly a sign of what's to come as Net connections speed up. We especially liked the blazing-fast search feature that quickly calls up stories on a topic of your choice. Can you survive without the reassuring voice of a news anchor? Sure, but just to feel more at home, you may want to try your best imitation of James Earl Jones intoning "This... is CNN."

The Daily News: Just the Links

http://www.cs.vu.nl/~gerben/news.html

News

Newshounds with international tastes will drool over this list of 200 links to various newspapers and information sources from around the globe. From Poland's *Donosy* (in Polish and English) to Costa Rica's *La Nacion*, the major and minor electronic world news sources are lined up, shotgun style, for your own exploration. It's fine for researchers who already know what they're looking for, but you'll have some leg-work to do if you're browsing on a particular topic (sites are arranged geographically only). We'd like to see more than just the links, however; connecting to a site from another country may leave many users confused at best. But if you already have a sharp journalistic eye, this list can keep you busy for a long time.

Daily Weather, Surf, and Traffic

http://paella.ucsd.edu/ccs/daily_weather.html

News

Here are the three things *everybody* in Southern California wants to know about: sun, surf, and cars. This clever service gathers together resources on weather and surfing conditions (*not* the digital kind, thank you) as well as real-time traffic graphics from both Los Angeles and San Diego. Several surfing pages—from Surfrider Online to the LaJolla Surfing Weather Page—can be accessed from here, and you can also get old-fashioned ocean conditions for non-surfers, too. A final bonus is the set of skiing links for Utah, Oregon, and Colorado. And, of course, at the very bottom of the Southern California site is earthquake news. (Why worry?) We love the concept, but it's almost into information overload. Then again, what could be more appropriate?

Federal Emergency Management Agency (FEMA)

http://www.fema.gov/homepage.html

News

In case of an ACTUAL emergency, this site is not "only a test." Here you'll find the latest news on relief efforts for floods, earthquakes, and hurricanes, and learn how you can get help or give it. Cut straight to the News Desk for the latest on current relief efforts. Then be prepared (are you listening, Boy Scouts?) for the next time: download documents on how to get ready for a hurricane or file a flood insurance claim. We'd like to see FEMA upgrade from its outdated gopher servers, (often clumsy to access from the Web) and nail some fresh plywood around the interface. But since the Net was originally designed in part for national emergencies, this site is still one of the most valuable resources going.

Mercury Center

http://www.sjmercury.com

News

The *San Jose Mercury News* was one of the first, and is still one of the best, of the Web's online newspapers. It's developed into a slick subscription-based service with some unique features. Instead of adopting a newspaper-like look, it stresses an innovative hyperlinking system that lets users move between related topics with little effort. Some features (headlines) are free, others (like in-depth articles and late-breaking news) require a subscription. San Francisco area residents will appreciate the online classified ads, and the "Merc's" home-town coverage of California's Silicon Valley high-tech industry. And for a modest monthly fee, "NewsHound" will scan the news services daily for topics you choose. We're not wild about the site's sometimes odd graphics, but we applaud its non-linear approach to delivering news.

MMWire Weekly

http://www.mmwire.com/

News

MMWire (which stands for Multimedia Wire) is a daily report on the multimedia industry, faxed daily to subscribers around the nation. Here MMWire boils its daily newsletter down to a weekly form. The emphasis is on commerce and corporations: you'll find reports on major players like Sony and IBM, along with little fish just starting to make a splash. The classifieds section has "help wanted" postings from companies with multimedia positions (if you're a freelance multimedia professional, go here NOW—there are some tasty jobs here for talented people). The Wire also provides eFlash, a free service that sends you hot info via e-mail, not unlike their faxed form. The site also includes back issues, reports on conferences and trade associations, and much more. Essential reading for multimedia pros.

NandO Times

http://www2.nando.net/nt/nando.cgi
News

The name *NandO Times* may sound like a newspaper from outer space, but it's actually "Netspeak" for the *News and Observer* of Raleigh, North Carolina. "All the news that's bits we print" is their cheerful, if slightly tortured, motto. Coverage includes one-sentence sketches of breaking stories, followed by one-paragraph summaries, presuming typical Web users have painfully short attention spans. For detailed stories (mostly from wire services), you have to register (it's free). The use of pictures is among the best from news sites on the Web, but we're not as thrilled with their cluttered roundup of news headlines. Don't miss the sports section (why not "SpandO"?), one of the largest collections of sports news and fan trivia we've seen.

Newsbytes Pacifica

http://www.islandtel.com/newsbytes/
News

Newsbytes is an international wire service covering the computer industry—and on the Web, it shines as a freshly updated source of techno-news.

WELCOME TO NEWSBYTES PACIFICA

NEWSBYTES 1995 UPDATE CD-ROM FREE WITH
SUBSCRIPTION SERVICE

From now until September 30, 1995, all new subscribers to the Newsbytes Subscription Service will receive the Newsbytes 1995 Update CD-ROM for free (a $29.95 value). We'll even ship the CD internationally - at no cost to you! Simply sign up for the Newsbytes Subscription Service (Japanese information is here); once your purchase has been confirmed, you'll receive an order form for your free CD with the next edition of your Newsbytes subscription.

Correspondents around the world contribute stories on new computer technology and hi-tech company news, although some of the material may be a little dry for the average user. (On a recent visit, we read about Conner Peripherals' increased investment in a Singapore facility, and Magnetic Software's release of a new version of BlankCheck software.) One especially useful resource is "Web Cites," which lists online sites of companies mentioned in the daily reports. We've found this the best source available for Japanese and Chinese high-tech news, and applaud its efforts to add visual elements with its "Newspix" section.

Newspaper and Current Periodical Room

http://lcweb.loc.gov/global/ncp/ncp.html

News

This is one great reading room. The Library of Congress has assembled here a collection of links, resources, and newspapers, both online and offline, from Greece to Colombia. The page also includes links to tax forms, Supreme Court decisions, and the United Nations, among others. But the real glory here is in the list of global publications: Austrian news summaries, *Noticias de Mexico y el Mundo*, and much more. Don't expect to find a lot of colorful pictures and wacky graphics: this is the straight dope. But while lots of sites talk about "virtual tours," this actually does turn out to be very much like wandering past the magazine racks in your own library.

Pilot Online

http://www.infi.net/pilot/index.html

News

Southeastern Virginia's *Virginian-Pilot* newspaper isn't bashful about showing its local news to the world here. The paper's visually friendly, easy to read, and best of all, free. Whether the news is interesting to you depends on where you live. A heavy emphasis on military news offers a unique resource for families who may have relatives stationed at one of Virginia's sprawling military bases. We're charmed by the paper's personal touch, featuring an online "public" editor to answer user questions by e-mail (but please, no broad questions like "So what's happening in the world today?"). But the best resource is CareerWeb, an international jobs database covering a broad range of job categories (not just computers). All in all, it's highly recommended for Virginians (and pilots, we suppose).

TimesFax

http://nytimesfax.com/

News

Despite the name, don't go rushing to your fax machine for "all the news that's fit to fax." The New York Times has expanded its fax service to the Web by enabling users to freely download a file here that can viewed with special software

(the free Adobe Acrobat reader program for PCs and Macs). And once you make it through the instructions on viewing the file, you're ready to experience an American journalism institution. This is not the full edition of the *Times*; instead, with ads from folks like Mobil, Advil, and AT&T, TimesFax delivers an eight-page news summary that covers the top stories of the day. Will it be free forever? Probably not, since most newspapers are experimenting with combinations of online subscriptions and advertising. For now, it's a winner.

TribWeb

http://www.tribnet.com/register.htm

News

Like the AP Wire Search page, this site from the Tacoma, Washington, *Tribune* offers access to Associated Press U.S. and international wire reports. The difference

here is that TribWeb has more categories (family news, education news, and so on) and extra features like restaurant and movie reviews. Another advantage is that the TribWeb archives its wire material for at least two weeks and sometimes longer; this helps because the *AP* writes a lot of undated pieces that can run at any time. Registration is simple, but required. (And don't get any smart ideas about using the stories to start your own online paper—this material is copyrighted.) Fine for news junkies, but it's wall-to-wall words, a bit of a shock for readers used to the eye-catching layout of newspaper stories.

USA Today

http://www.usatoday.com/

News

Flashy, splashy *USA Today* has been derided as "McPaper," but for Web users and their famous short attention span, this online version offers McNews with easy drive-thru service. Minute-by-minute sports scores, constantly updated news summaries, fresh stock market graphics, and those famous weather maps adapt well to the Web, carrying a familiar *USA Today* air about them. Once a subscription service, USA Today has decided to offer much of its news for free, and let advertisers pay the bills. Its visual layout is the best we've seen among Web news sites, and while most of the stories are from AP wire sources, the paper is beginning to embrace the digital world with more of its original content. If you like the paper, you'll like the site.

Women's Health Hot Line

http://www.soft-design.com/softinfo/womens-health.html

News

The flashing banner's gotta go, but we say "yes" to the informative, well-researched articles here. Edited by medical journalist Charlotte Libov, this online newsletter addresses women's health concerns frankly and with authority. "Sex is a serious topic for women with heart problems," reports Libov, who goes on to speak openly about its physiological and emotional consequences. In "50 Essential Things to Do When the Doctor Says it's Heart Disease," the author recommends taking control: "Back in the old days... you expected to be taken care of." Libov also addresses the risks of smoking, and provides readers with tips on how best to evaluate medical news from today's confusing media sources. A super and long-overdue reference for women of all ages.

Women's Wire

`http://www.women.com/`

News

When Mom's line is busy and your best friend's on vacation, the sisters are "in" at Women's Wire. This sharp, politically savvy page from San Francisco has everything from headline news to a forum

for "back talk," where women can share their opinions on controversial issues. "Question Authorities" provides women with opportunities to query experts in the fields of fashion, business, and sex (subtitled "carnal knowledge"). There's even advice for stargazers: asks Therese in California, "If my husband is an Aries and the oldest child and I'm a Pisces and youngest, do we have a marriage made in heaven? Or are we an accident waiting to happen?" (We'll keep the answer a surprise.) And lest we forget those irksome (and ubiquitous) troubles with men, you may want to consult "eMale: The Gender Challenged."

WWW WorldNews Today

`http://www.fwi.com/wnt/wnt.html`

News

This is another in the growing list of online news services that will tailor themselves to your reading interests. This one has all the usual topics—sports, headlines, travel—but for a monthly fee will also e-mail you articles on specific topics (say, "Bosnia") by 10 a.m. each day. Some of the good stuff: columns from all corners of the political spectrum, like Molly Ivins and Walter Williams (he sits in for Rush

Limbaugh) and, of course, the personal ads, which are free! (We found the standard "SWM is seeking fun-loving female pen pal.") It won't wow your eyes, with basic graphics and postage-stamp sized pictures, and we're not wild about its sometimes haphazard layout. But you can't deny it's useful as a free service that doesn't require registration.

Aether Madness

http://www.aether.com/Aether/
Reference

ary Wolf and Michael Stein's book "Aether Madness" is a slightly wacky guide to cyberspace. This online version is an excellent resource for many topics, including computer talk: GIF, MUD, packet switching, and so on. We recommend that you read the preface before skipping off to whatever looks cool. The authors rightfully state that this is not an encyclopedia; it is dependent on the whims of its creators, who take readers along on tours that range from "Budget" to "Kitchen Sink." This is a cool spot for new folks to visit because it doesn't just throw lists of Internet sources and sites in their faces. It answers some of the most common questions and complaints, like: "We tried to go there, but it didn't exist."

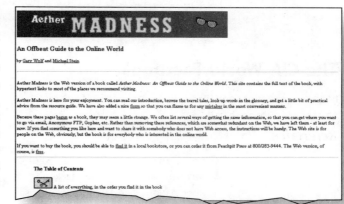

Barbara's News Researcher Graffiti Page

http://www.gate.net/~barbara/
Reference

resh from an actual newspaper librarian and researcher—Barbara Gellis Shapiro of Florida's *Palm Beach Post*—comes this extensive listing of the most useful Internet reference works. Shapiro's idea was to take the most useful links for news researchers and put them together in a convenient listing, so don't expect this to be everything about anything—and forget about pictures. Instead, the links provided here contain statistics, government information, and commercial information services. Whether it's banned books available online or the Divorce Home Page you want, the links are here. Florida resources are a big part of the list, as is journalism in general, but students and other researchers can find good starting points here, too.

Bill's Library

http://www.io.org/~jgcom/library.htm
Reference

Now *here's* a library and a half—at least. Bill Henderson, who lives in Toronto, Canada, and has a cool home page in his own right, has amassed an eminently readable collection of online magazines, literature, and the like. "'Twas brillig, and the slithy toves...'" from Lewis Carroll's "Jabberwocky" is among the many delights to be found in the Poet's Corner. For a "definitive guide to the postmodern scene," consult "The Panic Encyclopedia" (or *The New Republic*). You may not know what "The Morpo Review" is, but you sure can find out (it's an electronic magazine published by creative college students around the United States). This obviously is the work of a man who A) has a extraordinary interest in literature and B) has *way* too much time on his hands. But you'll be glad he does.

The CIA World Factbook

http://www.odci.gov/cia/publications/94fact/
fb94toc/fb94toc.html
Reference

The Central Intelligence Agency receives billions of dollars to keep tabs on other nations. The factbook at this site is one grand example of that work, with political, social, and economic information on places you didn't even know existed—for instance, the Ashmore and Cartier Islands, located between Australia and Indonesia. Together, the factbook says, they are about the size of the Washington D.C. mall. (Not bad research, considering that the isles have no permanent residents.) And if you know nothing about, say, Botswana (hello students!), this would be a very good place to start looking. The title is slightly misleading: you won't find classified information here. But you will find a lot of everything else.

DejaNews Research Service

http://www.dejanews.com/
Reference

Usenet, the Internet free-for-all that encompasses thousands of newsgroups, can be a mess. So how can you find your way to newsgroup postings on, say, kangaroos (and there are plenty out there)? This service makes trying to find something a little bit easier, especially for newcomers. When we searched for "Richard Nixon," for instance, we found postings on such diverse newsgroups as rec.pets (Checkers, no doubt) and sci.space.policy. Searching for "orangutan" yielded 86 hits. Searches can be for whole words, phrases, and even words with similar beginnings. And you can write to the author of the posts you find, too. The search menus are easy to use, making this both useful and a great way to pass the time.

Directorate of Time

http://tycho.usno.navy.mil/time.html
Reference

Clockwatchers will enjoy every second at the Directorate of Time, a service of the U.S. Naval Observatory in Washington, D.C. Not only can you get the exact time accurate to the nanosecond, but you'll be amazed to read just how much trouble it takes to keep the entire civilized world from losing a tick here and there. Of course, everyone knows it takes 50 cesium beam frequency standards and 10 hydrogen masers to keep a master clock like this from missing a beat, but it's nice to be reminded. The really big news when we last visited: the announcement of a leap second by the International Earth Rotation Service (it's actually very important, since many navigational devices depend on exact time). Extra-fun bonus gadget: a powerful sunrise/sunset calculator for your home town.

Foxy!

http://www.tumyeto.com/tydu/foxy/foxy.htm
Reference

Keva, Ivy, Deanna, Lauren, and Annie have put together the first-ever (they say) online 'zine exclusively for babes (and

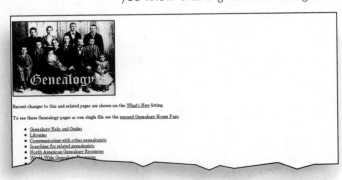

"Poot! jocks," whatever those are). This is Required Cruising 101 for twenty-somethings with attitude (not to mention a healthy sense of silly), especially when it comes to advice on dumping a jerk or dealing with a deadly case of the dorks. Send e-mail to Alex ("a real live boy") to have all those burning questions answered, like, "What's with that whole stripper fascination thing?" Or, just talk trash with your girlfriends in this lively twist on feminism from the irreverent generation. Tongue-in-cheek articles explore the vagaries of "fashion vixens" and beauty tips for battling the pesky pimple. Freelance vulpine submissions are encouraged.

The Genealogy Home Page

http://ftp.cac.psu.edu/~saw/genealogy.html
Reference

If you're stumped about your family roots, this page (the result of combined efforts by several genealogy buffs) may help you get the real story. For example, if you know that a great-uncle emigrated

from Leningrad, but was born in Berlin, the German-Russian genealogical library is a logical next step. Only a few genealogical libraries let you do online searching so far, but the site suggests other ways you can trace the names of your ancestors using the Net's growing resources. A staggering collection of genealogical software is available for downloading, including "Heraldry," a program for drawing your coat of arms, and several family chart and scrapbook applications. We suggest this site as a great way to begin a valuable family project, and to learn about the Web's powerful tools as you go along.

Geographic Nameserver

`http://www.mit.edu:8001/geo`

Reference

To call this just a geography site isn't fair; hey, geography should *always* be this fun. Visitors can enter a name (even their own) and seconds later receive a listing of all cities and towns in the United States with that name. For example, ten towns named "Elmer" exist in the U.S., two in Louisiana alone. This simply designed site also generates the county, zip code, area code, and latitude/longitude coordinates for each result, which makes it (would you believe) useful, too. Bill Clinton might be interested to know that seven places called "Clinton" are county seats. According to the database, "Fun" does not exist anywhere in the United States. Visitors to this site may beg to differ.

Global Encyclopedia

`http://204.32.221.16/`

Reference

Information, the saying goes, wants to be free. This pseudo-encyclopedia is a great example of that. The "Global" in this title means that people around the world are invited to provide entries on any subject. The content, therefore, is sometimes pretty casual. The entry for Liechtenstein, for example, begins: "Liechtenstein is a very small country in Europe, between Switzerland and Austria." Some are downright whimsical: shrimp are defined as "wonderful animals. They come in a variety of sizes." Maybe it's not professional writing, but it can be a lot of fun to read. And, the entry for Morse Code is well-written and includes the full code itself. Because volunteers do the writing and editing, many of the entries are themselves the relative size of Liechtenstein. But the originality of the entries is fantastic.

Inform Women's Studies Database

```
http://info.umd.edu:86/Educational_Resources/
AcademicResourcesByTopic/WomensStudies/
```
Reference

More than a database, this page provides loads of info for anyone interested in women's studies. Link to "Computing" for a discussion of gender issues in the computer industry, or use pointers to a host of electronic women's forums. An index of electronic and real-time conference announcements is impressive and eclectic: you'll find details on the Feminist Therapy Institute, the Black Women's Health Caucus, Feminism, and Postmodernism—there's even a downloadable conference report on Sexual Identities in the Middle Ages. An unusual collection of feminist film reviews puts a new spin on Hollywood: ever want to get the feminist perspective on *Home Alone*? Then there's the job bank, calls for paper submissions, and dozens more gender-related links. Solid photos and design do wonders for this academic material.

Library of Congress

```
http://www.loc.gov
```
Reference

If the question is reference, here's the answer. The Library of Congress home page is a motherlode of information that goes far beyond library paste. It affirms the

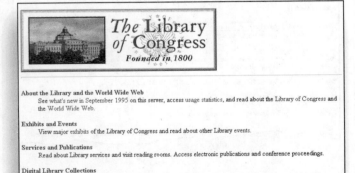

About the Library and the World Wide Web
See what's new in September 1995 on this server, access usage statistics, and read about the Library of Congress and the World Wide Web.

Exhibits and Events
View major exhibits of the Library of Congress and read about other Library events.

Services and Publications
Read about Library services and visit reading rooms. Access electronic publications and conference proceedings.

Digital Library Collections
Search and view items from digitized historical collections (American Memory); read about other special Americana collections held by the Library.

core democratic value of open access to information with special displays like the hitherto top-secret Revelations from the Russian Archives. Every month the server is updated with new exhibits, new prints, and photographs (we recommend the "Politics and Propaganda" and "Pictorial Journalism" series, which represent photographers from Matthew Brady to Leni Riefenstahl). Then, of course, there are the incredible reference resources and Americana to be mined by scholars, surfers, and anyone who still can't explain how a bill becomes law. Simply put, the Library of Congress is one of the best repositories on everything American.

My Virtual Reference Desk

http://www.intercom.net/user/rbdrudge/main.html
Reference

Remember when you visited your dad's office, and you played with all of the cool things he had there, and you really got on his nerves? This site gives you direct access to all of those cool things, without cluttery desks, chairs, and paper clips. Here you'll find links to the official Naval Observatory time, the word of the day, headline news and stock quotes, cross-word puzzles, and even a zip code search engine, a poker dictionary, and *Bartlett's Quotations*. Author Bob Drudge essentially offers his own list of the best and brightest sites in 26 different categories. It's certainly an easy place to kill some of that Naval Observatory time—we recommend a few dozen spins on the "random links" icon.

Newsletter Library

http://pub.savvy.com/
Reference

Maybe, just maybe, your favorite topic isn't well-represented on the Internet (although we doubt that). Well, the chances are good that somebody is publishing a *newsletter* about the subject, and here's a giant listing to check. Maybe it's banking (10 subject headings), high school sports or telecommunications (15 different subjects). Perhaps bilingual education is your cup of tea. Whichever it is, just fill out the handy form here and send it in, and you'll get sample copies of newsletters pertaining to the issues you request. For free! If you produce a newsletter and want to have it listed (along with over 10,000 others), you can register it online. Unfortunately, you can't browse through specific newsletters, but you do get the luxury of sitting in your home while free stuff is traveling toward you.

The Reference Desk

http://www-sci.lib.uci.edu/~martindale/Ref.html
Reference

This page at the University of California at Irvine library has plenty of reference links, especially for health and medicine centers. It also includes an unusual number of links to the time: we counted at least four links to clocks, plus a page that tells the time on the seven continents. And there's more. Want to know which movies Denzel Washington has appeared in?

Looking for a site online that can perform Chi-square statistical tests? You'll find them here. Visitors will find some pretty unique stuff, like the Cutaneous Drug Reaction Database in New Hampshire (a listing of drug reactions that affect the skin). Good college links, too! This is the Internet info equivalent of, say, the Mall of the Americas.

The Smithsonian Institution

http://www.si.sgi.com/
Reference

The Smithsonian isn't just 18 incredible museums in Washington—it's a cottage industry. This Web site proves it, with layers and layers of info on the famous museums (including the National Zoo), membership, D.C. sightseeing, policy statements on pets and strollers, and, inevitably, an online shopping mall. Among the museums available for electronic exploration are the Cooper-Hewitt National Design Museum, the National Museum of American History, and the National Air and Space Museum. There, a clickable floor plan guides you through ongoing exhibits like "Flight Time Barbie" and the fuselage of the Enola Gay (the B-29 that carried the atomic bomb to Hiroshima). In fact, you could spend hours in just one museum, let alone have time for all the resource and cultural centers, children's pages, and news releases that are here.

Tripod

http://www.tripod.com/
Reference

Become a member of this online service for college students and young professionals (sign-up is free and painless), and you can access their "Tools for Living": hot tips on travel, health, career, finance, and more. This is mainly aimed at generation sub-x (or whatever it is): for instance, the "Resumé Doctor" offers the winning fonts and phrases for that exotic life story. You'll need the resumé, too, if you hope to secure one of the many internships listed in Tripod's National Directory. Making healthy lifestyle choices is the focus of "Ask the Experts." And visitors can learn to build their own simple home pages. Tripod has a habit of running contests and surveys frequently, but that's not so bad. You might even win something. And if nothing else, it keeps things lively.

Virtual Reference Desk

http://thorplus.lib.purdue.edu/reference/index.html
Reference

Quick! What's the international country code for Benin? BN? Not! (It's BJ.) And just what *is* the Estonian word for torpor? You'll be hard pressed to name a fact that can't be found at this site. It's great for students, crossword fanatics, and anyone who's ever had to look up a zip code. How many acronym dictionaries do you need? This place has three, which is AWL (a whole lot). If you're having trouble understanding your college-age children (or if you're a geeky sophomore), check out the college slang dictionary. (Supposedly, in California, New England "preppie school types" are known as "bifftads," and "to slort" is to go to class with the express purpose of sleeping through it.) No slorting here, just a lot of cool stuff.

World Population Counter

`http://sunsite.unc.edu/lunarbin/worldpop`
Reference

This simple page gives you one straight fact: the current estimate of our world's human population. At our last check, it was just a shade over 5.76 billion and rising. (One estimate says we're due to stabilize at just about 11.6 billion in the year 2200.) And just so you feel abreast of the situation, it updates itself every 30 sec-

onds. If you like to deal in smaller numbers, visit the U.S. population "clock," where the number was only 263 million and change the last time we checked in. But there's something mesmerizing about watching the world population counter click up 190 or so new souls every minute.

The WWW Virtual Library

`http://www.w3.org/hypertext/DataSources/`
`bySubject/Overview.html`
Reference

Given only one place to begin the great Internet adventure, this ranks as a contender for top dog, a worldwide resource for information. Even words like "humongous" can't describe just how heavy with data the stacks are here, with categories that cover just about everything—facts, fantasy, and frivolity—wherever the information is, be it Web site or newsgroup or service organization. Games

and sports, "hard" sciences and social sciences, ghosts and angels and UFOs, and even home pages are only a fraction of the available categories. In addition, servers, browsers, and gophers get their due. Like a search engine, but without that mind-gone-blank attack that accompanies search forms. When you want to find out something, you go to the library!

Schools and Education

Schools and Education

Individual colleges and universities can be great places for Web exploration. At first glance, they often seem quite dull: lists of faculty addresses, dry explanations of library hours, and so forth. But do a little digging and you'll find whimsical faculty members showing off their vacation pictures—and student pages are, of course, geysers of weird creativity. Even piano teachers are getting into the act. We've included a few of our favorite colleges here, and you can always scan for your own school in the "College and University Home Pages" site reviewed in this chapter.

AskERIC Virtual Library

http://ericir.syr.edu
Schools and Education

AskERIC is a massive online question-and-answer service primarily for teachers, but parents will be amazed at the depth and breadth of resources here. For access to info on "Using Popcorn to Create a Reading Book," "MacBeth Made Easy," and scores of lesson plans... AskERIC! (Yes, we can't resist their cleverly catchy title.) Language arts teachers will find great guides to directing a "whole language experience," and science teachers can browse mini-lessons on topics from soil erosion to elementary astronomy. A super bonus: learning materials that can be used with children's programming on The Discovery Channel or PBS's "Newton's Apple" series. A tip of the mortarboard to Syracuse University, the U.S. Department of Education, and Sun Microsystems for sponsoring this terrific page.

Cal Band History

http://server.berkeley.edu/calband/history.html
Schools and Education

Some will find this dull; others, a delight. For the uninitiated, the marching band at the University of California at Berkeley is one of the more famous examples of its genre. Its battles with arch-rival Stanford have eclipsed the schools' football games at times. In "The Pride of California: A Cal Band Centennial Celebration," a group of alumni have collected a history of the band in 14 chapters. An oral history includes transcribed interviews with luminaries and regular folks who played in or worked with the Cal band. (Don't miss the story of Cal band members creating a replica of a Stanford treasure and racing through Stanford's gymnasium during a basketball game.) Big downside: no pictures and mainly gopher server text. But the stories are still a blast!

Carnegie Mellon University

http://www.cmu.edu/cmufront/cmu.html

Schools and Education

Other universities we could mention (but are too polite to) could take home page lessons from Carnegie Mellon U. Fitting, because Carnegie claims to be one of America's top 10 computer schools, and has long been an active player on the Internet. Even the college prez makes a special Web welcome here (and shows off one of America's top 10 presidential mustaches). In addition to a look at the school itself, this site also dispels any possible Pittsburgh phobias with its flattering look at the city's lifestyle, history, and commerce. (Particularly helpful is the Yellow Pages, an alphabetical guide, with maps, to everything from adoption services to travel agents.) Pittsburgh graphics

are good and transitions smooth. Excellent electronic admissions segment. Good student pages, too.

CEARCH: Cisco Educational Archive

http://sunsite.unc.edu/cisco/

Schools and Education

This site is swell for educators and schools hoping to "internetwork" via the WWW. CEARCH is a cute acronym for the Cisco Educational Archive and Resources Catalog. (It's a joint project between Cisco Systems and the University of North Carolina.) A "CEARCH" using the keyword "logic" turned up a pointer to "Cyborgs Are Us," a series of stories by Dr. Andrew Yeaman, and a tool for older students to use in considering the cyborg as

metaphor for "the movement from modern to postmodern society." Next, you're invited to the Virtual Schoolhouse, a "meta-library of K-12 links" to nearly every online education resource imaginable, from Doctor Fun to Mega Math to Declassified Spy Photos (honest!). If Cisco would just upload some stuff for custodians, then *everybody* on the K-12 staff would have good reason to visit this spot.

College and University Home Pages

http://www.mit.edu:8001/people/cdemello/univ.html
Schools and Education

At this site, MIT's Christina DeMello provides an extremely useful (and popular) service: a directory of university home pages. Visitors can download the entire list in compressed formats or search by letter. (For faster results, the data is "mirrored," or stored, at several sites around the world.) A glimpse at the "L" listings, for instance, yields La Salle University, Lycoming College, and dozens of other schools whose names you might not recognize. Click on "O" and you'll find the +stfold College page—all in Norwegian, natch. There's an English translation, though, and a nice map of Norway, too. And what tour of world colleges would be complete without the Beijing University of Chemical Technology? Terrific resource!

Columbia University

http://www.columbia.edu/
Schools and Education

"You don't have to be in New York when you come of age intellectually. But if you are, the city's vigor and sophistication will be yours for life." (Melvin

Schwartz CC '53) Such "vigor" comes through loud and clear on Columbia U.'s home page. Amid sparkling descriptions of student life in the Big Apple, the academic and administrative info is almost an afterthought. Especially swell is the Go Ask Alice health question and answer service. You'll also find extracurricular activities, ranging from an amateur radio club to the World Federalist Organization. Even the self-promotion is impressive: "As the poet Walt Whitman said, 'A great city is that which has the greatest men and women.' At Columbia, you'll have the freedom, the encouragement and the opportunities to become one of them." Woo!

CyberED

http://www.umassd.edu/cybered/distlearninghome.html

Schools and Education

Aiming to "rival the traditional classroom," the University of Massachusetts-Dartmouth offers electronic registration and full credit courses online here. Why choose CyberED? Because "asynchronous communications" (those lacking immediate face-to-face or phone-to-phone interaction) have their advantages, the school argues persuasively. Plus, after all, "On the Internet, no one knows you're a dog." There are no dogs among the course offerings here, which include "Technical and Business Writing," "Personal Finance," and "The Holocaust," a class the registrars describe as "carrying significant intellectual and emotional weight." Tuition is about what you'd expect at many real-time universities. (The lunches are better at your house, though.) The school says it strictly limits enrollment to encourage faculty-student interaction, so if you're interested, register early.

EdLinks

http://www.marshall.edu/~jmullens/edlinks.html

Schools and Education

John L. Mullens, a West Virginia high school principal, weaves some of the Net's best education sites into his Web. Biggies like Educom, AskEric (an amazing database of lesson plans and resources for teachers), and the Library of Congress are all here, elegantly categorized and succinctly described. There are also dozens of links to not-so-biggie-but-still-impressive sites, like "Kathy Schrock's Guide for Educators," which features a classified index of resource materials from arts and literature to world news. Or try "Teacher Talk," an online conferencing system for K-12 instructors to share advice and anecdotes about the latest classroom snafu... or miracle! This is a fine bookmark for anyone involved in education, and for parents who want to be more involved in the process.

Educational Software Institute

http://www.bonsai.com/q/edsoftcat/htdocs/esihome.html

Schools and Education

For parents, educators, and students, this "one-stop educational software center" features a catalog of over 7,000 titles for sale from more than 300 publishers, available for both PC and Macintosh. Middle-schoolers can learn critical-thinking skills using programs like "Granny Applebee's Cookie Factory," a virtual business where children must follow "recipes" to fill cookie orders, repair machines, and dream up advertising schemes. Selections for older students include "The Secret Island of Dr. Quandary" and "Museum Madness," a problem-solving application using a "mixed-up" virtual museum as its setting. This enormous, well-organized resource promises many items not available in the average retail market, some of which are offered in both Spanish and English. Take your time.

Welcome to Educational Software Institute Online!

ESI Online represents, explains, and sells the world's largest and finest collection of K-12 educational software (more than 7,000 titles) from over 300 publishers. If you're a parent, educator or student, you can use this easy-to-search online catalog to find just the right programs for your needs. You can order right here online, too! It's si...

The Edutainment Page

http://www.edutainment.com.au/

Schools and Education

Parents and educators can browse over 150 reviews of educational and home software on this page from Linda Bruce, an Australian psychologist and computer education specialist. Reviews are arranged according to subject, and include foreign language tutorials, art and graphics, music, science, and thinking skills. Bruce's Top 10 list includes her all-time favorite picks, like Crayola's Amazing Art Studio, which "contains everything from crazy lines, stickers, and drop-in animations, to magic effects... and exploding erasers." Bruce's reviews are plenty thoughtful, and designed to help parents choose the right software for their child's specific needs. Also included is a "Value for Money" page, an edu-savvy guide that takes parents step-by-step through the "how's" and "what's" of buying software for kids.

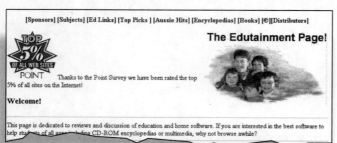

[Sponsors] [Subjects] [Ed Links] [Top Picks] [Aussie Hits] [Encyclopedias] [Books] [©][Distributors]

The Edutainment Page!

POINT   Thanks to the Point Survey we have been rated the top 5% of all sites on the Internet!

Welcome!

This page is dedicated to reviews and discussion of education and home software. If you are interested in the best software to help students of all ages including CD-ROM encyclopedias or multimedia, why not browse awhile?

Engines for Education

http://www.ils.nwu.edu/~e_for_e

Schools and Education

Author Roger Schank was a terrible student who became convinced that the education system simply does not work. In this hyper-book, Schank and his colleagues at Northwestern University try to solve problems ("Why Biology Lab is No Fun") and reform conventional education methods with the help of new technology. It's all aimed at professional educators, but anyone curious about American education will be stimulated (or irritated) here. For example, Schank asserts that most kids learn geography by traveling, not by memorizing state capitals ("in alphabetical order, no less"). He calls this "incidental learning," and says it works just as well for physics (try playing a baseball game) as for geography. Alas—because Schank argues that letter grades stifle creativity, we can't give this site the "A" it might deserve.

Environmental Education Network

http://envirolink.org/enviroed/

Schools and Education

This is an excellent electronic clearinghouse for environmental education information and materials. Students can explore the solar system, learn about deforestation in the world's rain forests, or poke around some old dinosaur bones in Honolulu. "Earth Viewer" generates instant real-time images of the Earth, as seen from the vantage point of the Sun, the Moon, or a satellite in Earth orbit—a virtual space shuttle for Web browsers! Teachers will find a wealth of K-12 resources, including air quality lesson plans designed to teach kids about acid rain, carbon monoxide, and the ozone layer. EnviroLink, which sponsors the site, also offers links to a "Green" Market that promotes and sells eco-friendly products, and a huge library containing shelf after virtual shelf of "EnviroEvents," activist info, and government resources.

eWorld: Learning Community

http://www.eworld.com/education/resources/

Schools and Education

This Apple-sponsored page is brimming with educational links, and the sharp graphics and clickable town map will delight parents, kids, and teachers alike.

Step through the doors of the eWorld Museum for links to The Smithsonian Institution and The International Museum of the Horse (no kidding!). The little red School House serves up news and projects from schools and colleges around the world, like an earthquake bulletin from students at Akatsukayama High in Kobe, Japan, or the legend of the Jackalope from Monroe Middle-Schoolers in Green River, Wyoming. Educators, students, and parents could probably spend eons here, if only they didn't have so many other things to do! One note of caution: this site tends to be extremely busy during the day; if you're connecting from home, you'll be much happier if you visit after regular school and business hours.

Financial Aid Information

http://www.cs.cmu.edu/afs/cs/user/mkant/Public/FinAid/finaid.html

Schools and Education

College grant and loan information doesn't come any straighter than this index, maintained by Mark Kantrowitz of Carnegie Mellon University. (He wrote *The*

Prentice Hall Guide to Scholarships and Fellowships for Math and Science Students, remember?) Students of all ages will appreciate these plain-vanilla links to bank student loan programs of all types, plus extras like the full text of *Don't Miss Out: The Ambitious Student's Guide to Financial Aid*. Direct links to fellowship databases will be of particular interest to grad students, and the grants and scholarship pages go on for days. Added bonus: fastWEB, a searchable database of over 180,000 private sector financial aid sources. A ton of good info here.

Global Schoolhouse Project

http://k12.cnidr.org./gsh/gshwelcome.html
Schools and Education

Here's a taste of interactivity on the global level. The GSP is a project funded in part by the National Science Foundation to show how high-speed Internet connections could be put to swell use in public school classrooms. The idea is to "link kids around the world," which Global Schoolhouse did in eleven states and Australia. Once linked, students focused their attention on four curriculum clusters: weather, "trash" (how to manage the world's garbage), energy, and space. Students used Net resources to amass information, then shared ideas, learning experiences, and problem-solving with other kids across the countries. The actual project ended in early 1995, but you can still read all about it and, if you like, communicate with the participants. A super resource for teachers and other education pros.

Global Schoolhouse Project

Linking Kids Around the World

The Global Schoolhouse Project was a technology demonstration project funded in part by the National Science Foundation. The project was designed to demonstrate the potential of high speed Internet connectivity in the public school classroom.

The Global Schoolhouse Project officially ended on December 29, 1994. The content of these pages will continue to be m̶ ̶ ̶ ̶ ̶ ̶ ̶ ̶ ̶ ̶ ̶final reports on school projects, reports from the project

Harvard University

http://www.harvard.edu/
Schools and Education

This isn't flashy, but then, neither is Harvard. This site provides everything a Harvard hopeful needs to know about each of the university's 10 schools. The Radcliffe College link, for example, explains that Harvard and Radcliffe remain "legally, fiscally, and physically distinct" (even if their students may not). You'll also find lots of useful directories, a Harvard map, and library resources. The most fun is the extensive list of student activities, including the "Arabidopsis thaliana database," Harvard Gay and Lesbian Caucus, and The Noteables singing group ("nicknamed 'Harvard-Radcliffe's Broadway Beat' because that is what we do... beat Broadway. To death"). From the looks of the Varsity Fencing Team page, though, the Harvard pen may still be mightier than the sword.

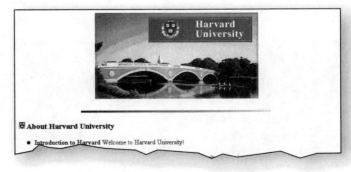

About Harvard University

• **Introduction to Harvard** Welcome to Harvard University!

Home Education Resource Center (HERC)

http://www.cts.com/~netsales/herc/
Schools and Education

This page of home schooling resources for browsers and buyers will also be of interest to conventional school teachers. HERC's catalog includes "American History Simulations," "Beginning Map Skills," math study kits, and much, much more. Valuable state-by-state home schooling regulations are outlined in detail: Colorado, for instance, does not require certification for parental home schooling, but your child must take regularly scheduled national achievement tests and score above the 13th percentile. An index of support groups across the nation provides added value for parents who are thinking of "opting out" of the system. Great links to other Internet education resources, and a special bonus: guidance for keeping kids out of the seamier "adult" (to use the term loosely) side of the Web.

Home Education Resources Center (HERC)

Presented by Net Sales, LLC

Welcome to HERC, your center for home schooling and educational resources on the Internet. In addition to being a great starting point for educational resources on the Net, HERC offers a full line of educational materials from some of the leaders in education for teachers, home schoolers, and involved parents. You can order direct via the Internet or call us anytime at (800)388-7800. Click here if you're not sure where to start

Humanities External Degree

http://dolphin.csudh.edu/~hux/huxindex.html
Schools and Education

Since 1974, California State University at Dominguez Hills has offered a fully accredited Master of Arts degree in the Humanities. Now they're doing it completely via the Net. Admission to the program requires a 3.0 undergraduate grade point average, the usual admissions application, and an "Intellectual Autobiography:" a personal essay describing your "most significant artistic, cultural, or intellectual life experiences." (Uh-oh.) The program sounds tricky, too: one three-credit course explores "the position of the individual in the classic and modern models of social and political organization; conservatism, liberalism, socialism, anarchism; study of the Utopian tradition; and study of aesthetic theories that connect the artist with society." (Whew!) Working professionals and stay-at-home parents may also want to consider this impressively modern college option.

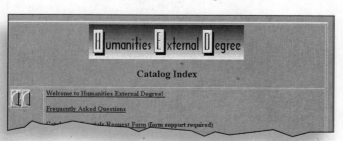

Catalog Index

Welcome to Humanities External Degree!

Frequently Asked Questions

Catalog Materials Request Form (form support required)

Lake Superior State University

http://www.lssu.edu

Schools and Education

It's hard to resist a university Web site where the president, Robert D. Arbuckle, confidently proclaims that "Tomorrow will be better than today because the University Community wills it." Set against a background as blue as the water itself, Lake Superior State U.'s home page grid is an efficient, lively read. Visitors can discover that the LSSU Lakers compete in NCAA Division I hockey (where they've won two championships this decade), but are relegated to the smaller NCAA Division II for all other sports. Tour the campus by way of an interactive map and don't miss the lovely images available at Scenes From Campus. For a smallish college, the Lakers put together a very solid home page.

Massachusetts Institute of Technology

http://web.mit.edu/

Schools and Education

At first glance, this page simply presents the staid sort of academic and administrative links you'd expect from an institution like MIT. You can get the lowdown and standard items like admissions (in 1994, about 7,150 students applied for admission; 2,200 of those applicants were accepted), *Counterpoint* (the MIT-Wellesley magazine), and nuclear engineering course descriptions. (We were especially interested in the Beginner's Guide to Athena, MIT's vast network computer system.) But "for informal information," click on the Student Information Processing Board, where we found Lurker ("an interactive web game/movie written at the MIT Media Lab"), The Cult of Safety Pup ("an organization dedicated to mayhem and... taking over the world in the name of our Lord Safety Pup"), plus other hijinks. The student pages here are especially impressive and entertaining.

Massachusetts Institute of Technology

MIT is an independent, coeducational university located in Cambridge, Massachusetts. For informal information see the MIT Student Information Processing Board's SIPB WWW Server. Our first campus information system was TechInfo.

Due to the high load, this server is currently slow. We're aware of the situation, and taking steps to resolve it. Thank you in advance for your patience.

General Information
MIT facts, news, student, faculty, and staff online directory, including homepage URLs. Visitor information and how to apply to MIT.

Academics and Research
Browse through ... on MIT schools, departments, research centers, labs, and programs. Access the MIT

One World Resource

http://www.nav.com/OWR/oneworld.html

Schools and Education

Location. Location. Location. If you're in the market for a college or university, this is what the creators of this site hope you'll keep in mind. Navigator Communications has teamed up with

Argyle in a frenzied attempt to "compile all the university sites of the world into one location." You say you've always wanted to spend some time in Latvia? No problem. Riga Technical University or the University of Latvia are at your educational service. Still undecided? Take a look at institutes of higher learning ranging from Stanford to Czech Technical University to the Fukuoka Junior College of Profanity—er—Technology. Special guest stars include Florida U.'s Department of Anesthesiology, and "Paper and Cathode" (a graphics exhibit from Kendall College of Art and Design). This project is far from finished, but it's a valiant effort, and the Webmasters say they're looking for more.

The Peters Projection Map

http://www.webcom.com/~bright/petermap.html

Schools and Education

The Peters Projection is a "newfangled" global chart created in 1974 by Arno Peters, which provides a "one-to-one" mapping of the Earth's surface. Why? Well, all maps of the world are "projections" because they attempt to portray the surface of a sphere in only two dimensions. The Mercator projection is the one most commonly used in today's classrooms, but it can be misleading—you wouldn't know

from using it that, say, Africa is 14 times the size of Greenland. Peters tries to fix all that. The text on this site tends toward the grandiose, and will sail over the heads of most children, but the map itself is a nice visual aid for geography teachers and parents. A companion tutorial (for DOS only) can be downloaded, providing an interactive explanation of the whole darn thing.

Peterson's Education Center

http://www.petersons.com:8080/
Schools and Education

From "the leading provider of information on U.S.-accredited educational institutions" (publishers of the popular *Peterson's Guides*), this is a comprehensive tour of American education from kindergarten through post-graduate school. Profiles of the Beaufort Academy, Texas Military Institute, and 1400 other "independent" schools are provided, along with 3300 colleges and universities. There's even a directory of summer programs for kids and teens, like the high-powered Madison Avenue Advertising Workshop in New York City. And it's all searchable, too. Wow! This is solid, no-nonsense information, geared toward folks who want "SAT Success," and who want to assure they're on the right side of this Peterson equation: "Of all the new jobs being created, 87 percent will require a high school diploma and at least 52 percent will require additional education." Hit the books, kids.

The Piano Education Page

http://www.unm.edu/~loritaf/pnoedmn.html
Schools and Education

Here, the West Mesa Music Teachers Association of New Mexico has compiled a grand array of keyboard resources. Both the Alfred and Suzuki teaching methods are explored (and no, the latter doesn't recommend you learn while riding a motorcycle). Studio etiquette admonishes the parent who arrives early to pick up a child from lessons to "remain quiet and do not interrupt." (Stage moms, this means you!) The buying tips advise that "It's worth the extra time and effort to seek a grand piano made prior to World War II," while adult students are counseled that they shouldn't "expect to learn as fast as [a] seven-year-old child." Good software reviews, too. It's a super (and serious) site—but what would Chopin think about the link to the Power Ranger's Home Page in the "Just For Kids" section?

The Piano Education Page Program

Premiering This Month on The Piano Education Page

Learning to Play the Piano

Just for Kids

Piano Teaching Software

Links to Other Web Pages of Interest

World-Wide Web Search Tools

School Psychology Resources Online

`http://mail.bcpl.lib.md.us/~sandyste/school_psych.html`

Schools and Education

Dr. Sandy Steingart at the University of Maryland maintains this extensive index of resources for school psychologists. Parents will find much to value, too! Mental retardation, attention deficit disorder, autism, and general learning disabilities are among the many issues that are thoroughly resourced here. Assessment and evaluation links include the Buros Institute of Mental Measurements (authors of *Tests in Print*), and a "Frequently Asked Questions" page about the validity and methods of psychological testing. Steingart's mega pointers include hip-type resources like "Psychology Cyber-synapse" and "Dr. Bob's Mental Health Links," plus old favorites like the American Psychological Association. The simple index makes it particularly easy to find specific topics like bi-polar disorder or Tourette's Syndrome.

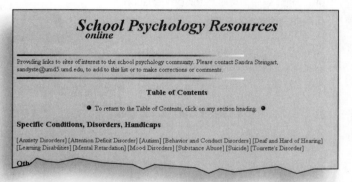

Stanford University

`http://www.stanford.edu/`

Schools and Education

An opening spread of blue skies above stucco and terra-cotta buildings surrounded by palm trees evokes Stanford's California appeal. Below the California dreamin' image, the usual features (academics, administration, labs) are neatly categorized for your perusal. Prospective undergrads may be inspired by "Minds in Motion" (on the admissions page), including anecdotes such as how President Gerhard Casper has discounted his theory that serious learning must be "accompanied by a modest degree of suffering." Extracurricular pages include the Chinese Christian Fellowship (with multilingual contacts), the Mendicants, an acapella singing group "with the express purpose of serenading (and subsequently wooing) Stanford women," and so forth. Information on the Bay Area includes an earthquake map, flood information, and "Devil's Slide Updates from the *Montara Mountain Free Press.*"

The Student Guide: Financial Aid from the U.S. Department of Education

http://www.ed.gov/prog_info/SFA/StudentGuide/

Schools and Education

According to the U.S. Department of Education (and they should know), more than 80 percent of all student financial aid comes from government sources. Another 19 percent comes from school-sponsored sources (one percent is stolen, apparently). You can find out about the first 99 percent right here, straight from Uncle Sam's mouth. So-so advice ("contact the financial aid administrator" is not going out on a limb) is supplemented by hard details on eligibility for Pell Grants, state grant programs, and student eligibility status. The section on borrower rights and responsibilities doles out this warning: "You must make payments on your loan, even if you don't receive a bill..." Still, grousing aside, this page goes a long way in unraveling some of the mystery over landing that first student loan.

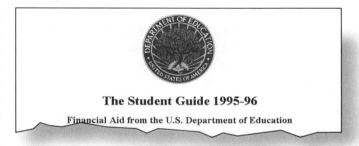

The Student Guide 1995-96

Financial Aid from the U.S. Department of Education

University of Virginia

http://jefferson.village.virginia.edu/~meg3c/uva_info/

Schools and Education

This unofficial UV home page was created as a Systems Engineering 301 project. (Check out the creators, all of whom look as if their picture could be placed in the dictionary next to "engineer.") Take a tour of The Lawn, and you'll learn that the University of Virginia is one of Thomas Jefferson's proudest achievements. In addition to other expected links like Academic Information and University Life, the site offers a delightful directory of home pages created by students and faculty. On our last visit, we chose at random the page of Brian Paco Hope, and he rewarded us with comical tidbits from his life, his position on the computer science racquetball ladder (#2 at last notice), and even a Fiancée Page featuring Miss Rebecca B., a geology student at North Carolina State. (She, in turn, thoughtfully provided us with a link to the U.S. Geological Survey.) No doubt Thomas Jefferson, himself a bit of an innovator, would approve.

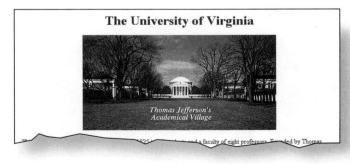

The University of Virginia

Thomas Jefferson's Academical Village

Web and Computer Resources for Indian Teachers and Students

http://www.fdl.cc.mn.us/~isk/

Schools and Education

Paula Giese, a computer consultant and "non-Status Canadian Anishnabeg, Treaty 6, Beaver Lake band" member, created this animated Internet guide for Native American K-12 students and educators. It includes "political prisoner" Norma Jean Croy's story—"part of that huge body of Indian history that nobody knows except those few who lived it"—as well as an extended library of book reviews for Indian young people. Terrific teachers' resources are linked via the "Tools" page, where educators can access everything from classroom planning guides to game shareware. Both kids and tribal leaders will enjoy the Pocahontas page, where Native youths share their unique thoughts about the Hollywood blockbuster: "In real-life," comments Majik Star Rising, "Pocahontas met John Smith at the age of ten, was not wearing clothing, and had her hair buzzed."

Science

Science

Where else but on the World Wide Web will you ever get a look at a relativistic heavy ion collider? Scientists, who were once the only users of the Internet, continue to provide some of its most incomprehensible pages as they swap quarks and stack up gravitational theories. But the Web has also given scientists the chance to proudly show off their handiwork, whether that happens to be fruit flies or nuclear reactors. Be prepared to see plenty of pictures of smiling technicians and mascot lab cats. And speaking of photographic glory, don't miss the "Sky and Space" portion of this chapter, with its enthusiastic coverage of space shuttles, hurricanes, and exploding comets.

earth sciences

earth sciences

Agriculture Online

http://www.agriculture.com/

Earth Sciences

The editor of *Agriculture Online* invites you to think of this magazine as "a huge country coffee shop" where farmers and ranchers can exchange ideas. That's a pretty good description. Like corn in Iowa, this site is growing at a rapid pace—adding new links and tools like @g Search, a handy device that finds agricultural stuff on the Internet. Visitors can buy or sell machinery, read about women in agriculture, or see rankings like the top 20 dairy farms in America. A wide variety of discussion groups allow ag folks to comment on important goings-on, like the current cattle markets. The site actively encourages reader participation, too, asking for farmers to become weather spotters for its online service. Who says farming isn't a hi-tech field?

The Amazing Environmental Organization Web Directory

http://www.webdirectory.com/

Earth Sciences

This directory is, as its title claims, "amazing." Aside from the usual suspects in land conservation and sustainable development (like the National Wetlands Technical Council and Yellow Mountain Institute for Sustainable Living), there are entries here that may surprise you. We found five listings for environmentally conscious arts organizations, including The Video Project, an Oakland, California, non-profit organization that supports and distributes environmental video productions to schools, libraries, and community groups—they helped sponsor the award-winning Bill Moyers' special, "Global Dumping Ground." You'll also find unique architecture and design links, like Enertia Building Systems, a manufacturer of do-it-yourself solar home kits made entirely from recycled materials. A complete and thorough site, this is practically a one-stop resource for environmentalists.

Arachnology

http://sesoserv.ufsia.ac.be/Arachnology/Arachnology.html
Earth Sciences

From Belgian spider-lover Herman Vanuytven comes an arachnid index the Addams Family would be proud to call their own. Experience the delights of anthropods as you spin through photos of jumping spiders, tailless whipscorpions, and the Australian paralysis tick. Ticks, by the way, are members of the arachnid family (they have eight legs, too), and browsers may be interested to know that ticks seek the emission of human pheromones—a sort of biological homing device—to track down suitable hosts for blood meals. (So *that's* how Dracula does it.) Home growers can seek advice on the care and feeding of tarantulas, or weave through a collection of spider societies, poison databases, and a student paper on spider romance. (Title: "Courtship behaviors that both stimulate the female and ensure the male is not mistaken for a prey item.")

Ask-A-Geologist

http://walrus.wr.usgs.gov:80/docs/ask-a-ge.html
Earth Sciences

Actual scientists at the United States Geological Survey are standing by right now to answer your pressing questions about geology. Maybe you're curious about all those California earthquakes—like, how come they have so *many*, while New York just sits there? And what about all those mud slides? Why is there so much oil in Texas, but not in Wisconsin? Is it cheese-related? The nation's geologists are ready with answers. While it's true this home page only offers instructions on how to format and transmit your question, and doesn't include the postings it receives, it's just quirky and unique enough to rate high marks from us. It's nice to know our team at the U.S. Geological Survey is on the job! Student questions especially welcomed.

CELLS alive!

http://www.whitlock.com/kcj/quill/
Earth Sciences

This "microscopy of living cells and organisms" from Quill Graphics is loaded with info on viruses, parasites, bacteria, and even "foodborne pathogenic microorganisms." Yow! Uncover the truth about *Cryptosporidium parvum*, which lurk in water supplies and look a lot like anemic Sugar Pops; discover how the worm-like

continued

CELLS alive!
continued

Streptococci threaten white blood cells. An interesting lesson on why penicillin works so well (we wouldn't expect less from mold in a petri dish) accompanies a fascinating look at cell regeneration, poetically dubbed "cell suicide." If you're inspired after this little visit, link to "Tom Terry's Microbiology Course," a virtual classroom sponsored by the University of Connecticut, complete with practice exams. Highly readable and informative, and a great teaching tool for kids aged 10 and up.

City Farmer's Urban Agriculture Notes

http://unixg.ubc.ca:780/~cityfarm/urbagnotes1.html
Earth Sciences

The folks who produce this site have been in urban agriculture for 17 years—so listen to them, dadgum it. City Farmer is a non-profit society in Vancouver, B.C., which has been promoting urban food production and environmental conservation since 1978. Its Web site shows off stuff like the "Demonstration Garden," which illustrates just how much produce one person can grow in a city backyard (a lot). Info is provided on city farms and community gardens, plus plenty on soil, worms ("Composting with Red Wriggler Worms" is a must-see!), and compost bins (like what to do when there's a rat in the pile). The site even includes a worm-related script idea that some of the society members sent in to *Seinfeld*—no, it's not terribly funny, but you've got to like their spirit.

Urban Agriculture Notes

The Cliff Ecology Research Group

http://www.uoguelph.ca/CBS/Botany/index.htm
Earth Sciences

Here we have a bunch of scientists from the University of Guelph in Ontario, Canada, who are excited about cliffs—they actually wrote the book, contributing an entry to *Encyclopedia Brittanica*. "Science on the edge of discovery" is their motto, and they do things like live-trap small mammals to determine what kind of crazy animal would hang out around cliffs. (Besides humans, that is.) In fact, most of the pictures here are of people hanging from cliffs, and they look like they're having a pretty good time. It all goes to show that when somebody else is excited about something, it's pretty easy to get interested in it yourself. An unusual specialty and an unusual Web site.

Coastal Ocean Modeling at the USGS

http://crusty.er.usgs.gov/

Earth Sciences

Get this: people at the U.S. Geological Survey get to dye water red and blue and then track the effects of tidal movements on the coastline. And they get paid! In addition to being expert water-colorists, they also check to see how the amount of effluent (that's a fancy word for stuff that comes from treated wastewater) affects whales in Massachusetts Bay. Or perhaps you were wondering how simulated particle trajectories react under a steady wind. Don't yawn: this site is brimming with great visual aids—many in movie form—that illustrate the USGS's unique experiments. Most of the tests described here were conducted along the New England coast, so it may not interest everybody, but for sheer uniqueness and quality of design this is an excellent example of modern science on the Net.

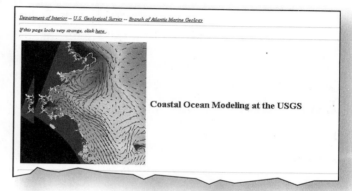

Coastal Ocean Modeling at the USGS

The Earth System Science Community

http://www.circles.org/

Earth Sciences

This page reports on projects conducted by ESSC, a consortium of teachers and students researching earth science phenomena from El Niño to greenhouse gases. It's an innovative program: high school and college instructors commit to a year-long curriculum that utilizes a global network of educators and multimedia resources, all designed to improve students' understanding of Earth systems and expand scientific literacy. Not surprisingly, students play a big role in reporting project results here. High schoolers in Washington, D.C., for instance, completed a study on Earth's radiation budget that showed how clouds affect the earth's surface temperature. It's a terrific resource for eco-nuts in general, and for earth science students in particular.

Earthquake Information

http://www.civeng.carleton.ca/cgi-bin/quakes
Earth Sciences

Darling, was that a 7.2 trembler or was that my heart pounding? Let the National Earthquake Information Service (NEIS) clear things up with this bulletin of the latest rumbles worldwide. NEIS serves up quake location, size, date, and even the precise longitude and latitude. There's nothing fancy here: it's a simple, straightforward presentation, and an astonishing record of just how many quakes the earth experiences in a day. In fact, we were surprised to find nearly a dozen recorded occurrences of 5.0 or greater in just one month (and whose fault is that, anyway?). A swell map lets you zoom in on a quake location, display it in relation to nearby rivers, and even choose your own directional points for markers. Great for kids and quake-watchers.

Earthwatch

http://gaia.earthwatch.org/
Earth Sciences

Keeping the planet healthy and whole is the focus of this page from Earthwatch, one of the largest private sponsors of scientific field research. The organization conducts remarkably varied global studies, ranging from "The Elephant Factor," a project exploring the impact of Zimbabwe's pachyderm population on biodiversity, to a look at threatened habitats in Ontario's ancient forests. (And who can resist a study titled "Giant Clams of the Great Barrier Reef"?) For a fee, Earthwatch members can actually travel to project sites and assist scientists in a variety of field activities. (On second thought, we'll skip the giant clams.) A list of available field work is offered, which includes expenses, details of project objectives, and accommodations. How does a grass hut in the Amazon grab you?

Environmental News Network

http://www.enn.com/
Earth Sciences

ENN's home page is a virtual environmental news clearinghouse, collecting info from sources as widespread as the Swedish government to U.S. green-beat reporters. The vast database is updated regularly to include breaking eco-news as it happens daily around the world. During the ruckus over French nuclear testing in the South Pacific, for instance, ENN fed continuous reports to its "Daily News" file, including an eyewitness account of a Tahitian riot and commentary from France's top political and environmental journalists. ENN also maintains an extensive library of resources: abstracts, articles, and papers can be searched by topic or date. Access to ENN's complete files is not free; the cost of total access is roughly that of an annual magazine subscription. This is a hot spot for students and journalists.

EnviroWeb

http://www.envirolink.org
Earth Sciences

Originally founded by a Carnegie-Mellon undergraduate student, the EnviroWeb has grown in just a few years from a mailing list of 20 to one of the world's largest electronic environmental info-banks. In addition to providing extensive indexes and links to all things environmental, they provide free Internet access ("in the spirit of a Freenet system"), a massive gopher library, mailing lists, and "EnviroChat," an Internet Relay discussion forum for the eco-inclined. Shop the Green Marketplace for environmentally friendly products like handmade, chemical-free soaps or "checks with a conscience," printed with soy-based inks on recycled paper. Handsome graphics, deep content, and an easy interface combine to make this a very crisp site indeed.

Farmer to Farmer

http://www.organic.com/Non.profits/F2F\
Earth Sciences

For those who say that without chemicals, life itself would be impossible, here's some gentle nose-thumbing. This online edition of the non-profit *Farmer to Farmer* newsletter promotes a booming organic farming industry. Features like "Building Your Soil" (earthworms can be your friends!) are aimed at supporting natural farmers and convincing others to abandon pesticides. "Farmer Speaks Out" takes a new look at the old problem of pest control: if killing pests really worked, the author says, "we would not be out there year after year killing them again and again." (Of course, plenty of alternatives are offered here.) Some articles are two years old or more, but this is fascinating reading that will be useful to farmers and organic home gardeners alike.

University of Florida—Institute of Agricultural Sciences

http://www.ifas.ufl.edu/

Earth Sciences

Did you know that agriculture is one of Florida's top three sources of revenue? All those oranges, don't you know.

(And you thought the economy would collapse without Disney World.) From citrus to sugar, the Sunshine State's land yields a lot of produce. To get all the facts, point your browser to the University of Florida's Institute of Agricultural Sciences, and discover why Florida ranks 8th in the nation for farming productivity. IFAS is the king of outreach programs; it has offices in all 67 counties and does research on the Everglades and bugs, too. We also liked the National Food Safety Database, which teaches readers ways to prevent illnesses spread through food (can you say "salmonella?"). Top-notch interactive maps lead you through a geographic array of beans, cabbage, carrots, tomatoes... whew!

Gateway to Antarctica

http://icair.iac.org.nz

Earth Sciences

Antarctica has long been dismissed as "that big, cold thing down there." Now ICAIR, the International Center for Antarctic Information and Research, is out to change all that. Based in New Zealand, the group shows here that Antarctica has a lot going for it: for one thing, it's the only continent where military activity is officially forbidden by treaty. It's the largest wilderness on Earth, home to some pretty impressive protected areas like McMurdo Sound and Mt. Erebus. Antarctica now hosts a fairly booming tourist industry: expeditions range from icy kayaking on the Southern Ocean to dogsledding expeditions across the tundra. Also, it has penguins. Does *your* continent have penguins? If ICAIR has its way, you may begin calling Antarctica "that *wonderful* big, cold thing down there."

Global Entomology Agriculture Research Server: GEARS

http://gears.tucson.ars.ag.gov/

Earth Sciences

This multimedia wonderland developed at Arizona's Carl Hayden Bee Research Center may have you dressing up like a beekeeper to hunt the elusive virgin queen (bee, that is). Learn why nasty Varroa mites are threatening the U.S. bee industry, and find out how to handle swarming African honey bees, a.k.a. the dreaded "killer" bees. (Step one: remain calm.) The Sound Room features "the year's best insect-related sounds," like a "stridulating" desert harvest ant (that's insect talk for "ant scaring off an attacker") and a piping queen bee. Before you go, don't forget to stop by the trivia hive for a fast game of "Tribeeal Pursuits". Quite simply one of the best ento-sites around.

Hydroponics, Hydroponics, Hydroponics!

http://www.aloha.com:80/~virhol/

Earth Sciences

What the heck is hydroponics? It's the unique science of growing plants without soil, and this enthusiastic industry-sponsored site hopes you'll give it a try. The practice has been around ever since the Babylonians strung up the Hanging Gardens, and according to these easygoing Hawaiians, it's a simple process that could provide cures for everything from "Sick Building Syndrome" to world hunger. Best bets for hydroponics: tomatoes, spinach, lettuce, and herbs (though the authors say almost any plant will grow with a little TLC). Best of all, it says here, hydroponic plants and vegetables take up less space than soil gardens, produce higher yields, and are less prone to pest invasion. When you feel ready to take the plunge, consult the list of suppliers to find out what you'll need to get started.

ION Science

http://www.INJersey.com/Media/IonSci/
Earth Sciences

I ON Science is a general science 'zine with *real* eye appeal, an electronic testimonial to the fact that not all science

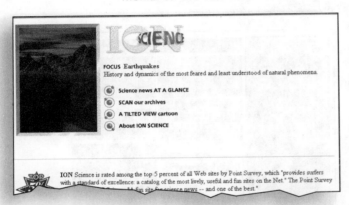

FOCUS Earthquakes
History and dynamics of the most feared and least understood of natural phenomena.

- Science news AT A GLANCE
- SCAN our archives
- A TILTED VIEW cartoon
- About ION SCIENCE

ION Science is rated among the top 5 percent of all Web sites by Point Survey, which "provides surfers with a standard of excellence: a catalog of the most lively, useful and fun sites on the Net." The Point Survey "A fun site for science news -- and one of the best."

geeks are graphically deprived (or depraved, for that matter). The editors aim to "demystify complex topics, because we don't think you should have to be a rocket scientist to gain insight into the natural world." So far, they're doing a bang-up job. Archives contain ripping accounts of the dinosaur exhibit at New York's Museum of Natural History, algorithms for monkeys, and "cockroach love," the story of how the household pests' own natural "seduction" secretions may result in their obliteration (from your kitchen, anyway). For a light-hearted spin on the world of science, check "A Tilted View," *ION*'s version of *The Far Side* for technologists.

Live Access to Climate Data

http://ferret.wrc.noaa.gov/ferret/main-menu.html
Earth Sciences

T he National Oceanic and Atmospheric Administration's Pacific Marine Environmental Laboratory hosts this live access climate data server, which extracts real-time weather info from an immense

NOAA / PMEL - Thermal Modeling and Analysis Project

Live Access to Climate Data [Help]

< Currently selected region

Change DATA SET . . . COADS Climatology

Change VIEW . . . Longitude-latitude

ocean climate database. The really cool part (aside from the fact that you can get a weather report from just about anywhere in the world) is that the page enables you to turn data into instant color graphics (or downloadable spreadsheet files) using a tool called Ferret (a goof on gopher?), which you download onsite. You pick a region (the whole planet, or a small portion), and decide how to slice the data (like surface temperature in January, or dissolved oxygen at 100m), and poof!, a stunning custom graphic pops out. Ferret is part of a science trend on the Web: easy visualization tools for humongous datasets, providing instant scientific (and eyeball) gratification. We like.

More Aquatic Ape Theory

http://huizen.dds.nl/~seismo/aat.html

Earth Sciences

Was there a time when our evolutionary ancestors lived in marshes as sea-apes? (Or sea monkeys?) The question is explored at length on this page hosted by Hollander Maarten Fornerod. The idea—called AAT, or "Aquatic Ape Theory"—is still considered laughable by some, but has a surprising cast of supporters like Desmond Morris (*The Naked Ape*) and Daniel C. Dennett (*Darwin's Dangerous Idea*). Maarten smartly keeps a running score of anthropologists both for and against AAT. A generous helping of comments and citations help shed light on the theory, even if it's all a bit on the academic side: "Perhaps the best suggestion is that the exertions involved, in a hot climate, required the maximum development of the cooling system by evaporation of sweat." We know the feeling.

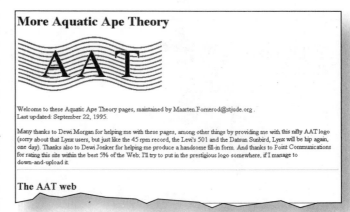

The Mouse and Rat Research Home Page

http://www.cco.caltech.edu/~mercer/htmls/rodent_page.html

Earth Sciences

This is *the* place for rodent researchers. When the intro refers to a "somewhat exhaustive" listing of resources, the authors are being modest. We counted hundreds of links and pointers to exotic-sounding places like the "Transgenic and Targeted Mutant Animal Database" and the "Internet Atlas of Mouse Development." "Mouse Nomenclature Rules and Guidelines" (do you have *your* copy?) sets forth standard symbols and language for scientific researchers—which only makes sense, after all. Lab techs can download sequence management software at the "BigBlue and MutaMouse Web Site," or send for details on the annual Mouse Molecular Genetics Conference. And for the homebody, the Pet Rat FAQ File offers a slightly more warm and fuzzy version of the critter we love to test.

National Audubon Society

`http://www.audubon.org/audubon/`

Earth Sciences

" The mission of the National Audubon Society is to conserve and restore natural ecosystems, focusing on birds and other wildlife for the benefit of humanity and the earth's biological diversity." And to spot the elusive yellow-bellied sapsucker! (Sorry—we got carried away.) The Society here provides news about their increasingly diverse environmental programs, like the "Living Oceans" project, a marine conservation initiative dedicated to long-term science-based protective policy reform. Audubon bird sanctuaries from Maine to Arizona help preserve vital natural habitats, and you'll find guides to all of them right here. Alas, although the info is superb and the graphics are nice, few alluring pictures of flora and fauna attend these pages, and the famous Audubon prints remain mostly out of your virtual reach.

New South Polar Times

`http://www.deakin.edu.au/edu/MSEE/GENII/`
`NSPT/NSPThomePage.html`

Earth Sciences

These news dispatches from scientists at the bottom of the world give a new meaning to the "lowest common denominator." Just about anyone should be interested in how the staff at the Amundsen-Scott South Pole Station in Antarctica survives the harshest climate on the planet. This bi-weekly chronicle is aimed at students, but we were charmed by the behind-the-scenes, diary-like tone of the writing. Whenever a fresh crew arrives at the station, for instance, the people already there "suffer from all the germs that the new folks brought with them." This site also contains various South Pole science reports on meteorology and wind chill, and promises another magazine—*The Blizzard*—which will take any Antarctic-related contributions. A fascinating glimpse at life from those living down under even Down Under.

Ocean Planet Home Page

http://seawifs.gsfc.nasa.gov/ocean_planet.html

Earth Sciences

This beautiful Smithsonian Institute project lets visitors explore the world's oceans with ease. Visitors can jump from room to virtual room, from "Sea People" in Sri Lanka to "Oceans in Peril," where we learned that the levels of toxic contaminants in our seas have reached unprecedented proportions. Audio files play back whale songs and seagull calls, a lonesome buoy, and the turbulent winds of a hurricane. And what museum would be complete without a gift shop? This "sea store" is one of the best: it even clued us in on the hidden environmental costs that may be involved in producing and distributing ocean products. The page aims for a non-technical audience, with plenty of visuals, making it a great spot for kids to learn about the mysteries of the deep.

Pacific and Yukon Green Lane

http://www.pwc.bc.doe.ca/

Earth Sciences

Sponsored by Environment Canada, this very green page links ecologists to Canadian environmental sites and offers a tour of "E-Town," an interactive graphical city filled with eco-facts and industry. Click on the schoolhouse, for instance, and discover a weather tutorial where budding meteorologists can soar through the virtual skies testing their knowledge of *altocumulus* and *cumulonimbus* clouds. The Science Lab is home to Canada's Pacific Environmental Science Centre, where ongoing biodiversity studies examine the health of Canada's soil, water, air, and wildlife. Corporate watchdogs can stop by the Hall of Industry to find out how pollution prevention and abatement programs are providing incentives for industrial polluters to clean up their acts. Informative and entertaining.

PIGVISION

http://toolshed.artschool.utas.edu.au/PigVision/pigvision.html
Earth Sciences

PIGVISION teaches pigs to draw. Really! The group describes itself as a collaborative project on "the interface between art and animal husbandry." This page comes from the Sunday Hill Research Station in Tasmania, where artists have somehow gotten hooked up with the agricultural labs. The site explains a few individual projects undertaken by PIGVISION, including research into how pigs see and think. Can pigs really draw a circle? How about a square? Can pigs wear black turtlenecks and do performance art? (That's our own question, actually.) Kidding aside, these folks seem serious enough, and photos confirm that several of these art-iculture projects have actually taken place. In any case, it's worth a visit just to tell friends, "I've been to PIGVISION!"

Planetary Coral Reef Foundation

http://pk.com/pcrf/
Earth Sciences

The PCRF ship *Heraclitus* is on a five-year mission to study fragile coral reef ecosystems in oceans around the world. At the same time, the *Heraclitus* (a handsome tri-masted sailing ship) will undertake the Sea People Project, an attempt to study civilization's origins via various cultures. That still isn't tricky enough, so the PCRF intends to staff the *Heraclitus* with a multinational group of youth who'll learn to live in global harmony, be crack oceanographers, and keep their bunks clean all at the same time. If it all sounds a bit Quixotic, well, this *is* from the people who brought you the Biosphere 2 project. Thank heavens *somebody* is out there dreaming. This site isn't much to look at, but we must admit they seem to be having a pretty good time.

Rainforest Action Network

http://www.ran.org/ran/
Earth Sciences

This page from the highly vocal public interest group can be described in just two words: way cool. Its lively, icon-driven, animated interface serves up the lowdown on global rainforest deterioration, and what you can do at home to help reverse the process. (Assuming you don't live *in* a rainforest yourself.) You've probably already heard the facts: though rainforests cover less than two percent of the

Earth's surface, they're home to nearly half the planet's known life forms. And rainforests are being destroyed at the rate of 214,000 acres per day. What to do? RAN offers simple, tree-saving activities like e-mailing your congressperson and boycotting products made from what they believe are irresponsibly harvested rainforest materials. As RAN puts it, "the Earth is your home. There aren't any others for sale or rent anywhere in the neighborhood."

Recycler's World

http://granite.sentex.net/recycle/

Earth Sciences

Paul Roszel, a "Recycler Extraordinaire" from Guelph, Ontario, dishes the dirt here on recycling efforts around the world. Ever-evolving and expanding, this ambitious project uncovers info on where and how to recycle waste products ranging from wood paper to stainless steel alloys. The impressive links to recycling associations and publications are fully operational, but in some instances provide only snail mail and vox instructions (look, not *everyone's* wired yet). For that hard-to-find used aluminum piping, be sure to stop by The Recycler's Exchange, an electronic bulletin board for trading, selling, and buying recyclable commodities. And if you're starting your own recycling business in a remote corner of Iowa (or anywhere else), Roszel can help with that, too: he specializes in "recycling start-up ventures."

Satellite Oceanography Laboratory

http://satftp.soest.hawaii.edu/

Earth Sciences

This site provides "real-time data for meteorology and oceanography." True enough, but the pictures are even better. If you're wild about oceans, you'll find terrific satellite images, technical reports, and access to mountains of data here. Some of

continued

**Satellite Ocean-
ography Laboratory
continued**

the features are unique—one set of satellite shots tracks canoes from a Polynesian
village society as they make their way
across the water. Volcanoes are well-
represented, along with regularly updated
weather information from Maui. (Hey, you
never get a bad forecast.) And you won't
have to wait for the 11 o'clock news anymore to get your "Doppler radar" or
"polar orbiting" movie fixes. They're all
right here, captured in real time. Even for
non-experts, this is a great site for poking
around.

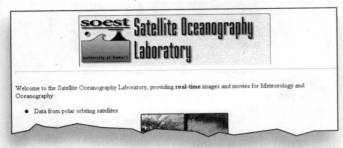

The Sierra Club

http://www.sierraclub.org/

Earth Sciences

One of the oldest nature organizations
in the U.S., the Sierra Club says it has
been promoting responsible enjoyment of
the Earth's resources since 1892. Track
down your local chapter here using a
clever interactive map, or get the skinny on
SC's famous outings. Trekkers can arrange
a relaxing ski holiday, or take a "service"
trip to help preserve an archeological site.
SC Action Alerts detail news of pending
environmental legislation and invite
browsers to sign the "Environmental Bill of
Rights." Activists will also find the congressional voting tracker very handy. The on-
site bookstore has colorful titles like *Blue
Potatoes, Orange Tomatoes*, as well as a first-
rate selection of eco travel guides.

Snakebite Emergency Web Page

http://www.xmission.com/~gastown/herpmed/snbite.htm

Earth Sciences

This plain-text site may not be the *fan-
ciest* place you'll ever visit, but it's a
worthy stop if you're planning a trip to the
Mojave or a hike in the Ozark Mountains.
Finding out what *not* to do about
snakebites may be the thing that saves
your life. For instance, your first instinct
might be to reach for the nearest painkiller
(or shot of Jack Daniels), but the experts
here say "no way," on both counts. (They
also say, "Don't apply electric shock of any
kind." Whose crazy idea was *that*?)
Antivenom resource numbers and a
snakebite hotline may not help you in the

desert, but you can always call ahead if you *plan* on a getting snakebit. Worth a sheet of your printer paper before that next camping trip.

Soil, Water, and Climate Web Server

http://www.soils.umn.edu/

Earth Sciences

"Just another Stuckey's on the Information Superhighway," boasts this page from the University of Minnesota. Visitors can forage through the "Farmstead Assessment Decision Support System," and download a software program designed to evaluate how well farmsteading (as opposed to mega-corporate farming) protects our drinking water. (There's a great online tutorial, too.) If dirt's your thing, link to a garden of earthy delights at the Earth and Environmental Science page from the U.S. Geological Service, or jump to the famous UMN gopher to peruse articles on climatology, rhizosphere studies, and "precision agriculture," a system designed to maximize soil-specific crop management for long-term environmental benefits. You'll also get the inside info on graduate programs at UMN and connections to other soddy sites around the country.

U.S. Coast Guard Cutter Polar Sea

http://www.compumedia.com/~jef/psea/psea.homepage.html

Earth Sciences

The U.S. Coast Guard ship *Polar Sea* and its sister ship, *Polar Star*, are the world's most powerful non-nuclear ice-breakers. You'll find a ton of specs here (they can crunch through six-foot-thick ice continuously, or, unbelievably, *21-foot-thick* ice in Ramming Mode). These are a friendly bunch of sailors (if maybe a tiny bit stir crazy) who actually drove their ship right smack through the ice all the way to the North Pole for a rendezvous with a similar Russian ship. They're rightly proud of their work, and in addition to icebreaker data, show off a great photo album, with pictures of stunning Arctic vistas and a funny-looking Russian helicopter. It isn't all fun and games, though. The crew conducts some serious research in sea ice physics and chemistry while they're out there rendezvousing. You can read the abstracts here, but trust us: the photo album is much more amusing!

United States Coast Guard

United States Department of Agriculture

http://www.usda.gov/usda.htm

Earth Sciences

This user-friendly tour of the United States Department of Agriculture starts at the USDA Visitor Information

Center, with basic info on programs like farm subsidies, food stamps, and school lunches. Some USDA agencies, like the Forest Service and the Foreign Agricultural Service, have their own pages under USDA Agencies and Programs; users researching a specific topic can check the National Agricultural Library for help. We also recommend the "Agriculture Fact Book," which essentially is the USDA in Adobe Acrobat format. The press releases at this site may be of interest to Net-connected farmers—however, at the rate the entries seem to be updated, they might do just as well to read the newspaper.

United States Geological Survey's National Marine and Coastal Geology Program

http://walrus.wr.usgs.gov:80/docs/pmg.html

Earth Sciences

This marine geologist's gold mine is loaded with interesting summaries of current research, photos of impressive-looking equipment, and tons of facts, facts, facts. The enthusiastic scientists at the USGS are out to share their findings on

marine ecology and resources. Read how the aftermath of the Prince William Sound oil spill (the largest in U.S. history) produced pollution consequences far beyond those resulting from immediate spill damage, or why research in the Great Lakes wetlands is focusing on the formation of beach ridges. In a disturbing twist, some pretty cool underwater photos reveal barrels of radioactive waste on the ocean floor, which the team has helped locate. How much longer can the USGS survive funding cutbacks and produce cool sites like these? Browsers can get the skinny direct from scientists, who are not above conducting a job search online!

VolcanoWorld

http://volcano.und.nodak.edu/vw.html

Earth Sciences

No, VolcanoWorld is not a new theme park. It's the result of combined efforts by volcano experts and educators who hope to answer everything you ever wanted to know about these strange mountains filled with molten rock. Hosted by a grinning flame-topped volcano named Rocky (and talk about a dandruff problem), VolcanoWorld combines text and graphics with hi-tech photos in a series of volatile lessons. K–12 teachers will find their own super lesson plans on "Hot Spots and Mantle Plumes" and "Mount St. Helens." Kids can find out how to become a volcanologist (this does not include studying old *Star Trek* episodes). Volcanic photos from around the world and a very groovy slide show give new supercharged meaning to the word "evacuate."

Photos Needed

Hawaii Volcanoes National Park Sep 19

Mount St. Helens - "Fire & Life" Sep 12

Whole Frog Project

http://george.lbl.gov/ITG.hm.pg.docs/Whole.Frog/
Whole.Frog.html

Earth Sciences

The first goal of this project was to provide high school biology students with a 3D imaging tool to use in studying frog anatomy. But it's so much more! Even non-science types will thrill to the tibio-fibula of the skeletal system, the detailed heart and lungs, and the rotating, transparent frog movie. (The authors say, "Ultimately we intend to be able to enter the heart and fly down blood vessels, poking our head out at any point to see the structure of the surrounding anatomy." Woo!) Among the advantages cited here are the ability to view more than one anatomical angle at once, and the nifty trick of "undissection"—plus, you don't have to "pith" your little green lab partner to do any of this. This is fun, unusual, and darned educational.

physical sciences
physical sciences

Amateur Science

http://www.eskimo.com/~billb/
Physical Sciences

This is a great home page from Bill Beaty, a full-of-wonder guy who wants everyone—especially kids—to know how much fun science experiments can be. Besides suggesting experiments to do at home, like the very amusing "TOUCH THE CLOUDS device," Beaty reports on some of his own experiments with infectious enthusiasm. (Our strong favorite is the frightening "Dangerous experiments with a big capacitor bank" article.) This is also the home of the Society for Amateur Scientists, where Beaty offers links to suppliers of stuff like surplus lasers. Bill seems to be involved with some pretty heavy "Weird Science," in which we discover text and images of dubious inventions for free energy and antigravity. Soon enough you'll want to photograph ghosts and auras or build electrostatic motors, or take the easy way out and just build a lava lamp.

DIII-D Fusion Home Page

http://FusionEd.gat.com:80/
Physical Sciences

The nice folks at General Atomics want you to know how close they are to practical atomic fusion energy. No girly-whirly cold fusion for them; they intend to achieve the too-cheap-to-meter dream the old-fashioned way: by brute electromagnetic force. They have the second largest Tokamak in the U.S. (the inside of which looks exactly like the central power core in the Death Star from *Star Wars*), and they're not afraid to use it. (A Tokamak is a huge doughnut-shaped plasma-containment vessel surrounded by men in lab coats.) The idea is to crush ultra-hot hydrogen plasma into helium, see? The lengthy tables of specifications are incomprehensible until you notice the links labeled "Huh?," which produce friendly explanations of Troyon factors and MeV. Real red-meat science.

Decavitator

http://lancet.mit.edu:80/decavitator/Decavitator.html

Physical Sciences

Check out the *Decavitator*, a pedal-powered hydrofoil created at MIT. It's the fastest human-powered watercraft in the world (18.5 knots). This enthusiastic Web site has videos (and stills for those of us with slow connections) of the funny-looking craft under construction, in testing, and then in action, chasing ducks and wiping out. Loads of serious design specs, configuration history, an account of the world-record competition, and tips for do-it-yourself hydrofoilers are also available (you'll learn to fear ventilation, for example, which is what happens when the wing pierces the water's surface, and sucks air down the lifting surface). Plus they're working on a successor, code-named "Skeeter." The best part, though, is the collection of graphics of the insectoid craft rocketing up Boston's Charles River.

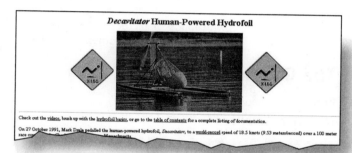

Decavitator **Human-Powered Hydrofoil**

Check out the videos, brush up with the hydrofoil basics, or go to the table of contents for a complete listing of documentation.

On 27 October 1991, Mark Drela pedalled the human-powered hydrofoil, *Decavitator*, to a world-record speed of 18.5 knots (9.53 meters/second) over a 100 meter race co...

Discovery Place

http://dp.worldweb.com/

Physical Sciences

The petroleum industry is huge—that much we know. It also turns out to have a nice Web site. Discovery Place, maintained by the oil industry in Alberta, Canada, is a global site for industry members or enthusiasts seeking information and links on the oil and gas business. An extensive list of resources is the most useful site for the lay person, offering everything from heavy construction equipment to rental geologists to emergency service provider Wild Fire International. In case you're a starving petroleum engineer (and who doesn't know one?), a few companies advertise job listings in the online career section. Or join a discussion on "finding reverse osmosis for glycol," if you dare. A well-structured site, which, considering the emphasis on engineers, isn't too surprising.

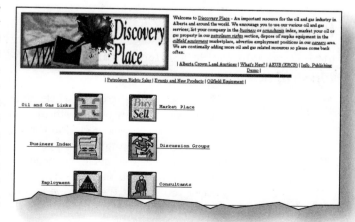

GE Lighting Institute Home Page

`http://www.ge.com:80/gel/index.html`
Physical Sciences

General Electric does more than just make light bulbs: they run a very swanky *Lighting Institute*, where "lighting professionals" can go to conferences and seminars to get "in touch with the innovative lighting products which will affect their businesses and their lives." This site offers a beautifully presented tour of the institute, with loads of pictures of exquisitely lit offices, factories, and homes. Check out the luminous conference table in the Vanguard Room, or the no-glare-on-the-computer-screen lighting techniques in the simulated offices (the technique looks like it'd work, but your office would look like it's having a flying-saucer invasion). The text can be a little pompous sometimes—hey, fellahs, they're just light bulbs!—but the graphics are inspiring (if sometimes slow to load).

The Geometry Center

`http://www.geom.umn.edu/`
Physical Sciences

Some of the best science sites on the Web offer interactive toys that suck you in by amusing you, and then show you the math or science behind whatever they've gotten you to play with. This is a great site in that mold. The Gallery of Interactive Geometry features amusing tools like the Penrose tile generator (start with two dimensions and work your way up to a baffling 13), a 3D CyberViewer, a tool to make M.C. Escher-style graphics, and an Orbifold Pinball machine (with which we explore the effects of negatively curved space). The math ranges from simple pictures (like the inscrutable Klein bottle) to heavy-duty graduate-level papers, but even these are presented in rich hypertext, with lots of pictures. There's software to download (mostly for Unix, unfortunately), and a graphics gallery of interesting geometric constructs.

Holography

`http://www.holo.com:80/holo/gram.html`
Physical Sciences

Try your hand at creating simple holographic patterns online with this fun interactive device, which gets you thinking about interference patterns. Then go on to learn how to actually create holograms. It ain't simple, but this site is serious about training you to do it. The extensive tutorial, with its loads of easy quantum mechanics illustrations, is cleanly written and often quite funny. The practical aspects of home holography are sort of reminiscent of the early days of still photography: ingredients for your home studio include 3/4" plywood, roofing tar, an inner tube, buckets of sand, and, of course, some lasers. Armed with your education, you can move to the advertisement section. Among the items you're offered here is the Liconix *Embosser II* laser, which "delivers a blistering 150mW TEMoo at 442nm." It all makes perfect sense if you were paying attention.

The Live Artificial Life Page

`http://www.fusebox.com:80/cb/alife.html`
Physical Sciences

Artificial life is a self-modifying (evolving) software construct that has simple genes and a simple visible structure that reflects the genetic makeup of real life. (Got that?) The Live Artificial Life Web page is the most amusing of several pages devoted to this new science, partly because it lets you try your own hand at evolving simple new artificial life forms: little stick figures that mutate into complex stick figures (based on a program described in *The Blind Watchmaker* by biologist Richard Dawkins). If you create a particularly cool one, post it to the Bestiary. This Web site may be the most god-like thing you do all day. (Note from The Professor: before you start evolving, please go to the Morph Watch page to see if anyone is in the lab at the moment. You don't want to reset the morphs while someone is busy evolving a masterpiece.)

Mathematical Quotations Server

`http://math.furman.edu/~mwoodard/mquot.html`
Physical Sciences

Think mathematics is boring? Here's an alphabetical list of quotations by people who love, loathe, or live with math. Douglas Adams' explanation of Bistromatics ("the first nonabsolute number is the number of people for whom the table is reserved") bumps up against more serious one-liners by Aristotle and Poincar. And the mathematical heavies reveal philosophical sides here, like Blaise Pascal ("Men despise religion; they hate it, and they fear it is true"). They slam other scientists ("If your experiment needs statistics, you ought to have done a better experiment"—Ernest Rutherford). They slam themselves ("You know we all became mathematicians for the same reason: we were lazy"—Max Rosenlicht). Non-mathematicians like Woody Allen, Malcolm X, and Edgar Allen Poe weigh in, too. Weird and likable.

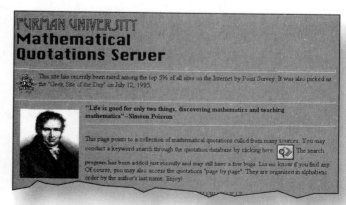

John Mount's International Interactive Genetic Art II

`http://robocop.modmath.cs.cmu.edu:8001/htbin/mjwgenformII`

Physical Sciences

This is an odd page: you're presented with nine Rorschach-blot-looking, computer-generated artwork images, and you're asked to rate (one to 10) how much you like each one. After you vote, the machine explains what the point is:

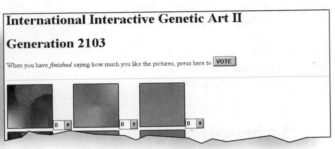

you're helping determine the "fitness" (as in evolution) of the current pictures. After every ten votes, the computer creates new images by "evolving" them from the old ones. That is: random mathematical mutations are made to the formulae that create the pictures, and the input from the humans determines which mutations survive in subsequent generations. There's a load of technical math stuff about exactly how the pictures mutate, but we preferred to just groove on the artwork. The gallery of past winners is great (although we're puzzled by the concept of "winner"), and the server-push Genetic Art Slide Show is a trip.

Mr. Solar Home Page

`http://www.netins.net:80/showcase/solarcatalog/index.html`

Physical Sciences

Imagine the famous painting "American Gothic," but with giant photovoltaic panels in the background, and the sourpuss farmer mutated into the jovial, outgoing

Mr. Solar (a.k.a. Charlie Collins, whose "passion is to help others become as self-reliant as he is"). Charlie and his wife Fran live on the DO IT Homestead, a self-reliant farm that serves as a proud example to all of us slackers who take electrical power for granted. There are more than 100 folksy, informative articles online about alternative energy, including wind and water power, in the form of archived "Ask Mr. Solar" columns. "Yes, Eric, rotary inverters are *very* inefficient." If you're interested (and who wouldn't be, after exposure to the infectious Mr. Solar?), answer the questionnaire, and Mr. Solar will hook you up with like-minded folks near you.

Nanothinc

http://www.nanothinc.com:80/NanoHome.html

Physical Sciences

Nanotechnology is the science of molecule-tiny engines. There are dozens of Web sites devoted to this emerging technology, but the Nanothinc folks actually hope to make money at this mostly theoretical pursuit. Their fascinating Web site (complete with NanoVideo and NanoSound) provides convincing evidence that this is the *big* technology of the future, supplying us with everything from analytical laboratories on a chip, to robotic microsurgery, to teensy machines that'll repair the cracks in your skyscraper. The introduction gives you the basics, like creation of custom proteins and buckyballs. And that's just the beginning (although some spots, like Consumer Products, were still under construction when we last visited). The site promises to let regular folks "explore a world of the future in which advanced nanotechnology is the norm, with profound effects on everyday life." Plus, they're hiring!

Physics Around the World

http://www.physics.mcgill.ca/physics-services/
physics_services2.html

Physical Sciences

Physics Around the World offers links to science resources and information. This site is a "Physics Yellow Pages for the Web," with a great search engine (which we dearly wish our telephone book had). It's funny to enter non-physics words, like "cow," and see what pops out. Also interesting is the Internet Market Place for Physicists, where scientists can buy or sell used instruments. We found one ad searching for a "differential sputter gun" (it's a real physics tool, we checked). Other links can get you a job, provide free software for download, show basic (and not-so-basic) physics tables and information, and let you sniff around the world's leading physics departments.

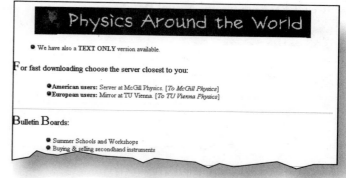

Relativistic Heavy Ion Collider

`http://acnsun10.rhic.bnl.gov:80/RHIC`

Physical Sciences

This is Big Science, baby. The Relativistic Heavy Ion Collider (RHIC to friends) is a 3.8 kilometer tunnel o' gadgetry that will collide subatomic particles called heavy ions at high energies to recreate the hot, dense plasma of quarks and gluons believed to have existed in the early universe. (Set it for defrost and it also works wonders with meatloaf.) You'll find tons of tech talk here, but head right for the brief photo tour of the RHIC site (it won't be ready until 1999), which looks pretty much like a billion-dollar irrigation pipe full of space-age cartoony gadgets like the Grumman dipole magnet. If you dig the RHIC, you'll probably also enjoy a visit to its parent page, the Brookhaven National Laboratory, for a look at similar Department of Energy brainstorms.

SUCCEED Engineering Visual Database

`http://succeed.edtech.vt.edu/`

Physical Sciences

What better teaching tool for engineers than pictures of other things that already have been built? As part of the

SUCCEED Engineering Visual Database

Welcome to the NSF SUCCEED Engineering Visual Database--an online repository of images for use by engineering faculty and students.

This web site is rated TOP 5% of all web sites by Point Communications Corporation.

The Engineering Visual Database contains a sample of images contributed by members of the SUCCEED Coalition and interested supporters.

For each image, a brief description and thumbnail are provided. To view the full screen image click on the thumbnail. The full screen will be displayed by the viewer program for your platform. From the viewer you can save the image to your hard drive. Some viewers may allow you to copy to the clipboard. All images are in the *jpeg* format. All jpeg images are 24-bit, compressed to an average size of about 100K each. If you wish to use these images in an application that does not support the *jpeg* format you will need another program to convert the images into a format that your application supports. This archive is currently under construction. Check frequently for additional materials.

National Science Foundation's SUCCEED program, Virginia Tech has gathered here hundreds of photographs displaying unusual or noteworthy structures and designs, ranging from aircraft carriers to lab procedures for measuring the specific gravity of cement. You can search categories like Aerospace and Ocean Engineering, or hunt by keyword. Check out places like King Khalid Military City in Saudi Arabia (you have 23 photos to choose from) or the bridge over Lake Jocassee, South Carolina. Images are presented in small thumbnails, which you can use to decide if you want the whole 100–200 KB image. And, if you have a favorite feat of modern (or ancient) engineering that deserves to be on the list, you can submit it.

WebChemistry

http://www.latrobe.edu.au/chejs/chem.html

Physical Sciences

So maybe you don't have time to find all the chemistry sites on the Web. Relax—Australian university student Joey Santos has done it for you. From file transfer sites to chemical societies and journals, this listing has most anything you're looking for. University chemistry departments from Japan to the West Indies outline course descriptions and faculty vitae (we're talkin' massive listings here), and better yet, Joey's included links to chemistry-related software—even for Macs. The online tutorials could be just what you need the night before that mid-term exam in Chem 101. This is the exhaustive work of a man who clearly has too much time on his hands. But you may thank him for it.

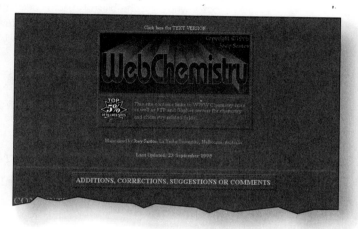

Web Elements

http://chemserv.bc.edu/web-elements/web-elements-home.html

Physical Sciences

Throw your dusty old periodic table into the round file: Web Elements is fast and easy. Here you can choose any known element (from one to 105) and get the full rundown, from atomic weight to isotopic abundances. The elegant program from England's Sheffield University also offers related scientific data and functions. Choose from a nifty set of isotope pattern or element percentage calculators. You can even decide for yourself whether element 104 should be called Rutherfordium or Dubnium. ("Dubnium"? We cast our vote for Rutherford.) The authors also suggest that you "use the data you obtain at your own risk...," which is probably good advice for any site popular with nuclear scientists.

World Submarine Invitational

`http://siolib-155.ucsd.edu:80/wsi/`
Physical Sciences

Here's a contest for *underachievers*: the World Submarine Invitational. And it's not a who's-got-the-biggest-reactor deal at all: this race is for human-powered submersibles. The site offers everything you'll need to enter: from diagrams of the course (lots of flashing underwater beacons), to the friendly rules (safety is emphasized throughout, so make sure your sub has an escape hatch and brakes). The

World Submarine Invitational encourages designers to "challenge the medium not the environment, and the clock, not each other." (In other words, no torpedoes allowed.) You only get to see rough drawings and schematics, so the rest is left to your imagination. But you've got to love the idea. And you can always make those "going to the submarine races" jokes.

WWW Spirograph

`http://juniper.tc.cornell.edu:8000/spiro/spiro.html`
Physical Sciences

For anyone who was asleep (or not yet born) in the 1970s, the Spirograph was a toy that used geared plastic circles with holes for a pen to make swirly cyclic mandalas. Sadly, they seem to have perished with the Pet Rock, but the concept lives on in cyberspace with this fun site. Here, you specify the sizes of the gears and the position of the hole, and let the robot create the resultant figure. Even complicated ones

pop out in a few seconds; this is both good (no tedious grinding away like we remember from childhood) and bad (no fun grinding away like we remember from childhood). The point of this demonstration is to introduce the user to a few simple parametric equations, presented gently at the end. Suggestion: vary only one parameter at a time, and you may get some surprises.

sky and space

Astronomy and Space on the Internet

`http://fly.hiwaay.net/~cwbol/astro.html`
Sky and Space

Leaving no celestial stone unturned, this fabulous site collects the greatest hits of Internet space pages and arranges them

over a handsome starry background. You'll have to visit to understand the vastness of the links, which are great for scientists and casual wanderers alike. There are links to sun pages, moon pages, star pages, and silly pages about Mars. There's one collection of links, for example, just to home pages for Shoemaker-Levy 9 (the comet that recently gave Jupiter a "bump in the night"). Poke around at random, and you're sure to learn something fascinating. On our last visit, for instance, we learned that the head of a comet is actually comprised of two parts, the nucleus and the coma, and that in the world of comets a head 10 kilometers wide is considered small. In our world, this site is a biggie.

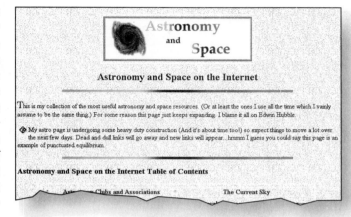

The Astronomy Cafe

http://www2.ari.net/home/odenwald/cafe.html

Sky and Space

Take an astronomy lesson... please. Astrophysicist Sten Odenwald has put together a page of astronomy resources that is part lesson and part fun. You can find out what it's like to be an astronomer (from personal accounts by Dr. Odenwald and other scientists about projects like high-altitude balloon-based research). Or learn how to write a real research paper.

You can even ask a question, which he may post—along with the response, of course. One such query: "If the sun is made of hydrogen and helium, why can't we see through it?" Hmm. Visitors can also read cool essays by Dr. Odenwald like "Hyperspace in Science Fiction," where he reviews how sci-fi writers have treated the topic of space travel.

Astronomy Picture of the Day

http://antwrp.gsfc.nasa.gov/apod/astropix.html

Sky and Space

One day we saw the face on Mars. Before that, it was the "string of pearls" comet that collided with Jupiter in 1992. Awhile back we saw the damaged Apollo 13 spacecraft; the next day the pieces were streaking back into the atmosphere. When we last visited, we saw Mimas, one of Saturn's smaller moons, which is remarkable for the colossal

impact crater occupying a third of its face. (There seems to be a theme of impacts and explosions developing here, which we think is great.) Every day a new picture or image of the universe is placed here, with a brief explanation full of hypertext links to extensive background information. Makes you want to look at the universe nearly all the time, doesn't it?

Avion Online

http://avion.db.erau.edu
Sky and Space

For one of the Web's best examples of student work, check out Avion Online, the virtual version of the student newspaper at Florida's Embry-Riddle Aeronautical University. No sophomore tomfoolery here, just a steadily piloted weekly specializing in aeronautical news gleaned from the Net (and reported by students). On our last visit, the issue offered a front-page story about a tragic midair collision that killed three students, and a load of national aviation news (including an article about a successful test flight of a solar-powered airplane). The Kennedy Space Center counts as "local news," so there's also lots of aeronautical and space info here, plus all the campus news, gossip, editorials, and sports you'd expect from a school paper. Crisp pics of air shows and shuttle flights are sprinkled throughout. Comics, too!

Center for Mars Exploration

http://cmex-www.arc.nasa.gov/
Sky and Space

Yet another great NASA page, this one has enough history, factoids, and images to keep you busy on an entire flight to the Red Planet. It's Martian overload: links to a newsletter, educational resources, missions past and future (the Pathfinder will set up weather stations on the surface in '97), and even "Mars today," which shows the daily position of the planet. One link offers a library of *all* of the unprocessed Viking Lander photos: you pick a mission and a camera, and then point at exactly what you want to see. (We recommend you start with the surface images rather than the global ones—they're much smaller to download.) It's a delight to wade through, as long as you can stomach the graphic of a weird green alien holding Mars on its back just like Atlas held Earth. Not exactly "Our Favorite Martian."

Welcome to the Center for Mars Exploration

The Center for Mars Exploration (CMEX) WWW server is currently under construction. This page will be adding many new features including historical references to Mars, previous Mars mission information, tools to analyze Mars, current Mars news, and much more.

The Mars Educational Multimedia CD-ROM

Images
NEW! Web part of the CMEX CD-Rom

Comet Shoemaker-Levy

http://newproducts.jpl.nasa.gov/s19/s19.html

Sky and Space

Comet Shoemaker-Levy vs. the planet Jupiter is the most spectacular catastrophe since Godzilla vs. Tokyo. In July of 1994, 21 chunks of comet, some as big as two kilometers across, collided with Jupiter, and the effects on the Jovian atmosphere have been simply spectacular. All the greatest hits from the clash are here in gorgeous color, with more camera angles than Monday Night Football. In fact, nothing shows better why we spent all those tax dollars on the Hubble telescope—it's all here on the screen. There's even a scary section on comets striking the Earth. The visuals can be slow to load, but the wait is well worth it. Shoemaker-Levy is doomed in the end, of course, but it wreaks havoc on its way out. Godzilla would be proud.

Current Weather Maps/Movies

http://rs560.cl.msu.edu/weather

Sky and Space

This multimedia weather server at Michigan State features one of the Net's best collections of satellite photos and weather animations. While waiting for them to download, you can whisk your hands across the screen, weatherman-style, and practice your best Willard Scott patter. (Don't forget to plug old Nellie's 128th birthday.) The pictures come to you compliments of geostationary satellites with names like GOES, and once you discover the shots that cover your area, you can be prognosticating in no time. Maps are available in GIF and JPEG (we recommend JPEG for faster downloads if your browser can handle them); the polar views and infrared maps are far more sophisticated than you'd ever see on a TV newscast. A fine resource that will appeal to both scientists and amateurs.

Earth Viewer

http://www.fourmilab.ch/earthview/vplanet.html

Sky and Space

You've seen images of the Earth. And the Moon. But how about real-time images of the day or night side of the Earth above any location? This page takes space imagery another step by enabling visitors to choose what they want to see: you pick the latitude, longitude, and altitude you want, or just select a particular satellite, and the machine pops out an image. (You must have a browser that can support forms.) You can choose to look at Earth with a cloud cover—or maybe just a topographical map suits you better. Whatever. This could come in mighty handy someday (although we can't quite think how), but in any case, it's rather god-like. Depending on your astronomical interests, this page is either too much of a good thing or another fantastic tool and toy. We pick the latter.

European Space Agency

http://www.esrin.esa.it/htdocs/esa/esa.html
Sky and Space

The European Space Agency (ESA) is NASA's equivalent in Europe, coordinating space policy for its members and researching new space technologies. Americans don't hear about them a lot, which is a shame, because they're important space-farers these days, and their great-looking Web site is a good place to start. While the Europeans lack some of the enthusiasm found on NASA pages, they still present lots of solid science. They offer online editions of technical publications, which include titles like *Microgravity News* (they're growing some interesting biological crystals out there) and *Earth Observation Quarterly* (on our last visit, they were studying the trees of Central Africa from space). ESA also contributes to setting telecom policy across Europe. Some of the graphics-heavy pages take some time to access, but it's still worth a visit.

INTELLiCast

http://www.intellicast.com/
Sky and Space

This is among the slickest-looking weather sites we've seen, scoring big points for ease of use. And if you live in one of its weather reporting cities, you can even get a local forecast. You pick your city (or one nearby) from a comprehensive list of U.S. locations; if you're in a big metro area, you can get detailed graphics and forecasts. INTELLiCast gets its forecast information from a growing network of local TV stations (and you know how accurate they are); don't miss the incredibly detailed radar maps tracking that cloud-burst just outside your window. For non-U.S. users, the reports of weather from around the world are sketchy at best. The ski report looks promising, offering descriptions ranging from "corn snow" to "powder" at ski areas across the U.S.

Jonathan's Space Report

http://hea-www.harvard.edu/QEDT/jcm/space/jsr/jsr.html
Sky and Space

Harvard astrophysicist Jonathan McDowell gives you all the space news that's fit to e-mail in his weekly report. When last we visited, Jonathan had the latest poop on the new extra-comfy spacesuits, along with a really cool (but regrettably unidentified) photo of some a complicated-looking orbital apparatus. We also found a catalog of all known geosynchronous satellites, with the status of each. ("Drift" does *not* sound good.) Jonathan knows which pad your favorite shuttle is resting on, what the Russians are up to, which launches are classified—frankly, he's starting to sound a little suspicious. Visitors can also link to Jonathan's Space Page or his other fave space program links. Fascinating stuff!

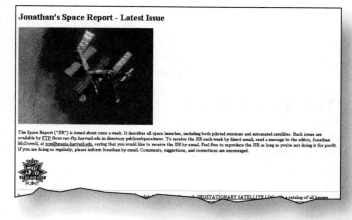

NASA Shuttle Web Archives

http://shuttle.nasa.gov/
Sky and Space

Ever wonder what astronauts *do* in space for, say, 12 days? You can find out the fascinating details and much more in this glossy NASA production. Visitors can look up just about everything they might care to know about upcoming or previous missions (there are separate sites for each), and even ask the crew questions (they won't get back to you immediately, mind you). Lots of pretty color pictures are available, just in case you can't make the launch. Heck, with this service, it might be cheaper to skip the trip to Cape Canaveral anyway. As the *Washington Post* puts it, "The only way you're going to get a closer look at the space shuttle is to fly to Houston and park yourself before a console in Mission Control." One question: mission schedules detail when the crew sleeps and when it conducts experiments, but why aren't meal times listed?

National Hurricane Center

http://nhc-hp3.nhc.noaa.gov
Sky and Space

Both schoolkids and scientists will find something to chew on at this fascinating hurricane research site, where you can gawk at some stunning photographs. (You can also learn how meteorologists give those human names to tropical storms.) It's all updated regularly, depending on what's happening with Arthur, Bertha, or Hortense. At the very least, find out if your name's on the list of future storms, so you can temporarily adopt a nickname and avoid the unpleasant associations. Some of the information is far too technical for simple weather gawkers, but the pictures more than make up for it.

The Nine Planets

http://seds.lpl.arizona.edu/nineplanets/
nineplanets/nineplanets.html
Sky and Space

Perhaps you can name Santa's eight reindeer faster than the nine planets. If so, this page can help. It's an excellent guide both for newcomers and for folks who were sharp enough in school to learn about moons. Take Europa, one of Jupiter's satellites, for instance. This page showed us how big it is (3138 km in diameter) and how far it is from Jupiter (670,9000 km), then offered an amazingly close-up photo (it's sort of brown, with interesting lines) and the history behind its name. The full tour consists of some 60 pages and includes the whole solar system (including some *really* obscure Neptunian moons, like Larissa); an express version is available, too. For those romantic journeys, snippets of Gustav Holst's "The Planets" can be heard.

The above composite shows the nine planets with approximately correct relative sizes (see Appendix 2 for more).

One way to help visualize the relative sizes in the solar system is to imagine a model in which it is reduced in size by a factor of a billion (1e9). Then the Earth is about 1.3 cm in diameter (the size of a grape). The Moon orbits about a foot away. The Sun is 1.5 meters in diameter (about the height of a man) and 150 meters (about a city block) from the Earth. Jupiter is 15 cm in diameter (the size of a large grapefruit) and 5 blocks away from the Sun. Saturn (the size of an orange) is 10 blocks away; Uranus and Neptune (lemons) are 20 and 30 blocks away. A human on this scale is the size of an atom.

Not shown in the above illustration are the numerous smaller bodies that inhabit the solar system: the satellites of the planets; the large number of asteroids (small rocky bodies) but also the comets (small icy bodies) which come and go from the inner parts of the

Penn State University Weather Pages

http://www.ems.psu.edu/wx/index.html
Sky and Space

An innovative use of virtual reality and a nice collection of offshore weather data make Penn State's pages unique among weather sites. With Apple's free Quicktime VR software, users can simulate navigating through cloud cover across the planet (watch out for that 747!). It's not likely to give you vertigo, but it's an impressive use of a new technology. Those heading for the high seas can also check wave conditions, surface temperatures, and wind speeds, all updated every hour; perfect for that next outing on Lake Erie or the Indian Ocean. You also get the standard satellite pictures and meteorological data, only for the most schooled of weather gurus. If you just want to know if it's going to rain tomorrow, this is probably overkill.

SEDS (Students for the Exploration and Development of Space)

http://seds.lpl.arizona.edu/
Sky and Space

Why let NASA have all the fun? SEDS is a club for college and high school kids who are fascinated by space travel. Completely run by students, and founded in 1980 at MIT, SEDS promotes learning, talking, designing, and just plain spitballing about space exploration. Hey, these kids are serious: check the pictures of SEDSAT, the student-built satellite scheduled to be released by a NASA space shuttle in 1997. (It looks like a flying breadbox, but has an interesting accelerometer experiment aboard.) Don't fret, there's still time to lend a hand: here you'll find a call for students wishing to contribute scientific work to the satellite. The kids are also into some pretty heavy-duty amateur rockets, political activism to support NASA's space station, and loads of links to space-related sites.

Space Movie Archive

http://www.univ-rennes1.fr/ASTRO/anim-e.html
Sky and Space

This monster archive contains nearly 500 movies of space imagery, from comets smacking into Jupiter (there are dozens of these) to the creature from *Alien* (or even the lip-smacking Captain from *Star Trek*). Many of the animation or film sequences are VERY big (a starship *Enterprise* flyby is small, at 97 KB, but most of them exceed 1 megabyte), but what a catalog! 11 days of the *Mir-Atlantis* encounter, a day-by-day account of other shuttle missions, and hundreds more films, including meteorological overheads of Europe and the great 1991 eclipse. We found cometary motion movies, an exploding Atlas booster, and old films from Lunar Ranger series of impact probes (space exploration's gotten a lot easier since then). The archive even includes a massive 14 MB tour of the *Enterprise* quarters of *Star Trek: The Next Generation*'s Deanna Troi.

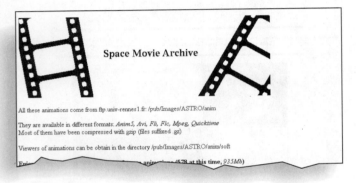

Suns'n'Roses

http://www.Stars.com/Roses/
Sky and Space

"Why is there something instead of nothing?" "Where do the laws of physics come from?" Suns'n'Roses is a jumble of metaphysical thought and specula-tion from astrophysicists and futurists, compiled by NASA systems whiz Alan Richmond, who provides his own perspective. After the introductory warning ("Reality under construction"), there's lots of very interesting talk about cosmology, quantum fluctuation, and Heisenberg's Uncertainty Principle, which "allows you to have a free lunch—as long as you eat it quickly enough." Quotes from notables like William Gibson, Carl Sagan, and even William Wordsworth are supplemented by color graphics of space, planets, and cool, swirly, abstract color-things. You can also link to places like Stanford's Metaphysics Research Lab. Not for the casual surfer (or for readers of *Cosmo*), but it *will* make you think.

Weather Processor

http://thunder.atms.purdue.edu
Sky and Space

Here's a heavy-weather site for cumulo-nimbus junkies—just the kind of high-tech, up-to-the-minute stuff that makes the Internet so irresistible for the obsessive. Coming to you live (well, hourly) from a GOES geostationary satellite orbiting 22,000 miles above the equator, this Purdue University site offers a hailstorm of images and a flood of data from strangely-named places like the European Center for Medium Range Forecasting. Wind-chill factors! Water-vapor readings! Up-close maps of Indiana! Still not satisfied? Then play dueling rainbows by jumping to other university weather sites nationwide... if you dare. But go lightly on the millibars, please.

Web Nebulae

http://seds.lpl.arizona.edu/billa/twn/
Sky and Space

Bill Arnett, creator of The Nine Planets, produces this beautiful gallery of photographs of nebulae, sampled from the many sources on the Web. The archive sources are listed, and there is a tiny bit of information about each photo, but this isn't a "science thing." This is the art of the universe. A glossary and index make things easy, but the stars of the show are the stars: big, colorful pictures that are far prettier than even sad clown paintings. It's hard to resist famous names like the Pleiades, and even harder to resist names like Eskimo, Keyhole, Horsehead, and Little Dumbbell. Highly recommended viewing: the Cat's Eye Nebula.

Shopping

Shopping

As worries about hackers and credit cards have cleared away, online shopping has started to take hold. A popular creation is the "virtual mall," in which multiple vendors band together as part of a single Web site. As you browse from one shop to the next, it can seem vaguely like a real shopping mall (especially since there are no restrooms). Another popular sales approach is the superstore: take a look at Amazon.com Books, which seems to plan on carrying every single book in print on Earth. Perhaps most charming, though, are the single small vendors, such as the Virginia Diner with its peanut recipes and White Rabbit Toys with its college-town atmosphere. As in real life, a friendly shopkeeper is still the best selling point of all.

Amazon.com Books

http://www.amazon.com
Shopping

Billed as "Earth's biggest bookstore," Amazon.com Books features a database of one million titles. Proprietors aspire to the lofty goal of listing *every* book in print. A quick search for obscure titles leads us to believe they aren't kidding around, either. Ordering is quick and easy, and more than 20 categories can help ease the burden of browsing such a huge stack. The real achievement here is the *free* personal notification service. Subscribe and the folks at Amazon.com will notify you of new titles in your category (say, insect taxidermy), or tell you when a new book comes out by your favorite author. Perhaps most impressive is the speed of searching—nearly any combination of keywords brings a quick list of related titles. Sound impersonal? It may be, but a daily spotlight on favorite titles offers recommendations from the staff, capturing at least a little of the coziness of a small bookstore.

Archie McPhee

http://www.halcyon.com/mcphee/
Shopping

Archie McPhee is a catalog-turned-cyberstore billed as the "Outfitters of Popular Culture since 1986." It is, quite simply, a repository of useless-but-cool consumer items like rubber chickens ("the pinnacle of American humor"), voodoo dolls, and a miniature Easter Island head: "worship it, use it to contact aliens, or just look at it." Dip into munchies like bubble gum that tastes like pickles, or "Cricket Lick-Its" (lollipops with real dead bugs in them! Yow!). Actually, just browsing the catalog's endless array of lines ("Lost your mind? Buy a replacement" and "Give yourself a hand!") is amusing enough. But if you really *need* an alarm clock that wakes you up and freaks you out, this is where you can make that purchase. Archie McPhee: because a home can never have too many gargoyles.

BookWire

The Big Daddy of online book resources, BookWire is thick and heavy with information for readers, publishers, and dealers. *Publisher's Weekly* and *Boston Book Review* run the show, so new titles are whisked to review desks, and the authors are promptly sat down and interviewed. The amount of options for visitors here is daunting, so we recommend using the site's Navigator page. From there, link to the "Reading Room," an amazing online library of books for download, mostly classics from Abbott to Wolff, with a particular strength in children's titles. Or skip to the *BBR*'s page of essays and interviews with people like Camille Paglia and Art Spiegelman. Looking at books always seems to lead to spending money, and of course that's easy enough to do here, too.

Carnivorous Plants Invade the Net!

Peter Pauls Nurseries wants you to know that flesh-eating plants are "exciting, educational, and make a distinctive statement in any setting." ("Distinctive" is the operative word.) They're also hoping you'll buy a few bug-biting beauties (or at least seed packets) from this virtual greenhouse. We found the Butterwort a particularly virulent assassin (it oozes gooey slime to trap its victims), though the dependable carnage of Venus Flytrap is always a crowd-pleaser. And the prices ($4.95 for the venomous Cobra Lily) won't bury *you*, either. And if you've already been bitten by these verdant jaws, you'll really enjoy the site's offering of Carnivorous Plant Links, including a searchable database and a Carnivorous Plant Society Homepage.

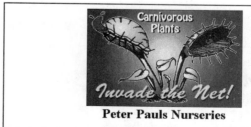

Codpiece International

http://www.teleport.com/~codpiece/codpiece.shtml
Shopping

What is a codpiece? Well, a man wears it, ah... ahem... it covers the... well, let us quote Codpiece International: "The codpiece... had to be invented to fill up the gap between the hose in the front,

through which the breeches gaped." That's it. The codpiece was all the rage in the 15th and 16th centuries, before it went the way of the blunderbuss (if that's not too suggestive a statement). Codpiece International (run by a company called Pegasus Printing) is determined to bring back the codpiece as "a new dimension in men's clothing." Actually, you can't buy codpieces here, though you *can* buy funny T-shirts about them—perhaps the true purpose of the campaign. But it's fun to read the amusing history of the codpiece and check out fashion illustrations of new-fangled designs.

Cybershop

http://cybershop.com
Shopping

This digital shopping mall injects an element that online shopping tends to lack—fun! (If you can make it through the elaborate-but-slow intro and registration process, that is.) Time spent registering here won't be wasted, as Cybershop puts

your personal information to good use for a birthday greeting and reminders of your loved one's special days. The site promises "the ultimate shopping experience!" and we won't spend much time arguing with that. After browsing everywhere from home electronics to personal fitness, we nearly spent $2,929 on Fisher-Price bedroom furniture—for kids we don't even have! Fortunately, the check-out point displays photos of and prices for everything—and a convenient, cart-emptying chicken exit. Cybershop may be more salesroom than playground, but it's well-organized, dazzlingly displayed, fully searchable, and extremely easy on the feet.

CyberTown

http://www.directnet.com/cybertown/

Shopping

CyberTown is a huge shopping and services center that sprawls over the entire galaxy and across several centuries—or perhaps it just *seems* to sprawl that far. The creators hope that CyberTown will become a central point for Web access and a sort of self-contained virtual village. By the look of things, they're well on their way. The graphic theme is space-age (the town is set in "the latter half of the 21st century"); so far, most of the in-house stuff is shop storefronts, where you can in fact order things. But the site is linked "back in time" to our modern Earth and history resources, and plans are in the works for several interactive gizmos, like CyberHood, a virtual walk through the seedier side of CyberTown.

Dr. Duey Neadham's Wacky Web Pages

http://scitech.lm.com/

Shopping

The snappy graphics here will grab you right away, but Dr. Duey's page has much more to offer. SciTech (the site's founder) is a friendly company specializing in fun science projects ("just add water... for cleanup") and educational games. You can buy them all here, of course. (We can't wait to learn about superabsorbent polymers by dissecting a disposable diaper lining!) The site also has details on ChemCamp, a touring series of five-day science programs for kids. Why are they doing this? "We're crazy," the site asserts. "We're kind of scientific renegades because of our humor, hands-on (and hands-in) style and our measurable degree of boingy thinking." Perhaps it's attributable to "boingy thinking," but SciTech manages to push its products in a refreshingly cheerful way, never resorting to the hard sell.

WorldWideWeb **Distributors**

of Summer Science Activities & Museum-Quality Gifts.

Flower Stop

http://www.rmii.com:80/fstop/fstopmain.html
Shopping

This online fresh-flower market offers next-day delivery (in the U.S.) of bouquets, vases, and that grand standby, the single long-stemmed rose. (The blooms come from Pikes Peak Greenhouses in Colorado Springs, in case you were wondering.) Shoppers can frolic among an "Enchanting Alstomeria Bouquet" or "Exotic Orchids"; if necessary, they can select a "nice" clear plastic vase or a nicer etched crystal one for delivery. The "Romance and Roses CD Set" features two centuries of the world's greatest love themes ("for lovers only!") to accompany your flower purchase. The prices are probably higher than your local florist, but this is still a nice example of online shopping. It's colorful, quick, and lets you see the product without provoking your allergies.

Fuji Publishing Group Cigar Page

http://www.netins.net/showcase/fujicig/
Shopping

With the next annual StogieFest right around the corner, you might want to puff up on your cigar knowledge. (Brush those ashes off your vest while you're at it.) This jam-packed humidor of information from Fuji Publishing—gunning to be "the place for cigars on the Internet and outside of cyberspace"—is just the ticket. Here, puffing surfers can download the Windows Online Cigar Guide (all 4 MB of it), flip through pages of the Web magazine *The Double Corona*, browse smoking-related newsgroups, and—take a breath here—jump to a host of other smoky pages. (You'll be surprised at how many are out there.) A "Cigar Brand Information" section will keep you abreast of notable cigar-makers and hook you up with a box of 25 Churchills (or whatever your pleasure).

The Gigaplex!

This "whopping 600-plus page Webmagazine devoted to arts and entertainment" definitely delivers the giga-goods: excellent coverage of film, music, food, theater, and photography, among other fields. The fabulous Filmplex offers Hollywood interviews galore with stars like Richard Gere (who tenderly reveals a moment when ·he and Jodie Foster watched the Oscars with friends, "lying on this bed... and throwing things at the screen"). Musicplex interviews Zubin Mehta and k.d. lang. And the Theaterplex features excellent Q&A with movers and shakers of the stage like Terrence McNally and Anna Deveare Smith. There's even a YogaPlex! However subtly, some of these pages want to sell you something—A Hawaiian retreat, a photojournalism book—which makes the Gigaplex part shopping mall, part magazine. And wholly entertaining.

A billion pleasures await you!

Hold on to your seat!

Green Market

Made from "100% recycled electrons," this environmentally friendly market hosts listings of "green" companies. It's a partnership with EcoNet and the Institute for Global Communications, and claims to feature "some of the hippest companies around." A super-efficient search function enables shoppers to locate specific products quickly. Browse the index and you'll find companies like Dancing Tree Recycled Paper and Printing, who make chemical-free papers from raw materials like garlic, chili peppers, and hemp (you use the paper for *writing*, mind you). And Island Press, an environmental book publisher, offers dozens of titles of solutions-oriented reading. You'll also find "earthwise" paints and computer peripherals (no electron-wasting online catalogs here). Much of the rest of the site is devoted to listing environmental education and discussion groups on the Net.

Hall of Malls

`http://nsns.com/MouseTracks/HallofMalls.html`
Shopping

The Hall of Malls features direct links to The Bizarre Bazaar, Downtown Anywhere, and dozens more Web shopping venues. Site creator New South Network Services has been "attracting mice and analyzing their tracks" for quite some time; they don't take themselves too seriously, and that's part of the appeal here. (Rather than sticking the visitor with a ready-made link description, a game lets you match words to make your own: we chose "Infobahn Strip-Center.") "These things are sprouting up everywhere!" the Webmaster writes. "You want to cruise the malls? Our challenge to ye cruisers is this: Imagine a day, maybe two to five years hence, when there are 10,000 online." Enthusiastic Infobahn Strip-shoppers that we are, we relish the thought. With its links to Yahoo and other sharp search sites, Hall of Malls makes a great launch pad.

Hot Hot Hot

`http://www.hot.presence.com/g/p/H3//index.html`
Shopping

This self-professed "culinary headshop" lives up to its hype hype hype by offering an entertaining array of more than 100 "products of fire." Search the catalog by "heat level" to find chili sauces with progressively scary names: "Bats Brew," "Ring of Fire," and the horrific "Nuclear Hell." Or search the "origin of hot sauces" using a clickable map. We fell upon "Capital Punishment," a unique blend of paste, peppers, and more peppers imported from Merida, in the Yucatan Peninsula. These folks don't stop at chip, dips, and spicy barbeques, either—we found ourselves quite curious about the Jalapeno Peanut Butter Fudge Sauce (for the ice cream anti-social?). The Surgeon General may not approve, but Hot Hot Hot is way cool.

Movie Madness Merchandise

http://www.moviemadness.com/

Shopping

This online mover of movie merchandising claims to have the largest selection of movie- and television-related stuff in the world. *Melrose Place* addicts, for instance, can hook up with a neat "Mondays are a bitch" black coffee mug. *Bridges of Madison County* buffs will fall in love with the Meryl Streep and Clint Eastwood action figures and durable plastic pickup truck (just kidding on that one, but there IS a nice selection of bridge/truck/sunflower-themed clothing here). Vinyl keepsakes for the kiddies are readily available in the Batman and Jim Carrey varieties, while cult TV shows such as *Star Trek* and *The X-Files* generate more mature trinketry—like shot glasses, key chains, and business-card holders. "I'm Captain James T. Kirk of the starship *Enterprise*—here's my card."

Welcome to Movie Madness Merchandise!

We have the largest selection of movie and television-related merchandise in the world. We offer t-shirts, caps, mugs, and collectibles from your favorite movies and television shows. Movies like: Star Trek, Batman Forever, Pocahontas, Lion King, James Bond, and much more! Also we have products from your favorite television shows like: X-Files, Babylon 5, Friends, Seinfeld, Frasier, E.R., Mad About You, and much more!

We offer you many easy ways to get your merchandise: You can order online or through our Toll Free Number 1-800-382-2311 within the U.S. If you are calling from outside the U.S. 1-916-344-4028, or FAX ORDER TO 1-916-649-1209. Either way it is quick and easy. You can also Mail a Check or Money Order to: Movie Madness Merchandise. 1731 Howe Ave #302, Sacramento, CA 95825 Questions?? Email John T. Wells at movie@caleweb.com

We continually add to our store as products for new movies and television shows become available, so please don't forget to add us to your hotlist and check back often!!

Please click here to visit the Movie Madness Home Page

NetMall

http://www.ais.net:80/netmall/

Shopping

Maybe they should have named this HyperMall, as the on-site shop selection is limited to a couple-dozen names, while the main attraction is a searchable index of links to more than 3,000 other online merchandisers. NetMall's on-site shops are pretty interesting, though. One, "Find a Friend," claims it will help you "reunite with long lost relatives or friends" and "collect on an old debt." (The word "friend" is used loosely in the latter example.) And L'eggs Online offers a new way to purchase panty hose. The "shopping cart" ordering system automatically obtains billing info, price totals, and the like, enabling surfers to add or subtract items while browsing through "ARTEFACTA," "Maine Lobster Direct," "Zarahemla Book Shoppe," and thousands more inventory options. Definitely a bookmark page for Internet commerce.

Nuke

http://www.nuke.com
Shopping

Sendai Publishing presents more than 2,000 pages of multimedia extravaganza here, with a dense (yet lively) interface. It's meant to be the starting point for fans of video games, computer entertainment software, movies, television, comics, and trading cards on the Net. It includes news, reviews, shopping, and much more. (And faced with this many options, you're likely to go reeling for the site's Frequently Asked Questions section for an orientation.) Past TVScape items have included an interview with *Star Trek's* Patrick Stewart ("What a pompous ass," he said of himself); on our last visit, the computer game "Alien Virus" received respectable ratings from the Review Crew. And the Shelter will always sell you loads of PC software. The site continues to mushroom. Wow!

Onsale

http://www.onsale.com/
Shopping

Here's a fresh twist in Net commerce: Onsale has created a vibrant, photo-filled online auction, in which you outbid other Web users for products ranging from digital cameras to fine wine to automobile radar jammers. Sale formats include straight sales, markdowns, and Dutch auctions. When we last visited an Onsale Dutch auction, they had placed 15 modems worth $200 each (or so they said) on sale for a minimum bid of $10, with actual bids running up to $65. The items remain on auction for a few days, and bidders even get e-mail updates on the proceedings. You can also read up on the Onsale merchants on display, like Bob Pace Boxing Memorabilia and Murray's Tickets. The selection can be limited, but this is a novel idea nonetheless.

Oxford University Press

http://www.oup.co.uk/ouphome.html
Shopping

Don't think for a moment that Oxford University isn't ready for the electronic age. This promotional site proves that the renowned academic book and journal publisher is ready to move smoothly into selling you CD-ROMs or online services. If you register—It's easy! It's free!—you can sample online magazines like *The Computer Journal*, *Nucleic Acids Research*, and *Postmodern Culture* (which features a virtual reality facility with "asynchronous discussions"). For an engaging look into the making of the "Oxford English Dictionary," don't miss the *OED Newsletter*, which discusses the origin of words like "kinkily" and "libidinally." That kinky bit notwithstanding, the site tends to be a little stuffy. But it's an essential stopover for the bibliophile.

Real Estate Straight

http://www.baynet.com/inman/
Shopping

With acres and acres of real estate questions, answers, news, and reference materials (even a few funnies), Real Estate Straight is a real motherlode of info. Brought to you by Inman News Features, a California-based real estate journalism venture, this remarkable site covers topics from permits and zoning to the legal ramifications of a neighbor who won't part with a pet pot-bellied pig. The Q&A Library includes more than 10,000 real estate questions from consumers ("How is the price set?" "How does a seller get rid of a house that has been on the market for six months?"), broken down into clear categories and subcategories. Sales pressure here is surprisingly low (considering the business), while the information comes in a freeflow. It's simply an excellent source for buyers, sellers, and agents.

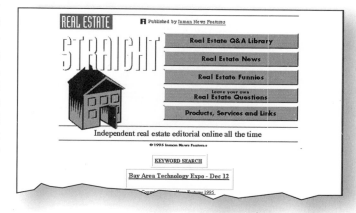

Sam's Wine Warehouse

http://www.ravenna.com/sams

Shopping

Sam's Wine Warehouse, Chicago's top wine merchant, has extended its storefront to the Web, where it delivers a bubbly temptation to online connoisseurs of hooch. And it might just be the best service since the drive-thru daiquiri stands in Louisiana closed down. Sam's offers the full complement of spirits, from Vielle #5 Louis Phillippe 1840 Vintage cognac ($5,800 per bottle, thank you very much) to Monopolowa Potato Vodka ($12.99). And hey, you can't put cognac in a screwdriver. The site also includes "tasting notes from the best wine minds in the industry" (Sam's staff, who else?). Click "Spanish and Chilean Wines" and get a nice price spread of summery selections. The site also offers links to "A Napa Valley Virtual Visit" and "The Making of Single Malt Whiskey." Order online, by phone or fax. Cheers!

Ticketmaster Online

http://www.ticketmaster.com:80/

Shopping

You won't hear Pearl Jam singing the praises of this ticket-selling giant, but those who don't mind attending events in its shadow may find this promotional site helpful. (It's another slick production from Starwave Corporation, which like Ticketmaster is partly owned by Paul Allen.) Rock groupies and theater people can peruse "onsale" tickets across the country here (Thrill Kill Kult in Phoenix! *Fiddler on the Roof* in Buffalo!). The weekly "Tipsheet" dishes up gossip and celebrity news (Liz Taylor on Michael Jackson: "I think he's like litmus paper"), and fills visitors in on the previous week's top-grossing concert acts. As of our last visit, you still couldn't order tickets here online—but surely that's just a matter of time. Besides, what fun is it camping out in front of your own computer, waiting for tickets to go on sale?

Upscale Wholesale Page

http://www.upscale.com
Shopping

Upscale Wholesale is the name; cool, hard-to-find (even hard-to-imagine) gear is the game. Specialty and fun are top priorities at this virtual storefront, where prices are supposed to be 20 to 30 percent lower than they would be on retail tags—provided you could even find some of these gadgets. Affordable night vision equipment and audio/video surveillance goodies reflect a military inclination, but animal lovers could go for the Australian chew-proof trampoline dog bed. Channel-surfers with an itchy trigger finger should appreciate the "Gunvertor," a handgun-shaped remote control. And what kind of motorist could resist at least taking a peek at Granny's featured auto product? When you're done shopping, stop by the upscale offering of funky links, which run from supermodels to Al Gore.

Virginia Diner

http://www.infi.net/vadiner/index.html
Shopping

Virginia (put your hand on your heart when you say it) reigns as peanut capital of the world—at least according to the Virginia Diner of Wakefield. Its goober-filled menu makes this site a natural Web shopping outlet for the popular Virginia variety, which (we discover) is larger than other peanuts. (And did you know the average American eats 12 pounds of peanuts per year?) Copy the recipe for southern peanut pie, or mail-order raw peanuts and learn how to roast 'em yourself. Amid all the reasons to "break out the nuts," the diner also offers ham smoked and cured in a process "developed by Indian tribes over three centuries ago," and two-pound bags of hushpuppy mix to go with it. It's a friendly, straightforward page, and ordering is a snap.

White Rabbit Toys

http://www.toystore.com/

Shopping

This Ann Arbor toy store looks like a kindergarten classroom, but claims to be on the Web, in part, so that those leaving the University of Michigan can keep in

touch. The White Rabbit's pride-and-joy is its selection of hard-to-find toys from companies like Sweden's Brio (cranes, cars, tunnels, and towns), Germany's Ravensburger ("spend a rewarding evening with a game that intrigues all family members"), and, from the U.S., Primetime Playthings ("created by a team of child psychologists..."). The spirit of the store is best captured on the staff page, with its childhood pictures of store employees ("Ever since 1991, Jo Ann has wanted to own a toy store. Her wish came true in 1992."). The site itself is nothing spectacular, but we have to admit that it *does* seem like a fun store.

A World of Tea

http://www.teleport.com/~tea/

Shopping

Steep a mellow bag of chamomile and settle in here for tales and trivia from the fascinating world of tea. Brought to you by the Stash Tea Company, an

Oregon-based mail-order firm, this surprisingly entertaining sales site spins in some tea history ("Three great Zen priests restored tea to its original place in Japanese society") and news ("Animal studies suggest tea is a cancer-preventing agent"). Stash's online catalog makes it easy to order teas, gift packs, kettles, and mugs. Basically, you'll find everything here but the tea party, including tea quotes. "There is a subtle charm in the taste of tea which makes it irresistible," said Kakuzo Okakura in 1906. "It has not the arrogance of wine, the self-consciousness of coffee, nor the simpering innocence of cocoa."

Weird and Wonderful

Weird and Wonderful

Weird and Wonderful is a favorite category around the Point offices (where it's also known as "the road less traveled"). If there are two people in the world who believe that George Washington was secretly from Venus, they can find each other on the Web and start their own society. And depending on how much time they want to put into their home page, they can even make it seem pretty plausible. (Remember those strange wooden teeth? And the powdered wig? What was he hiding?) To be fair, many of the pages in this chapter are done by serious, levelheaded people. There are important topics discussed, such as spirituality and freedom of information and death. There are also some terrific pages here done by colorful kooks. You'll have to decide for yourself which is which.

The Alberta UFO Research Association

`http://ume.med.ucalgary.ca/~watanabe/ufo.html`

Weird and Wonderful

This site from the Canadian UFO research group, the centerpiece of which is the AUFORA *Journal*, not only details UFO sightings from around the world (and you can report yours here with a handy form), but also tries to follow up on the sightings with international government agencies. The regularly updated "News" section reports on unusual sightings and occurrences across the globe: UFOs, crop circles, and even the more puzzling recent cat mutilations in British Columbia (cleanly severed, exsanguinated half-cats, "hauntingly similar" to 1970's cattle mutilations). The *Journal* is skeptic-friendly, and it's clear that AUFORA is serious in its attempt to gain respect worldwide, making full use of the Web to gather and distribute information on this increasingly *mainstream* topic.

Alcor Foundation

`http://www.webcom.com/~alcor/`

Weird and Wonderful

"Cryonics is the ultra-low-temperature preservation of terminally-ill patients, as soon as possible after legal death." The goal of cryonics is to keep you in the back of the freezer (behind the strawberry jam, perhaps) until medical technology has advanced to a point where they can fix whatever killed you. But let's not be too flippant, because this page has lots of really fascinating info on molecular repair of the brain via nanotechnology and reversible logic (the body may be dead, but the *information* isn't necessarily gone), cryonics and overpopulation, Deism, and even cryo-humor. Most of the information comes from offsite links, but Alcor will freeze you (they currently have 28 patients in suspension) for just over $100,000. (You can pay it affordably with a life insurance policy listing Alcor as the beneficiary.) Interestingly creepy.

Angelnet

http://alive.mcn.org:80/angelnet.html/

Weird and Wonderful

Celestial souls will want to hover over this page of cherub chat, spiritually hosted by the cleverly-titled EcoCre8ive Community. Seraphs can visit an Angelic Virtual Altar to "rub" a magic lamp, breathe deeply, and express hope for world peace (or at least a faster modem connection). Embark on "an alchemical interactive journey" in the labyrinth of the Secret Mystery, where discovering the lost treasure of Atlantis could result in some heavenly prizes. Scribes can share their angelic encounters online or add canonical wit to the "world's largest cyberactive poem." And whether you're swimming with the dolphins, flying with angels, or exploring the work of "self-taught, left-handed soul inspired musician" Scott Huckabay, keep headphones handy at all times for out-of-this-world aural activity. Stellar animation and clever interactivity.

Astral Projection Home Page

http://www.lava.net/~goodin/astral.html

Weird and Wonderful

Enter this page and you may find yourself floating in the ethereal abyss, only to look down and discover... yourself! That's astral projection (or "OOBE," an out-of-body experience), detailed and resourced nicely here by host Charles C. Goodin. Nebular surfers can fly through newsgroups and links galore, like the Altered States of Consciousness home page or "A Discussion of Psychic Powers and How to Develop Them." "Ask Robert Bruce" invites queries on lucid dreaming and astral planing; once you're armed (or winged) with info, glide over to "Joe's Garage" for some meditation and relaxation techniques. Voyagers, don't forget to pick up your Astral Projection Tips of the Month.

Aunt Agatha's Occult Emporium

http://www.direct.ca/Graphics/agatha/
Weird and Wonderful

Everything for the pagan ritualist can be found in Aunt Agatha's online cupboard. A panoply of Voodoo dolls, gargoyles, and conjure kits (honest!) await the shaman or witch with the virtual touch—simply complete the order form and a Zodiac talisman could be winging its way to you in no time! Literary sorcerers may want to submit a whimsical spell or two to Auntie's Newsletter—consider the "Chocolate Ritual" (provided by Hoo-Chuan Tan of Ontario), which assures that "Chocolate sprinkles where thou art cast/No calories in thy presence last." (Pagans like chocolate, too?) And the "Uncle Fynyx Rage Page" serves up thoughts on the origins of crop circles: "Those highly defined, articulated shapes? Ball lightning? I don't think so."

The Burning Man Project

http://www.well.com/user/burnman/index.html
Weird and Wonderful

Since 1990, the northern Nevada desert has been the site of "The Burning Man Project," a wild festival of perhaps mystical, certainly spontaneous, audience participation. Seventy-two hours of pyro-technics, trance-dancing, drumming, bocce ball or... whatever! Towering over the party is the 40-foot Burning Man, fiery inspiration for what seems to be a M*A*S*H unit of Deadheads with gunpowder. Photos and video clips help show the fun (they really do!), and there are plenty of tips on how to party in the desert (hint: bring water), so that you can avoid being the annual winner of the "Donner Award" for gross stupidity.

©Tyree Lynch

The Burning Man Festival 1995

Now in its tenth year, **Burning Man** is a unique annual celebration held in the high desert wilderness of Northern Nevada. Over the course of a long weekend, a temporary community is established on the largest flat expanse of land in North America, a small city complete with its own radio stations, daily newspaper, community centers and civic monuments. Three days of art, music, dance, and performance climax in the ritual destruction by fire of a four-story human effigy known as the Burning Man. Next year's festival will take place over Labor Day weekend, August 29th - September 2nd, 1996, and is expected to draw 4,000 participants.

Contact Information
    Check it out if you're interested in attending next year, if you have anything to contribute to this site, or if you maintain a site of your own that includes Burning Man-related material.

Jonathan Cainer's Daily Horoscopes

http://www.realitycom.com/webstars/index.html

Weird and Wonderful

This page looks great, it's highly entertaining, and it covers all the signs. Direct from London's *Daily Mail*, columnist Jonathan Cainer pronounces the weekly forecast in either text or RealAudio. (And doesn't everyone want an astrologer with a British accent?) Cainer had us scrambling to harness our creative Venusian potential for the week with his enthusiastic cheerleader's style: "It'll be a great week, no doubt about that." And of course, for a fee he'll send you a personalized Year-Ahead Horoscope. A relatively new development is Astro-Chat, a bulletin board system where you can chat with other like-minded individuals, or find a good astrologer to draw up a personal chart for you.

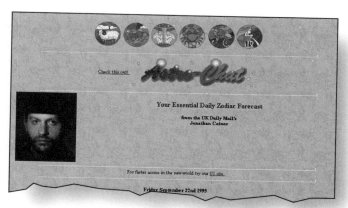

COGWEB—The Covenant of the Goddess

http://www.cog.org/cog/

Weird and Wonderful

This page is home to international Wiccan congregations and sole practitioners around the globe. Wicca, an offshoot of Neo-Paganism, claims to be one of the fastest growing religions in the U.S., and the discussions here of witchcraft as a "life-affirming... nature-oriented religion" run contrary to the cauldron-boiling, spell-casting bunch traditionally thought of at Halloween. ("Most Witches consider their practice a priest/esshood," the authors say.) Anyone worried about catching a hex should consider COG's Code of Ethics, which states, "An ye harm none, do as ye will." (Translation: no harm, no foul.)

Those intrigued by the practice can study criteria for forming a coven and applying for membership with the National Council. It's different, all right, but it's engrossing reading.

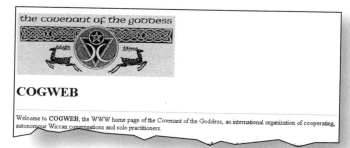

The Conspiracy Pages

http://ROCK.SAN.UC.EDU/~TAYLORRM/index.html
Weird and Wonderful

Now it can be told: Wyatt Earp and Doc Holliday were stagecoach robbers who set up the OK Corral to bump off "those who could make a case against them." That's no surprise at this index, where there's always a hidden plot just around the coroner. Conspiracy's greatest hits are here, from JFK to UFOs, from mind control to Masons, from John Birchers to Iran-Contra, all presented in appetizer-sample quotes from a variety of sources. Choose between the "intimate and furtive relationship" between Gerry Ford (*Mr.* Warren Commission) and the F.B.I., or the same between Bill Clinton and anything in a skirt. It's truly hard to tell if Robert Taylor, the page's linkmeister, is paying campy tribute to single-bullet theorists or if he is one himself. Whichever, it's a lot of fun.

Cosmic Connections

http://www.primenet.com/~cosmic/
Weird and Wonderful

Cosmic travelers can hitch a Web ride from this far-out dock, which probes out-of-body-experiences (OOBEs), UFOs, Merkabahs, and hosts (no pun intended)

of other altered realities. At last, a sign that the New Age movement has a sense of humor, or in proper terminology, "playful energy." (On our last visit, the opening message read: "Please pardon our mess... We're in the middle of a PARADIGM SHIFT!") If those mysterious crop circles have been bugging you (and you *know* they bug the farmers), find out why Sharon Warren calls them "galactic calling cards." You can also accelerate your consciousness using "Mind Gymnasticks"—if you order the tapes (the site is packed with promos for tapes and seminars). Well, as true UFO believers say here, "ships happen."

Dead Pool 1995

http://www.pitt.edu/~jwast8/Deadpool.html

Weird and Wonderful

The Dead Pool is a morbidly amusing contest to see who can most accurately guess which celebrities will pass on in the coming year. Each participant picks 10 candidates, folks they think just won't make it for whatever reason. Some of the choices are obvious: Milton Berle, Abe Vigoda, and other guys you thought were already dead. Some surprises keep it sporting, however: one daring past choice was TV's Olsen Twins ("must be both—no half-points awarded"). Cheating is strictly prohibited: the rules state that "the participant may in no way affect the demise of a person." Some may find this distasteful (especially those who make the list), but others will find themselves checking up every time a celebrity passes away.

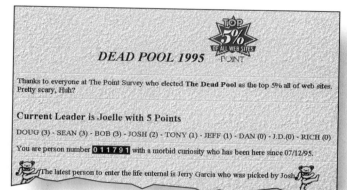

DEAD POOL 1995 TOP 5% OF ALL WEB SITES POINT

Thanks to everyone at The Point Survey who elected **The Dead Pool** as the top 5% all of web sites. Pretty scary, Huh?

Current Leader is Joelle with 5 Points

DOUG (3) - SEAN (3) - BOB (3) - JOSH (2) - TONY (1) - JEFF (1) - DAN (0) - J.D.(0) - RICH (0)

You are person number `011791` with a morbid curiosity who has been here since 07/12/95.

The latest person to enter the life enternal is Jerry Garcia who was picked by Josh.

DeathNet

http://www.IslandNet.com:80/~deathnet/

Weird and Wonderful

The Right to Die Society of Canada doesn't mince words on its titles, does it? Here they offer a virtual library of resources on human mortality. Asserting its respect "for every point of view," the society has assembled an impressive collection of info on its chosen topic: articles like "Then it was Birth Control, Now it's Euthanasia," a complete toxicology and poisons database from the University of Singapore, or the official transcripts from Canada's Senate Special Committee on Euthanasia and Assisted Suicide. It's not *all* doom and gloom, however—there's some mild whimsy here, like an audio clip of a bell tolling. Overall, it's an exhaustive look at the Last Roundup.

DeathNET: an international archive specializing in all aspects of death and dying -- with a sincere respect for every point of view.

DeathNET is the result of hundreds of hours of volunteer work, gathering together a wide range of materials related to the legal, moral, medical, historical and cultural aspects of human mortality. Most of these materials are not readily available from any other source on or off the Internet. Constructive comments are welcome.

September 23, 1995: What's NEW on DeathNET?

All About DeathNET

Earth Portals

`http://alive.mcn.org:80/earthportals/`

Weird and Wonderful

Transcend your earthly moorings to pass through these portals of spiritual cosmology in search of "tools and ideas... intended to enlighten our collective human condition." Your host, Willard (who sounds as if he's talking from a very deep well), welcomes you to a journey "through all the various metaphors of consciousness." You begin with "Music From the Galaxies," make a stop for a Zen reading, and wind up with a list of eco-conscious links (EnviroLink, the Whole Earth Catalog). One of the catchiest stops is Willard's Portal Ether Ship, a mock spacecraft the author built in 1972 following a close encounter on a Minnesota country road (true story!). Willard also invites you to shop the Portal Market, where products embodying "Gaia consciousness" are a reminder that "we are all cosmically endowed links in the Great Chain of Being."

Earth Portal Controls

Welcome to Earth Portal Controls

Below are four control buttons which will bring you to new transformational products, new locations on the Internet which deal with making the Earth a better place on which to live, people who are offering new ideas about how to understand our place in the universe, and flights of the imagination. Each of these areas will grow and change as we approach the turn of the century, so make a note to periodically pay a visit, and see the many new additions to these Earth Portals.

| The Portal Market | The Portal Net |
| Portal Messenger | Portal Ether Ship |

——— Return to Earth Portals

Electric Italy

`http://www.nettuno.it/electric-italy/`

Weird and Wonderful

Sub-dubbed "Inspiration, Omens, and Tools for the 21st Century," this server is positively beefy with New Age healing pointers to Systemic Shiatsu, Postural Integration, and Character Analytic Vegeto-Therapy. Based in Praiano, Italy, the page also serves up some odd accompaniments to its holistic fare: a link to *Ciao Manhattan*, an Italian high fashion catalog; a guide to metropolitan Rome; and restricted access to "The House of Erotic Art" for Electric Italy Club members aged 21 and over (membership details and prices are provided, of course). The "Dumb's Guide to Psychoanalysis" adds yet another dimension to this eclectic page. The title "Electric" Italy could mean almost anything... and apparently does. Unless you're in Italy yourself, expect the graphics-heavy front page to take a while getting to you.

The Electronic Chronicles

http://www.awa.com/artnetweb/projects/ahneed/first.html

Weird and Wonderful

This futuristic spoof from "The Casaba Melon Institute," in collaboration with "Dr. Eleanor Musing and her team of cognicians," presents *The Electronic Chronicles*, news of the past from an undisclosed point in the future. Welcome to a world where electronic technology is replacing the "communicative invention called language" and where The Newsetta Stone, found at the Twin Lions Excavation site (discovered in 5486 Lapsumatera), reveals a civilization obsessed with microwaves and point and shoot cameras. Considering The Newsetta Stone is a page ripped from an electronics store ad, this might also be considered a spoof on historians who compile "complete" pictures from limited data (it's difficult to get through all the levels of parody here, occasionally). Extremely witty, often obscure, this is a cynic's dream come true.

Esther and Son Daily Astrological Currents

http://www.teleport.com/~esson/

Weird and Wonderful

This one-size-fits-all astrology page (from a mother-son team in Portland, Oregon) offers a daily forecast based not on individual Zodiac signs, but on where the sun is positioned in relation to planet Earth. No muss, no fuss, no need to call mom for your exact time of birth. Think of it as an astrological weather forecast—it announces the directions life in general is supposed to be heading, rather than portents for each specific sign. Believers can find out when to "send signals wildly into the atmosphere," and when to lay low, and then pass this universal advice on to friends and business associates. (Or not.) You can have the daily Currents report sent to you automatically via e-mail, or even via postal mail. Or you can pay extra for the full treatment.

Astrological Services

Welcome to Esther and Son's Astrology on the World Wide Web.

Euthanasia World Directory

http://www.efn.org/~ergo/
Weird and Wonderful

Sponsored by the Euthanasia Research & Guidance Organization (ERGO), this is an extensive worldwide reference list for right-to-die issues and advocacy groups.

Iron-age burial stones in Cornwall, England

Euthanasia World Directory

Compiled by Euthanasia Research & Guidance Organization (ERGO!)
ergo@efn.org
Home Page http://www.efn.org/~ergo

1. List of 36 <u>organizations</u> which are members of the <u>World Federation of Right to Die Societies</u>.

Emphasis is given to U.S.-based organizations in the form of philosophical stances and recent accomplishments, but contact information and the like is provided for groups worldwide. Cemetery surfers can access the full text of the Oregon Death With Dignity Act or browse the shelves of ERGO's online bookstore to order titles like "Final Exit: The Practicalities of Self-Deliverance and Assisted Suicide for the Dying." A lengthy biography of Hemlock Society's Derek Humphrey, founder of ERGO, is also included, including a bit on how he became involved in this business: he assisted his first wife's suicide in 1975. It's a sobering, and sincere, resource.

The Extraterrestrial Biological Entities Page

http://sloop.ee.fit.edu/users/lpinto/index.html
Weird and Wonderful

This sharp page on UFO subjects covers the major "events" with an appropriate degree of skepticism. Extraterrestrial Biological Entities (you know, EBEs) used to be called simply "aliens." Although coverage of classics like Area 51 and Groom Lake sightings is standard, autopsy photos of the famous Roswell EBE (New Mexico, 1947) are offered here without comment, and a good chunk of this page is devoted to abduction stories, some of them de-bunked. This page is a good catch-all for UFOs or EBEs, well-organized and with plenty of images of those "big, friendly eyes" and, of course, saucer shapes. Buried little gems here include "UFO trivia" (10,000 reports worldwide in 1990, and January is their busy season, it seems), and the full text of CFR 1211, the federal regulation that gives NASA authority to quarantine anyone having extraterrestrial contact.

Fatima Home Page

http://www.cais.com/npacheco/fatima/fatima.html

Weird and Wonderful

In 1915, in a little village about 70 miles north of Lisbon, Portugal, three children sat down in the fields to pray the rosary and saw an angel. Two years later, on the same ground, they spotted an apparition of the Virgin Mary. So begins the story of the Miracle of Fatima, outlined in precise detail on this page from the same people who brought you The Shroud of Turin page. An abridged eyewitness account of the "Miracle of the Sun" recounts the October, 1917 day when some 70,000 people reported seeing a "pulsating sun" that "spun around on itself in a mad whirl," then seemed to dive from the sky. Believe it or don't, it's a beguiling tale. Link to a wealth of other Fatima and Catholic resources.

Fortean Times

http://alpha.mic.dundee.ac.uk/ft/ft.cgi?-1,ft

Weird and Wonderful

Freak shows on the Net don't get much better than this. Charles Fort (1874-1932) was a New York writer, pal to Theodore Dreiser and "iconoclastic philosopher." That means he liked weird stuff, and didn't accept common scientific explanations for strange phenomena such as raining fish and the like. The "Journal" follows this Fortean attitude with a collection of weird photos and stories, but doesn't act as an advocate. In fact, they openly question the veracity of some of the photos, but that didn't keep us from enjoying the others, such as "Chicken Love Tragedy" or "Cleric with Fish." If you have the time and inclination, watch the movie of the exploding whale (with this odd commentary: "KABOOOOOM Splut Splut Splut"). Just another day at the beach!

FringeWare, Inc.

http://www.fringeware.com/

Weird and Wonderful

FringeWare is a group of high-tech "fringe" entrepreneurs who compile, synthesize, and peddle twisted products

and weird ideas. Need a set of Bondage Pig Earrings for that special someone? If these are too flashy, try the Wicked Hand Dangle Pendant. Cover that unsightly prom night pimple with the "life size" *Alien* Face Hugger Kit. Distributing weird ideas naturally translates into their online e-zine, *TAZMEDIA*, a grade-A work covering weirdness ranging from JFK to OKC. Catch also the text on Applied Memetics ("Memetics is to media as genetics is to biology"), which shows they're truly on the fringe—they know where Power lies and what tactics are required to get it. An inspiring link for those skirting the edge; a survival manual for those already over.

50 Greatest Conspiracies of All Time

http://www.webcom.com:80/~conspire/

Weird and Wonderful

At last: an online 'zine that shows just how entertaining conspiracy theories can be! This page is kind of a Noam Chomsky-David Letterman hybrid: the authors provide the grain (sometimes chunk) of salt required to digest some

mighty wacky theories—without calling anyone a liar (exactly). Hardcore fans of conspiracies can still get their JFK-UFO-Vince Foster fix here—they don't mess with tradition, and the layout is slick enough to have come from a CIA photo lab! The true spirit of 50GCAT, however, lies in Lyndon LaRouch explaining why British intelligence "grew" the Grateful Dead out of mind control experiments, and stories like "Jonestown: Population Zero," complete with Mr. Kool-Aid icon (sensitive types beware!). Every month new features are "brought to light" with an irreverent, cynical, and funny edge at this glossy site.

The Gaia Page

http://www.maui.net/~team/gaiapage.html

Weird and Wonderful

"Consciousness is universal and fractal; the universe is fractal and conscious." If this doesn't *quite* answer everything you wanted to know about the world, consider the Gaian Hypothesis. This page from the Maui Institute ("Vortex of the Pacific Century") asserts that the Earth is a giant, self-sustaining organism and that humans have started mucking it up just a little too much. Humans, the theory goes, have contributed to the growing hole in the ozone layer, the depletion of natural resources, and increasing levels of water toxicity. But it's not too late to reverse the process: practical solutions include recycling and being a "greenhouse gas miser" at home (with great tips on how to do that). Sometimes convoluted, this site is never dull, and gets high marks for its sound ecology pages.

... Rated as one of the Top 5% by Point ...

...The Gaia Page ...

Hastings UFO Society

http://www.santarosa.edu/hufos/

Weird and Wonderful

Flash! "Possible UFO Abductee assaults Rural Deputy with her Bosoms!" (The distinctive gray color of the deputy's uniform was consistent with alien skin color; who knew?). Following in the footsteps of the Firesign Theater, these students from Hastings College will peddle no hoax before its time. The time has come for this all-audio probe into the unidentified realms of the universe. Saucer fans can plug into Psychic CB Channel 22 for the latest bulletins on possible alien births (followed by a cover-up in Albania), or tips on avoiding impact with the Giant Space Blob, "the fastest moving bulk of matter ever detected in the galaxy." No, that's *not* another Orson Welles reference. You may be downloading for hours, but where else can you hear "The Mystery of Blackie the Chicken"?

Idea Futures

http://if.arc.ab.ca/IF.shtml
Weird and Wonderful

Just like a regular "futures" market, this one bets on ideas. Think the Amiga computer system will be out of business by 1997? Put your money (not real, of course) where your mouth is. Computer types trade ideas online and bet on their outcome. It's sort of like those stock market exercises you did in 10th grade, but a lot more fun, because you get to submit your own ideas for trading, and hit the full range of human experience: past topics have included whether North and South Korea would unify, and whether Michael Jackson and Lisa Marie Presley would get a divorce (trading was pretty heavy on this one). To be a member, you have to subscribe to at least one e-mail list, but it's worth it if this is your bag. Just remember: it's not real money.

Impropaganda

http://www.impropaganda.com/~street/detour/yo.html
Weird and Wonderful

Impropaganda has some gems on the alleged secret organization, the Illuminati, the main course in this meal for conspiracy theorists. For the uninitiated, a "Cliff Notes-style" outline of Illuminati history describes significant events, from the origins of Atlantis on up to the Watergate scandal. To learn more about this supposed secret sect, enter Chapel Perilous and check your paradigm at the gate. Co-founder of Discordianism Kerry W. Thornley ("I determined... that when I grew up I was going to be a crackpot"), whose book "Zenarchy" is online here ("don't leave *OM* without it"), also owns the corner on "Kutcha," a soapbox for ranting about the government in the name of Art. We admit it—this stuff is entertaining in an anachronistically charming way, and it proves that the Web is the best thing to happen to the world of counterculture since tie-dyed shirts.

Institute for the Study of Contact with Non-Human Intelligence

http://www.catalog.com/cgibin/var/denniso/index.html

Weird and Wonderful

This groupis determined to "bring you the most up-to-date and reliable information on all aspects of human contact with other intelligent life." Followers of the Whitley Strieber "abduction" case can read his adamant denials of epilepsy as the cause of his experiences, or ponder the authenticity of the "Roswell Film." ISCNI doesn't limit itself: the focus is "non-human intelligence," and this includes apes, dolphins, computers, and even angels. As told here, more people have had encounters with angels (or "divas") than have even *seen* a UFO. Without discussing the nature of angels, who seem to be a darn-sight more helpful than space bugs, ISCNI retells a few fascinating encounters. Our favorite was of Dorothy MacLean, who got some life-saving gardening advice from the diva of sweetpeas.

The Kooks Museum

http://www.teleport.com/~dkossy/

Weird and Wonderful

Can the book be as fun as this museum? Kooks are respected as sincere weirdos in this splashy tribute, whether it's because they are just plain mental, or because they have PROOF that Jimmy Carter is Bill Clinton's biological father. With graphics that are slightly disturbing in their own right, we are directed to several of the Museum's wings: in the Hall of Hate hang the details of the Society to Cut Up Men (yes, that's "SCUM"); in the Schizophrenic Wing you'll hear voices like that of Dan "Am I Insane?" Ashwander. Elsewhere you'll learn about goat gland science, the demons of rock music, salvation by spaceship, and even scientific proof that Satan created dinosaurs just to irk God. Lovely to look at, delightful to know, and absolutely chubby with weird stuff.

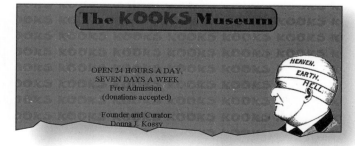

Magic Show

http://www.uelectric.com/magicshow.html

Weird and Wonderful

It's what it says—a virtual magic show, with plenty of tips and revelations for wannabe David Copperfields. Consider the all-important card throw, which has been a simple, yet effective display of dexterity for

over 150 years—five articles from master magicians describe the most effective methods here. There's also a Q&A page where Mister Magic (who "sees all, hears all, can riffle shuffle with the best of them, and does a mean triple lift") fields questions about the best way to incorporate a snake into one's act. The real treat here is a rare digital animation of the great Valadon, made from a series of 1902 photos (though the hand is quicker than the modem on this download). The page is sponsored by Robinson Wizard, makers of the computerized conjuring apparati like "The Sponge Ball King's Cups & Balls," which are for sale here.

Magical Blend

http://www.eden.com/~magical/

Weird and Wonderful

A virtual companion to the popular New Age magazine of the same name, Magical Blend ("the cutting edge in world transformations") covers dream

psychology, alternative healing, deep ecology, and even world music. Shamanism and "new" vision tend to inform the publication, which also serves up interviews with Timothy Leary and the late Jerry Garcia (*before* he was late; just in case you were wondering). Full text articles from current and past issues explore the controversial work of Carlos Casteneda, and a suggestion that time can be "mapped" using the ordering of Tarot card trigrams and hexagrams as a model. The colorful graphics will appeal to both magical and prosaic types.

Mensa Home Page

http://www.intac.com/~mensa/faq/index.html

Weird and Wonderful

Mensa, the international high-IQ club, has a home page geared toward both current and prospective members. (To join, you've got to score in the top two percent of the population on a standardized intelligence test.) Opportunities for mingling with other Mensans include onsite personal ads and notices of upcoming genius-type gatherings (maybe you'll meet Marilyn Vos Savant or Geena Davis, two famous Mensa members). The page also links to some special interest groups (SIGs) started for or by Mensa members, including a glossopoeic SIG for the discussion of invented languages (what other kinds are there?) and a practical-joke SIG that posts in-joke signs like the one for "Schroedinger's Cat-Sitting Service" at Mensa conventions. You'll find a few Mensa personal ads, too. Beyond that, this no-frills site is strictly business.

Motherheart

http://www.afn.org/~mother

Weird and Wonderful

This resource, which "encourages nurturing in all aspects of life," is a massive index to Internet sites dealing with community, health, wholeness, spirituality, and more. Visitors can search for their ideal co-op in the Intentional Communities Database; on our last visit, we found a pointer to Dancing Rabbit, a Berkeley, California co-op that hopes to eventually form its own self-sustaining town. If you're a fledgling clairvoyant, harness that spiritual energy with a quick lesson in channeling and learn to ground and clear chakras (it has nothing to do with that back 40 we've been meaning to plow). Expectant parents can link to an online "birth center" for info on midwifery and healthy birthing, or try the Alternative Medicine Home Page for advice on "unconventional, unorthodox, unproven... alternative, complementary, innovative, integrative therapies" for a winter cold.

Motherheart is a resource that encourages nurturing in all aspects of life. There is no limit set for the ways in which Motherheart can achieve this and we welcome suggestions as to ideas, networkers in allied fields and Home Page or Gopher links to include here. Currently, Motherheart enjoys - but not necessarily endorses - these resources:

Community
Real Life
Spirituality
Birth, Children and Parenting
Care Giving
Health and Wholeness
Caring for Gaia

Museo de las Momias

`http://www.sirius.com/~dbh/momias.html`
Weird and Wonderful

This "Mummy Museum" from Guanajuato, Mexico, the birthplace of muralist Diego Rivera, celebrates the town's unusual practice of digging up its buried citizenry for display in the local museum. If you're buried in the cemetery in Guanajuato, your descendants have to pay fees for the upkeep of your burial plot. As the story is told here, if they can't pay up, out you come. While the practice may seem morbid to some, the Mexican fascination with the afterlife and the traditional fiestas of "El Dia de Los Muertos" ("Day of the Dead") are part of the culture. Pictures of selected bodies are here for browsing—though not gory, they're probably not for the squeamish. And perhaps we understand Rivera's work just a little better now.

The New Age Web Works

`http://www.newageinfo.com/`
Weird and Wonderful

More than 450 links to New Age-related resources give this page from California (where else?) a warm inner glow. The services index can help you

organize that next big drumming circle, or arrange for a little transformational travel. Or, tune in to Lisa Theil's goddess music and join the Pagan Poets Circle to read the latest musings on "Man's Milk." (Don't ask.) On the lighter side, you can explore the power of chaos with a tarot reading and learn how Larry, Moe, and Curly have contributed to your good fortune today. Find out where the 32nd Annual National UFO Conference is being held, and leave your calendar open for the Crone Oracles Workshop. Druidism, astrology, magic spelled with a "k"—it's all cheerfully presented here.

The Paul Is Dead Story

http://catless.ncl.ac.uk/Obituary/paul.html
Weird and Wonderful

Paul McCartney is really alive and well, but there was a time when Beatlemaniacs were convinced he was secretly as dead as a doornail. This page recaps all the incredibly meticulous evidence, from the play-it-backward brouhaha over "I'm So Tired" to Paul's mysterious barefoot appearance on the cover of *Abbey Road*. This site is simply a long text file, and (appropriately) is based on the faulty memory of someone who heard the rumors a long time ago (hey, good enough for us!). Nonetheless, the degree of sincerity is unmistakable: "Paul did indeed die, spiritually, as he was reborn in the ways of the Maharishi." Whatever! This is great fun for fans of pop hysteria, and for those who feel Paul *really* died when he recorded "Ebony and Ivory."

Psychedelic Tabby Cabal

http://www.paranoia.com:80/~fraterk/index.html
Weird and Wonderful

Whispering an invocation to "Goddess Chaos," this page is a guaranteed gateway to the realm of "fringe" ideas. What sets this apart from similar sites is its slick interface and the quality of the suggested sites. Links to like-minded sites are, in fact, the bulk of the page, but it's a very good, quick catch-all stop to feed your hunger for weirdness, whether it's Timothy Leary or Buckminster "Bucky" Fuller. Good collection of conspiracy links, too. The name is never really clearly explained; it's bound to attract a certain number of confused cat fanciers, but even they may dig the psychedelic graphics that are a signature here.

Shroud of Turin

`http://www.cais.com/npacheco/shroud/turin.html`

Weird and Wonderful

Whether you believe it's the actual burial cloth of Jesus, or just another chic headstone rubbing, there's no denying

The Shroud of Turin

Welcome to the Shroud of Turin Page

And he bought a linen shroud, and taking him down, wrapped him in the linen shroud, and laid him in a tomb which had been hewn out of the rock; and he rolled a stone against the door of the tomb. (Mark 15:46, RSV)

Learn about this fascinating Christian historical artifact, which may be the burial cloth of Christ. If this is so, then this is undoubtedly the most important relic in Christianity. If not, this is still one of the most fascinating items not only for Christianity, but for science as well

Last Updated: **13 June 1995**

For believers no amount of proof is necessary. For nonbelievers, no amount of proof is sufficient.

Whether you are a believer or a nonbeliever, the Shroud of Turin is not easily dismissed. In this page we will present some of the known facts about the Shroud, historical and scientific. We will let you be the judge of its authenticity.

the world's fascination with the Shroud of Turin. The Shroud's true origins are a mystery, and have been the subject of speculation for some time. At this unusual site, good photo reproductions let you get about as close to the Shroud as you ever will, while the excellent question-and-answer file reveals the cloth to be made of linen and just over 14 feet long. A discussion of the 1988 Carbon 14 dating test (which asserted that the Shroud's origin is medieval, not biblical) directly contradicts some researchers' findings that the cloth is a Mandylion relic. The final decision, as always, must be the viewer's.

Smitty's UFO Page

`http://www.best.com/~schmitz/ufo.html`

Weird and Wonderful

Dave "Smitty" Schmitz is a software engineer from San Francisco. He thinks the government is up to something

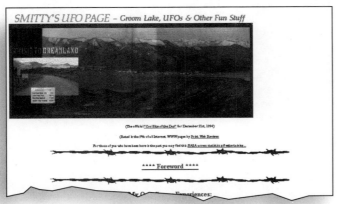

SMITTY'S UFO PAGE - *Groom Lake, UFOs & Other Fun Stuff*

ENTRANCE TO DREAMLAND

(The official "Cool Site of the Day" for December 21st, 1994)

(Rated in the 5% of all Internet WWW pages by Point Web Review)

For those of you who have been here in the past you may find this NASA screen statistics of interest a bit ...

**** Foreword ****

in the middle of the Nevada desert. There are rumors, in fact, that this is where the Air Force parks all the UFOs it has recovered and hidden from the public all these years. Do you think Smitty is crazy, or do you agree there's something out there? This site merely offers the stories—not as proof, but in an effort to engage others in the debate of what *should* be proof, if anything. Because of this approach, skeptics will probably enjoy this page as much as believers. Smitty's recaps of his two trips to the Nevada Test Site at Groom Lake are fun road adventures in search of *something*.

Sovereign's WWW Content Page

This really ought to be called the "Malcontent Page." Bring your axe and grind it here, or just watch others rant on about the ATF, AIDS, gun control, and all the other bad dogs that are threatening to wee on the carpet we call the Constitution. (That metaphor comes from the page's section "Conspiracy, Control and ??????".) This is for those who think the U.S. government is "out of control"—or rather, frighteningly *in* control. Their motto, "If you don't believe in something, you'll fall for anything" is fittingly murky in its meaning, but it sounds terrific. Unsurprisingly, "Sovereign" believes in honoring capitalism—check out the "Freedom Shop," where a measly ten bucks buys you proof that the limo driver shot JFK. This is a marvelously packaged bunch of pixilated notions.

Spirit-WWW

Spiritual seekers may well find they've hit the motherlode at this site, which is a virtual encyclopedia of strange phenomena and alternative realities. Selections available on this "personal, not-for-profit" home page include channeling, astrology, faith healing, meditation, and UFOs. The site points out that "the term alien or extraterrestrial shows our ignorance of the interconnectedness we live in." (At last, political correctness comes to the galaxy.) Thoughts on reincarnation ponder the meaning of karma and "How Past and Future are perceived and realized finally by the Soul." Contortionists will enjoy the Yoga page, which provides an overview of the different practices, including Karma, Bhakti, and Vedic movements. Plus New Age art, movies, audio clips, and more.

The Spot

The Spot is a fun sort of online soap about twentysomethings, supposedly emanating from a seven-bedroom beach house with an infamous history of wild partying and debauchery. Typical resident: Tara, a 23-year-old film student trying to make it as a director. Zany pet: Spotnik, a "Cyberian Husky." It's a "microcosm of a generation," so naturally there's always a party cooking! Visitors can read regular postings from the residents, see the snapshots ("Love on the Beach"), and read the

continued

The Spot
continued

diary entries ("Did Jeff realize I had missed my plane... the morning I found him in bed with Tomeiko?") It's pretty much like your own life, probably, but you may enjoy visiting anyway. This extremely glossy site is the brainchild of Fattal & Collins, a California advertising agency that is perhaps now deciding what to do with all the fans it has attracted.

Tarot Resources

http://www.iii.net/users/dtking/tarot.html
Weird and Wonderful

This extensive list of tarot resources will please expert readers and curious amateurs alike. Besides laying out the

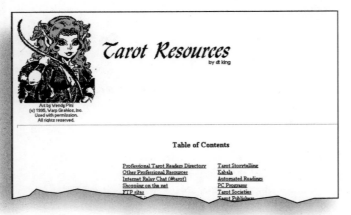

basics, the page offers a few tips on finding a professional reader: questions like "What deck do you use?" and "What is your basic approach?" may help you weed out those with which you won't be comfortable (assuming the answers will make sense to you in the first place). There are other, more obvious tips, like "don't bring your life savings with you." Seasoned pros may want to browse "Tapestry," an e-zine for forecasters. Among the more colorful links are the pictures of the Rider-Waite deck (a popular tarot deck style), and instructions for waxing your tarot cards when their coating gets worn down.

Taos Hum Homepage

http://www.eskimo.com:80/~billb/hum/hum.html
Weird and Wonderful

" The 'Taos Hum' is a low-pitched sound heard in several places across the U.S. and U.K.," earning its name from the many reports received in New Mexico beginning in 1991. It is usually heard only in quiet environments, and is described as sounding like a distant diesel engine (its common "signature"). "Since it has proven undetectable by microphones or VLF antennae, its source and nature is still a mystery." Wait, don't laugh! This quirky Web site isn't much to look at, but the blend of solid scientific inquiry and off-the-edge speculation is fascinating. Reports from "hummers" reveal as much of the mystery as they can (bio-iron in the brain tissue?), but it remains a big question mark. There are clippings from both the straight and the "unconventional" press, revealing a sincere effort to help those unfortunate few who "sense" the hum.

UFO Phenomena

http://zeta.cs.adfa.oz.au/Spirit/ufo.html

Weird and Wonderful

This is about as one-stop as it gets in the world of alien Web surfing. From info and discussion to pictures, this server from the Czech Republic has all its saucers covered. Earth-bound terrestrials seeking intimate contact can scope out the Pleiadians ("dimension travelers"), or investigate the more familiar Zeta Reticulis (the little gray hairless dudes with bug eyes).

Abductees will feel reassured by Budd Hopkins' controversial report on "Implants and Group Abductions," and visitors can splashdown with the Allagash Four (theirs was not a warm-n-cuddly ET tale). Many more cosmic particles and full online images will keep rocketeers happy for hours.

Vampyres Only

http://www.vampyre.wis.net/vampyre/index.html

Weird and Wonderful

Coming to you direct and undead from the Vorld Vide Veb... it's Vampyres Only. The entries here are alternately spooky and funny, and host Vlad III is given to puns likely to stick in your craw, such as "Thirsty for more? Here are links to similar veins of interest...." The hefty catalog of vampirobilia includes a collection of movie and sound files, from Orlok and Dracula to

Barnabus Collins (from TV's "Dark Shadows") and, of course, Lestat. A list of shops from around the world is helpful to those creatures of the night who feel the burning desire to...*accessorize*. The Vampire Vulnerability Test is a fang-in-cheek check of your Draculattractiveness. As they say back on the farm, this page puts the "ick" in slick.

Web-o-rhythm

http://www.qns.com/html/weborhythm/

Weird and Wonderful

Web-o-rhythm creates a swell full-color GIF of your personal bio-rhythm chart. You might remember biorhythm machines from amusement parks in the '70s: you put in a quarter, enter your birth date, enter the month for which you want your biorhythm, and it prints it out for you. Web-o-rhythm is essentially the same, but you save the quarter. The computed chart shows you

when you're supposed to be up and when you'll be down in the month to come. Biorhythm fans will notice the addition of a new cycle—intuitive—to the traditional three of mental, physical, and emotional. (Does Biorhythm Local 329 know about this?) As an added bonus, after your chart is computed, you're provided with a direct link to your horoscope at another site.

Whitewater & Vince Foster

http://www.cris.com/~dwheeler/n/whitewater/whitewater-index.html
Weird and Wonderful

The "extremely complex, tortuously convoluted" Whitewater investigation is the focus of this valiant attempt to get a handle on the most troublesome of the Bill Clinton scandals. The many alleged transgressions—Swiss bank accounts, drug trades, money laundering, murder, and of course, *cover-ups*—are divided here into categories of "Suspicious," "Shocking," and "Mindboggling." The most "mindboggling" we found was a series of allegations that Vince Foster "was being investigated as a traitorous spy working for Israel" and that his death was "'arranged' and 'necessary' for 'national security.'" It says here that "the small band who have accused the government of an elaborate cover-up in the Foster case can no longer be glibly dismissed as conspiracy theorists." Are you listening, Oliver Stone?

The World Wide Times

http://www.aloha.com/~k/
Weird and Wonderful

This is a beefy online news source for all UFO-related material. Sightings can be reported using the official Alberta UFO

Research Association form, or you can scan the experiences of others, ranging from brief sightings to abductions. The handy encyclopedia has entries for dozens of different types of space visitors, from Venusians to Railoids (does *that* spell "relief?"), and there's plenty of discussion about cover-ups, ominous tales of black helicopters, and those MIBs ("Men in Black"): are they supernatural/extraterrestrial visitors, or G-men in formal wear? Heaps of photos and other images flesh out the stories. Another fine resource for those who can't get enough of the UFO business.

Index

I

N

R

T

WANT MORE INFORMATION?

CHECK OUT THESE RELATED TOPICS OR SEE YOUR LOCAL BOOKSTORE

CAD

As the number one CAD publisher in the world, and as a Registered Publisher of Autodesk, New Riders Publishing provides unequaled content on this complex topic under the flagship *Inside AutoCAD*. Other titles include *AutoCAD for Beginners* and *New Riders' Reference Guide to AutoCAD Release 13*.

Networking

As the leading Novell NetWare publisher, New Riders Publishing delivers cutting-edge products for network professionals. We publish books for all levels of users, from those wanting to gain NetWare Certification, to those administering or installing a network. Leading books in this category include *Inside NetWare 3.12*, *Inside TCP/IP Second Edition, NetWare: The Professional Reference,* and *Managing the NetWare 3.x Server*.

Graphics and 3D Studio

New Riders provides readers with the most comprehensive product tutorials and references available for the graphics market. Best-sellers include *Inside Photoshop 3, 3D Studio IPAS Plug In Reference, KPT's Filters and Effects,* and *Inside 3D Studio*.

Internet and Communications

As one of the fastest growing publishers in the communications market, New Riders provides unparalleled information and detail on this ever-changing topic area. We publish international best-sellers such as *New Riders' Official Internet Yellow Pages, 2nd Edition*, a directory of over 10,000 listings of Internet sites and resources from around the world, as well as *VRML: Browsing and Building Cyberspace, Actually Useful Internet Security Techniques, Internet Firewalls and Network Security,* and *New Riders' Official World Wide Web Yellow Pages*.

Operating Systems

Expanding off our expertise in technical markets, and driven by the needs of the computing and business professional, New Riders offers comprehensive references for experienced and advanced users of today's most popular operating systems, including *Inside Windows 95, Inside Unix, Inside OS/2 Warp Version 3*, and *Building a Unix Internet Server*.

Orders/Customer Service **1-800-653-6156**   Source Code **NRP95**

New Riders Publishing   201 West 103rd Street ◆ Indianapolis, Indiana 46290 USA

REGISTRATION CARD

World Wide Web Top 1000

Name _____ Title _____

Company _____ Type of business _____

Address _____

City/State/ZIP _____

Have you used these types of books before? ☐ yes ☐ no

If yes, which ones? _____

_____

How many computer books do you purchase each year? ☐ 1–5 ☐ 6 or more

How did you learn about this book? _____

Where did you purchase this book? _____

Which applications do you currently use? _____

_____

Which computer magazines do you subscribe to? _____

_____

What trade shows do you attend? _____

_____

Comments: _____

_____

_____

Would you like to be placed on our preferred mailing list? ☐ yes ☐ no

☐ **I would like to see my name in print!** You may use my name and quote me in future New Riders products and promotions. My daytime phone number is: _____

New Riders Publishing 201 West 103rd Street ◆ Indianapolis, Indiana 46290 USA

x to `317-581-4670` Orders/Customer Service `1-800-653-6156` Source Code `NRP95`

Fold Here

- -

‖‖ ‖ ‖

BUSINESS REPLY MAIL

FIRST-CLASS MAIL PERMIT NO. 9918 INDIANAPOLIS IN

POSTAGE WILL BE PAID BY THE ADDRESSEE

NEW RIDERS PUBLISHING
201 W 103RD ST
INDIANAPOLIS IN 46290-9058